THE DIARY OF
EDWARD GOSCHEN
1900–1914

THE DIARY OF
EDWARD GOSCHEN
1900–1914

edited by
CHRISTOPHER H. D. HOWARD

CAMDEN FOURTH SERIES
Volume 25

LONDON
OFFICES OF THE ROYAL HISTORICAL SOCIETY
UNIVERSITY COLLEGE LONDON
GOWER STREET, WC1
1980

ISBN: 0 901050 69 5

Printed in Great Britain by Butler & Tanner Ltd
Frome and London

CONTENTS

ACKNOWLEDGMENTS

The papers of Edward Goschen are the property of his grandson, Sir Edward Goschen, Bt, of Lower Farm House, Hampstead Norreys, Berkshire, by whose permission the extracts from his diary and from other documents that are among his papers are now published. I am deeply indebted to Sir Edward and Lady Goschen for innumerable kindnesses.

I acknowledge the gracious permission of Her Majesty the Queen to make use of material in the Royal Archives at Windsor Castle.

I am most grateful to the Marquis of Salisbury, to Viscount Simon, to Lady Salisbury-Jones and to Sir Anthony Rumbold, Bt, for allowing me to use documents of which they are the owners.

Extracts from Crown Copyright Records in the Public Record Office appear by kind permission of the Controller of Her Majesty's Stationery Office.

I should like to thank Elizabeth, Countess of Abingdon, Lord Hardinge of Penshurst, Sir Herbert Butterfield, Professor M. Balfour, Professor A. J. P. Taylor, Professor H. N. V. Temperley, Dr T. H. Aston, Mr N. Bruce and the Head Master of Rugby School for courteously complying with my requests concerning a variety of matters.

I also wish to express my appreciation of the valuable cooperation extended to me by the Queen's Librarian and by the Registrar of the Royal Archives, Windsor Castle; by the Danish Embassy in London; by the Librarian of the Italian Institute in London; by the Politisches Archiv of the Auswärtiges Amt, Bonn; by the Archivist and Librarian at Hatfield House; and by the Archivist of *The Times*.

Finally, I should like to thank those friends and colleagues who have given me the benefit of their expert knowledge, and especially Professor John Röhl, Dr F. R. Bridge, Dr Geza Jeszenky, Dr Láslo Peter and Dr Hedwig Pollak.

NOTE

The diary of Edward Goschen is contained in twenty-four red, cloth-bound, octavo volumes, published by the firm of Charles Letts, and providing one page with a printed heading and ruled lines for each day of the year. The entries are all in Goschen's own hand-writing. The first is that for 12 February 1891; the last that for 30 December 1914.

Although Goschen did not by any means make an entry for every day, the total number of words in the twenty-four volumes must be very large indeed. It would be rash to estimate their number, even to the nearest hundred thousand. However, not all this material calls for publication. Much of it is trivial; much may reasonably be regarded as private. Some entries repeat statements—often of doubt-ful accuracy—at second or third hand; some summarize what was printed in the newspapers; many merely consist of the words: 'Noth-ing partic.'

The earlier diaries, that is, those for the years 1891–1900, when Goschen was successively secretary of the Lisbon Legation (1891–3), Washington Embassy (1893–4), St Petersburg Embassy (1895–8) and Minister in Belgrade (1898–1900), are of limited general interest. I have, however, incorporated a number of extracts from these early diaries, more especially those that shed light on Goschen's own character, in the Introduction. The diaries that Goschen kept while Minister in Copenhagen (1900–5) are more interesting, partly because from 1903 onwards the post of Russian Minister in the Danish capital was held by Alexander Isvolsky. I have accordingly included a small selection from the Copenhagen diaries in the text printed below. The most important diaries are, of course, those kept by Goschen during his years as Ambassador, first in Vienna (1905–8) and then in Berlin (1908–14), from which I have included a more copious selection. Even so, I have omitted much material that is either trivial or, despite the lapse of years, still private. It should be empha-sized that a number of the individuals mentioned in the diary are still alive.

Goschen's grammar, orthography, capitalization, punctuation and use of abbreviations all raise problems of the kind with which editors of historical documents will be familiar. Goschen made grammatical mistakes, sometimes as a result of inserting an afterthought into a sentence and overlooking the syntactical consequences. His French grammar was not invariably correct. He sometimes misspelt words, especially proper names. His spelling of Slavonic names was in-consistent. His capitalization was idiosyncratic. He employed numerous abbreviations. I have not attempted to correct grammatical or orthographic errors, but where it has seemed necessary, I have drawn attention to them. I have retained Goschen's capitalization, his punctuation, in so far as to do so is compatible with intelligibility, and his abbreviations, apart from ampersands. I have italicized the names of ships and the titles of plays, operas, ballets, books and newspapers.

I have done my best to identify persons mentioned in the text wherever that has seemed necessary and been possible. Where Goschen was uncertain as to a person's name or identity he often indicated his uncertainty by means of a question-mark. I wish to emphasize that such question-marks in the text are Goschen's own. Where I myself am unsure of a reading I have indicated the fact in a footnote. On the other hand, where Goschen through inadvertence ended a sentence with a full stop, instead of the question-mark that the sense required, I have replaced the full stop by a question-mark.

The diary records Goschen's receipt of numerous letters, dispatches and telegrams from the Foreign Office. Unfortunately, very few of these are to be found among his papers, which, apart from the diaries, are extremely meagre for the years 1900–14. Goschen more than once notes having destroyed unwanted documents; many more must have been burned on 5 August 1914. Fortunately, numerous drafts or copies of communications sent to him by the Foreign Office have been preserved, some of which have been printed in *British Documents on the Origins of the War*. However, it would seem that the Foreign Secretaries and the permanent officials of the period did not by any means keep copies of every communication that they sent.

There are holograph letters by Goschen in the Royal Archives at Windsor Castle, and among the papers of Salisbury (Hatfield House), Lansdowne, Grey, Lascelles and Nicolson (Public Record Office), Hardinge (Cambridge University Library), Cartwright (Northamptonshire Record Office), de Bunsen (Mill Down, Hambledon), Rumbold (Bodleian Library), Wickham Steed (Archives of *The Times*) and Charles Trevelyan (Library of the University of Newcastle-upon-Tyne). His official dispatches and telegrams are in the Public Record Office. There are documents relating to Goschen among the papers of Simon (The Wharfe, Topsham), Bell and Chirol (Archives of *The Times*) and Leopold Maxse (West Sussex Record Office) and in the Haus-, Hof- und Staatsarchiv, Vienna, the Politisches Archive of the Auswärtiges Amt, Bonn, and in the Deutsches Zentralarchiv, Merseburg.

ABBREVIATIONS IN THE TEXT

(The abbreviations employed by Goschen are extremely numerous. This list is not exhaustive: I have listed merely those abbreviations which might puzzle some readers.)

A.D.	Archduke, Archduchess
Ä.	Aehrenthal
A.H., A.-Hy.	Austria-Hungary
B.	Bannerman, Barrington, Boss, Bülow, Bunt
B.H.	Bethmann Hollweg
B'h.	British
B.P.	Budapest
Brock	Brockdorff
C.	Cambon, Crozier
C.B.	Campbell-Bannerman
Ch. d'Aff.	Chargé d'Affaires
C—n	Cambon
Crack	Crackanthorpe
Cz.	Czar
D.	Danneskiold, Demidoff
D'Ä., D'Äh., D'Ähr.	Aehrenthal
D.C.O.	Duke of Cambridge's Own
D'off	Demidoff
F.	Fairholme
F. and G.	Fruhling and Goschen
F.F., Fr.F.,	Franz Ferdinand
F.J.	Franz Joseph
G.	George
Golu	Goluchowski
H.	Hardinge, Harrison
H. of C.	House of Commons
I.	Isvolsky
J.	Johnstone
K.	Kahn, Kiderlen-Wächter, King
Kr.	Kaiser
L.	Lansdowne, Lichnowsky, Lister
Ll. G.	Lloyd George
M.	Malcolm, Maud, Mensdorff
N., Nico, Niko	Nicolson
N.F.P.	*Neue Freie Presse*
O.	Ouroussoff, Osten-Sacken
P.	Plunkett

R.	Raikes, Reverseaux
R.R.	Representatives
S.	Salisbury, Schoen, Steed
T.	Teck, Ted, Tentschach, Tittoni, Tyrrell
V.	Victoria, Vienna
W.	Wales, Wilhelm, Windsich-Graetz

ABBREVIATIONS IN THE FOOTNOTES

Unless otherwise stated the place of publication is London

B.D.	*British Documents on the Origins of the War 1898–1914*, ed. G. P. Gooch and H. Temperley, 11 vols. (1926–38)
B.H.L.	*Briefwechsel Hertling-Lerchenfeld 1912–1917*, ed. E. Deuerlein, 2 vols. (Boppard am Rhein, 1973)
D.A.B.	H. Beyens, *Deux Années à Berlin 1912–1914*, 2 vols. (Paris, 1931)
D.D.F.	*Documents diplomatiques français 1871–1914*, 60 vols. (Paris, 1929–59)
D.D.K.	*Die deutschen Dokumente zum Kriegsausbruch*, ed. M. Montgelas and W. Schucking, 4 vols. (Berlin, 1927)
De B.P.	De Bunsen Papers
F.O.	Foreign Office
G.P.	*Die grosse Politik der europäischen Kabinette 1871–1914*, ed. J. Leipsius, A. Mendelssohn-Bartholdy and F. Thimme, 40 vols. (Berlin, 1922–7)
Go. P.	Edward Goschen Papers
Gr. P.	Grey of Fallodon Papers
H.P.	Hardinge Papers
Lan. P.	Lansdowne Papers
Las. P.	Lascelles Papers
M.P.	Maxse Papers
N.P.	Nicolson Papers
Ö.U.A.	*Österreich-Ungarns Aussenpolitik von der bosnischen Krise 1908 bis zum Kriegsausbruch 1914*, ed. L. Bittner and H. Uebersberger, 9 vols. (Vienna 1930)
P.A.	Politisches Archiv
R.A.	Royal Archives
R.P.	Rumbold Papers

INTRODUCTION

I

William Edward Goschen, best remembered as Sir Edward Goschen, was British Ambassador in Berlin at the time of the outbreak of the First World War. It was he who, on 4 August 1914, delivered the British ultimatum to the Secretary of State at the Imperial Foreign Office, Gottlieb von Jagow, and subsequently had a celebrated interview with the Imperial Chancellor, Theobald von Bethmann Hollweg. According to Goschen's report of his last days in Berlin, written later for the Foreign Office, Bethmann Hollweg complained that Britain was going to make war on a kindred nation 'just for a scrap of paper'—the 'scrap of paper' being the London Treaty of 19 April 1839, which had provided for the independence and neutrality of Belgium, under the guarantee of the five Great European Powers.[1] Goschen's report, which was laid before Parliament, helped to make the words 'scrap of paper' a catch-phrase, which was exploited over and over again for purposes of war-propaganda.[2]

The name of the author of what must be one of the most frequently quoted diplomatic documents of the early twentieth century naturally figures in numerous historical monographs. Goschen's character has been delineated by several of those who knew him personally: by Maurice Baring, who served under him in Copenhagen and later became well known as a novelist and journalist, in *The Puppet Show of Memory* (1922); by Henry Bruce, who was his private secretary in both Vienna and Berlin, in *Silken Dalliance* (1946); by Frank Rattigan, who was second secretary at the Berlin Embassy in 1913–14, in *Diversions of a Diplomat* (1924); and by Baron Hubert Beyens, who was Belgian Minister in Berlin from 1912 until the outbreak of war, in *Deux Années à Berlin* (Paris, 1931, 2 vols.). The story of his conduct of his mission in the summer of 1914 has been related by Horace Rumbold, who was Councillor at the Berlin Embassy at the time, first in a 'rough account', set down shortly after its author's return to England,[3] and then in *The War Crisis in Berlin*, published more than a quarter of a century later (1940; 2nd ed. 1944). His qualities as a diplomat have been appraised by Henry Wickham Steed, who, as correspondent of

[1] Goschen to Grey, dated 6 Aug. 1914, F.O. 371/2164; *B.D.*, xi, no. 671; cited hereafter as 'no. 671'; for a discussion of the real date of this document see below.
[2] See below, p. 51; also Appendix B.
[3] R. P. Rumbold wrote on the envelope containing this document: 'A rough account by me of the crisis at Berlin during the 12 days which preceded the European war. This account was written immediately after I returned to England on 7 August, 1914.' Martin Gilbert in his *Sir Horace Rumbold* (1973), pp. 104–25, to which I am much indebted, quotes at length from this document, cited hereafter as 'Rough Account'.

The Times, was in close touch with him during the years of his Vienna ambassadorship, in *Through Thirty Years* (1924, 2 vols.). However, so far as the editor is aware, his diary and other private papers have not previously, been used by any historian.

An 'Ancestral Tree', evidently drawn up towards the end of the nineteenth century by a professional German genealogist, provides a considerable amount of information concerning Goschen's descent. It shows that he was the youngest child of Wilhelm Heinrich Göschen, a native of Leipzig, who was born in 1793, and of Henrietta Ohmann, who was born in London in 1805. Wilhelm Heinrich Göschen was the fourth and youngest son of Georg—or Jürgen—Joachim Göschen, a native of Bremen, born in 1752, who moved to Leipzig, where he founded a publishing firm. Goethe and Schiller were among his authors. His wife was Johanna Henriette Heun of Sonnenschein. Wilhelm Heinrich Göschen emigrated to London while still in his early twenties, and, together with another young German, Peter Frühling, set up what proved to be the successful finance house of Frühling and Göschen. His marriage to Henrietta Ohmann, daughter of Wilhelm Alexander Ohmann (according to the 'Ancestral Tree', an Irishman of German descent) and Henrietta Sim, took place at Liverpool on 12 May 1829.[4]

Henrietta bore her husband six daughters and six sons. Five daughters and five sons reached maturity. The eldest son, George Joachim, born in 1831, entered the House of Commons in 1863 as a Liberal, was a member of Russell's second and Gladstone's first Cabinets, but, having broken with Gladstone, served under Salisbury as Chancellor of the Exchequer from 1887 to 1892 and as First Lord of the Admiralty from 1895 to 1900. He had a house in Portland Place and another, Seacox Heath, at Flimwell, near the Kentish village of Hawkhurst, but on the Sussex side of the county border. In 1900 he was raised to the peerage. Henry, Charles and Alexander, respectively the third, fourth and fifth sons, pursued successful careers in banking. Two daughters, Emily and Marion, married brothers, Gustav and Georg von Metzsch, who were both in the service of the King of Saxony. William Edward, the youngest child, was born at Eltham in Kent on 18 July 1847. He was known by his second Christian name. Wilhelm Heinrich Göschen lived until 1866; his wife until 1895.

Edward Goschen—to give his surname in the form that the family after a time adopted—spent much of his childhood at Templeton House, Roehampton. He was, like his eldest brother, educated at Rugby, where in due course he became, according to his fellow-ambassador, Maurice de Bunsen, who had been with him at the school, although a few years his junior, 'a great swell in the cricket

[4] 'Ancestral Tree,' the property of the family.

eleven'.[5] He went on to Corpus Christi College, Oxford, and twice represented the University at tennis—real tennis, as it is now often called—against Cambridge. In 1869 he entered the Diplomatic Service. After being employed for a few months at the Foreign Office he was posted to Madrid. He subsequently served in Buenos Aires, Paris, Rio de Janeiro, Constantinople, where he was for a time attached to George Joachim's Special Embassy, Peking and Copenhagen. In 1891 he proceeded to Lisbon. It is at this point in his career that his diary begins.

In 1874, while serving as third secretary at the Buenos Aires Legation, Goschen married an American girl, Harriet Hosta Clarke, daughter of Darius Clarke. According to the 'Ancestral Tree' Hosta— she too used her second Christian name—was born in 1849 at Marshall in the State of Michigan; the wedding took place near New York. To judge from a portrait in oils by Archibald Stuart-Wortley, which is in the family's possession, Hosta must in her younger days have been strikingly good-looking. She figures frequently in her husband's diary as 'Boss' or 'Bossie'—nicknames that are probably the outcome of some family joke. She seems to have retained few roots in her country of origin and to have preferred life in Europe, although she evidently found the so-called entertainments of diplomatic life uncongenial. The marriage was a happy one. Hosta bore her husband two sons, Edward Henry, born in 1877 and known variously as 'Ted', 'Teddie', 'T. Wee', 'Twee' or 'Fry', and George Gerard, born in 1887 and known as 'Bunt' or 'Bunty'. She died, after a long illness, in February 1912.

II

It would be interesting to know whether Goschen kept any record of his activities before 1891, when this diary begins. No such document is to be found among his papers. One would also like to know his motives for keeping a diary. No doubt he did so, partly at least, for his own amusement. He probably found that to write an account of an important conversation soon after it had taken place helped him subsequently in the composition of a dispatch or private letter to the Foreign Office. He certainly found his diary a useful means of refreshing his memory concerning past events.[6] He evidently also intended it to be read by his wife, from whom he was often parted and to whom

[5] De Bunsen to Hilda von Deichmann, 9 Jan. 1910, de B.P., MB/I/11. I have made enquiries at Rugby School, but have been unable to confirm de Bunsen's statement. However, there seems to be no reason to question its correctness: Goschen was a good athlete.

[6] Goschen to Rumbold, 21 March 1915, Gr. P., F.O. 800/1107.

it contains numerous references—even an occasional mild reproof (Diary, 30 May 1891, 1 March 1903). He must surely have written some of his long and detailed narratives of royal or imperial occasions with her in mind. He makes it clear that he allowed her to see what he had written (Diary, 31 May 1891). Moreover, it is significant that after, on 23 February 1912, recording her funeral, he made no further entry in his diary for more than five months. Whether he ever intended his diary to serve as raw material for a volume of memoirs is hard to say. At all events, he published no such volume.

The volumes in which Goschen kept his diary were, unlike those used by some of his contemporaries, not fitted with locks. Unless, therefore, he took appropriate precautions, they could easily have been read by some unauthorized person. It is significant that on two occasions, 1 December 1895 and 16 October 1910, he refrained from confiding information to his diary on the ground that it was 'too secret'. On the other hand, he did enter a number of remarks that he would certainly not have wished to be seen by a malicious, indiscreet or venal reader.

One must not, of course, expect the diary to overturn one's fundamental notions concerning the period that it covers. Goschen was never in a position to make major decisions as to policy. Moreover, at a time of crisis he did not always, understandably, write up the events of each day. This was the case, unfortunately, in October 1908 and in late July and early August 1914. Nevertheless, his diary is of considerable interest. It supplements his correspondence in an important respect in that it records what occurred on his occasional visits to the Foreign Office, as on 5 February 1912, or when he was just about to go on leave, as in the last few days of June 1914. It illustrates the daily round, including the frustrations, of a career diplomat. It gives candid and often amusing first-hand impressions of many of the leading personalities of the day. It sheds light on Goschen's relations with the personnel of the foreign ministries in the capitals in which he served, with other members of the various Diplomatic Corps, and with the Foreign Office—more especially with the successive permanent under-secretaries, Sir Thomas Sanderson, Sir Charles Hardinge and Sir Arthur Nicolson. It illustrates the extent and the limits of his understanding of the changing international situation. In places it is revealing because of what it does not mention. Together with Goschen's letters, by no means all of which have been published, it also constitutes a self-portrait of a centrally placed participant in the events that led up to the outbreak of the First World War.

Goschen shows himself to have been an affectionate husband, who nevertheless frankly enjoyed the company of young and pretty women. He was a devoted father to his sons, in whose education and careers he took a keen interest. He was a member of the Church of England. He had a great capacity for enjoying all sorts of harmless pleasures, including some not usually associated with a senior member of the Diplomatic Service. On the other hand, he had little taste for many of the formal entertainments inseparable from his career, although he certainly appreciated the good things of the table. His most conspicuous failing, of which he was himself fully conscious, was irascibility. After winning a tie in a lawn-tennis tournament during his first summer in St Petersburg he acknowledged that it had been expected that he would lose his temper—although on this occasion he had not (Diary, 5 July 1895). He sometimes expressed contrition for displays of bad temper in the family circle (Diary, 11 and 17 September 1896). He was not always contrite (Diary, 6 July 1898). He also had a marked tendency, which he likewise frankly acknowledged and of which the diary affords numerous examples, to take a dislike to a new acquaintance before he had had time to form a considered judgment.

Unfortunately for himself, and no doubt for the members of his family and for his subordinates, Goschen was much plagued by minor ailments. They occur frequently in his diary and correspondence—lumbago, sciatica, rheumatism, gout, influenza, head-ache, tooth-ache, gripes, boils, cysts—he had to endure them all and others as well. No doubt they were to a large extent the consequence of the artificial and unhealthy way of life that his profession imposed on him—frequent and exhausting journeys by train and boat, long waits on station-platforms or in church-porches for unpunctual or absent royalty, heated arguments with foreign ministry officials, hours spent standing about in draughts at *cercles* and other receptions, rich, indigestible food consumed in restaurants or at innumerable dinner-parties. These maladies interfered both with his performance of his duties and with his enjoyment of his leisure pursuits. They probably help to explain his many bouts of irritability. They may also have delayed the progress of his career.

Despite his recurring ailments Goschen engaged in a great variety of sporting activities. He was a good shot, a successful angler, a skilled yachtsman, a skater, a golfer (albeit an erratic one), a player of both tennis, in the original sense of that term, and of the more recently invented lawn-tennis. He was particularly fond of cricket, which he still played occasionally when in his early fifties (Diary, 2 and 3 August 1897, 18 June 1898). According to Bruce, who was for some years an 'honorary member of the family', the cricket news was always, except on 'lumbago days or days when we had had some flaming row', the first part of *The Times* to be studied and discussed.[7] When in

[7] Bruce, op. cit., p. 122.

London he enjoyed watching matches at Lord's. Thus, early in the 1909 season, when the Australians under M. A. Noble were touring England, he wrote from Berlin to Hardinge:

> I am thinking of, if there is no objection, running over to London for a few days; it is long since I have seen the Australians and the test match on the 14th at Lords has attractions for me. If this comes off I would suggest (if you were not such a busy man) that you might come up to Lords with me one day—and during that odious innovation the tea interval, we might have a talk about the situation. But we shouldn't—we should probably only talk cricket![8]

It can scarcely be a coincidence that the day, 28 May 1909, on which Goschen wrote this letter, was also the second day of the first test match, which was being played at Edgbaston. The Ambassador was no doubt impatiently waiting for news of the latest score.

In many respects Goschen was a typical member of the British Diplomatic Service of his day. He had been educated at a public school that nurtured two other ambassadors among his near-contemporaries—Arthur Nicholson and Maurice de Bunsen. He was a competent linguist. His diary indicates that he spoke French and wrote it, although not without a few trifling errors. He knew German, although less well than might have been expected in view of his background. He was not bilingual. He made spelling mistakes when confronted with unfamiliar proper names. While in Belgrade and perhaps finding time heavy on his hands he took lessons in 'German composition' (Diary, 29 March 1900). In 1913 he wrote that while on a shooting-party in Silesia he had been keeping up his German, implying that he did not speak it much when in Berlin.[9] However, in another letter, written in 1909, he quotes Bethmann Hollweg at some length as having spoken to him in German.[10] Moreover, the passage in Goschen's letter is correct and idiomatic. He knew Spanish, which he evidently enjoyed speaking and writing, Portuguese and some Danish. The *Foreign Office List* records that while at the Constantinople Embassy he passed an examination in Turkish. He did not, so far as can be judged from his diary, speak Russian or the language then known as Serb. After 1870 he did not serve in the Foreign Office. He did his best to collect reliable information from foreign ministers and their staffs, from colleagues in the Diplomatic Corps, from other British diplomats *en passage*, and from newspaper correspondents. He embodied the information which he had gathered in dispatches and telegrams to the Foreign Office, and, increasingly as he rose in the

[8] Goschen to Hardinge, 28 May 1909, H.P., 15.
[9] Goschen to Nicolson, 29 Nov. 1913, N.P., F.O. 800/371.
[10] Goschen to Hardinge, 'Xmas Eve', 1909, H.P., 15.

service, in semi-private letters. These communications give the impression that writing came easily to him. Bruce recalls seeing him 'with one of his beloved Servian cigarettes dangling perilously in his beard', drafting dispatches 'without hesitation or correction'.[11] The results were both legible and readable.

He was not, of course, any more than any other British career diplomat of his generation, an expert on the history and institutions of any of the countries in which he served. Nor was he an economist or a geo-politician. Indeed, on one occasion he listed certain subjects that he hated. They were: statistics, finance, commerce and boundaries (Diary, 17 July 1911). Although he once, on 12 November 1900, recorded that he had been reading Pepys, he generally noted little concerning his reading, apart from that of correspondence, official papers and newspapers. In short, he was not an 'intellectual', in the way that his eldest brother might justly be so described. On the other hand, he accumulated a vast store of experience. By 1914 he had been head of successive missions for a longer period than any other serving British Ambassador.

In being of mainly non-British descent[12] and married to a foreign-born wife, Goschen was in no way untypical of the diplomatic profession of his day. In any case, the fact that he was of predominantly German descent does not mean that he identified himself with his father's country of origin. On the contrary, he acknowledged, some years before his appointment to the Berlin Embassy, that his feelings towards Germans in general were the reverse of affectionate and that he disliked being descended from one (Diary, 1 December 1901). His outlook was completely British, or as he himself would no doubt have said, English. Beyens observed the contrast between Goschen's ancestry and his character. Although, the former Belgian Minister wrote, Goschen was 'd'origine germanique', 'rien en lui ne trahissait cet atavisme, hormis son nom'. He gave the impression of being 'un agréable gentleman du plus pur sang britannique'. Nor was this merely a matter of appearance. Beyens found 'anglais aussi, très anglais ses sentiments et sa façon flegmatique d'envisager les événements et d'en tirer des conséquences'.[13]

Goschen's diary and letters bear out Beyens's judgment. They abound with references to the delights, which he was able to enjoy only at intervals, of life in England. 'English Country House life *is* jolly—how hateful it is never to have any of it!!' he observed while

[11] Bruce, op. cit., p. 122.
[12] It has sometimes been stated or implied that Goschen was of Jewish descent. To prove that he had no Jewish ancestry at all would be impossible. However, the 'Ancestral Tree' affords no evidence of any. Several of Goschen's forebears were Lutheran pastors.
[13] *D.A.B.*, i, p. 26.

on leave from the Lisbon Legation and staying at Ballards, his brother
Charles's Surrey home (Diary, 25 June 1892). During his first year
in St Petersburg he entertained some Embassy friends to tea at a café
overlooking a branch of the Neva, and noted with mixed enthusiasm
and nostalgia that 'one might be sitting in a Pub at Teddington or
Maidenhead' (Diary, 21 May 1895). 'The only place I am ever
decently well in is dear old England,' he lamented while in Belgrade
and suffering from one of his periodic ailments. 'How I wish I was
there now out of this horrible place,' he added (Diary, 15 December
1898). 'I am overjoyed at the prospect of a few days in my native
country,' he wrote to Nicolson in the spring of 1911.[14] Moreover, he
held that his duty was not to the country of his forebears, but to that
of his own birth and upbringing. In 1912, after an article in a German
newspaper had criticized him, arguing, as he put it in another letter
to the permanent under-secretary, 'that what makes it worse is that
I am really a German—like de Bunsen and to a certain extent Cartwright', he left no doubt as to his sentiments on the matter: 'after all
I am here not to push German ideas and interests, as the Article would
seem to think, but those of my Govt. and country'.[15]

In certain respects, nevertheless, Goschen was not a typical member
of the Diplomatic Service. It was, for example, unusual for a member
of that service to have an elder brother who was a member of the
Cabinet and who wrote him indiscreet letters, couched partly in the
language of Goethe. A few of these letters, written by George Joachim
Goschen in the later eighteen-nineties, when he was First Lord of the
Admiralty and a member of Salisbury's Cabinet and his youngest
brother was at the St Petersburg Embassy, have been preserved.

In March 1896 George Joachim wrote that Salisbury had been 'low
and bothered—no wonder'. Not only Britain but Europe had had
'to climb down in face of the Turk'—on the Armenian question.
Newspaper talk about 'the influence of public opinion' was: 'Stuff'.
'You and I wissen das besser,' added the eldest Goschen, concluding
quasi-paternally: 'Adieu mein Sohn, mache deine Sache gut!'[16]

In the following month, after seeing Nicholas O'Conor, the newly
appointed Ambassador in St Petersburg, George Joachim wrote: 'I
said to myself "Why on earth is this man made Ambassador over the
heads of so many?" I could see no "esprit". Er imponierte nicht.'[17]
In December 1897, after the German landing at Kiaochow Bay, he
commented: 'The F.O. took the German escapade very lightly. What
a "send off" at Kiel! How offensive! How absurd!' Of the Russian

[14] Goschen to Nicolson, 5 May 1911, N.P., F.O. 800/348.
[15] Goschen to Nicolson, 18 May 1912, N.P., F.O. 800/355.
[16] G. J. Goschen to Goschen, 5 March (1896); year not specified, but evident from
contents; Go. P.
[17] G. J. Goschen to Goschen, 29 Apr. 1896, Go. P.

action at Port Arthur he observed: 'We have been rather befooled.' He also showed his awareness of the risks attending these 'interesting letters', warning his brother that 'the fire, if you *have* an open fire, is the best place for those *you* receive'.[18]

However, there seems to be no reason to believe that Edward Goschen's career benefited from his eldest brother's exalted position. At all events, George Joachim's accounts of his contacts with the Prime Minister—who was also the Foreign Secretary—were not encouraging. 'Nach seiner Art, Salisbury never speaks of you to me,' he wrote in March 1896.[19] A few weeks later he informed his brother that, although Sanderson had spoken 'very nicely' of his work as chargé d'affaires in St Petersburg, 'that queer Salisbury has said never a word'.[20]

Indeed, during the years when George Joachim was a member of Salisbury's Cabinets his youngest brother enjoyed no particularly rapid promotion. In a draft letter, evidently written in 1896, the Secretary of the St Petersburg Embassy relieved his feelings by dwelling jokingly on the First Lord of the Admiralty's powers of patronage:

I want you to use your influence in getting me a naval appointment. I am tired of diplomacy and feel that I should shine as an Admiral....[21]

After a disquisition on the unfairness of the system of promotion as operated by 'the Markis'—that is, the Marquis of Salisbury—he added:

You may show all this to Lord S. if you like and tell him that if he hates the service as he is said to do, the service perfectly loathes him.[22]

Goschen was also unusual among British diplomats serving abroad in being a keen amateur musician. He attended numerous recitals, concerts and performances of operas, often making critical comments on what he heard. Thus in 1895, while in Dresden on a visit to his sister, Emily von Metzsch, he attended a rehearsal of a symphony concert, at which ' "Aus der neuen Welt" by Dvořák was the pièce de Résistance'. He liked only the first movement of the then still recent work, questioning 'whether the motives themselves were worthy of the excessively clever and complicated Treatment' (Diary, 22 March 1895). However, he was not only a listener and critic; he was

18 G. J. Goschen to Goschen, 21 Dec. 1897, Go. P.
19 G. J. Goschen to Goschen, 5 March (1896), Go. P.
20 G. J. Goschen to Goschen, 29 Apr. 1896, Go. P.
21 Goschen to G. J. Goschen (draft), undated, but evidently written early in 1896, Go. P.
22 Ibid.

also an executant—on the violin. He seems to have taken up the in-
strument comparatively late in life (Diary, 4 November 1891). While
in Lisbon he took part in a benefit concert in the presence of the King
and Queen of Portugal, who 'laughed to see me playing in the Orchestra' (Diary, 8 March 1892). In St Petersburg, after a dinner at the
French Ambassador's, he made his 'début as a violinist (save the
mark)'. Accompanied by the Ambassadress, he played 'lots of things'.
'I played very poorly—but not badly for me,' he noted modestly
(Diary, 3 March 1897). In 1910, when Ambassador in Berlin, he took
part in duets with the heir-apparent at the latter's residence. 'It may
amuse you to hear that after dinner the Crown Prince and I played
duets for two violins. He had got in a Pianist on purpose!'[23] he
reported to Hardinge. Together with his younger son, a gifted pianist,
he composed some pieces (Diary, 9 April 1902, 16 April 1903 and
2 July 1911). Unfortunately, efforts to trace these compositions have
not proved successful. So far as can be judged, he was not a highly
skilled performer. Bruce, who used to accompany him at the piano,
refers disparagingly to his 'scrapings on the fiddle'.[24] Goschen, for his
part, was fully aware of his technical limitations. However, his love
of music probably made it easier for him to establish friendly relations
with some of those with whom he had official dealings.

From 1900 onwards Goschen was also exceptional in being a Carinthian landowner. In that year, on the death of a first cousin, Oskar
Göschen, a retired major in the Austro-Hungarian Army, to whom
he had previously paid a number of visits, he inherited Schloss Tentschach, together with an estate, a few miles to the north-west of Klagenfurt. The Schloss is a loftily situated structure with three massive
corner-towers and an arcaded court-yard, erected in the sixteenth
century on the site of an earlier building. Bruce, who often stayed
there as Goschen's guest, described it as 'gloriously situated with a
sublime view and a stillness such that you could hear a dog bark in
the valley miles below'.[25] This inheritance provided Goschen and his
family with what they had hitherto lacked—a home of their own,
although not one where they could live the whole year round. Tentschach, as the property is invariably called in the diary, was a never-
failing source of delight to its owner.

If the stereotype of a British diplomat of his era as a man with a
comfortable private income can be said to correspond with reality,
Goschen was certainly not a typical member of the Service. In fact,
he himself demolished the popular image of the affluent professional
diplomat. 'Nobody has ever succeeded in making money out of Diplo-

---

[23] Goschen to Hardinge, 10 June 1910, H.P., 20.
[24] Bruce, op. cit., p. 132.
[25] Bruce, op. cit., p. 115.

macy yet—and most dips. that I know have spent all their modest
capital, by the time they arrive at Ministerial or Ambassadorial age,'
he wrote, while in St Petersburg.[26] His connection with the world of
merchant-banking should not be regarded as proof that he himself
possessed large independent means. His Carinthian property involved
him in considerable outgoings. Moreover, his way of life was not of
the simplest.[27] His diary affords abundant evidence that even after
he had risen to ambassadorial rank he was beset by financial
problems.

It is clear where Goschen's political sympathies lay. He revered
monarchical institutions in general and the British monarchy in particular. He wrote of successive British and most foreign crowned heads
with respect and affection—the principal exceptions being 'German
Bill' (Diary, 26 October 1895) and the members of the Obrenović and
Karadjordjević dynasties. He avowed his love for 'Austria-Hungary
and her Ruler'.[28] He regarded the proposed payment of members of
the House of Commons as 'the first nail in England's coffin as a
great and politically pure country' (Diary, 28 March 1893). At the
time of the British advance into the territory of the Boer Republics
he supported the view that 'complete and unconditional surrender'
was the only thing to which Salisbury could listen. 'Well done! Mar-
kiss,' he wrote with unwonted approval of the attitude taken by the
Prime Minister (Diary, 14 March 1900).

As far as the organization and functioning of the Foreign Office
and the Diplomatic Service were concerned Goschen was a tradi-
tionalist. While in St Petersburg he commented that Salisbury was
'always for the Blue Book' (Diary, 11 March 1897). He thought, in
other words, that the Prime Minister and Foreign Secretary, when
writing his dispatches, had Parliament and the press, rather than the
ambassador to whom they were addressed, in mind. He did not welcome the innovations of the Hardinge–Crowe era. 'Oh! How I hate
all these new schemes,' he wrote from Vienna in 1907 to Lascelles,
now his colleague in Berlin, on the subject of commercial attachés.
'I don't care about any of these new fangled schemes,' he added,
apropos of the annual reports that were now expected of him.[29] In
the completion of these reports he was not a model of punctuality.
His report for the year 1911 is dated 21 February 1913 and, understandably, begins with an expression of 'great regret for its tardy
arrival'.[30] He was, moreover, sceptical as to the number of those at

[26] Goschen to G. J. Goschen (draft), undated, but evidently written early in 1896, Go. P.
[27] Bruce, op. cit., p. 121.
[28] Goschen to Hardinge, 4 Dec. 1908, H.P., 12.
[29] Goschen to Lascelles, 4 Feb. 1907, Las. P., F.O. 800/13.
[30] Goschen to Grey, 21 Feb. 1913, F.O. 371/1650.

the Foreign Office who would actually read what, after much travail, he finally consigned to the diplomatic bag.

A diary cannot be expected to reveal its author's entire personality. Although Goschen's diary fully illustrates his weaknesses, it tells one only a limited amount concerning the more agreeable side of his character. For this one must rely on the writings of those who knew him. Baring recalled his 'inimitable humour', 'minute observation of detail' and his 'keen eye for the ludicrous'.[31] Rattigan testified to his 'kindness and thoughtfulness', 'ripe experience' and 'wise judgment'.[32] Bruce, who of all those who served under Goschen probably knew him best, after describing in some detail the Ambassador's 'lumbago days', when 'it was well to get out of the room as quickly as might be', added that such days were not too frequent, and that in the long bright intervals between them Goschen's charm was disarming and his affection sincere.[33]

Nor does the diary tell one much about its author's appearance, although it does record (6 December 1904) that he had his portrait painted. Efforts to trace this portrait have not, unfortunately, proved successful. There is, however, in the possession of the family, a fanciful oil-painting by James Bowie, showing Goschen with Bethmann Hollweg, who is in the act of literally tearing up the famous 'scrap of paper'. There are also a number of photographs of Goschen in existence, of which the best known to the editor is that reproduced in Bruce's *Silken Dalliance*.[34] Probably taken when Goschen was Ambassador in Berlin, it shows him as an elegantly, but not ostentatiously, dressed man, with abundant, greying hair, parted on the left, bushy eyebrows, a mainly white moustache and beard, and a genial expression. Beyens described Goschen as a man 'aux cheveux d'un gris d'argent, au teint fleuri, à la barbe en pointe mise à la mode par Édouard VII'.[35] So far as the shape of the beard was concerned, the former Belgian Minister's memory was, however, at fault.

III

Our detailed knowledge of Goschen's career begins with the first entry in his diary, that for 12 February 1891, the day on which he, his wife and his younger son, 'Bunt', sailed for Lisbon, where he was to serve as secretary at the Legation. In recent years Britain's relations with Portugal had been strained by rivalries in south-central Africa.

[31] Baring, op. cit., p. 214.   [32] Rattigan, op. cit., p. 134.
[33] Bruce, op. cit., p. 93.   [34] Facing p. 92.
[35] *D.A.B.*, i, p. 26.

On the day following his arrival in Lisbon Goschen noted having been told that the under-secretary at the Ministry of Foreign Affairs had remarked that his name 'stank in the nostrils of the Portuguese who had been swindled out of a lot of money by F. and G.!!' (Diary, 16 February 1891). However, on 11 June 1891 Petre, the Minister, signed a treaty with Portugal. Thereafter relations between the two countries approximated somewhat more closely to those customary between allies.

Some two months later Goschen travelled by train with a party of friends—all male—to Badajoz, in Extremadura, just across the Spanish frontier. The trip was of no political significance, but his account of it is of interest as an illustration of his love for Spain, where he had served his first tour of duty in the early eighteen-seventies, and of his great capacity for lively enjoyment.

On Thursday 13 August he and his companions set out, occupying a 'salon'. After a midnight supper they 'sat outside on the verandah till any hour', Goschen and a friend 'singing Spanish songs'. Next morning at Badajoz the heat was 'enormous'. Goschen drove into the town with a Spanish friend, the military attaché in Lisbon; they 'walked about—chaffed the niñas—drank lemonade, bought fans'— and amused themselves generally:

> Liked Badajoz very much—every body looked so gay—the niñas were so pretty—and the whole appearance—the noises and the smells brought back memories of happy days spent in Spain. There is no country in the world that touches my heart so much. I like the life and I like the people—and I always get on well with them.

After lunch the party went to a bullfight, Goschen's lengthy description of which reveals him as an *aficionado* with an impressive command of the technical vocabulary of the *corrida*. After dinner they 'sat in the limelit Plaza till midnight'.

The following day, Saturday 15 August, was a holiday of obligation and a fiesta. Dancing began at nine o'clock in the morning and continued until noon. The party then went to Mass. After a late breakfast in a restaurant Goschen and a Spanish friend teased 'a very pretty niña in the next house—until arrival of brother or novio'. In the afternoon the party went to another *corrida*, in which a well-known *torero* took part and which was 'magnificent'. In the evening they drove back to their hotel in—or rather on top of—a horse omnibus:

> What a drive—*full* galop for the last quarter of a mile—'garreta— garreta—jaca—mula—macho' and all the old cries—glad to arrive safe but a most exhilarating drive.

After dinner at the hotel, at which Goschen made the acquaintance of the *torero*, the party once again sat in the plaza:

> How nice it was—what gaiety and animation amongst the people and how different from Portugal. Viva España—viva la gracia—olé—olé.

On the following day Goschen and his friends took the train back to Lisbon. 'I have never enjoyed a trip much more,' he commented. In the evening he reached his summer quarters at Cintra, a few miles from Lisbon, and was 'delighted to find my dear ones all well'. (Diary, 13–16 August 1891.)

In May 1893 Goschen received an offer from Rosebery of the secretaryship of the Embassy—it had only just been raised to that status—in Washington. 'I accepted gratefully but with curses in my heart against the ill luck of W'n having been just made an Embassy in time for us to be hunted out of Europe again,' he wrote. 'Boss perfectly miserable,' he added (Diary, 29 May 1893). Unfortunately, he did not explain the reasons for Hosta's reaction to the prospect of returning to her native country. The Goschens left for the United States in October 1893 and returned to England in December 1894. Life in Washington seems to have been agreeable and not over-strenuous.

An incident that occurred during Goschen's stay in the American capital deserves, in the light of subsequent events, to be at least briefly mentioned. In March 1894 the well-known English actors, William and Madge Kendal, gave a short season of plays in a Washington theatre. Goschen recorded having, on 16 March, seen them perform *A Scrap of Paper*, which was, in fact, a translation of a play by the French dramatist, Victorien Sardou, the original of which was entitled *Les Pattes de Mouche* and had first been produced in 1860; he noted that it was 'very good and very amusing' and that after the performance he had supper with the Kendals, had 'a good theatrical talk' and stayed until half-past one. It is interesting to speculate as to whether there was any connection in Goschen's mind between the title of the then popular play which he saw performed in Washington on 16 March 1894 and the words that he attributed to Bethmann Hollweg just over twenty years later in his famous report of his final interview with the German Imperial Chancellor. (See Appendix B.)

Goschen's next posting was as secretary at the St Petersburg Embassy. On 12 March 1895 he set out, much worried about his mother's health. He first went to Dresden to visit his sister Emily and her family. While there he learnt of his mother's death (Diary, 14 March 1895). He finally reached St Petersburg on 27 March. On the same day he was taken to the Foreign Ministry by Lascelles, the Ambassador, and introduced to Lobanov, on whom his characteristic verdict was: 'I did not care much about the latter's face' (Diary, 27 March 1895).

Early in April news arrived of the terms demanded from China by the victorious Japanese. They included the cession of the Liaotung Peninsula. He considered that Britain was right not to intervene, although he recognized that her attitude would 'rather disturb the entente' (Diary, 7 and 9 April 1895). After the signature of the Treaty of Shimonoseki he placed on record his belief that Rosebery had been right not to join in advising Japan not to annex the peninsula, which was 'much more important to the Russians than to us' (Diary, 21 April 1895).

The Goschens enjoyed a splendid summer in Finland. In October Lascelles left to become Ambassador in Berlin, Goschen taking over as chargé d'affaires. The winter of 1895–6 saw Britain beset by difficulties. 'The old year closes with black clouds all round—America, Ashanti—Transvaal and Germany—and always the East—where things are as bad as ever,' commented the chargé, adding: 'Outlook for 1896 very fair to medium' (Diary, under 31 December 1895, but evidently added later).

Nevertheless, despite alarms elsewhere, Britain's relations with Russia remained comparatively tranquil. Early in 1896 Goschen had a brief conversation with the Tsar, which he thought worth reporting to his brother:

When I was presented to the Emperor the other day he suddenly knocked me all of a heap by asking me what the Queen thought of the Transvaal business. I told H.M. that I didn't know but that I expected that there were things connected with it that must have come upon Her Majesty with rather a shock. He shook his head solemnly and said 'Her eldest grandson!' and then passed on![36]

At all events, the chargé d'affaires in St Petersburg provoked no crisis in Britain's relations with Russia.

In May 1896 Goschen was in Moscow, together with the new Ambassador, O'Conor, for the Tsar's coronation. Once again he and his family spent the summer in Finland. On the outward journey he had the misfortune to leave a dispatch-box in the train. He foresaw that 'it will be rather awful if it is lost as it contains all my correspondence with George and Sanderson' (Diary, 25 June 1896). While in Finland he learned with regret of the death of Lobanov, recalling that 'he was always kind and genial with me' (Diary, 1 September 1896). In November he, Hosta and 'Bunt' returned to England on leave. Two days after arriving he called at the Foreign Office and spoke

[36] Goschen to G. J. Goschen (draft), undated, but evidently written early in 1896, Go. P.

to the permanent under-secretary. 'Saw Sanderson—who was friendly—he insists upon it that the Russians have an understanding with Turkey,' he wrote. He for his part was unconvinced, believing that 'they can do what they like without one' (Diary, 16 November 1896).

Early in 1897 Goschen returned to St Petersburg, and not long afterwards, at an Embassy dinner-party, made the acquaintance of Lobanov's successor, Muraviev, whom he described, a trifle oddly, as 'a shiny looking chap—of a very marked Russian type'. 'I expect his character is also rather typical of his race,' he added (Diary, 16 February 1897). Meanwhile, a revolt had broken out in Crete, and war between Greece and Turkey soon followed. O'Conor was ill, and for several months Goschen had to bear much responsibility.

The year 1897 also saw a succession of imperial occasions. On 27 April Goschen recorded the arrival in St Petersburg of the Emperor Franz Joseph—'full, I expect, of German William's ideas on the Eastern Question'. On the following day Goluchowski, the Austro-Hungarian Foreign Minister, lunched at the Embassy. 'I was introduced to Goluchowski who seemed cheery—but he looks like a cook,' wrote the disrespectful secretary. That afternoon he was presented to Franz Joseph, of whose conversational gambit he was critical (Diary, 28 April 1897).

In August the Emperor Wilhelm II and the Empress Augusta arrived. 'I was interested at seeing him,' wrote Goschen, after attending a reception for the Diplomatic Corps at the Winter Palace. He recorded what was evidently his first encounter with the Kaiser and Kaiserin at some length (Diary, 8 August 1897):

> The Emperor with energy stamped on his face—and denoted by his walk—knocked us off very quick: he spoke to me warmly of George—who, he said, had given him a capital dinner in London 10 years ago. 'He has a charming family and an excellent cook.'!! He spoke to very few people—bowing to almost all. The Empress looked nice I thought—and certainly she has still a beautiful figure notwithstanding her 8 children—but those who knew her said she had aged very much latterly.

Later in the month it was the turn of the French President, Faure, accompanied by the Foreign Minister, Hanotaux. 'I noticed much enthusiasm in the streets—much more than for German William,' Goschen commented (Diary, 24 August 1897). However, he thought that 'many Russians see great danger in this and are afraid of the people being inoculated with republican and radical ideas' (Diary, 25 August 1897).

Goschen was once again chargé d'affaires when the Russian fleet moved on Port Arthur. On 2 April 1898 Hosta and 'Bunt' left for London, and after their departure he set down his impression of the Russian Foreign Ministry in the light of recent events. 'What liars these people are—what is the value of their assurances I wonder.' A fortnight later he too left for home. On 18 April he chronicled his arrival in 'dear old England' and his enjoyment, in the company of his family, of his 'first piece of English mutton'.

On calling at the Foreign Office he saw Bertie, then an assistant under-secretary, who 'seemed to think everybody a b— fool except himself', and was 'perfectly furious with Lamps' (Sanderson) because of the part that he had played the previous January in the withdrawal from Port Arthur of the British ships which had been sent there by the local commander-in-chief. Salisbury had been 'furious at the ships being there at all'. George Joachim had been 'pleased' and had 'refused to send them away at once'. Bertie's final comment, as recalled by Goschen, was: 'Lord Salisbury never does put his foot down now—or if he does—he takes it up again directly' (Diary, 20 April 1898).

While on leave Goschen received an offer, which he promptly accepted, of the Belgrade Legation. After a final spell of some ten weeks in St Petersburg he set off for his new post on 17 September, travelling by way of Vienna. He reached his destination on 20 September and the following day noted in his diary that Belgrade was 'not a bad little town—fearfully dusty and dried up'.

The small country, known at this time to English people—as far as it was known to them at all—as 'Servia', had achieved independence from the Ottoman Empire in 1878 and had become a kingdom in 1882. In 1888 King Milan, of the Obrenović dynasty, had obtained a divorce—not valid in the eyes of the Orthodox Church—from his Bessarabian-born queen, Natalia, and in the following year had abdicated in favour of his thirteen-year-old son, Alexander. However, after some years spent abroad he had returned in 1897 and had been appointed by his son commander-in-chief of the army. He was the most powerful figure in the country. King Alexander was unmarried. Vladan Djordjević was Prime Minister and Foreign Minister. The Radicals constituted the opposition but their representation in the Skupština was negligible. Peter Karadjordjević, head of the rival dynasty, was in exile. On most sides the kingdom was bordered by territories, a considerable proportion of the populations of which consisted of Serbs, or of people alleged to be Serbs. However, the treaty concluded by Milan with Austria–Hungary in 1881 was still in force. In 1885 Milan had led his forces against Bulgaria and had been overwhelmingly defeated. In April 1897, on the occasion of Franz Joseph's visit to St Petersburg, Austria–Hungary and Russia had agreed as

to the necessity of maintaining the *status quo* in the Balkan Peninsula
for as long as possible, and, in the event of that proving impossible,
of laying aside all spirit of conquest in that region. Moreover, since
Milan's return Serbian relations with Russia had deteriorated.[37]

Goschen's first stay in Belgrade was brief. After three days he went
on to Tentschach to visit his cousin Oskar, and thence to England.
As a minister-designate he was invited to stay at Balmoral, where he
arrived on the afternoon of 18 October. That evening he dined with
Queen Victoria, who, he recorded, spoke kindly and sympathetically
about George and, more especially, his wife Lucy, who had died a
few months previously. She also spoke a good deal about the Tsar
and Tsarina, 'of whom she seemed very fond'. On the other hand,
Goschen noted: 'She did *not* speak as if she was very satisfied with
her other Imperial grandson—and spoke rather bitterly about his visit
to the Sultan and the time he had chosen to make it' (Diary, 18
October 1898).

On 4 November Goschen called at the Foreign Office. He was not
detained for long. He recorded that he had seen Salisbury 'for exactly
2 minutes' and that 'the only thing he said to me was that he "supposed" the chief thing for me to do was to watch King Milan'. A
few days later he recalled Salisbury's remarks at greater length: 'All
he said about Belgrade was "Let's see—King Milan is there—well
I suppose we had better keep our eye upon him".' 'These were all
my instructions!' commented Goschen, adding: 'Except that he said
that he supposed things would go on quietly as long as Austria held
together—but that he had his doubts about it after the Emperor's
death.' As for the permanent under-secretary: 'Sanderson was not
much better—his instructions were—"I think on the whole we lean
rather towards Austria than to Russia".' Brodrick, the parliamentary under-secretary, cross-examined him 'horribly'—but about
Russia. After these interviews the new minister can have had few
illusions as to the importance that the Foreign Office attached to his
Belgrade mission (Diary, 4 and 9 November 1898).

Goschen arrived back in Belgrade on 14 November 1898. Before
long he made the acquaintance of the leading figures of the regīme.
After some three months at his new post he set down his impressions,
which were not favourable. Milan was 'an arrant scoundrel'; Alexander 'a conceited boy—weak and obstinate at the same time'; as
for Vladan Djordjević and the members of his Government—'those
who have any hand in the direction of affairs are King Milan's
creatures and the scum of Servia' (Diary, 17 February 1899). A few
weeks later he wrote of Alexander that 'his social proceedings and

[37] See M. B. Petrovich, *A History of Modern Serbia 1804–1918* (New York, 1976), ii,
p. 474, to which I am much indebted.

conversation are simply idiotic—it is the only word' (Diary, 29 March 1899). He noted some speculative gossip concerning the young King's matrimonial intentions and his ability or inability to perpetuate the Obrenović dynasty (Diary, 27 November 1898, 21 January 1899). He also met Madame Draga Mašin, formerly lady-in-waiting to Queen Natalia, 'said to be the King's Lady', and recorded a story that the Queen had dismissed her, 'having found her in "flagrante delicto" with the King' (Diary, 11 and 12 March 1899). As far as the country as a whole was concerned, he considered that it was 'difficult to imagine a country in a more hopeless and difficult position than that in which Servia finds herself at present placed'.[38]

Goschen also noted, on the authority of the Belgian Minister, the prevalence of 'the "great Servian" idea'—that is, 'the old Servia of Dushan' (Diary, 8 January 1899). However, he discounted the likelihood of any single-handed attempt to realize such an aspiration by force. There was 'no one for the Serbs to make war on'; the Turks were 'too strong' (Diary, 16 December 1898). 'Poor Servia' had 'no arms, no men and no money' (Diary, 16 April 1899).

In the summer of 1899 a young Bosnian made an unsuccessful attempt on the life of Milan. During the months that followed Goschen recorded a number of remarks concerning the kingdom's situation, both internal and external. He quoted Alexander to the effect 'that in Servia Russia was always called "L'Oncle" and Austria "La Tante"' (Diary, 22 July 1899). He wrote that the Minister of Finance, Vukašin Petrović, whom he found 'an interesting talker', had told him that 'his policy and that of King Milan was to eliminate from the public mind—as they had from their own—all Utopian dreams of a greater Servia'; it was not 'to talk of getting slices of Macedonia here—and to have an eye on Bosnia and Herzegovina'; that 'what was necessary was to improve Servia proper—and legislate for its actual inhabitants—not Serbs in other places'; and that 'the Bosnian and Macedonian Serbs were much happier as they were—and it was useless to think that there was anything in Servia as now constituted to attract them' (Diary, 15 August 1899).

A few weeks later war broke out in southern Africa. Early in 1900 Goschen became personally involved when his elder son volunteered for service. He returned to England and on 17 February saw 'Ted' off at Southampton. Two days later he learnt that Oskar Göschen had died and that Tentschach was to be his. Shortly after resuming his duties in Belgrade he received an offer from Salisbury of the Copenhagen Legation, where he had already served as secretary from 1888 to 1890. 'Oh dear Oh dear! I am not thrilled—tho' it has great advantages and I suppose I must accept it,' he wrote, adding: 'But

[38] Goschen, draft memorandum, undated, Go. P.

another move! and it was so nice and quiet here—while there there are Royalties and British Subjects' (Diary, 31 March). 'Accepted but with misgivings,' he noted the following day. On 8 April he, Hosta and 'Bunt' arrived at Tentschach for their first stay there together. 'What a delight to be in a home of our own at last,' he commented. After a final spell of duty in Belgrade he left for London on 5 June, enjoying 'a very "beau départ"'. *En route* he read that his son's battalion had suffered heavy losses. 'Ted' was indeed a prisoner. Fortunately, his period of captivity proved to be brief.

IV

On 31 July Goschen arrived in Copenhagen. It is from this point in his career that entries in his diary have been selected for inclusion in the text printed below, and his movements and activities generally can be followed by reference to it. His new post presented no insuperable problems. However, as he had foreseen, the octogenarian King Christian IX's close links with not only the British but also the Russian and Greek dynasties kept him busy on the social level.

Goschen greatly enjoyed his years in Copenhagen. He yachted, he fished, he played golf and ping-pong. He was the guest of members of the Danish aristocracy at their country-houses. He was especially friendly with Count Danneskiold-Samsøe, the fortunate father of eight daughters, the youngest but one of whom, Mary, 'Ted' later married. On 13 September 1901, in Copenhagen, King Edward VII knighted him and invested him with the order of St Michael and St George, and on 8 April 1904, also in Copenhagen, conferred on him the knighthood of the Royal Victorian Order. Nevertheless, after a time Goschen began to feel that professional advancement was passing him by. Fortunately, he had had the opportunity to gain favour in what was still, as far as diplomatic appointments were concerned, a powerful quarter. On 3 March 1905 he received the welcome news of his appointment as Ambassador in Vienna. According to Mensdorff, the Austro-Hungarian Ambassador in London, who was Edward VII's second cousin and had formerly been Goschen's colleague in St Petersburg, Lansdowne knew him only slightly—a statement that the diary (12 December 1901 and 9 December 1902) confirms—but the King had apparently desired his appointment.[39]

Goschen was delighted at his appointment to a post which, at the time, he probably expected to be his last. At the end of March he

[39] Mensdorff to Goluchowski, 8 March 1905, P.A. VIII/134, Haus-, Hof- und Staatsarchiv, Vienna. I am indebted to Dr F. R. Bridge for transcripts of this document and of that quoted immediately below.

paid a visit to Vienna to prepare his take-over of the Embassy, situated in the Metternichgasse, and renewed his acquaintance with Goluchowski. In May he and Hosta returned to England. On 29 May they were the guests of Mensdorff, who found Goschen 'ein netter sympathischer Mensch', but thought Hosta 'verlegen'.[40] After a week-end at Windsor Castle they set out for the Austrian capital on 22 June. On the morrow of his arrival Goschen again saw Goluchowski. Three days later he presented his credentials to the Emperor. He also paid another call on Goluchowski, who, he reported to Lansdowne, said 'that it was too hot to talk politics, and that he, like every body else, was going to leave Vienna as soon as possible'.[41] After spending a good part of July and early August at Tentschach, Goschen and his wife arrived, on 13 August, at Marienbad, where Edward VII was due shortly to take his annual cure, and where, accordingly, the Ambassador was expected to be in attendance.

With the aid of Henry Wickham Steed, *The Times*'s young and energetic Vienna correspondent,[42] Goschen made a real effort to grasp the complicated issues involved in the 'Hungarian Crisis', which had arisen three years previously with the introduction in both the Reichsrat and the Hungarian Parliament of bills to increase the size of the army. In December 1905 he sent Grey, who had just become Foreign Secretary in the new Liberal Government, a long account of the problems of the Habsburg Empire, with special emphasis on the Magyar question. However, he set limits to the scope of his enquiry into what he rightly called 'the extraordinarily complicated internal affairs of the Austro-Hungarian Monarchy':

> There is certainly no doubt that the objects, aims and political relations of Pan Germans, progressive Germans, moderate Germans, Poles, Slovaks, Slovenes, young Tchecks, old Tchecks, Ruthenians, Croats, and all the other different nationalities of which the Empire is composed, require an almost lifelong study before they can be thoroughly understood.[43]

Goschen found Goluchowski, who began before long to appear in his diary and correspondence as 'Golu', amusing and agreeable, as far as personal relations were concerned, but uncommunicative on political matters. 'I love Golu socially and we get on first rate,' he wrote in April 1906 to Lascelles, now in his eleventh year at the Berlin Embassy; 'but I hate going to see him officially as he sits and blinks

[40] Mensdorff, Tagebuch, 29 May 1905, Nachlass Albert Mensdorff-Pouilly-Dietrichstein, Karton IV, Haus-, Hof- und Staatsarchiv, Vienna.
[41] Goschen to Lansdowne, 30 June 1905, Lan. P., F.O. 800/117.
[42] For Goschen's relations with Steed see P. Schuster, *Henry Wickham Steed und die Habsburgermonarchie* (Vienna, 1970).
[43] Goschen to Grey, 13 Dec. 1905, Gr. P., F.O. 800/40.

at me and it is difficult to extract anything from him.'[44] Goluchowki resigned some six months later, not altogether to Goschen's regret, and was succeeded by Alois Count Aehrenthal, whose acquaintance Goschen did not make until the following January, but of whom he came to form a favourable impression. 'The more I see of d'Ährenthal the more I like him,' he wrote to Grey; he found the Foreign Minister 'rather slow and *very* cautious', but 'charming to do business with'.[45] However, whether Goluchowski or Aehrenthal was at the Ballhausplatz, there was one thing that remained constant. That was Goschen's belief that Austria-Hungary's conduct of foreign relations was controlled by Germany. As early as April 1897, at the time of Franz-Joseph's visit to St Petersburg, he had recorded his conviction on this point in his diary. In Vienna he adhered to it. In December 1905 he informed Grey that 'as regards the Foreign Policy of Austria-Hungary it is scarcely too much to say that she is well under the thumb of Germany'.[46] In 1907 he reported that Aehrenthal 'buttons himself up tightly when he is waiting for instructions from Berlin'.[47] Events did not confirm the correctness of this assumption.[48]

Goschen was destined to enjoy a briefer tenure of the Vienna Embassy than he himself would have wished. In November 1907 the Foreign Office reminded the King, who was expecting a visit from the Kaiser, that Lascelles's appointment as Ambassador in Berlin, which had already been extended once, would finally expire the following October and would not be renewed.[49] In January 1908 the Clerk of the Privy Council, Almeric FitzRoy, another diarist, recorded having discussed the impending vacancy with Metternich, the German Ambassador; he gathered that Nicolson, at that time Ambassador in St Petersburg, would not be acceptable in Berlin, because of the part he had played two years previously at the Algeciras Conference.[50] In June Grey proposed the name of Fairfax Cartwright, the Minister in Munich. The King passed on this proposal to his nephew, who displayed no enthusiasm, expressing a preference for some public figure of the calibre of Curzon, Cromer, Rosebery or Bryce. Grey also heard from Metternich that Cartwright had once written a book containing reflections on Berlin society. Grey did not respond favourably to the Kaiser's suggestion. Eventually the name of the Ambassador in Vienna was suggested. On 11 August the King,

[44] Goschen to Lascelles, 11 Apr. 1906, Las. P., F.O. 800/13.
[45] Goschen to Grey, 19 Apr. 1907, Gr. P., F.O. 800/40.
[46] Goschen to Grey, 13 Dec. 1905, Gr. P., F.O. 800/40.
[47] Goschen to Grey, 19 Apr. 1907, Gr. P., F.O. 800/40.
[48] F. R. Bridge, *Great Britain and Austria-Hungary 1908–1914* (1972), p. 18.
[49] 'Views of the Foreign Office on subjects which the German Emperor may possibly raise during the visit of His Majesty to Windsor,' 9 Nov. 1907, R.A., W. 52/55.
[50] A. FitzRoy, *Memoirs* (1925), i, p. 337; see also H. Nicolson, *Sir Arthur Nicolson* (1930), p. 290.

who was *en route*, by way of Ischl, to Marienbad, met the Kaiser at Friedrichshof, a royal Schloss near Cronberg. There Wilhelm agreed to accept Goschen as Ambassador.[51] However, he long resented the unwillingness of the British Government to send a well-known public figure to Berlin as Ambassador.[52]

On the day following the Friedrichshof meeting the contented occupant of the house in the Metternichgasse boarded the royal train, now bound for Ischl. Soon afterwards the King sent for him and informed him of his destiny. In the circumstances he could scarcely refuse to accept the promotion thrust upon him. He could not even talk the matter over with his wife. His diary clearly reveals what his feelings were and what he foresaw hers would be.

Goschen had obvious private reasons for not wishing to leave 'dear Vienna'.[53] But, if we may believe Wickham Steed, who had a conversation with him at Marienbad only two days after he had learned from King Edward of his appointment to Berlin, he foresaw that the question of German naval expansion, which Hardinge had raised unsuccessfully with the Kaiser at Cronberg, would present him, as Ambassador, with an insoluble problem. On 14 August Steed wrote to Moberly Bell, the manager of *The Times*:

> Sir Edward Goschen told me this afternoon of his appointment to Berlin as successor to Frank Lascelles. . . .
>
> Hardinge hinted to me at Ischl and Goschen told me today in so many words that the King's visit to William at Cronberg was by no means a political success. It seems that the King and William avoided serious political talk but that Hardinge took the bull by the horns and frankly raised the question of armaments. He pointed out that the constant increase of the German navy would compel us constantly to go one better and that this would engender such discontent in England that Anglo-German relations might be very seriously affected.
>
> The Germans proved quite intractable, so much so that Goschen tells me he regards his appointment to Berlin with dismay as things appear to be going straight towards a conflict which neither he nor any diplomatist will be able to prevent and by which his reputation may be ruined.[54]

It is open to question whether Goschen was wise to associate so closely and so publicly with the highly polemical Steed. Earlier in the year Steed had been warned by Bell that he was 'credited among

[51] For the history of Goschen's appointment see S. Lee, *King Edward VII* (1927), ii, pp. 612–19.
[52] H. F. Young, *Prince Lichnowsky and the Great War* (Athens, U.S.A., 1977), p. 206.
[53] Goschen to Cartwright, 27 Aug. 1908, Cartwright Papers.
[54] Steed to Bell, 14 Aug. 1908, Steed Papers. See also Steed, op. cit., i, p. 282.

other things with having converted into our bitterest enemies one of the few nations that stood by us during the Boer War'.[55] Towards the end of August Steed sent the manager what purported to be a report of a conversation at Marienbad, in which he declared that King Edward and Goschen had taken the view 'that if France is ever attacked by Germany, it will be because of French friendship for England and that, as France would be in that case involved in a struggle against heavy odds, England is bound to lend her prompt and efficient military aid'; both men, he added, strongly favoured 'the maintenance and development of our present friendships coupled with thoroughgoing Army Reform, based on some form of obligatory service'.[56]

Another visitor at Marienbad that year was Paul von Schwabach, a wealthy Berlin banker, who was also honorary British Consul-General. His strikingly wide circle of acquaintances included Friedrich von Holstein, to whom he wrote from the spa on 22 August, informing him that he had made the acquaintance of the Goschens (the appointment to the Berlin Embassy having by this time been announced). He had, he related, called at the wish of the Ambassador, and had found him to be 'der Typus des freundlichen, wohlgewaschenen älteren Engländers'. Goschen was, he thought, approaching his new task with the best possible will, but without enthusiasm, and with the feeling that he had a not exactly comfortable time ahead of him—'ohne Begeisterung und in dem Gefühl eine nicht eben bequeme Zeit vor sich zu haben'. Lady Goschen, he added, was American—'liebenswürdig und anspruchslos, good class, but not smart'.[57]

The last weeks of Goschen's Vienna ambassadorship proved to be eventful. Franco-German relations were disturbed by the Casablanca incident. The Foreign Office showed concern at the possibility, as a consequence of the Young Turk Revolution of the previous July, of a declaration by Bulgaria of her independence of the Ottoman Empire. On 2 October, accordingly, Grey asked the Ambassadors in Paris, St Petersburg and Vienna to urge the governments to which they were accredited to instruct their representatives in Sofia to deprecate any such step;[58] he asked Goschen in particular to urge the Austro-Hungarian Government to use its influence on Ferdinand of Bulgaria himself[59]—Goschen and Aehrenthal both being in Budapest and the Prince also in Hungary at the time. On 4 October Goschen

[55] Bell to Steed, 10 July 1908, Bell Papers.
[56] Steed to Bell, 19 Aug. 1908, Steed Papers.
[57] Schwabach to Holstein, 22 Aug. 1908, P. von Schwabach, *Aus meinen Akten* (Berlin, 1927), p. 149.
[58] Grey to Bertie and others, 2 Oct. 1908, *B.D.*, v, no. 278.
[59] Grey to Goschen, 2 Oct. 1908, *B.D.*, v, no. 279.

reported that he had spoken to Aehrenthal, who had expressed disbelief as to rumours of an impending Bulgarian declaration of independence, and had declined to take the course urged upon him.[60] On the following day Bulgaria proclaimed her independence. Grey was indignant, and incredulous as to Aehrenthal's veracity.[61] On 6 October Austria-Hungary announced the annexation of Bosnia-Herzegovina. The Treaty of Berlin had thus been violated twice within two days.

The British press, *The Times* particularly, denounced Austria-Hungary's conduct. Even Valentine Chirol, the head of that newspaper's Foreign Department, while considering the Austro-Hungarian Government's action 'really inexcusable', felt that *The Times* had perhaps been 'slightly more vehement in denouncing it than was necessary or expedient'.[62] This press campaign produced a vigorous reaction.

In the normal course of events Goschen would have gone home to receive instructions and kiss hands on his new appointment. However, the situation was not normal. Moreover, Lascelles having left, the Berlin Embassy was under a chargé d'affaires. It was accordingly decided that Goschen should proceed direct to the German capital as soon as possible; on the other hand, his successor in Vienna, Fairfax Cartwright, was not to take up his post for a month or so, as there had been 'such a display of unfriendliness towards England'.[63]

Goschen was still in Vienna when, on 28 October, the *Daily Telegraph* published, under the headline, 'The German Emperor and England', a 'personal interview' with a 'representative Englishman', the unnamed author of which explained that he had decided to make public the substance of a 'lengthy conversation', which it had been his 'recent privilege to have with the German Emperor'. The 'representative Englishman' was, in fact, Brigadier Edward Montagu-Stuart-Wortley, of Highcliffe Castle, on the Hampshire coast. In the previous year Montagu-Stuart-Wortley, at that time a colonel, had lent his house to the Kaiser; more recently he had been that monarch's guest at manœuvres. The 'interview' took the form of a monologue. When reports of the Kaiser's remarks appeared in the German press there was an uproar.[64] (See Appendix A.)

On 3 November Hardinge wrote to Goschen to express the hope that, 'with the Emperor exploding bombshells in the newspapers' and in view of Germany's possible importance in the negotiations concerning the Balkans, he should proceed to his new post 'at once'.[65] Meanwhile,

[60] Goschen to Grey, 4 Oct. 1908, *B.D.*, no. 289.
[61] Grey to Goschen, 5 Oct. 1908, *B.D.*, v, no. 299.
[62] Chirol to Steed, 19 Oct. 1908, Chirol Papers.
[63] Hardinge to Knollys, 26 Oct. 1908, R.A., W. 54/120.
[64] O. J. Hale, *Publicity and Diplomacy* (New York, 1940), p. 319.
[65] Hardinge to Goschen, 3 Nov. 1908 (copy), H.P., 13.

the outgoing Ambassador was being made to feel the chill that had descended on Austro-British relations. His Viennese friends displayed a tendency to be out of town. On 4 November, during a *cercle*, which followed a state banquet in honour of the King of the Hellenes, he had an exchange with Aehrenthal, which he described in a dispatch as 'short, but somewhat sharp'[66] and in his diary more graphically. The mutually unfavourable opinions expressed by the Foreign Minister and the Ambassador on this occasion did not by any means disappear with the latter's departure on 7 November. Aehrenthal is on record as having a few weeks later described Goschen as a sleepy-head—'eine Schlafmütze'.[67] For some time he continued to criticize 'den unfähigen Goschen'[68] and the 'wenig hervorragenden Sir Edward Goschen',[69] whom he held partly responsible for the imperfect information concerning Austro-Hungarian policy possessed by the British Government, which, at the time of the Sandjak railway episode, had been under the impression that 'wir hätten jeden Schritt auf Befehl Deutschlands unternommen'.[70] Goschen, for his part, blamed Aehrenthal, according to a French acquaintance, whom he got to know in Berlin, for the irresponsibility with which he had rushed into an affair that might lead to war.[71]

V

The Berlin Embassy, where on 8 November Goschen took up his duties, was, like the Imperial Foreign Office, situated in the Wilhelmstrasse. A substantial stone structure with a classical portico, it stood only a short distance from the junction with Unter den Linden. Rumbold described it later as 'a fine but somewhat gloomy building', which had originally been built for a railway magnate.[72]

It soon became apparent that the new Ambassador need not have come to Berlin so soon. When, on the day following his arrival, he called at the Imperial Foreign Office, he found that Schoen, his former colleague in Copenhagen and now Secretary of State, was absent, and that Kiderlen-Wächter, the German Minister in Bucharest, who was temporarily in charge, was unable to say when the Kaiser or Bülow would be able to receive him.

[66] Goschen to Grey, 5 Nov. 1908, *B.D.*, v, no. 430.
[67] *Das politische Tagebuch Joseph Redlichs*, ed. F. Fellner (Graz, Köln, 1953), 9 Dec. 1908, i, p. 3.
[68] Aehrenthal to Mensdorff, 17 Dec. 1908, *Ö.U.A.*, i, no. 768.
[69] Aehrenthal to Mensdorff, 25 Feb. 1909, *Ö.U.A.*, i, no. 1055.
[70] Aehrenthal to Mensdorff, 17 Dec. 1908, *Ö.U.A.*, i, no. 768.
[71] Marie Radziwill to Robilant, 5–7 Dec. 1908, *Lettres de la Princesse Radziwill au Géneral de Robilant* (Bologna, 1934), iv, p. 52.
[72] Rumbold, op. cit., p. 7; for a picture of the Embassy see p. 6.

On 10 November, Jules Cambon, the French Ambassador, called. He had clearly lost no time in making the acquaintance of his new colleague. On the same and the following day the Reichstag debated the *Daily Telegraph* 'interview'. Bülow, Goschen reported, 'was looking worn and ill'; the speech delivered by Kiderlen-Wächter, who sported a yellow waistcoat, was 'received with derision and noise on every side'.[73] On 13 November Goschen met the Chancellor, who did all the talking'.[74] The talk, though copious, was evidently not substantial.

A week later, at Potsdam, Goschen presented his credentials to the Kaiser, whom he had already met briefly twice—in St Petersburg in 1897 and in Copenhagen in 1903. He found the first part of the audience 'rather an ordeal', he acknowledged to Hardinge. Wilhelm 'looked so absolutely stiff and unbending', and on being presented with the King's letter, looked straight at him 'without saying a word—and without a smile or an encouraging look of any kind'. Goschen thereupon improvised a short speech, 'which was evidently expected'. As soon as he had finished, Goschen continued, 'the whole man changed'. The Kaiser 'shook hands warmly' and talked to him 'in the kindest and most friendly manner'. 'He said that I should find my task of maintaining and strengthening the relations between the two countries an easy one as no one could possibly entertain any doubt with regard to *His* friendly and affectionate sentiments towards England,' reported Goschen, adding, however: 'He did *not* however mention on this occasion what the sentiments of a large portion of his subjects were.' The Empress was 'exceedingly gracious and kind'. 'But the first few minutes of my Audience took it out of me,' confessed Goschen.[75]

A few days later Goschen sent Hardinge a comparison of the locum tenens at the German Foreign Office and the absent Secretary of State:

> Kiderlen-Wächter is the man whose yellow waistcoat gave such offence the other day in the Reichstag. He is not a bad fellow and tells amusing stories. But I should prefer to deal with Schön. Their procedure is, I expect, about the same—that is to say they both are prone to agree with me at first, then see the Chancellor, and then give one an entirely different answer. But Schön has a good manner and is always agreeable and polite. Kiderlen is more nonchalant and apt to meet one's arguments with that terrible German expression 'Ach was!'[76]

[73] Goschen to Grey, 12 Nov. 1908, *B.D.*, vi, no. 134; for Kiderlen's waistcoat see Goschen to Hardinge, 27 Nov. 1908, H.P., 11, quoted below.
[74] Goschen to Grey, 13 Nov. 1908, *B.D.*, vi, no. 136.
[75] Goschen to Hardinge, 21 Nov. 1908, H.P., 11.
[76] Goschen to Hardinge, 27 Nov. 1908, H.P., 11.

Goschen accordingly welcomed Schoen's return at the beginning of December. He had already learned to appreciate how complex were the arrangements for the conduct of Germany's foreign relations, as he explained in another letter to the permanent under-secretary:

> I am glad that Schoen has come back as he is always pleasant to deal with—but practically, except as regards current work when it is always more agreeable to have to do with a pleasant rather than an unpleasant man, it does not make much difference who is at the Foreign Office here. I now cease to wonder that Tschirschky was ever Minister of Foreign Affairs. But honestly the system of *three* Foreign Ministers is a nuisance.... It is of course a very convenient system for the German Government as it is apt to knock the bottom out of all *personal* diplomacy.[77]

Early in February 1909 there took place the long postponed visit to Berlin of King Edward and Queen Alexandra. Towards the end of the month, in another letter to Hardinge, Goschen enlarged on his previous account of the German Foreign Office, emphasizing how difficult it was 'to deal with so many Ministers of Foreign Affairs', and asking:

> How do I know when talking to Schoen how much of what I say reaches Bülow? How much does Kiderlen tell Schoen? for Kiderlen is much more Bülow's man than Schoen is. How much of our conversations with any of these reaches the Emperor who has the final decision? One cannot tell. I must say that on coming to Berlin I expected to find order in affairs developed to the highest point. What I *do* find is more muddle—more confusion—than I have found in any country during my 35 years experience. Chaos is the only word for it—and the admitted failures of German diplomacy during recent years is [*sic*] the result thereof. These failures have greatly contributed to the distrust with which they regard nearly every other country. They are trying to change their F.O. system but there will have to be considerable improvement before they satisfy either their own, or any other, country.[78]

Another passage in this letter affords a good illustration of the working in Berlin of Britain's *entente* with France. 'I like Cambon—we get on excellently together—but I always have the feeling that he has got an axe of his own to grind,' wrote Goschen.[79] Cambon, for his part, clearly desired to collaborate closely with his British colleague from the start. Before long there was regular consultation between the British and French Ambassadors.

[77] Goschen to Hardinge, 4 Dec. 1908, H.P., 11.
[78] Goschen to Hardinge, 26 Feb. 1909, H.P., 15.
[79] Ibid.

On the other hand, Goschen's relations with his Russian colleague, Osten-Sacken, were anything but intimate. 'Osten-Sacken of course one never sees and moreover his proclivities are decidedly German,' he explained to Nicolson, soon after the latter had succeeded Hardinge at the Foreign Office.[80] A few weeks later he wrote:

> Osten-Sacken's absence is immaterial, as, charming though he is, he never tells either Cambon or me *anything*, and seems to live, as far as Anglo- and Franco-Russian Relations are concerned, in the period of the Crimean War. He would appear to be ignorant that Russia has an Entente with one and an alliance with the other.[81]

Meanwhile, the problem of the naval rivalry of Britain and Germany remained. In March 1909 McKenna, after a struggle within the Cabinet, produced naval estimates which provided for four new battleships to be laid down at once, and four more if in any future contingency they were needed. In the following month Goschen reported having had conversations with Kiderlen-Wächter, who, he wrote, had more than once hinted at the desirability of an understanding between their two countries. (A few weeks previously Goschen in a private letter to Hardinge had expressed his lack of confidence in Kiderlen's sincerity when he protested his 'anxiety for a close understanding'.[82]) The idea of the man whom Goschen described as 'Bülow's mouthpiece' was, he explained to Grey, that such an understanding should take the form either of a political *entente*, such as would render increased naval construction on either side a source of satisfaction rather than of suspicion, or of a naval convention, under which each party would bind itself for a fixed period not to make war against the other, to join in no coalition directed against the other, and to observe a benevolent neutrality, should the other party be involved in hostilities against any other Power or Powers.[83]

Kiderlen-Wächter's overture was not well received by the Foreign Office.[84] Goschen himself was robustly sceptical. In May he wrote to Hardinge:

> I still hold the opinion that the best way to be friends with Germany, or at all events to retain her respect is to shew clearly, without too much talk, that we intend to maintain our maritime supremacy—whatever it may cost us and whatever they may do. They

[80] Goschen to Nicolson, 14 Oct. 1910, N.P., F.O. 800/344.
[81] Goschen to Nicolson, 4 Nov. 1910, N.P., F.O. 800/344.
[82] Goschen to Hardinge, 26 March 1909, H.P., 15.
[83] Goschen to Grey, 16 Apr. 1909, *B.D.*, vi, no. 174.
[84] Minutes by Grey, Hardinge, Crowe and others, ibid.

understand that sort of thing, being bullies, much better than invitations to reduce armaments.[85]

A few days later he developed this theme:

The only thing the modern German understands and respects is force—and, as I have often said to you, the best and only understanding we can have with them is to make them understand that we mean business and intend, whatever it may cost us, to maintain our maritime supremacy.[86]

In July Bülow resigned. He was succeeded as Chancellor by Theobald von Bethmann Hollweg, hitherto Secretary of State at the Ministry of the Interior, whom Goschen, although without actually having met him, described to Hardinge as 'a solid steady man—not so brilliant as Bülow but more reliable I should think and hope'.[87] Later in the month the Admiralty announced that the four 'contingent ships' were to be included in the current programme.

A few weeks after taking office the new Chancellor drew up a statement of policy. Germany should try to reach an agreement with Britain, if possible in the form of a treaty, under which Britain would pledge herself to neutrality in the event of Germany being either attacked by her neighbours or being obliged to go to war under the terms of her alliance with Austria-Hungary. A naval agreement would be a means to such a treaty.[88] On 21 August he had a conversation with Goschen, who telegraphed Grey that Bethmann Hollweg had told him that Germany was ready to make proposals for a naval arrangement, but that discussion of such an arrangement would lead to no practical result, unless it formed part of a general understanding.[89] In October the Chancellor again saw Goschen, on this occasion Schoen also being present.[90] There were further talks in November, and Goschen pointed out to Grey that what the Chancellor was proposing resembled strikingly what Kiderlen-Wächter had suggested in April.[91] No real progress was made.

These contacts afforded Goschen a number of opportunities to appraise the character and outlook of the new Chancellor, whom he evidently came to like personally and whom, he informed Hardinge, he found 'honest and straightforward', 'always excessively nice and pleasant', and 'very friendly and cordial'.[92] However, in comparison

[85] Goschen to Hardinge, 22 May 1909, H.P., 15.
[86] Goschen to Hardinge, 28 May 1909, H.P., 15.
[87] Goschen to Hardinge, 17 July 1909, H.P., 15.
[88] Bethmann Hollweg, Memorandum, 13 Aug. 1909, G.P., xxviii, no. 10,325.
[89] Goschen to Grey, 21 Aug. 1909, B.D., vi, nos. 186–7.
[90] Goschen to Grey and to Hardinge, 15 Oct. 1909, B.D., vi, nos. 200–1.
[91] Goschen to Grey, 4 Nov. 1909, B.D., vi, no. 204.
[92] Goschen to Hardinge, 28 Aug. and 'Xmas Eve' 1909, and 28 Jan. 1910, H.P., 15, 20.

with Bülow, 'a supple many sided Cosmopolitan', he thought Beth-mann Hollweg 'a Prussian of bureaucratic tendencies'.[93] After a conversation early in March 1910 he reported that 'while the Chancellor was talking to me I could not help thinking that in Foreign Affairs and diplomatic conversations Bethmann-Hollweg was a novice'; he considered the novice 'intellectual and, in certain respects, very able', but 'not, at all events yet, what one would call a European Statesman'.[94]

It should be noted that it was at this time, February 1910, that Goschen's wife, Hosta, was taken seriously ill. She never fully recovered. Goschen's work as Ambassador during the two years that followed has to be understood as having been carried out in the shadow of his wife's illness.

On 6 May 1910 Edward VII died. Goschen's diary and letters shed some light on the much discussed question of the King's role in the conduct of foreign relations. He clearly found Goschen a valuable source of information. This was especially true of Serbian affairs, concerning which Goschen possessed considerable knowledge, based on first-hand experience.[95] The King's share in the appointment of Goschen first to Vienna in 1905 and then to Berlin in 1908 was clearly important. He knew Goschen personally better than did either of the Foreign Secretaries of the period. In this connection there seems to be no reason to question the accuracy of Mensdorff's assessment of the decisive nature of the part played by the King in 1905. Moreover, he could exercise pressure on a reluctant appointee in a way that would have been difficult for a Foreign Secretary. It is most doubtful whether in 1908 Grey, who was a decade and a half younger than the Ambassador in Vienna, and, except when the latter was in England, could communicate with him only by bag or by telegram, could have talked him into exchanging the Metternichgasse for the Wilhelmstrasse, as did the King in the royal train on the way to Ischl.

In the summer of the same year Schoen was succeeded as Secretary of State at the German Foreign Office by Kiderlen-Wächter. Goschen told Hardinge that he regarded Kiderlen's appointment as a 'misfortune'.[96] A few months later in a letter to Nicolson, he predicted, on this occasion without great insight, that the new Secretary of State 'would never go in for cheap and showy successes at the expense of a rival'.[97] Before the end of the year he expressed his conviction that 'Kiderlen has already got the whole direction of Foreign Affairs into

[93]Goschen to Hardinge, 14 Jan. 1910, H.P., 20.
[94] Goschen to Hardinge, 4 March 1910, H.P., 20.
[95] Goschen to Edward VII, 1 Dec. 1905, R.A., W. 47/345.
[96] Goschen to Hardinge, 1 July 1910, H.P., 20.
[97] Goschen to Nicolson, 25 Nov. 1910, N.P., F.O. 800/344.

his hands and that the Chancellor, as regards that department is like wax in his hands'.[98]

However, irrespective of questions of personnel, it was apparent that Britain's relations with Germany were not improving. On 7 November 1910 a prominent article in the *Daily Chronicle* complained that, since the Liberals had come into power, Britain's relations had improved with every country in the world—except Germany; with Germany her relations had grown worse. The article was date-lined 'Berlin'. The entry in Goschen's diary for the following day shows that the article had not escaped his attention.

As it happened, the year 1910 passed without an international crisis. In November Goschen was the guest of the Duke of Trachenberg at a shooting-party in Silesia. A few days later he sent Nicolson his impressions of the view taken by the Kaiser by his subjects in general, and, more especially, by those fortunate ones who had been present:

> Talking of the Emperor it is a strange thing how much he has lost in the eyes of his people. I hear it from all sides—and I have come to the conclusion that it is now only abroad that He is looked upon with the respect and belief in his Powers which he used to enjoy in Germany. I was perfectly astonished at my shooting party the other day to hear how he was criticized. For instance they were talking of the present Chancellor and bewailing the fact that there was now not a single great man in Germany capable of directing the affairs of the Empire. I said, 'Well at all events you have the Emperor.' They as much as said God help us if we have only the Emperor to rely on—what they *did* say any way was that His Majesty had certain high ideals and thought he could do a lot of things better than any one else—but 'as for directing the affairs off the Empire—why—he is not in the least in touch with his people and has no notion whatever of politics—either external or internal'.! This, mind you, was from men who know him well and are continually about him. This is what the *big* people say—the lower ranks are still harder on him.[99]

When, on 1 July 1911, the *Panther* anchored off Agadir, Goschen was in England. On his return to Berlin he was under no illusion as to his popularity. On 12 August, after a dinner-party at Friedrichshof, he had a vigorous exchange on the subject of Morocco with the Kaiser, who, he assured Grey, nevertheless desired a settlement and was merely temporarily irritated by the charges of timidity brought against

[98] Goschen to Nicolson, 17 Dec. 1910, N.P., F.O. 800/344.
[99] Goschen to Nicolson, 18 Nov. 1910, N.P., F.O. 800/344.

him so freely by the Pan-German press.[100] In September he warned Nicolson that 'the feeling against England is very widespread'.[101]

At 6.30 on the evening of Saturday 2 February 1912 the Foreign Office dispatched a telegram to Goschen, informing him that some communications had taken place with the Kaiser and the German Chancellor through Albert Ballin (the Hamburg shipowner) and Ernest Cassel (the Cologne-born London financier), and asking him, somewhat optimistically, to come to London 'at once', so that Grey could talk things over with him on 'Monday', that is 4 February.[102] It was, in fact, on Monday 4 February that Goschen left Berlin. He reached London the following morning. His diary tells in considerable detail the story of his contacts in the course of the day with Nicolson, Grey and Haldane, about which little or nothing has hitherto been known.[103] Haldane wrote later somewhat patronizingly in his *Autobiography* that 'Goschen was an excellent man, but had hardly sufficient imagination to be capable of getting on to more than agreeable terms with the Germans'.[104] The target of this criticism had made the acquaintance of the Secretary of State for War at Marienbad during the 1906 season and had not been favourably impressed. The renewal of that acquaintance on 5 February 1912 clearly did not cause him to change his opinion.

After a stay in London of, according to Paul Cambon, only twenty-four hours,[105] Goschen returned to his post. Early on 8 February Haldane, accompanied by his younger brother, John, the distinguished physiologist, reached the German capital. 'I arrived at Berlin at 7.30 this morning, and was met at the Friedrichstrasse by Sir Edward Goschen's motor and the embassy porter,' he recorded, evidently not without pique; he was received by the Ambassador himself at the more civilized hour of 10 o'clock.[106]

Goschen did not participate in the subsequent conversations on naval and cognate matters with Bethmann Hollweg, the Kaiser and Tirpitz. However, in his correspondence with Nicolson he showed his appreciation of the difficulties. On 9 February he recalled having pointed out in London that 'the difficulty to be foreseen in the whole business was—Tirpitz'; it was his 'firm opinion that if Lord Haldane had talked to him till Doomsday [*sic*] he could not have persuaded him to diminish the number of ships for which he has applied and

[100] Goschen to Grey, 16 Aug. 1911, *B.D.*, no. 476.
[101] Goschen to Nicolson, 22 Sept. 1911, N.P., F.O. 800/350.
[102] Grey to Goschen, 2 Feb. 1912, *B.D.*, vi, no. 494.
[103] On this point see R. T. B. Langhorne, 'Great Britain and Germany, 1911–1914', in *British Foreign Policy under Sir Edward Grey*, ed. F. H. Hinsley (Cambridge, 1977), p. 604, n. 19.
[104] R. B. Haldane, *Autobiography* (1929), p. 240.
[105] Paul Cambon to Poincaré, 7 Feb. 1912, *D.D.F.*, 3, i, no. 628.
[106] Haldane, Diary, 8 Feb. 1912, *B.D.*, vi, no. 506.

which there is little doubt the Reichstag will sanction'.[107] On the following day he wrote that he had before him Haldane's memorandum of his conversation with the Kaiser and Tirpitz, reporting what it was possible to obtain from the German Government. 'And what does it amount to?' he asked. He himself supplied the answer:

> That if what has been suggested is carried out the Germans get what under Grey's instructions, I have been opposing for two years—namely a political understanding without a naval agreement.[108]

On 15 February 1912—four days after Haldane's departure from Berlin—Hosta Goschen died at Arco, a health-resort in the south of Tyrol, as it then was, where she had been staying since the previous autumn in the hope of regaining her health. Goschen went to Arco, and then on to England for the funeral, which took place at Flimwell on 23 February. He made no further entries in his diary until August.

Goschen was not perturbed by the unfruitfulness of discussions, as to the utility of which he had been sceptical. 'I am afraid it is quite true that I have never cooperated very warmly in the endeavours of Germany to bring about an understanding that would tie our hands and free theirs,' he wrote to Nicolson in May 1912.[109] In any case, the lack of any positive outcome to the intermittent talks of the last three years did not in itself undermine Britain's relations with Germany, as to which he continued to be cheerful. In June of the same year he reported having told Marschall von Bieberstein, who was about to proceed to London as German Ambassador, that relations between their two countries 'were better than they had been'.[110] He was optimistic as to the prospects of preserving peace, at least among the Great Powers. Although he commented on the existence among German officers of 'a strong feeling against France' and on the activity of the Great General Staff, he declared that he could not believe that 'they contemplate *making* war'. As for Bethmann Hollweg, he 'was a man of peace to the core'.[111] In April 1913 he sent Nicolson another appraisal of the Chancellor's outlook:

> That he earnestly desires good relations with England is certain; and I have every hope that he is beginning to share the opinion of the growing number of his countrymen who realize that the two countries can be on perfectly good terms with each other and help

[107] Goschen to Nicolson, 9 Feb. 1912, N.P., F.O. 800/353.
[108] Goschen to Nicolson, 10 Feb. 1912, N.P., F.O. 800/353.
[109] Goschen to Nicolson, 18 May 1912, N.P., F.O. 800/355.
[110] Goschen to Nicolson, 21 June 1912, N.P., F.O. 800/357.
[111] Goschen to Nicolson, 3 May 1912, N.P., F.O. 800/355.

each other in moments of international difficulty without any political or naval formula.[112]

In this connection it should be emphasized that Goschen's feelings towards Germany and the German people evidently mellowed during the years of his Berlin ambassadorship. He made numerous friends. He enjoyed much hospitality both in the capital and on country estates. There was plenty to delight him in the musical life of Berlin. He found his duties absorbing. 'Of course I thoroughly enjoy the work, the most interesting I have ever had in my long career,' he wrote to Nicolson in 1910.[113] In December of the following year he acknowledged in his diary that he did not think that everyone at Court liked him and that he was sure that the Emperor did not; but he thought that the Crown Prince did, and that he certainly got on well with the Empress. In fact, after the death of Hosta the Empress showed him much sympathy, which he appreciated. In 1912 he wrote, apropos of his relations with Bethmann Hollweg, who shared his love of music,[114] that 'he and I have always been such good friends'.[115] Although in moments of stress he occasionally made animadversions on the German character,[116] he does not appear to have been unhappy in Berlin. Right down to the summer of 1914 his diary and correspondence contain nothing to suggest that he was pining for a transfer.

However, it was a fact that the Kaiser did not like or at least did not have a high opinion of Goschen. No doubt he compared the Ambassador unfairly with his predecessor, with whom he had been on unusually intimate terms—too much so from the British point of view, according to some critics.[117] Such intimacy Goschen did not achieve and probably did not desire. In August 1912, after an encounter at Homburg, Arthur Davidson, one of George V's equerries, reported to Nicolson that 'the Emperor had one side slap at Goschen, with whom I take it he is disappointed, because he can't treat him in the free and easy way he did Sir Frank'.[118]

An episode that occurred in the following month served to demonstrate the Kaiser's feelings. Marschall von Bieberstein, after only a brief spell at the London Embassy, had died; a successor had to be found. On 30 September the Kaiser sent a strongly, indeed, an oddly, worded telegram to Bethmann Hollweg, complaining that England kept Goschen, whom, he claimed, even his fellow-countrymen

[112] Goschen to Nicolson, 18 Apr. 1913, N.P., F.O. 800/365.
[113] Goschen to Nicolson, 28 Oct. 1910, N.P., F.O. 800/346.
[114] Goschen to Nicolson, 26 Jan. 1912, N.P., F.O. 800/353.
[115] Goschen to Nicolson, 18 May 1912, N.P., 800/355.
[116] For example, Goschen to Hardinge, 22 and 28 May 1909, H.P., 15; to Nicolson, 17 Nov. 1911, N.P., F.O. 800/352.
[117] Lee, op. cit., ii, p. 612.
[118] Davidson to Nicolson, 22 Aug. 1912, N.P., F.O. 800/358.

referred to as a 'darned ass', in Berlin; so long as England did not change her Ambassador, even a Marschall had no prospects; a replacement for Marschall should not be found unless England showed good will and sent to Berlin the best man that she had; if London did not respond to Germany's hint and Goschen stayed, the conclusion to be drawn would be obvious; he emphasized his point with a reference to taking mobilization plans out of the drawer.[119]

Later that year the outbreak of war in the Balkans and the Serbs' advance to the Adriatic aroused fears of an Austro-Serb conflict, in which Russia might intervene, with the possibility of further complications. 'Do we know yet what *we* are going to do supposing War breaks out between Austria and Russia, and France has to cut in?' Goschen asked Nicolson in a letter of 25 November 1912.[120] To this leading question the permanent under-secretary replied promptly but by no means categorically. He foresaw that a war involving Austria-Hungary, Russia and Germany would bring France's treaty obligations into play—'and then we shall ourselves be face to face with the problem as to what part we must assume'. He declined to speculate as to what that part would be, but avowed that he had very little doubt in his own mind 'as to what it should be'. Clearly Nicolson could not on his own responsibility give a ruling on the delicate question that Goschen had put to him. He took refuge in the doubtless correct statement that he had 'several other letters to write to other capitals' and that there were 'piles of boxes' awaiting his attention.[121]

However, in another letter, dated only a day later, Nicolson gave some guidance, at least of a negative kind, as to Britain's probable action in the event of a continental war. Benckendorff, he wrote, had spoken to him about the conviction held by Marschall's successor, Lichnowsky, 'to the effect that under no circumstances whatsoever, except in the case of a direct attack, would this country go to war'— an impression that he had no doubt conveyed to Berlin. 'I think it is possible that Grey may give a private hint to the German Ambassador that he has somewhat misinterpreted the feeling in England,' he added.[122] In fact, on 3 December Lichnowsky reported to Bethmann Hollweg that he had been told, not indeed by Grey himself, but by Haldane, that, in the event of a general European conflagra-

---

[119] Wilhelm II to Bethmann Hollweg, 30 Sept. 1912. Professor John Röhl has kindly supplied me with the text of the surviving part of this telegram, the original of which is in the Deutsches Zentralarchiv, Merseburg, Rep. 53J, Lit. B No. 7. It is quoted in Professor Röhl's *Zwei deutsche Fürsten zur Kriegsschuldfrage* (Düsseldorf, 1971), p. 116. The words 'darned ass' are in English in the original. It would be interesting to know the source of the Kaiser's belief that Goschen's fellow-countrymen regarded him in this way. See entry for 7 Dec. 1911.

[120] Goschen to Nicolson, 25 Nov. 1912, N.P., F.O., 800/360.
[121] Nicolson to Goschen, 26 Nov. 1912 (copy), N.P., F.O. 800/360.
[122] Nicolson to Goschen, 27 Nov. 1912 (copy), N.P., F.O. 800/360.

tion, resulting from an Austrian invasion of Serbia, it was hardly likely that Britain would be able to remain a silent onlooker; she could not, in any circumstances, consistently with her adherence to the principle of the balance of power, tolerate the overthrow of France by Germany.[123] On the morning of Sunday 8 December the Kaiser held a meeting at his Berlin Schloss. Moltke is recorded as having expressed the opinion that war was inevitable, and, therefore, the sooner the better, and Tirpitz as having voiced the Navy's preference for the postponement of the great struggle for a year and a half. Meanwhile, on 6 December King George had given a not dissimilar warning to Prince Henry, the Kaiser's brother.[124]

At the end of December 1912 Kiderlen-Wächter died suddenly at Stuttgart in his native Württemberg, whither he had gone for the Christmas holiday. Early in the New Year Goschen told Nicolson that he would miss the late Secretary of State, who had been 'very amusing' and had had 'a strong sense of humour'; he and Kiderlen had latterly been 'very good friends indeed'. He speculated as to how the Chancellor would manage:

> But what will Bethmann Hollweg do without him? Because, as far as one can judge, he has lately retired completely from the direction of Foreign Affairs. I could see that by the way he talked of them for a few minutes the other day. He seemed to know very little about them—and to think that every thing was going splendidly and the future without a cloud.

As far as the general international situation was concerned, Goschen was still apprehensive. Although he hoped that Nicolson would have 'a happy and prosperous year', he added:

> Politically it does *not* open well—and I cannot think that its prospects are rosy; nor shall I think so as long as Austria and Russia stand opposite to each other armed to the teeth![125]

Kiderlen's successor was Jagow, who was brought back to Berlin from the German Embassy in Rome. Goschen at first regarded him as a misfit. 'Poor Jagow, sitting reluctantly in his thorny seat at the Foreign Office, looks very harrassed,' he reported in February 1913.[126] In reply to an enquiry from Nicolson,[127] he compared the new Secretary of State with 'a man who is besought, and compelled against his will, to make a fourth at Bridge and then sworn at for playing

[123] Lichnowsky to Bethmann Hollweg, 3 Dec. 1912, *G.P.*, xxxix, no. 15612.
[124] J. Röhl, 'An der Schwelle zum Weltkrieg,' *Militärgeschichtliche Mitteilungen*, xxi (1977), p. 77.
[125] Goschen to Nicolson, 5 Jan. 1913, N.P., F.O. 800/360.
[126] Goschen to Nicolson, 1 Feb. 1913, N.P., F.O. 800/363.
[127] Nicolson to Goschen, 11 Feb. 1913 (copy), N.P., F.O. 800/363.

badly'. He contrasted Kiderlen, who 'had the skin of a rhinoceros', with 'this poor little man, who is deeply mortified and says so, and who told me only the day before yesterday that he didn't think I should see him very long sitting in the Secretary of State's room'. Nevertheless, his over-all opinion, of Jagow was favourable. 'Generally speaking,' he wrote, 'it is a pleasure to have to deal with such an un-Prussian, pleasant mannered man, and, moreover, with one who is obviously well disposed towards England.'[128]

In the autumn of 1913 Albert, King of the Belgians, came to Germany. On 6 November he was the Emperor's guest at a dinner in his honour at the Neues Palais, Moltke, the Chief of the General Staff, being also present. On 4 December Granville, the chargé d'affaires in Paris, wrote to inform Nicolson that Paléologue, of the French Ministry of Foreign Affairs, had told him 'in the strictest confidence' that the Emperor had declared to the King that 'war between France and Germany was inevitable', and that Moltke had 'used the same expression' and had added further observations which were even more disquieting.[129] Nicolson wrote to Goschen avowing his confidence in the Emperor's pacific inclinations.[130] Goschen fully agreed. His judgment on the Emperor deserves quotation:

> He *is* pacifically inclined and I think he would surprise a great many people by his prudence and patience—particularly those who judge Him entirely by the outbursts in which he occasionally indulges. I think it would take a great deal to drive him into war and he would require the whole nation behind him, which in these days when finance plays such a big part is scarcely likely to happen.[131]

VI

The first entry in the diary for the year 1914 shows that Goschen was aware of difficult problems ahead. However, the problems that he had in mind were not of a kind likely to precipitate a general European war. The Foreign Office, for its part, was optimistic. 'I think there is no likelihood of serious friction arising among the big European Powers,' wrote Nicolson on 19 January.[132] 'Since I have been at the Foreign Office I have not seen such calm waters,' he added early in May.[133]

[128] Goschen to Nicolson, 11 Feb. 1913 (probably misdated), N.P., F.O. 800/363.
[129] Granville to Nicolson, 4 Dec. 1913, N.P., F.O. 800/371.
[130] Nicolson to Goschen, 8 Dec. 1913 (copy), N.P., F.O. 800/371.
[131] Goschen to Nicolson, 12 Dec. 1913, N.P., F.O. 800/371.
[132] Nicolson to Goschen, 19 Jan. 1914 (copy), N.P., F.O. 800/372.
[133] Nicolson to Goschen, 5 May 1914 (copy), N.P., F.O. 800/374.

Towards the end of February 1914 Charles Hobhouse, the Post-master-General, came to Berlin on official business, and stayed at the Embassy. He too was a diarist, who, although he did not record his doings in Berlin at the time, set down his impressions on his return home. The Ambassador, who struck him as 'pleasant and exceedingly astute', unfortunately caught a chill, as Goschen's own diary records, after a dinner at the Schloss, and could not accompany Hobhouse when, on 1 March, he was the guest, also at the Schloss, of the Kaiser and his Consort. Hobhouse found the former vivacious and unstable, the latter unaffected and charming, and recalled that 'Goschen liked her much better than the Emperor'.[134]

On 3 June Goschen was entertained by the Kaiser to a luncheon at the Neues Palais in honour of the birthday of King George V, to whom he reported direct. His host 'was in the highest possible spirits and looked extremely well in health'. On the question of Albania, which was then exercising the foreign ministries of the Great Powers, the Kaiser interpreted a statement by Grey as meaning that the British Foreign Secretary would see certain persons 'jolly well d— first', and explained that that was exactly his own sentiment, enjoining his guest: 'When you report this don't say that I made this remark after lunch!' He had something to say, too, on the subject of one of Britain's current domestic problems:

His Majesty also discoursed very freely on the mild treatment which has hitherto been meted out to the Militant Suffragettes and expressed the fervent hope that severer measures would soon be adopted.[135]

Goschen's report is of interest for the light that it throws on his relations with the monarch to whom he was accredited. Perhaps the Kaiser's opinion had changed since September 1912. At all events, his remarks to Goschen at the Neues Palais on 3 June 1914 seem to have been genial enough.

On 23 June Goschen reached Kiel, where he was the guest, on board the battleship *King George V*, of Admiral Warrender, the commander of the Royal Navy squadron that was paying a visit during the yachting week.[136]

On the afternoon of Sunday 28 June the head of the Kaiser's naval Kabinett, Admiral von Müller, who was on board the *Hohenzollern*, received a telegram, giving the news of the assassination at Sarajevo of the Archduke Franz Ferdinand and the Duchess of Hohenberg.

[134] Hobhouse, *Inside Asquith's Cabinet*, ed. E. David (1977), p. 163.
[135] Goschen to George V, undated, but evidently written in June 1914, R.A. G.V. P.586/3.
[136] Rough Account, p. 1.

He at once put out in a steam-launch, overtook the imperial yacht *Meteor*, and informed the Kaiser of what had occurred.[137] Goschen himself learnt the news while at luncheon as Tirpitz's guest on board the latter's ship.[138] Personally he was sorry. He realized, too, that the crime might have most serious repercussions.

Back in England, on leave and with no international crisis having as yet arisen, Goschen's anxiety subsided. On 11 July he wrote to Rumbold, who was acting as chargé d'affaires in Berlin, telling him that he had seen Grey, who 'seemed rather nervous as regards Austria and Servia'. 'But I don't think he need be—do you?' he added. He observed that everybody was 'more concerned about home, than about foreign, politics', and seemed 'to think we are on the brink of something awful'. He went on to discuss the 'Varsity Match'—'the dullest I have ever seen'—and the 'Eton and Harrow', which had been 'fairly lively'.[139] The 'something awful' was of course not a European, but a civil, war, arising out of the deadlock in Ireland.

On 22 July Goschen began another letter to Rumbold, in which he discussed routine matters. He intended to return to Berlin on Tuesday or Wednesday of the following week, and after that he wanted to go to Nauheim, a German spa—'but l'homme propose etc.' On 23 July he completed this letter, commenting on talks which he had had the previous day with Grey, Nicolson and Imperiali, the Italian Ambassador:

> But I saw Grey last night and Nicolson in the afternoon and they both seemed to think that it was possible that Nauheim would have to go to the wall. Mais nous verrons! I dined with Imperiali last night and found myself in a hotbed of radicalism. Grey, Morley, [140] Lulu Harcourt,[141] Weardales[142] etc.! No one seems to think that the Buckingham Palace Conference will end in a settlement—but the King's speech was, I thought, excellent.[143] Imperiali was very pessimistic about Servia—and hoped Austria would not be foolish. Austria-Hungary's two allies seem very dubious as to her capability of behaving with any prudence or moderation.[144]

The day on which Goschen completed this letter was also the day of the delivery of the Austro-Hungarian ultimatum. On Sunday 26

---

[137] G. A. von Müller, *Regierte der Kaiser?*, ed. W. Görlitz (Göttingen, 1959), p. 30.
[138] A. von Tirpitz, *Erinnerungen* (Leipzig, 1919), p. 205.
[139] Goschen to Rumbold, 11 July 1914, R.P.
[140] Lord President of the Council.
[141] Colonial Secretary.
[142] Liberal peer and his wife.
[143] On 21 July 1914. The conference had been summoned in the hope of finding a solution for the Irish problem.
[144] Goschen to Rumbold, 22–23 July 1914, R.P.

July he left for Berlin by way of Flushing. Albert Ballin, who had been in London on a mission in connection with Britain's naval conversations with Russia, information concerning which had been leaked to the German Government,[145] was a fellow-passenger. The entry in the diary for 26 July was the last that Goschen made until the following December.

On Monday 27 July Goschen reached Berlin,[146] where, the holiday season being at its height, the Embassy staff was much depleted.[147] On the day of his arrival he saw Jagow, to whom he put the proposal, telegraphed on the Sunday afternoon by Nicolson, with the authority of the absent Grey,[148] for a conference in London of representatives of France, Germany and Italy, together with the Foreign Secretary himself.[149] This proposal Jagow declined.[150]

On Tuesday 28 July Austria-Hungary declared war on Serbia. That evening Goschen was summoned by Bethmann Hollweg, who confirmed Germany's rejection of the British proposal for a four-power conference.[151]

On Wednesday 29 July Goschen was Cambon's guest at dinner at the French Embassy. Polo, the Spanish Ambassador, and Beyens were fellow-guests.[152] Later that evening Goschen was again summoned by the Chancellor, who had just returned from a council at Potsdam, and, evidently acting on information supplied by Ballin, offered an assurance that, provided Britain remained neutral, Germany, in the event of a victorious war, would make no territorial acquisitions in Europe at the expense of France. Bethmann Hollweg declined, however, to give any assurance as to France's colonies, or, so far as Belgium was concerned, to promise more than that, provided she did not take sides against Germany, the integrity of her territory would be respected when the war was over.[153]

Early the following day, 30 July, wrote Goschen in a letter intended for Nicolson, but not sent at the time, Jagow called at the Embassy and spoke of a report received from Lichnowsky of a conversation that he had had with Grey; this, the Secretary of State explained, had arrived after Goschen had left Bethmann Hollweg the previous evening; had it been received earlier the Chancellor would have

[145] L. Cecil, *Albert Ballin* (Princeton, 1967), pp. 201–9.
[146] Goschen to Nicolson, begun 30 July, but not sent, *B.D.*, xi, no. 677; cited hereafter as 'no. 677'.
[147] Goschen to Nicolson, undated, but evidently written on 1 Aug. 1914, N.P., F.O. 800/375.
[148] Grey to resident clerk, 26 July 1914, *B.D.*, xi, no. 139.
[149] Foreign Office to Bertie, and also to Goschen, 26 July 1914, *B.D.*, xi, no. 410.
[150] Goschen to Grey, 27 July 1914, *B.D.*, xi, no. 185.
[151] Goschen to Grey, 28 July 1914, *B.D.*, xi, no. 249.
[152] *D.A.B.*, ii, p. 251.
[153] Goschen to Grey, 29 July 1914, *B.D.*, xi, no. 293; no. 677; Bethmann Hollweg, version of draft prepared by Jagow, 29 July 1914, *D.D.K.*, ii, no. 373.

spoken differently.[154] Lichnowsky had related how, on the afternoon of 29 July, Grey had warned him that, if France and Germany were to be involved in war, it would be impossible for the British Government to stand aside and wait for any length of time.[155] Jagow added, according to a telegram sent by Goschen to Grey, that he had heard the contents of Lichnowsky's telegram with regret, but not exactly with surprise.[156] On the same day Lerchenfeld, the Bavarian Minister in Berlin, informed his government that Bethmann Hollweg had told him that, in the event of war, Britain would take the side of the *Entente* powers.[157] At all events, the Imperial Government had now been apprised of the Foreign Office's view of Britain's probable course of action in the event of a Franco-German war, quite apart from any question of a hypothetical German violation of the neutrality of Belgium.[158]

On 31 July the German Government, following Russia's mobilization order of the previous day, proclaimed a state of war-emergency— 'Kriegsgefahrzustand'—and, after delivering an ultimatum to Russia, required from the French Government a statement of its intentions. On the same day Grey twice telegraphed Goschen, first proposing that the four disinterested powers make offers for a settlement to both Austria-Hungary and Russia,[159] and then instructing him to ask the German Government for an undertaking to respect the neutrality of Belgium, so long as no other power violated it.[160] Goschen saw Jagow that evening, but was unable to obtain a satisfactory answer on either count.[161] According to Rumbold, it was past midnight when the Ambassador returned to the Embassy, 'very depressed', and saying that 'he had done his utmost for peace'.[162]

On 1 August Goschen passed on a warning from Russell, the military attaché, to the effect that, in the event of war, Germany would send part of her forces through Belgium.[163] That evening Germany declared war on Russia. Early on the morning of 2 August German troops occupied Luxemburg. On the evening of the same day the German Minister in Brussels delivered an ultimatum, requiring a passage for his country's forces through Belgium. On the evening of 3 August Germany declared war on France.

[154] Goschen to Nicolson, begun 30 July 1914, but not sent, *B.D.*, xi, no. 677.
[155] Lichnowsky to Imperial Foreign Office, 29 July 1914, *D.D.K.*, ii, no. 368.
[156] Goschen to Grey, 30 July 1914, *B.D.*, xi, no. 305.
[157] Lerchenfeld to Hertling, 30 July 1914, *B.H.L.*, i, no. 111.
[158] For a full account of this episode see Young, op. cit., p. 111.
[159] Grey to Goschen, 31 July 1914, *B.D.*, xi, no. 340.
[160] Grey to Goschen, 31 July 1914, *B.D.*, xi, no. 348.
[161] Goschen to Grey, 31 July 1914, *B.D.*, xi, nos. 383 and 385.
[162] Rough Account, p. 20.
[163] Goschen to Grey, 1 Aug. 1914, *B.D.*, xi, no. 404.

At this point a passage in another diary should be mentioned. Under the date 4 August 1914 Berta de Bunsen, the wife of Maurice de Bunsen, now Ambassador in Vienna, recorded that Heinrich Count Larisch had called. The Count's son, Friedrich, was Councillor at the Austro-Hungarian Embassy in Berlin. Berta noted some gloomy remarks by the Count concerning the effects of mobilization and the inadequacy of the preparations in Austria 'for the thousands of wounded who will shortly be brought in'. On the following page she wrote: 'We feel sick at heart to think we may be forced to fight against these nice people.' Between these two sentences she subsequently, to judge from its position right at the top of the page, added another: 'He rather indiscreetly read us a letter from his son in Berlin who had been walking with E. who told him the great moment w'd be on *10th*.'[164] This passage raises an interesting question. Was 'E.' Edward Goschen? We know from the entry in his diary for 6 January 1914 that he was on friendly terms with the Larisch family in Berlin. We also know that he was a friend of de Bunsen.[165] On the other hand, it is difficult to see how at this juncture he could have foretold what was going to happen on 10 August. Moreover, there was another 'E.' in Berlin, who is perhaps a stronger candidate: the German Emperor himself.[166] We know that on at least one previous occasion he had walked and also talked matters of state with Friedrich Count Larisch.[167]

On the afternoon of the same day, Tuesday 4 August, soon after three o'clock according to Rumbold,[168] a telegram arrived from Grey, stating that the King of the Belgians had appealed to King George for diplomatic intervention on behalf of his country; that the British Government had been informed that Germany had asked Belgium for free passage through her territory; that this demand had been refused; and that the British Government protested against the violation of a treaty to which both Germany and Britain were parties, and requested an assurance that Germany would not proceed with the demand made upon Belgium and would respect her neutrality; Goschen was to ask for an immediate reply.[169] He accordingly embodied Grey's request in an *aide-mémoire*.[170] However, at the time when he had to make this important communication, Jagow was not

[164] Berta de Bunsen, Vienna Diary, 4 Aug. 1914, *Bulletin of the Institute of Historical Research*, li (1978), p. 223.
[165] Goschen to de Bunsen, 16 Dec. (1913); year not specified, but evident from contents, de B.P., IVb.
[166] Cf. Berta de Bunsen, Diary, 8 Dec. 1914, de B.P., BB/III/a, quoted below.
[167] Szögyény to Austro-Hungarian Foreign Ministry, 30 May 1914, *Ö.U.A.*, viii, no. 9775.
[168] Rough Account, p. 28.
[169] Grey to Goschen, 4 Aug. 1914, *B.D.*, xi, no. 573.
[170] Goschen to Imperial Foreign Office, 4 Aug. 1914, *D.D.K.*, iv, no. 823.

at the Imperial Foreign Office. Together with his ministerial colleagues he had gone to hear Bethmann Hollweg address the Reichstag. Goschen accordingly set out for the Reichstag Building.[171]
Manneville, the French Councillor, later recalled having encountered
him as he was leaving the Embassy. Goschen, he wrote, 'se rendait
au Reichstag pour écouter le discours qu'allait pronouncer le Chan-
celier; il allait entendre son vieil ami, M. de Bethmann-Hollweg,
annoncer officiellement la décision prise par l'Allemagne de violer
la neutralité de la Belgique'.[172]

In fact, by the time that Goschen reached the Reichstag Building
his 'vieil ami' had concluded his singularly infelicitous speech.[173]
According to some accounts his interview with Jagow took place at
the Reichstag Building.[174] Indeed, it may well be that he spoke to the
Secretary of State, at least briefly, there. But it seems likely that he
would have preferred to make a communication as important as the
one with which he had been charged at the Imperial Foreign Office
itself and in a formal manner. Moreover his own report states that
he went to the Foreign Office twice on 4 August;[175] presumably this
was the first occasion. In *The War Crisis in Berlin* Rumbold states that
Goschen communicated the text of Grey's telegram to Jagow in the
form of an *aide-mémoire* at the Imperial Foreign Office.[176] What is certain is that Goschen saw Jagow, handed over the *aide-mémoire*, but
failed to obtain a satisfactory reply.[177] He then returned to the
Embassy, where he composed a telegram to Grey, reporting his lack
of success.[178] This telegram did not reach its destination.[179] A version
has been preserved in printed form at the Public Record Office and
has been published in *British Documents on the Origins of the War*;[180]
it was supplied to the Foreign Office by Goschen after his return to
England.[181] However, there is no need to doubt its general accuracy.
Jagow was evidently polite but adamant.

Meanwhile, Grey had sent another telegram, informing Goschen
that Belgian territory had now been violated, repeating his request
for an undertaking by Germany to respect Belgium's neutrality, and

---

[171] Rough Account, p. 29.
[172] H. de Manneville, 'Les derniers jours de l'ambassade de M. Jules Cambon à Berlin', *Revue d'histoire diplomatique*, xli (1935), p. 453.
[173] Lerchenfeld to Hertling, 5 Aug. 1914, *B.H.L.*, i, no. 118; *Berliner Tageblatt*, 5 Aug.
1914.
[174] Ibid.; in his Rough Account, p. 29, Rumbold certainly gives the impression that
the interview with Jagow took place at the Reichstag Building.
[175] No. 671.
[176] Rumbold, op. cit., p. 316.
[177] No 671; Rough Account, p. 29.
[178] Rough Account, p. 29.
[179] Clerk, minute, 13 Aug. 1914, *B.D.*, xi, no. 667.
[180] Goschen to Grey, 4 Aug. 1914, F.O. 371/2164; *B.D.*, xi, no. 666.
[181] Clerk, minute, 13 Aug. 1914, *B.D.*, xi, no. 667.

asking for a satisfactory reply, to 'be received here by 12 o'clock to-night'; if no satisfactory reply were to be forthcoming, Goschen was to ask for his passports and say that the British Government felt bound to uphold the neutrality of Belgium and observance of the treaty, to which both Britain and Germany were partners.[182] This telegram, according to Rumbold, reached the Embassy at six o'clock in the afternoon; it constituted Britain's ultimatum to Germany.[183] Once again Goschen composed an *aide-mémoire*, paraphrasing Grey's telegram.[184] He then went once again to the Imperial Foreign Office.[185]

James Gerard, the United States Ambassador, relates in his memoirs that he also called at the Foreign Office that afternoon. In the waiting-room he found Goschen, who told him that he had come to ask for his passports, Gerard was sure that this statement was over-heard by another man who was sitting in the room and who had the appearance of a German journalist.[186]

At all events, in due course Goschen, for the second time that day, saw Jagow. As before, he failed to obtain a satisfactory reply. He then asked whether he might see Bethmann Hollweg. His request was im-mediately granted.[187]

Although Goschen's interview with Bethmann Hollweg at the Im-perial Chancellery on the evening of 4 August 1914 constituted by far the most celebrated incident of his career, our knowledge of what the two men actually said to each other on that occasion is limited. We do not even know for certain in what language they conducted their exchange. Each was perfectly capable of speaking the other's language; each could also speak French;[188] they may even have used more than one language. In his 'Rough Account' Rumbold stated, on the strength, according to James Headlam-Morley, of what Goschen had told him on the very day of the interview,[189] that Beth-mann Hollweg 'made a set speech in English', declaring that 'England was responsible for the war', and that 'for the sake of "a piece of paper" she had gone in against Germany'.[190] However, as far as the linguistic point was concerned, when a good many years later he wrote his book, *The War Crisis in Berlin*, he had second thoughts. He took the view that a man as agitated as was Bethmann Hollweg would probably have used his native language. He also raised the possibility

---

[182] Grey to Goschen, 4 Aug. 1914, *B.D.*, xi, no. 594.
[183] Rough Account, p. 30.
[184] Goschen to Imperial Foreign Office, 4 Aug. 1914, *D.D.K.*, iv, no. 839.
[185] No. 671.
[186] J. W. Gerard, *My Four Years in Germany* (1917), p. 91.
[187] No. 671.
[188] For Bethmann Hollweg's linguistic ability see K. H. Jarausch, *The Enigmatic Chancellor* (New Haven, 1973), p. 110.
[189] J. W. Headlam-Morley, Note, *B.D.*, xi, no. 671, no. 4.
[190] Rough Account, p. 30.

of the Chancellor having spoken French.[191] There are several other pieces of evidence, relating both to the question of the language used by Bethmann Hollweg on this occasion and to the actual words that he uttered. None of them is altogether conclusive. (See Appendix B.)

After returning to the Embassy Goschen composed another telegram for dispatch to the Foreign Office.[192] Like its immediate predecessor this telegram never reached its intended destination.[193] In this case, too, Goschen subsequently supplied the Foreign Office with a text, a printed version of which has been preserved.[194] Once again, one cannot be certain that the printed version is identical with what Goschen actually wrote in Berlin on the evening of 4 August. Nevertheless, there is no need to doubt his statement that he failed to obtain from either the Secretary of State or the Chancellor a satisfactory reply to the British Government's request, and that his final interview with Bethmann Hollweg was 'very painful'. The Chancellor was probably feeling the strain of the events of the last few days, and more particularly, as Rumbold states, that of his oratorical efforts in the Reichstag that afternoon.[195] He may well have lost his temper and, in the heat of the moment, uttered words that were singularly ill-chosen.

According to Nicolson's son and biographer the Foreign Office did later that evening receive from Goschen an urgent telegram *en clair*, reporting that Bethmann Hollweg had informed him by telephone that Germany would not reply to the ultimatum, and that, therefore, a state of war would arise by midnight.[196] However, no such telegram has come to light in the Foreign Office archives. Nor is such a telegram mentioned in Rumbold's 'Rough Account' or in Goschen's own report of his last days in Berlin.[197]

In this report Goschen related that Zimmermann, the under-secretary at the Foreign Office, called at the Embassy that evening, and after some civil and regretful preliminary observations, asked him whether a demand for passports was equivalent to a declaration of war. Goschen pointed out that there had been numerous cases of diplomatic relations being broken off, without war ensuing, but referred him to the instructions sent by Grey, of which he had given Jagow a paraphrase, and the main point of which he now reiterated— the British Government expected an answer to a definite question by twelve o'clock that night, and, in default of a satisfactory answer,

---

[191] Rumbold, op. cit., p. 322.
[192] No. 671; Rough Account, p. 30.
[193] Clerk, minute, 13 Aug. 1914; *B.D.*, xi, no. 667.
[194] Goschen to Grey, 4 Aug. 1914, F.O. 371/2164; *B.D.*, xi, no. 667.
[195] Rough Account, p. 30.
[196] Nicolson, op. cit., p. 424.
[197] See also L. Albertini, *The Origins of the War of 1914* (Oxford, 1965), iii, p. 500.

would be forced to take such steps as their engagements required. Zimmermann replied that this was in fact a declaration of war, as the Imperial Government could not possibly give the assurance required either that night or any other night.[198]

Theodor Wolff, who at this time was editor of the *Berliner Tageblatt*, has related that at about half-past seven that evening he met Wilhelm von Stumm, the head of the Political Section of the German Foreign Office, from whom he learnt of the latest development; he asked whether he might publish the news in an *Extrablatt*; to this request Stumm agreed; the *Extrablatt*, announcing that Britain—or, rather, England—had broken off diplomatic relations with Germany, that Goschen had asked for his passports, and that this meant, in all probability, war with Britain, appeared on the streets at about half-past eight.[199] (Gerard believed that the *Extrablatt* was the outcome of the remark dropped by Goschen in Jagow's waiting-room;[200] on the other hand, Wolff was in a good position to know the true story.)

Beyens has given an account of the distribution of the *Extrablatt* and of its effect. He dined alone that evening, he wrote, at the Kaiserhof. On leaving he passed one of the *Berliner Tageblatt*'s cars, from which a handful of printed sheets was thrown out. After reading one of the sheets he decided to hasten to the British Embassy to make enquiries. He found the stretch of the Wilhelmstrasse that lay in front of the Embassy filled with people. 'Deutschland über alles' was sung; there was an outbreak of whistling; and a hale of projectiles broke the first-floor windows. The two policemen on duty outside the Embassy were helpless.[201]

Rumbold, who was inside the Embassy at the time of these events, has told how, while the staff were dining with Goschen that evening, the butler brought in an *Extrablatt*, and simultaneously the hostile crowd gathered outside; later he and his colleagues went into one of the front rooms to smoke; they heard the noise of breaking glass; some people climbed on to the window-sills.[202] Rattigan has described how with much difficulty he got a message put through to Jagow.[203] After order had been restored in the street Jagow called in person and made, in Goschen's words, a 'full and complete apology' for the crowd's behaviour.[204] Later, according to Wolff, he called a second time to raise, on the authority of the chief of police, who was his cousin, the question of provocation from inside the Embassy.[205]

[198] No. 671.

[199] T. Wolff, *Der Krieg des Pontius Pilatus* (Zürich, 1934), p. 371; the *Extrablatt* of 4 Aug. 1914 is reproduced in F. Wile, *The Assault* (1916), p. 134.

[200] Gerard, op. cit., p. 91.

[201] H. Beyens, *L'Allemagne avant la Guerre* (Paris, 1915), p. 344.

[202] Rough Account, p. 30.   [203] Rattigan, op. cit., p. 137.   [204] No. 671.

[205] Wolff, op. cit., p. 373. On the question of the alleged provocation see Lerchenfeld to Hertling, 5 Aug. 1914, cited above.

According to Rattigan, the Secretary of State, who was 'stricken with grief', sat on a sofa with the Ambassador, to whom he declared: 'There are three very unhappy men in Germany, the Kaiser, the Chancellor and myself.'[206] Rattigan does not specify whether Jagow made this avowal on his first or on his second visit. Nor, unfortunately, does he state whether he actually heard the words from Jagow's own lips.

Late on the evening of 4 August the last steps towards war were being taken in London. The actual formal declaration took place at Buckingham Palace and was recorded by King George V—yet another diarist:

> At 10.30 the Prime Minister telephoned to say that Goschen had been given his passports at 7.0 this evening. I held a Council at 10.45 to declare war with Germany, it is a terrible catastrophe but it is not our fault.[207]

As a matter of fact, the telephone message mentioned by the King was incorrect. At this juncture Goschen had not yet received his passports.[208] At all events, at eleven o'clock that evening, Greenwich Mean Time—twelve o'clock midnight, Central European Time—the Admiralty sent out a signal to the Fleet to commence hostilities against Germany.[209] The Foreign Office did not, so far as can be judged, attempt to inform Goschen of the final declaration of war.[210] To communicate with the Berlin Embassy at this late stage would certainly have been difficult—perhaps impossible.

On the morning of Wednesday 5 August, according to his report, Goschen asked in writing for his passports. Later he received a tart message from the Kaiser, brought by an aide-de-camp. At about eleven o'clock his passports were delivered to him by Botho von Wedel, Councillor at the Imperial Foreign Office, who informed him that arrangements had been made for him to leave for England the following day, travelling by way of the Hook of Holland. Wedel also brought what Goschen called a 'charming letter', which unfortunately does not appear to have survived, from Jagow. In the course of the morning Goschen handed over responsibility for British subjects and interests to the United States Embassy. In the afternoon Joseph

[206] Rattigan, op. cit., p. 139. A similar story has appeared in more than one book, according to which Goschen was told by Jules Cambon that there were three people in Berlin who regretted that war had broken out—Goschen, Jules Cambon and the Kaiser. In a letter to Goschen, dated 4 Aug. 1914 and preserved in the diary, Cambon wrote: 'J'ai vivement regretté de ne m'être pas trouvé à l'Ambassade quand vous y êtes venu. J'aurais voulu vous dire adieu après les années que nous avons passées ici ensemble, si unis et si associés dans une politique commune.'
[207] R.A., King George V, Diary, 4 Aug. 1914.
[208] No. 671; see also FitzRoy, op. cit., ii, p. 561.
[209] Admiralty to all H.M. ships and naval establishments, 4 Aug. 1914, R. S. Churchill, *Winston S. Churchill*, ii, Companion 3, p. 1999.
[210] FitzRoy, op. cit., ii, p. 561.

Grew, the American Councillor, accompanied by one of the secretaries, came to the Embassy. The archives were formally entrusted
to him. The rest of the day was devoted to sealing up the archives,
burning papers and packing.[211]

Rumbold has related that he arranged with an obliging lieutenant
of police for the Embassy party to leave early on the morning of Thursday 6 August and to be driven to the railway-station by way of side-
streets; at about seven o'clock Goschen and he left the Embassy
together, deploring the manner in which they were quitting their
post.[212] On the way to the station—the Lehrter Bahnhof—the
Embassy caravan joined a similar but smaller party from the Belgian
Legation.[213] Wedel was at the station and so was Grew, who had
brought an American journalist, Frederic Wile, who was to travel
with the British party. 'Poor Sir Edward—what a way to end his
career,' commented Grew, who likewise was a diarist. He noted that
Goschen had observed sadly: 'I am too old a man for all this.'[214] The
British and Belgian groups travelled together on the same train,
which, after a slow but not unduly eventful journey, crossed the Dutch
frontier on the morning of Friday 7 August. At the Hook of Holland
the British party went on board the steamer *St Petersburg*, which,
although at one point pursued by some British warships, reached Har-
wich safely that evening. At dinner in the special train to London
Goschen drank his staff's health in highly complimentary terms; the
staff responded appropriately.[215] At Liverpool Street he was met by
'Bunt'. He then went to a hotel to spend the night.[216] The following
day he called at the Foreign Office and was received by the King
at Buckingham Palace.[217]

The compliments exchanged in the train were, as far as one can
judge, sincere. In his final report Goschen gave full credit to those
members of the Embassy staff who had been at their posts during
the crisis.[218] He himself had stood the strain well. Rumbold wrote
at the time that he was head and shoulders above his colleagues in
the Berlin Diplomatic Corps.[219]

A few days later Goschen had a visit from Chirol, who promptly
reported to Hardinge, now Viceroy of India:

I have just been to see Goschen. The way in which he was treated

[211] No 671; Rough Account, pp. 32–4.
[212] Rough Account, pp. 35–6.
[213] *D.A.B.*, ii, p. 277.
[214] J. C. Grew, Diary 6 Aug. 1914, in *Turbulent Era* (1953), i, p. 139.
[215] Rough Account, pp. 37–8.
[216] *Times*, 8 Aug. 1914.
[217] *Times*, 10 Aug. 1914; R.A., King George V, Diary, 8 Aug. 1914.
[218] No. 671.
[219] Rumbold to his wife, 1 Aug. 1914, Gilbert, op. cit., p. 118.

shows the sort of people they are. He was, at any rate, given railway facilities and enabled to reach the Dutch frontier without hindrance, which is more than was done for either his French or his Russian colleagues, whose treatment was quite infamous. This he puts down solely to the attack upon the Embassy itself, for which the railway facilities were granted as a sort of compensation. But the mob outside the Embassy was absolutely fiendish, and, amongst other indications of the hatred there is of us, he told me that every one of the tradespeople who had battened on the Embassy for years past refused, on the last day, to supply him with anything. He would not even have got any food for the house but that he had an Italian under-chef who went out buying odds and ends of things, so to say, incognito. His last interview with the Chancellor was most painful. Bethmann quite lost his head and was almost insolent. We were responsible for the whole war. What business had we to fall upon Germany from behind when she is fighting for her life, 'just for a bit of paper'? And when Goschen pointed out that the bit of paper was a treaty which bound us in honour, he snorted and said 'How about the risks you are taking?' and snorted again when Goschen observed that, after all, when one's honour is concerned, one was not in the habit of counting risks. The only one who behaved like a gentleman was von Jagow.[220]

On 13 August Goschen gave the Foreign Office texts of the two telegrams that he had attempted unsuccessfully to send home from Berlin nine days previously.[221] The versions that have been preserved are both printed.[222] Goschen may well have supplied them orally and from memory.

At some time not easy to determine precisely but evidently a few days later, he completed his detailed report of his experiences during his last few days in Germany, including the interviews with Jagow and Bethmann Hollweg on 4 August and the journey to the Dutch frontier. The original typescript, signed by Goschen, is headed, in the handwriting of an amanuensis, 'British Embassy/Berlin/August 6th 1914'. Thursday 6 August was, in fact, the day on the morning of which Goschen and his staff left Berlin. The report is typed, not on the die-stamped writing-paper of the British Embassy in Berlin, but on the embossed paper of the Foreign Office. It was not originally dated 'August 6th'. The original date has been deleted, and is now only partly legible. It appears to be August 18th'.[223] The Foreign

[220] Chirol to Hardinge, 11 Aug. 1914, H.P., 71.
[221] Clerk, minute, 13 Aug. 1914, B.D., xi, no. 667.
[222] Goschen to Grey, two telegrams, 4 Aug. 1914, F.O. 371/2164.
[223] Goschen to Grey, dated 6 Aug. 1914, F.O. 371/2164; printed, B.D., xi, no. 671, without indication of original date.

Office recorded the receipt of the document on 19 August.[224] The report was printed with the heading 'London' and the date 'August 8, 1914'. It was laid before Parliament on 27 August.[225] On the following day it appeared in the press.

The passage in Goschen's report that attracted most attention was that in which he described his interview with Bethmann Hollweg at the Imperial Chancellery on the evening of 4 August. This passage still warrants quotation. Goschen related how, at the end of his second meeting on that day with Jagow:

> I then said that I should like to go and see the Chancellor, as it might be perhaps the last time I should have an opportunity of seeing him. He [Jagow] begged me to do so. I found the Chancellor very agitated. His Excellency at once began a harangue which lasted for about twenty minutes. He said that the step taken by His Majesty's Government was terrible to a degree, just for a word 'neutrality' a word which in war time had so often been disregarded—just for a scrap of paper, Great Britain was going to make war on a kindred nation who desired nothing better than to be friends with her.[226]

The phrase 'a scrap of paper' caught the fancy of the press. It figured in numerous headlines.[227] It was quoted over and over again in polemics concerning the origins of the war. It was regarded as a clear expression of German cynicism in regard to solemn promises. One contemporary wrote: 'Bethmann Hollweg's view of sacred obligations written on a scrap of paper is only that to be expected of those who have been brought up in the gospel of military might and doctrine of "vae victis".'[228]

As was to be expected, Bethmann Hollweg wrote a rejoinder. To be precise, he wrote two. Indeed, he may have written others that have not survived. His first rejoinder was embodied in a memorandum, written in longhand and dated 4 October 1914.[229] His second is contained in his *Betrachtungen zum Weltkriege*, published in 1919.[230] Bethmann Hollweg's version of what passed on the evening of 4 August 1914 differs from Goschen's in a number of respects. The Ambassador, he states, entered his room in a state of profound agitation—'in tiefer inneren Erregung'[231]—and began the conversation by

---

[224] Date stamp, 19 Aug. 1914, F.O. 371/2164.
[225] Cd. 7445, *Accounts and Papers*, 1914, ci, p. 95.
[226] Text as in F.O. 371/2164. The text given in Cd. 7445 differs slightly from the original. However, so far as this passage is concerned, the differences are unimportant.
[227] *Times, Daily Mail*, 28 Aug. 1914, *Punch*, 2 Sept. 1914, etc.
[228] Abinger to Maxse, 1 Sept. 1914, M.P.
[229] Bethmann Hollweg, Aufzeichnung, 4 Oct. 1914, Auswärtige Amt, Bonn, Hauptquartier, no. 2285, Eingangsstempel 13 Nov. 1914.
[230] T. von Bethmann Hollweg, *Betrachtungen zum Weltkriege* (Berlin, 1919), i, p. 180.
[231] Bethmann Hollweg, Aufzeichnung.

asking him whether he could give a different answer to the British request from that already given by Jagow.[232] On his declining to do so, Goschen asked whether, if war between their countries were, to his regret, to be decided upon, they might have a private and personal conversation about the appalling situation that had arisen. To this he at once agreed, inviting the Ambassador to sit down.[233] He recalled that since becoming Chancellor his aim had been the improvement of relations between Germany and Britain, and reviewed the efforts that he had made with this object in view.[234] He spoke in strong terms of the disaster that would come upon the world as a result of Britain's entry into the war.[235] However, neither in his memorandum nor in his book did he deny having uttered the words attributed to him by Goschen, or, at least, some similar expression.

In his memorandum of 4 October 1914 Bethmann Hollweg wrote of having asked Goschen a rhetorical question concerning respect for Belgian neutrality and the evil of a world war that certainly contained a reference to paper—'Schrumpfe die Achtung dieser Neutralität gegenüber dem Unheile eines Weltkrieges nicht zu einem Blatt Papier zusammen?'[236] In his *Betrachtungen zum Weltkriege* he recalled having referred to 'ein Fetzen Papier, *a scrap of paper*'. He acknowledged that in his indignation at the repeated and hypocritical stressing of Belgian neutrality, which was, in fact, not really what drove Britain into the war, he had made a slip – 'eine Entgleisung'. He also claimed that Goschen, on taking his leave, burst into tears and requested permission to wait for a time in the ante-room, so that his distress should not be visible to the Chancellery staff. Even after a lapse of five years the recollection of this denouement, which may well have grown in the telling, evidently afforded the former Chancellor considerable satisfaction.[237]

There can be no doubt that Bethmann Hollweg expressed himself most foolishly in the course of the famous interview, and that he fully deserved the censure that was later heaped upon him. However, in fairness to the Chancellor, it should be stressed that he had grounds for his belief that concern for the maintenance of the neutrality of Belgium was not the real motive behind the British Government's impending declaration of war. After all, Lichnowsky had twice sent warning that, in the event of a Franco-German war, Britain would take the side of France. Both these intimations of Britain's probable course of action had been given quite independently of any

[232] Bethmann Hollweg, op. cit., i, p. 181.
[233] Ibid.
[234] Bethmann Hollweg, Aufzeichnung.
[235] Bethmann Hollweg, op. cit., i, p. 181.
[236] Bethmann Hollweg, Aufzeichnung.
[237] Bethmann Hollweg, op. cit., i, p. 181.

mention of her attitude towards a hypothetical German invasion of Belgium.

It is noteworthy that when, on 1 September 1914, Grey wrote to Goschen to express his interest in the latter's 'despatch', he maintained the fiction that its date of composition was 6 August.[238] This fiction is maintained also in *British Documents on the Origins of the War*, in which the document is printed with the heading, 'Berlin, August 6 1914'.[239]

It would be interesting to know whether Goschen wrote at this time—we know that he did later—an analysis of the interplay of forces in Germany that resulted in the disastrous miscalculations of July and August 1914. At all events, no such document has come to light.

However, some weeks after the outbreak of war and in response to an enquiry from Leopold Maxse, the strongly anti-German proprietor and editor of the *National Review*, Rumbold, who had collaborated closely with his chief during the last days of the crisis and had no doubt discussed with him on the homeward journey the factors that lay behind the German course of action, wrote a long letter, setting forth what he claimed were the former Ambassador's views, which he evidently shared:

It is quite true that Sir E. Goschen believes that the German Emperor did not want war. That was certainly our impression shared by the French Ambassador, Jules Cambon, a competent observer. We had had some sidelights on the Emperor some little time previously. Our information was that he was averse to taking vital decisions—also that he shrank from the idea of the bloodshed which a war would cause.[240]

A few days later Rumbold wrote to Maxse again 'on the subject of the German Emperor's responsibility for the war', explaining that he wanted 'to put the matter in the light in which it presents itself to us who were at Berlin', which was that:

We believe that neither he [the Kaiser], nor the Chancellor nor Jagow really wanted war *now* and certainly not a war against 4 Great Powers at once.[241]

[238] Grey to Goschen, 1 Sept. 1914, *B.D.*, xi, no. 675.
[239] No. 671.
[240] Rumbold to Maxse, 18 Sept. 1914, M.P. 469.
[241] Rumbold to Maxse, 27 Sept. 1914, M.P. 469.

VII

For a time Goschen stayed with his nephew, George Joachim's son, at Seacox Heath.[242] He then took a flat in Chelsea, at 9 Wilbraham Place.[243] He made himself useful by attending meetings of the Privy Council.[244] On 7 December he resumed his diary, recording that 'Bunt' had received notice that he was to be sent to the Front.

On 8 December he entertained Maurice and Berta de Bunsen to luncheon. Berta described the occasion in her diary:

M. and I lunched with Sir E.G. at 9 Wilbraham Place in a flat he has taken as all his things like ours in Vienna, are at Berlin. Of course he c'd not tell us much we did not know as all had come out in the print, but it was interesting hearing details of his life in Berlin and intercourse with the Royal family, how in spring King George had given a pack of hounds to the G. Dragoon G'ds and he himself at Kiel *Peter Simple* to the Emperor who was a great lover of our English naval story books for boys. He told us that the E. feeling his son more popular is jealous of him. Also what friends latter and wife were at our Embassy especially with the Rattigans. How 'sans façon' in bad taste sometimes the E. was with people even the Ambassadors, catching Sir E.G. once by the breeches when he was passing and he wanted to speak to him and once when Cambon had to pass the E. in a narrow place the latter gave him a blow on the backside. Also what a blow and surprise England coming in against Germany had been the G.'s information from here having led them to expect that Civil War in Ireland w'd prevent our participating.[245]

Little more than a week later 'Bunt' left for France. Within a few days he was reported wounded and missing. The last entries in the diary testify to Goschen's distress.

'Bunt' was indeed severely wounded and a prisoner. Moreover, the gravity of his wound was not appreciated by the doctor who examined him. To make matters worse, he became a victim of reprisals for British treatment of German submarine prisoners, and was confined to the gaol at Magdeburg. Fortunately, he was visited by Gerard, who was struck by his condition. He was transferred to a hospital, where the seriousness of his wound was realized. As a result of representations made by Gerard to Jagow, 'Bunt' was eventually repatriated.[246]

[242] Goschen to Nicolson, 4 Sept. 1914, N.P., F.O. 800/375.
[243] Berta de Bunsen, Vienna Diary, 8 Dec. 1914, de B.P., BB/III/a.
[244] FitzRoy, op. cit., ii, pp. 577 and 587.
[245] Berta de Bunsen, Vienna Diary, 8 Dec. 1914, de B.P., BB/III/a.
[246] Gerard, op. cit., p. 115.

One day in March 1915, after a meeting of the Privy Council, Goschen had a conversation at luncheon with Almeric FitzRoy, whom he had known for a number of years.[247] The Clerk of the Privy Council recorded his impression of the former Ambassador, whom he found a man of 'unobtrusive sagacity'. Few people, he thought, had reached a fuller understanding of the German Emperor than Goschen, who during his first two years in Berlin had been 'inclined to think him true', but afterwards, and to the end, knew him to be 'as false as hell'.[248]

After a time Goschen gave up his Chelsea flat and moved to Beacon Lodge, a house in the park of Highcliffe Castle, overlooking the sea. Montagu-Stuart-Wortley was now his landlord, neighbour and friend.[249] However, the fact of this relationship with the man who had played so important a part in the *Daily Telegraph* episode should not be regarded as a proof that Goschen himself had been involved in the events that had led up to the publication of the famous 'interview'. Nothing to support any such conclusion has come to light in the papers of either Goschen or Montagu-Stuart-Wortley.

Despite the disagreeable termination of his Berlin mission and his son's ordeal, Goschen, who in 1916 was made a baronet and formally retired from the Diplomatic Service, was able to take a balanced view of the international situation. In June of that year he wrote a letter to a Swiss journalist, setting forth his ideas. Peace, he argued, could only be concluded on terms acceptable to the *Entente* Powers; such terms must include reparation for wrongs committed and the provision of means to reconstruct what the Central Powers had destroyed; this was the one condition of peace. His letter was published in the *Neue Zürcher Zeitung*, in *The Times*, and in pamphlet form.[250] By the standards of the period his attitude was not vindictive.

In the following year he was able to put his musical knowledge to public use. He was a member of the Privy Council committee that heard a petition for a charter of incorporation from Trinity College of Music. The committee, with Goschen's concurrence, decided against granting the charter.[251]

Early in 1923 Goschen wrote an interesting letter to a friend of the younger generation, Alan Lascelles, whom he had known in Berlin. Lascelles had sent him an article by Lewis S. Gannett on the question of responsibility for the outbreak of the war, entitled 'Who dropped

[247] FitzRoy, op. cit., ii, p. 587; i, p. 253.
[248] FitzRoy, op. cit., ii, p. 587.
[249] Information kindly supplied by Elizabeth, Countess of Abingdon, daughter of the late Major-General Edward Montagu-Stuart-Wortley.
[250] Goschen to Julian Grande, 9 June 1916, *Neue Zürcher Zeitung*, 17 June 1916; *Times*, 23 June 1916; E. Goschen, *The One Condition of Peace* (1916).
[251] FitzRoy, op. cit., ii, pp. 645–7.

the match?', which had appeared in *The Outlook*, a weekly edited by
J. L. Garvin.[252]

Goschen expressed his conviction that 'neither the Kaiser, nor Bethmann nor Jagow wanted war—at that moment anyway'. He recalled
Jagow's attitude towards the Austro-Hungarian ultimatum:

> Jagow thought the Austrian ultimatum to Servia too sharp. He said
> so to me, but I never knew for certain whether he had only known
> of it *after* it had been presented to the Servian Government. It is
> true that Jagow said so, but Cambon for one, never believed it.
> As regards Servia's reply Jagow's comment to me was that in it
> Servia had gone as far as any self-respecting country could possibly
> go, or be expected to go.

He discussed the German reaction to Russia's mobilization:

> I remember trying to persuade Jagow that the Russian mobiliza-
> tion was only against Austria, but he said that Germany could not
> afford to take chances; her assets were readiness and speed; delay,
> that is giving Russia time to complete a general mobilization would
> render those assets valueless and would add enormously to their
> difficulties, so they proclaimed as the Article states 'a state of
> threatened war' and the fat was in the fire.

Finally he dealt with the question of responsibility:

> It comes to what I have always maintained ... that the first re-
> sponsibility lay with Austria, in fact that she dropped the match,
> that the Kaiser, Bethmann and Jagow were against the war but
> that they were in the second, but in a high degree responsible for
> it, for at the same time they might have stopped Austria and didn't,
> and moreover, would not back up Grey's efforts to secure peace
> until at all events it was too late. You must scratch out Grey as
> one of the villains of the piece.[253]

The letter is a proof of the continued intellectual vigour of its
seventy-five-year-old author. It makes one regret that he never wrote
a full-length account of the events in which he had been a participant.

Goschen died in London on 20 May 1924. He was buried at
Flimwell.

On the day following that of Goschen's death *The Times* published
a long and eulogistic obituary notice, and devoted its second leader,
written by Harold Williams, director of its foreign department,[254] to

[252] *Outlook*, 23 Dec. 1922.
[253] Goschen to 'Tommy' (Alan Lascelles), 25 Jan. 1923 (copy), Go. P.; *Times*, 2
Dec. 1926.
[254] Editorial Diary, 21 May 1924, Archives of *The Times*.

an appraisal of his career and achievements. Entitled, as was to be expected, 'A Scrap of Paper', the article conceded that Goschen had not been one of the original geniuses of diplomacy who carry out a policy of their own devising in defiance both of foreign governments and of orders and prohibitions from home; there had been nothing striking in his diplomatic career; nevertheless, he had been faithful, diligent and loyal; his manner had been pleasant and unobtrusive; he had won the attachment of his colleagues; his general attitude had been one of cool and practical common sense; as Ambassador in Berlin he had earnestly striven to develop the policy of friendly association with Germany, which Asquith and Grey had regarded as 'the only possible preventive of European war'.[255]

The year 1924 also saw the publication of *Through Thirty Years* by Wickham Steed, who recalled Goschen's account of his final interview with Bethmann Hollweg, declaring that, when it had been published, he had felt glad that the world at large should at last have been enabled to appreciate its author's sterling qualities. Goschen, thought Steed, had not previously been considered specially eminent as a diplomatist. The easy-going good fellowship that marked both his official and his social relationships had·concealed from superficial observers the real strength of his character. But he had always been at his best in a tight spot. His place in history among Britain's great ambassadors had been assured by his handling of the German Chancellor on 4 August 1914.[256]

There is substance in the comments of both these writers. Until comparatively late in his career Goschen seems not to have been particularly highly rated by the Foreign Office; promotion did not come to him speedily; in 1905 he was not, if we may believe Mensdorff, the Foreign Office's choice for Vienna; in 1908 he was not the first choice for Berlin. He certainly showed himself on a number of occasions, as his diary illustrates, a tenacious upholder of his own government's standpoint. He did not in his correspondence persistently press suggestions concerning matters of the highest policy on the Foreign Office. Indeed, we have Francis Oppenheimer's testimony to the effect that, at the time of the war crisis of 1914, he specifically stated that he made it a rule not to ask for instructions[257]—he evidently meant that he did not make suggestions for instructions. However, it should not be thought that he never made suggestions at all. At the time of the First Balkan War, for example, he asked Nicolson whether 'Servia' could not be told that if she went to war with Austria-Hungary over the question of territorial access to the

[255] *Times*, 21 May 1924.
[256] Steed, op. cit., ii, p. 29.
[257] F. Oppenheimer, *Stranger Within* (1960), p. 229.

Adriatic, she would 'have to do it *alone* and at her own expense'.[258]
His correspondence reveals a number of other examples.

Goschen's conception of his functions as an Ambassador was
grounded on a number of firmly held convictions. He believed in the
essential integrity of Britain's foreign policy. In his diary (24 June
1907) he claimed that, although Britain seldom had a policy, when
she had one, it was always straightforward. He also believed in the
continuity of Britain's foreign policy, not merely as a desideratum,
but as a fact. Towards the end of 1910, when the second British general
election of the year was imminent, and a change of government
seemed possible, he reported to Nicolson, after a conversation with
Bethmann Hollweg:

> I always tell him that I cannot see into the future and that the
> only thing I know about politics at home is that our Foreign Policy
> is always continuous. Men may change and perhaps Methods
> but the groundwork of our Foreign Policy always remains the
> same.[259]

He believed, too, in the wisdom of Britain's conduct of foreign relations, as it evolved in the early years of the twentieth century—what
he termed in a letter to Nicolson, undated, but evidently written in
late November 1912—'the work of the last decade'—and more especially in that of the 'Ententes' with France and Russia, by means of
which 'all our old anxieties' had been 'set at rest'.[260] 'It is extraordinary to me how many people even including our own countrymen,
fail to see the importance of our maintaining our Entente with Russia,'
he wrote in May 1914.[261] As for the 'Entente' with France, numerous
entries in his diary testify to the fact that it was especially close in
Berlin.

How clearly, if at all, did Goschen foresee the outbreak of the conflict that, six years after his appointment to the Berlin Embassy, was
to engulf most of Europe? Like many of his contemporaries he passed
during those years through alternating phases of apprehension and
relief, as each successive international crisis was succeeded by a settlement and an encouraging *détente*. However, in August 1908 he foresaw
the serious consequences of the naval rivalry of Britain and Germany.
In his undated letter to Nicolson, evidently written towards the end
of November 1912, he stressed the danger of an extension of the Balkan
War. He was sure that, if Russia moved against Austria-Hungary,
Germany would join the latter; 'then of course France must also chip

[258] Goschen to Nicolson, 10 Nov. 1912, N.P., F.O. 800/360.
[259] Goschen to Nicolson, 25 Nov. 1910, N.P., F.O. 800/344.
[260] Goschen to Nicolson, undated, N.P., F.O. 800/363; evidently written in reply
to Nicolson's letter of 26 Nov. 1912, of which there is a copy in N.P., F.O. 800/360.
[261] Goschen to Nicolson, 23 May 1914, N.P., F.O. 800/374.

in'; and Britain would 'be confronted with a perfect beast of a problem'. This problem he proceeded to analyse:

> To my mind it means a catastrophe which ever way we solve it. Because it would be a catastrophe in itself to be dragged into a terrible war for a question originally paltry in itself and one in which we have no interest whatever. *But*—where should we be if we were to hold aloof? I shudder to think of it. What friends should we have left? And what figure should we cut?

In the short term Goschen considered that there was a good chance that the problem would not have to be faced. However, he expressed his fear of the 'Russian Panslavists' and his wish that 'both Sazonov and the Czar were stronger men'.[262]

It is interesting to compare Goschen's analysis, made in the autumn of 1912, of the possible repercussions of the Balkan situation with the gloomy warnings concerning a future 'Servian crisis' sent to the Foreign Office by his successor in Vienna, Fairfax Cartwright, in the following year.[263] It is also interesting to compare it with the actual events of July–August 1914. Goschen probably did not foresee precisely every stage in the concatenation of disasters that was to occur in the summer of that year. It is doubtful whether anybody else did. But he did perceive the dangers to the peace of Europe that lay in Austro-Serb tension, in Russian pro-Serb feeling and in the rival alliances of the two groups of great continental powers.

As far as his conduct during the actual crisis of 1914 is concerned, Goschen has been criticized on the ground that he was excessively passive. It has been argued that he should have taken steps to ensure that Grey did not wait until the last minute to make clear to Germany the nature of Britain's relations with her allies; had he been a great diplomatist, he would have ensured that the Foreign Secretary made this matter plain immediately the Austro-Hungarian ultimatum was delivered, so that Berlin might have been in a position to bring pressure to bear on Vienna.[264] However, to criticize Goschen on this score is to make highly questionable assumptions about Britain's foreign relations and her decision-making process. In any case, at the time of the delivery of the ultimatum Goschen was on leave. His diary shows that he called at the Foreign Office the next day. It does not tell us what advice, if any, he gave Grey.

The man in charge of the Berlin Embassy at the time of the delivery of the Austro-Hungarian ultimatum was, in fact, Rumbold, who, as

---

[262] Goschen to Nicolson, undated, N.P., F.O. 800/363.
[263] Cartwright to Nicolson, 31 Jan. and 23 May 1913, N.P., F.O. 800/363 and 367, quoted Nicolson, op. cit., p. 390.
[264] *Times*, 22 May 1924, quoting German press comment.

a mere councillor and chargé d'affaires, cannot justly be blamed for not having told his superiors in London what to do. Indeed, that the Foreign Office should not have asked Goschen to return to his post until after the Belgrade Government had replied to the ultimatum is symptomatic of its lack of prevision of the impending crisis. For almost four weeks the British Government was dependent for information from Berlin on a man who, because of his junior status, could not talk to the German Secretary of State as an equal, and who did not once in that period, so far as one can judge, have any direct contact with the Imperial Chancellor.

Nor would it be fair to criticize Goschen himself for not having been able, after his arrival in Berlin on the day before that on which Austria-Hungary declared war, significantly to influence the course of events. For one thing, reliable information concerning the German Government's actions was difficult to obtain. As Rumbold wrote, 'the fact is that, to us foreigners, the situation in Berlin during the crisis was obscure'.[265] Goschen recalled in 1923 that, after Russia's mobilization, 'the situation then became very obscure'.[266] There was little that he could do in the circumstances, except carry out his instructions to the best of his ability and report to London on the deteriorating situation.

One point in regard to which Goschen's record as Ambassador in Berlin does lay him open to criticism is the tendency that he showed in his correspondence with the Foreign Office to convey the impression that those who exercised power in the German Empire, or at least some of them, were more pacifically inclined than was in fact the case. His accounts of the political disposition of Bethmann Hollweg, in particular, cannot have prepared the British Government for the course pursued by the Imperial Chancellor during the weeks that followed the Sarajevo assassinations. Early in 1914 Nicolson, in a letter to Goschen, described Bethmann Hollweg as 'sensible and straightforward'.[267] It is difficult to see from what source the permanent under-secretary could have derived this impression, except from the Ambassador in Berlin. As late as the end of July 1914 Goschen expressed his conviction that 'the Chancellor and Jagow would like to avoid a general war'.[268]

How much responsibility, then, must Goschen bear for what it is tempting to call the 'failure of a mission'? The threat to peace inherent in the Southern Slav question, the alliances and arms rivalry of the Great Powers and the extra-European ambitions of several of them,

[265] Rumbold to Maxse, 27 Sept. 1914, M.P., 469.
[266] Goschen to 'Tommy', 25 Jan. 1923 (copy), Go. P.; *Times*, 2 Dec. 1926.
[267] Nicolson to Goschen, 19 Jan. 1914 (copy), N.P., F.O. 800/372.
[268] No. 677.

the aggressive mentality and excessive power of the military in more than one capital, and the inelastic planning of the Great General Staff, were not problems that any ambassador could be expected to solve. It is unlikely that any other hypothetical occupant of the Berlin Embassy would have succeeded in eradicating causes of conflict so deep-rooted and intractable.[269] In any case, Goschen did not exert in Berlin, nor in all probability did he ever expect to exert, influence of the kind enjoyed in London by Paul Cambon. As it was, he maintained good relations with Bethmann Hollweg and Jagow until the time of the final crisis. He did not exacerbate the international situation. Nor, so far as one can judge from his correspondence, did he urge extreme measures on his own government.

At all events, quite apart from the consequences that it would entail for the people of Britain as a whole, the British declaration of war on Germany constituted for Goschen a personal disaster. It meant the end of his ambassadorship, indeed of his career; unless the war were to prove to be a brief one, he could hardly expect to return to Berlin as Ambassador. It meant that his mission had ended in what could not appear as other than failure, however little he himself might be held to blame; for him there would be no 'beau départ'. It meant separation from the circle of friends that he had formed in the German capital and from his sister and her children. His younger son was of military age. The declaration of war on Austria-Hungary, which followed on 12 August, cut him off from Tentschach, his only real home. In August 1914 there can have been few persons in British official circles who had a stronger interest in the maintenance of peace with the Central Powers than had the Ambassador in Berlin.

[269] A point made by Z. S. Steiner, *The Foreign Office and Foreign Policy, 1898–1914* (Cambridge, 1969), p. 183.

THE DIARY OF EDWARD GOSCHEN
1900–1914

1900

Goschen arrived in Copenhagen to take up his post as Minister on 31 July. On 9 October he left again for England in order to welcome his elder son on his return from the war in South Africa. Accompanied by his wife, he set out again on 20 October for Copenhagen. The Goschens remained in the Danish capital for the remainder of the year.

Tuesday 31 July

Copenhagen

Left Berlin and after a frightfully rough passage from Warnemunde[1] to Gedser[2]—arrived safe (but scarcely sound) at Copenhagen at 7 p.m. Alan Johnstone[3] met me, accompanied by Captn. Boyle[4] (to whom my heart went out) *and Ole*[5]—the same as ever but slightly fatter.

Dined with Alan at Phoenix.

Wednesday 1 August

Went out to the Johnstones' luxurious villa (King of Greece's[6]) and dined with them. . . .

Thursday 2 August

Called on the few colleagues who are here, i.e. Beck Friis[7]—Jusserand[8] (n.b. didn't care for him) v. Schoen[9] and Benkendorf.[10]

Sunday 5 August

Went to Church—but could scarcely get there for rheumatism. P'cess Charles[11] did not turn up—so I need not have waited in the cold porch. Felt too seedy to go to Alan's who wanted me to stay.

---

[1] Warnemünde; port of Rostock. [2] Gjedser; on island of Falster.
[3] Secretary. [4] Consul. [5] Danish servant at Legation.
[6] King George I of the Hellenes; second son of Christian IX of Denmark.
[7] Swedish Minister. [8] French Minister. [9] German Minister.
[10] Benckendorff; Russian Minister.
[11] Princess Maud; third and youngest daughter of Prince and Princess of Wales; wife of Prince Charles, second son of Danish Crown Prince.

Monday 6 August

Rec'd by King Christian.[1] He seemed to me who had not seen him for 10 years very much changed.[2] He didn't say much—except to inquire after the Queen[3] and Princess.[4] A *very* short business—nearly as short as the same ceremony at Windsor.

Tuesday 7 August

Rain
Allan Johnstone left. I got lumbago in the morning—and had to have Melchior[5]—who after boiling a specimen—came back and told me that I was full of uric acid and must be treated for gout. Such a bore—the weather is beastly.

Wednesday 5 September

Dined at Tivoli in the evening with Rothe.[6] Also present Mrs Alan, Benckendorf, and Knagenhjelms.[7] Good dinner—and afterwards all the old amusements of Tivoli—Switchback, Wheel—Rifle galleries etc. Not a bad evening but *pretty damp*.

Thursday 6 September

Got a tel. from Twee[8] through George[9]—saying that he is well. As he tels. via Cape I presume he is free. Splendid news and now I feel a little less anxious.

Tuesday 9 October

Left for England by night train—Baring[10] came with me to station.

Thursday 11 October

Arrived in London very late as the Captain of the Flushing boat lost his way in the fog—much to Princess Aribert's[11] annoyance. Found Boss[12] in the best of health and spirits. Alic[13] dined with us and after dinner I went down to Southampton.

[1] Christian IX.
[2] That is, since being secretary of Legation at Copenhagen, 1888–90.
[3] Queen Victoria.
[4] Alexandra, Princess of Wales; Christian IX's eldest daughter.
[5] Physician.
[6] Aide-de-camp to Prince Christian, eldest son of the Crown Prince.
[7] Secretary, Swedish Legation, and wife.
[8] Goschen's elder son, Edward.   [9] George Joachim Goschen.
[10] Attaché; later well known as a writer.
[11] Princess Marie Louise; daughter of Prince Christian and Princess Helena of Schleswig Holstein; wife of Prince Aribert of Anhalt.
[12] Goschen's wife, Hosta.   [13] Alexander Goschen.

Friday 12 October

Twee arrived from S. Africa. I was on the Quay bright and early—and the *Carisbrooke Castle* steamed in—in bright sunshine. Saw our dear dear old Ted on the deck—in Khaki: he gave the old whistle. I rushed on board as soon as possible and soon found the dear old chap looking the picture of health. He had had fever and been in hospital—but had put on 3 stone since his escape. I say escape as he told me that the Boers had meant to take all the D.C.O. to Barberton—but that he (and others) had escaped in the dress of a highland Tommy. It was jolly seeing him again and we feel deeply grateful that he has been spared to us.

Saturday 13 October

Bunt[1] came up from Eton—and we four were together once more. How jolly it all is.

Sunday 14 October

We four went to Church—and thanked God for the safety of our boy—who has come back to us—as nice and boyish as ever—with a touch of gravity about him which adds to his charm.

Monday 15 October

Bunt went back. We three dined with Alics—George.... George looked rather wan and old—but only because his hair wanted cutting: it makes all the difference to him.

Wednesday 17 October

Lunched at Admiralty with George—who shewed me Salisbury's letter about a Peerage—which G. has decided to accept. But he wants an Earldom and I doubt if he gets it—a Viscounty is more probable—and Viscount Hawkhurst will probably be the Title.[2] Salisbury has been rather lukewarm—being amazed that George would not stop on till after the Elections. The Queen wanted G. to go on—and asked Lord S. to try and persuade him—Salisbury answered that he had exhausted his eloquence already. The eloquence, George told me, consisted in Lord S. asking him to defer his resignation till after the Elections!!

---

[1] Goschen's younger son, George Gerard.
[2] He took the title of Viscount Goschen of Hawkhurst.

Saturday 20 October

Left for Copenhagen leaving Old Ted with great regret—but still happy that he is near us again. Had a very rough crossing to Flushing and I was *nearly* seasick.

Monday 22 October

Copenhagen
Arrived at 10 a.m. and were met by Baring and Ewen[1] *and* Ole. Boss was delighted with the house and to my great relief liked Baring too. . . .

Monday 12 November

Miss Carstensen[2] came to lunch—and afterwards she took me to the Drummond Hays[3] to call—they were out! Then Boss and I had a short walk which we did not enjoy very much—and so home—to a very bad dinner—whereat I was wroth but did not visit it on my wife with hard words—as she had a headache—and so to bed where I passed an uneasy night. (I have just been reading Pepys.)

Friday 16 November

Same horrid weather and nothing partic: except heard that an attempt had been made on the Emperor of Germany—which turned out to be that a madwoman had thrown an axe at him—not very grave I fancy.

Saturday 17 November

Called on Schön to congratulate on German Emperor's escape! And on Schevekos[4] to ask how Czar is—he is suffering from Typhoid in a mild form and is going on well. A good thing because 1st he is a nice chap 2nd a friend to England.

Sunday 18 November

Church in the morning—and nothing else. Boss and I played in the evening—but as sometimes happens it did not finish well: but it is very rare nowadays.
Czarewich[5] left.

[1] Queen's Messenger.　　　　　　　[2] Lady-in-waiting to Princess Charles.
[3] There were several families of this name.
[4] He was secretary, Russian Legation.　　　[5] Grand Duke Michael.

Tuesday 20 November

Baring dined and went with us to Joachim quartett concert—which was very fine.

Mozart—Brahms and Beethoven. I enjoyed the last with a most beautiful 'Adagio molto expresivo'—which was divinely played. But all was good—only at a first hearing I couldn't made head or tail of Brahms. But a most delightful concert—Joachim leading as well as ever—only now and then—probably owing to deafness a little out in his intonation. But his style—his breadth and his bowing still the most perfect things in violin playing.

Saturday 8 December

Nothing partic. here: but news seems fairly good from S. Africa—many little successes and De Wet[1] seems rather cornered—and at all events is being hustled about. His attempt to get into Cape Colony failed. Read Chamberlain's[2] speech on the address[3]—very clever and full of fight—but to my mind not the speech of a high minded British Statesman. Still he gave better than he got.

Sunday 9 December

Did Tentschach[4] accounts all day: I think things are still done in much too ramshackle and extravagant a way. But things are getting more into order.

Monday 10 December

Chamberlain made a very good quiet speech on 2nd day of Address debate[5]—and gave a sort of Bird's Eye view of the Govt. policy after the War. The Egregious Tim Healy[6] made a speech in which he expressed the hope that the English troops might be beaten. I should have thought that it was an indictable offence—but anything in the way of treason seems allowed to the Irish Division of the H. of C. Perhaps he was best punished by no one taking any notice of it.

Rather seedy and out of sorts.

Thursday 27 December

Played football with Baring and boys in Ball room and got a severe hack from Bunt—on the shin! 50 trying to be 25.

[1] Commander, Orange Free State forces.
[2] Colonial Secretary.   [3] 6 Dec. 1900.
[4] Goschen's property in Carinthia; see Introduction.
[5] 7 Dec. 1900.   [6] Irish Nationalist M.P., Louth, North.

1901

The Goschens remained in Copenhagen until the beginning of June, when they moved out to 'Qui si sana', a house on the coast that they had rented. In July they made a trip to Frijsenborg, an estate in Jutland. On 2 October they left for Tentschach. On 21 November they left Tentschach for England. On 14 December Goschen set out alone for Copenhagen.

Tuesday 1 January

A rather bothering day. In the morning went to the Palace to congratulate the King. He looked very strong and well and said that he wished a happy New Year to the Queen—the Royal Family and England. Then on to Crown Prince's Palace where I was received by the Crown Prince,[1] Prince Xtian[2] and Harald[3] and little fat Prince Gustave.[4] In the meantime Boss had been rec'd by the Crown Princess[5]— and then we joined forces and wrote our names down on the Waldemars[6]—Xtians and Prince John.[7]

In the evening a very smart dinner at the Palace—attended by all the Royal family—Ministers and Heads of Mission. Things were very well done and the old costumes of some of the Footmen (Runners in former times) were very quaint and effective.

I sat between the Ministre des Cultes[8] and Admiral Weldahl.[9] The latter spoke English well—but the former said 'I speak very little English—but I love the English and hate the Boers.' I sh'd have enjoyed it all if I hadn't sat in a fearful draught. Afterwards talked to P'cess Thyra[10] and P'cess Alexandrine[11]—the latter very nice but with very yellow teeth. We had some Hock of *1598* which had to be drunk with sugar.

Thursday 7 February

Very low about money matters—don't know what is the best way to settle up—must consult Charles the Bk. Merchant![12]

---

[1] Frederick.   [2] Crown Prince's eldest son.
[3] His 3rd son.   [4] His 4th son.   [5] Princess Louise.
[6] Christian IX's 3rd son and his wife, Princess Marie.
[7] Prince John of Glücksburg; Christian IX's younger brother.
[8] Aagesen.   [9] Uldall.
[10] Christian IX's 3rd daughter; wife of Ernst August, Duke of Cumberland, son of the last King of Hanover.
[11] Prince Christian's wife.   [12] Charles Goschen.

Saturday 16 February

Young Schiörring[1] called—a very nice looking young fellow and we arranged a violin lesson twice a week—Wednesdays and Saturdays at 5 o'clock.

Wednesday 20 February

Schiörring

Didn't go out as I found my leg (wound)[2] was worse after skating so much yesterday. Had my first lesson with young Schiörring and it went off very nicely.

No news from the War but it would seem as if we must here [*sic*] important news soon—both as regards De Wet and Botha.[3] Chamberlain gave the Pro Boers in the House of Commons a good doing in the House of Commons on Monday.[4]

Saturday 9 March

Our Old Ted's birthday—I sent him a tenner and paid some bills for him. Fancy his being 25. Poor old boy—I am afraid his look out is not very brilliant—I doubt if he will pass his exam:[5] and what is he to do to earn a living if he doesn't? Not that diplomacy offers much in the way of a living except facility for spending. Baring dined with us and we drank the dear old chap's health.

I wrote a letter to Bunt in dog Latin in answer to such a charming letter in Latin from him to Boss.

Countess Benckendorff[6] called having got back yesterday—she was as nice and cheery as ever.

Schiörring—he brought me a sonata of Tartini's to learn which seems rather difficult—but very attractive.

Tuesday 2 July

Schoens lunched with us. He a true German snob and she ditto[7]— but we get on all right with them.

Friday 4 October

Arrived at Tentschach. . . .

---

[1] Johannes Schiørring; violinist; son of Christian Schiørring, also a violinist, from whom Goschen had taken lessons during his previous stay in Copenhagen.

[2] See Diary, 27 Dec. 1900.   [3] Commandant-General, Transvaal.

[4] 18 Feb. 1901.   [5] For the Diplomatic Service.

[6] Wife of Russian Minister.   [7] She was Belgian.

Thursday 21 November

Left Tentschach....

Friday 22 November

Left Vienna for England....

Saturday 23 November

England
Arrived pretty late after fair passage: arrangements at station for luggage etc. worse than ever. Old Twee and Bunt were there to meet us—B. looking awfully nice in Tails and Stick-ups—he was up for his long leave.

Jolly to be in England again.

Friday 29 November

Ballards[1] to Seacox[2]
Ted left for Tangier.[3] Boss and I Burchie[4] and Gar[5] went down to Seacox.... Old George looks a bit older but was very cheery and going very strong....

Sunday 1 December

Seacox
Went to the dear old church[6]—but alas! Mr Eagleton[7] didn't preach....

George is full of his book[8]—and works hard at it—but I *can* not see how it will interest the *general* public. The part about Schiller and Goethe may interest a certain section—but the love letters of my grandfather—tho' excessively spirituelles and full of fine thoughts—and even fascinating in their way will I expect be Caviare to the general crowd. Well—we shall see one of these days. Personally I would rather that the book had not appeared—for—tho' I oughtn't to—I hate the Germans and dislike being descended from one.

[1] Charles Goschen's house near Croydon.
[2] Seacox Heath, George Joachim's house at Flimwell, in Sussex.
[3] Where he was to serve as honorary attaché under Arthur Nicolson.
[4] Burchell; manservant.   [5] Dog.
[6] At Flimwell; the church is not in fact old.
[7] Vicar of Flimwell.
[8] His biography of his and Edward Goschen's grandfather, the Leipzig publisher.

Thursday 12 December

Ball.—town

... I went up to town to the F.O. Saw Lord Lansdowne for a minute—and Eric B.[1]—and just caught the 4 o'clock train back with Boss who had also been up to shop.

Saturday 14 December

Left London

Started on my journey—via Flushing—Hamburg—Kiel etc. Awful weather—rain and gale in the Channel—I was seasick. Train was late—Boat was late and missed connection at Flushing. Boat crammed with Germans—all sick.

[1] Barrington; Lansdowne's private secretary.

1902

Goschen was in Copenhagen during the early months of 1905. On 4 June
he and Hosta moved out once again to 'Qui si sana'. Later in June they visited
Gisselfeld, the country home of Count Danneskiold Samsøe. On 28 August they
left for Tentschach. Goschen returned to his post in mid-September, but rejoined
his wife at Tentschach some five weeks later. In November they left for London.
Goschen returned to Copenhagen in mid-December.

Wednesday 1 January

Court at 12.30. King did the job quickly and looked very well indeed. Then Crown Prince—who received with Harald and *Gustav*—
then names written on Valdemars and John—then dinner (Gala) at
6 o'clock in K'g Christian VII Palace—in the beautiful Rococo Hall.
I sat between Hansen—the Minister of Agriculture and Danneskiold Samsoe[1] (Kick). The latter was very nice—but the former only
spoke Danish and I didn't understand a word he said. He seems quite
a nice unpretentious man—and looked, tho' a peasant, quite at ease
in his uniform—more so than Alberti[2]—who didn't look otherwise
than the scoundrel *I* believe he is. The King sent round to me that
he drank to the health of the King and Queen of England and all
the B't Royal Family.

Sunday 5 January

Baring told me he had been offered Rome: he said that he didn't
want to move—but that if he had to he would prefer Rome to any
other place except St P. What he really wanted was to exchange into
the 'F.O. I told him that I sh'd think twice about going into the F.O.
as it was no career: but I also said that it was not easy to refuse a
transfer to an Embassy.

Saturday 11 January

Suddenly remembered that I was dining with Deuntzer.[3] Prince
Valdemar was dining and was very nice. He talked about Sonnenberg's
speech in the Reichstag and spoke of 'That fellow daring to speak
like that'. But I couldn't make H.R.H. angry with Bülow too....[4]

---

[1] Count Christian Danneskiold (or Danneskjold) Samsøe; he was half-English, his
mother having been Lady Elizabeth Brudenell-Bruce, daughter of the 1st Marquis of
Ailesbury. 'Ted' subsequently married his 7th daughter, Mary.
[2] Minister of Justice.　　　[3] Prime Minister and Foreign Minister.
[4] This refers to the debate in the Reichstag on 10 Jan. 1902, which arose out of
Chamberlain's speeches at Edinburgh, 25 Oct. 1901, and Birmingham, 6 Jan. 1902.

Saturday 18 January

Got the papers giving the opening debate in Parliament.[1] Both Salisbury and Balfour made excellent and firm speeches: neither they nor any body else seems to understand what the opposition want as regards peace: but it looks as if they thought that after the Boers have made war upon us and invaded our colonies we should beg them to make peace with us. The Irishes were awful of course—but it is at all events easy to understand what *they* want—viz. the humiliation of the Empire. I don't suppose C.-B. and his party want that.

Monday 17 February

Ball at P'ce Xtians. *I* enjoyed it—tho' it was very hot and crowded and the supper arrangements queer. The six Princesses sat down at a big table—while all our Ladies and the principal Danes stood up and eat as we could!! The Schoens were furious and Schoen said it was a 'Thierfütterung'....

Wednesday 19 February

Called on Deuntzer to congratulate him on his having been elected to the Folkething.[2] He told me that the Russians were furious about our Treaty with Japan[3]—and he said he had had a conversation with a Russian who had finally said—'Well we don't care we can soon have 250000 men out there!' He said that what annoys them all is that they thought England was a 'quantité négligeable' owing to the War—and that lo! we sprang up suddenly with a strong policy in the far East—and brought forth a political event of more importance than any of later years.

Played violin with C'tess Raben[4] in the afternoon.

Monday 10 March

Wedding day of King and Queen

Went out for a brisk walk to see whether that w'd do my back good—it didn't. Me Scheveko and Benckendorff called—and then the latter played with me till 7, when Burchell rushed in to remind me that I was dining at half past seven with Princess Maud. B. like most people who are fond of fireworks on the piano—does not accompany well. He bangs rather and allows for no rilenntos[5] or feeling of any sort. Still it was good fun and I think we both enjoyed it.

---

[1] 16 Jan. 1902.   [2] Lower house of Rigsdag.
[3] Anglo-Japanese agreement; announced 12 Feb. 1902.
[4] Her husband was Foreign Minister, 1905–8.
[5] The word Goschen probably had in mind was 'rallentamento'.

Thursday 20 March

Went to Deuntzer's day. I found him depressed about Antilles[1]—and state of Russia. He told me that his friends in Russia described that country as a smouldering volcano liable to burst out at any moment.

Thursday 3 April

Prince and Princess of Wales arrived. He looks very jolly and she rather imposing. I met them at the Station—and as I didn't know either of them and there was no one to present me it was rather embarrassing.

Wednesday 9 April

Prince and Princess of Wales and Prince Charles[2] and Princess Maud dined with us—also Rabens . . . and Bunt—the birthday boy. Afterwards about 70 people to dance.

The Queen had meant to come but couldn't as Duchess of Cumberland leaves tomorrow.

Great success I think. P'cess of Wales—who was very nice all thro' went before supper—but P'cess Maud stayed till nearly 3.

Couldn't enjoy it much because of ancle and throat.

Bunt and I composed a walse for the occasion—the Tappeur played it very badly—but people said it was pretty.

Sunday 16 November

London. Fine and cold.   N.E.

Arrived in London—being met by dear old Alic at Charing X in his *electric carriage*, which whirled us across the town in no time. . . .

Tuesday 9 December

Went up to London and was rec'd by the King—he was very nice and cordial and sent many messages to Denmark. He said that the Empress[3] and Queen had interfered rather too much in West I. islands business—etc. Saw Lord Lansdowne afterwards who said 'I suppose the King rec'd you very cordially as H.M. always speaks so well of you!' He deplored the loss of George from the Cabinet and spoke very nicely of him. I talked to him about Benckendorff.[4] He passed me out after ¼ of an hour's very pleasant talk. He was really very nice.

---

[1] The negotiations for the sale of the Danish West Indies to the United States.
[2] Crown Prince's 2nd son; later Haakon VII of Norway.
[3] Maria Fyodorovna; Christian IX's 2nd daughter; widow of Tsar Alexander III.
[4] Russian Ambassador in London from 1903.

Monday 15 December

Left for Copenhagen. Just caught George for a few minutes: he is as dubious about our Venezuelan policy as I am. Both he and I have a sort of feeling that we are being led by the nose by Germany.

Wednesday 17 December

Copenhagen

Arrived at Cop'n in pouring rain....

1903

The Goschens spent the first nine months of 1903 in Copenhagen, apart from a visit that Goschen himself paid to Gisselfeld in February. On 7 October Hosta Goschen left for Tentschach, where her husband joined her later in the month. On 25 November they left for England. Goschen returned to Copenhagen at the end of December.

Monday 12 January

Prince Xtian called—and gave his opinion about the Crown Princess of Saxony[1] and Giron[2]. He said, the young rascal—that the best plan for her would have been to have remained at home and had Giron with her all the same! *Not* a very elevated view for the future King of Denmark[3] to take.

Thursday 15 January

Boss had her first drive.... Went to Deuntzer's day and talked about a rumoured visit to Copenhagen from the German Emperor. He doesn't want him to come. He said one never knows what he will be up to—he may have as often happens a sudden attack of want of tact and may say or do something which will put up everyone's back and undo all the efforts of the last years to make the relations between Denmark and Germany more friendly. 'His visits are not always lucky or successful.'

Tuesday 27 January

It seems that the Venezuelan blockade will be raised soon—all the better. It has been a nasty business—and it has proved once more that it is not well to enter upon adventures in concert with Germany. If the Govt. thought that it would be a way of improving the relations between England and Germany they have been mistaken—as all it has done has been to accentuate the bitter resentment of England against the German campaign of traduction and insult during the Boer War. The business might have involved us in a quarrel with the U.S. but I am glad to say that all through they have been friendly to us and put what blame there was upon Germany.

---

[1] Crown Princess Luise, against whom the Saxon Crown Prince, Friedrich August, was about to bring divorce proceedings.

[2] Teacher of French; third member of the triangle.

[3] Succeeded, 1912, as Christian X.

Saw Charlie Hardinge's[1] app't. to succeed Bertie[2] at the F.O. as an Under Sec'y. of State! Another job—which is to be (and is) represented as a sop to the Dip. Service in view of Bertie's appointment. It is no sop whatever—as Bertie will stay in the Service and Hardinge will come back as soon as a good billet is vacant—like Gosselin.[3] It is all very hard.

Saturday 7 February

Read a very favourable and sympathetic criticism of George's book—*G. J. Goschen and his times*[4]—in the *Times*.[5] The *Daily Mail*[6] also had a column on it. Not a very good moment for its publication—when all England is bitter against everything German.

Wednesday 11 February

Peto's birthday. Reggie Lister[7] turned up—Boss liked him rather—I didn't—but then I never do at first. He got round me after a bit. He 'bounces' so and gasses—*but* there is always his redeeming sense of humour. He told me the Queen was furious about Venezuela and said that she knew there was something on when that 'snake' (Germ. Bill) came over. How she does hate him! He, Reggie L., told us that Egerton[8] was heartbroken about Rome—particularly as he had been told that he should not be forgotten.

Sunday 1 March

Church. In the afternoon went out on a message! ... Afterwards Elizabeth[9] brought her husband[10] into tea to introduce him to Boss—and unfortunately Falkenberg[11] and Wydenbruck[12] came in—wh. made it awkward as both Boss and I wanted to talk to the Moltkes.

They all went and Wydenbruck stayed on and was very bright and cheery. He said George's book was immensely talked about both in Germany and Austria—and was looked upon as a great event. He said the newspapers in both countries were full of it—as it treated of an interesting man and interesting times. W. is such a charming man spoilt—he would be such a nice colleague if he wasn't so queer and kept himself so aloof.

[1] Secretary, St Petersburg Embassy.   [2] Newly appointed Ambassador, Rome.
[3] Minister, Lisbon.
[4] Viscount Goschen, *Life and Times of Georg Joachim Goschen: Publisher and Printer of Leipzig 1752–1828*, 2 vols. (1903).
[5] *Times Literary Supplement*, 6 Feb. 1903.   [6] *Daily Mail*, 6 Feb. 1903.
[7] New secretary.   [8] Minister, Athens.
[9] Danneskiold's eldest daughter.   [10] Aage Moltke.
[11] Councillor, Swedish Legation.   [12] Austro-Hungarian Minister.

Boss and I played in the evening—but—well it never seems to be quite a success—I am keen and she is sensitive—and I never mean to put the dear girl out—but she doesn't quite understand me as regards music.

Thursday 5 March

Went to Deuntzers but missed him as he was late. Heard that the German Emperor is coming to Copenhagen—and on the 2nd. So telegraphed to that effect. How about Duke of Cumberland?[1]

Friday 6 March

Crown Prince's Ball—and before that a big dinner (and a very good one) at the Frijs[2]. . . . Miss Oxholm[3] took me on one side and wanted me to do what I can to get the German Emperor to express a wish that the Duke of Cumberland should meet him here. As it is—he will go—and the Duchess will go with him and that will distress the old King very much—while it would give H.M. enormous pleasure if things between the Emperor and Duke could be settled at Copenhagen! I must try—but it is rather delicate as I have no guarantee that if the Emperor *did* express the wish—the Duke wd. stop. That is the crux!

Monday 9 March

5 Danneskiolds came in to wish Twee many happy returns of the day and play Ping Pong. They also sent some flowers in—which was very nice of them.

Tuesday 10 March

Clara[4] and Mary[5] came to lunch—and ping-pong—then I showed them the citadel and monument wh. they had never seen before— and in the evening we went to a gorgeous dinner (P'ce and P'cess Xtian) followed by a large Ball—at the Langeland Ahlefeldts.[6] I took in Miss Oxholm—and we talked Cumberland affair: it appears that the matter is now solved by one of the Cumberland princes being ill—so that that will be made the excuse for H.R.H. Departure.

---

[1] Ernst August; son of last King of Hanover; Duke of Cumberland in British peerage; rightful Duke of Brunswick; husband of Thyra, Christian IX's 3rd daughter.
[2] She was Danneskiold's sister.
[3] Lady-in-waiting.
[4] Danneskiold's 6th daughter.
[5] Danneskiold's 7th daughter.
[6] Aristocratic Danish family.

Thursday 12 March

... *Very* good dinner—afterwards about 70 people and a really good dance....

Friday 13 March

All the better for last night—but with my grey hair—ought I to dance all night? I must—I can't hear a walse and see people dancing without joining in.

Monday 16 March

The Duke of Cumberland and his family left—such a pity—but there was nothing to be done as Schön wouldn't and I had no means of doing so—hint to the Emperor that He should ask the Duke to stop. Schön and I both jibbed because there was no guarantee that if the Emperor *was* asked to do so—the Duke w'd really stop. If the Duke had not been so obstinate things might have been arranged— as after all the Emperor had fixed his visit *knowing* the Duke was here— and had thereby indirectly showed that he w'd be glad to see Him.

It is further a pity because it is believed that the Emperor wanted to make the acquaintance of P'cess Alexandra[1]—with perhaps a view to a marriage between Her and the Crown Prince. This would have suited very well.

Tuesday 17 March

Had a walk with the D.s and went to Countess Raben's day. In the evening ... I had a long talk with the Crown Princess who was miserable about the Duke of Cumberland's departure. She said He might have good reasons for going—but the reasons for stopping were really far better and stronger. She said she had tried not to be annoyed about it—but had failed and was furious. The King had tried to keep him but could not and was much 'affligé'....

Thursday 19 March

Nothing partic.—except that the Empress arrived—so now we shall soon see the Queen....

---

[1] Cumberland's 2nd daughter.

Friday 20 March

... Had a very pleasant visit from Wydenbruck—who agreed with me that the Duke of Cumberland had not only been foolish but also very uncivil to the dear old King.

Tuesday 31 March

... Our dear Queen arrived and looked lovely as usual.

Thursday 2 April

A hard 'uniform' day—at 5 o'clock we were all at the landing place—which was prettily decorated. The *Hohenzollern* arrived *pretty* punctually. Then the Old King went on board—coming back very soon—and then the Kaiser came on shore in a twelve oared barge just like ours—and to the strains of *our National Anthem*—wh. made me sick.[1] The reception was cordial if not enthusiastic amongst the people—and every one was glad that there was no jarring note to mar the success of what was really a very pretty and brilliant reception. I got home at 6.15—and then had to get ready again for a Gala Banquet at the Palace at 7.30. I was in luck, I took in a charming Swede....

The Emperor made rather a nice speech—but his voice is harsh and disagreeable.

Friday 3 April

Emperor on the job. In the evening there was a gala reception at the Crown Prince's: very fatiguing but fairly amusing. *But* we were told to be there at 9.15—and we needn't have been there till 10 as no royalty appeared till then. We were all penned up in different rooms.... The Emperor—came round. He said to me exactly what he said to me years ago at St Petersburg (about George having asked him to dinner and having a good cook)[2]—didn't even glance at Boss— and enraged Lister by asking him whether he played Golf or Tennis!! So *we* didn't like him—but he has worked hard and has I think made a very good impression here.

Saturday 4 April

Awful day. Emperor changed his mind and is now only going tomorrow.

[1] 'Heil dir im Siegerkranz' has the same tune as 'God save the King'.
[2] See Introduction.

Sunday 5 April

Did not go to church—as cold and toe rather bad. Emperor left in the evening.

Wednesday 8 April

King's Birthday. Usual function in the morning—when the King looked splendid. The Queen received me today—after the Court—and then rec'd Lister at 2. It is almost annoying that after 2 years never receiving us (wh. we quite understood) She should now receive us solely because she must receive Lister—and that Miss Knollys[1] and Co. should say that it is so nice of the Queen to insist on receiving us before she received Lister. It may be well meant—but if one comes to look at it—it is rather galling. The Emperor seems to have captured the Queen to certain extent—because she said she *liked him personally* (what a change) but hated his politics.

Thursday 16 April

Nothing particular: but Möller[2] came and we arranged to have our walse printed—we also worked at our 'Romance for Violin and Piano'.

Thursday 23 April

Queen left—tearful as usual on saying goodbye to Her Relations. Empress left too and the two sisters travelled together as far as Neumünster.[3]
Messenger Waller also left—and now there will be peace for a bit.

Wednesday 2 September

Iswolskys[4] called. He seems a good chap—but I am doubtful about Mimi[5] tho' she seems very inclined to be friendly.

Friday 4 September

Iswolskys—Badeni[6]—Lady Ribblesdale[7] and Miss Lister[8] and the Boyles dined. We did not like Mimi much—but Iswolsky gains on acquaintance. Badeni awful.

---

[1] Bedchamber woman.   [2] Møller; violinist.
[3] In Schleswig; railway-junction.   [4] New Russian Minister and his wife.
[5] Isvolsky's wife; daughter of Count Toll, former Russian Minister, Copenhagen; Goschen had evidently known her during her previous stay there.
[6] Possibly Kasimir Count Badeni; more probably another member of the family.
[7] Wife of 4th Baron.   [8] Presumably a relative of the secretary.

Wednesday 16 September

Iswolsky in an after dinner conversation gave me his views upon our Treaty with Japan. Witte was just getting the upper hand against the Military party with his policy of the Commercial Assimilation, as opposed to the Military occupation, of Manchuria—when s'd Treaty appeared. It finished him and his policy—and won the day for the Military Party—whom Witte had been fighting for so long. He c'd not see how that could be an advantage to us—unless we considered it advantageous that Russia sh'd be forced to keep 200000 men out there. What advantage did we expect to get? Commercial? Japs would in that respect treat us just as badly as other nations. He knew them well—they were *not* clever—they were no statesmen—they were only fighters—and he admitted freely their military genius. The treaty had so swollen them with pride that there was no bounds [*sic*] to their military ambition. They were the only people who could organize Chinese immense forces [*sic*] and they *were* doing it—and that might mean that the Yellow Peril might some day become a fact and not a phrase.

Russia had no designs on Corea—but Japs had—and Russia would never stand having such a warlike nation established just on their frontier, etc.

Friday 18 September

... I sent a private letter to Lansdowne recording Iswolsky's views about the effect of the Anglo-Jap Treaty.[1]

Saw in the telegrams that Chamberlain, Ritchie[2] and Lord G. Hamilton[3] have resigned. It seems strange that *both* Ritchie *and* Chamberlain have resigned—as one was for Free Trade and the other preferential Tariffs etc. I can only suppose that Balfour and those who remain are in favour of something half way between the two—such as elastic retaliatory Tariffs.

Thursday 1 October

Saw in the paper that poor Mungo Herbert[4] is dead—poor chap he has not enjoyed his Ambassadorial honours very long. I wonder who will go to Washington—I hope not us—as Bossie would hate it so—but I don't *think* there is the slightest chance. I also hear that Scott[5] is leaving Petersburg soon—and that Bertie is anxious to leave

---

[1] Goschen to Lansdowne, 17 Sept. 1903, Lan. P., F.O. 800/122.
[2] Chancellor of the Exchequer.   [3] Secretary of State, India.
[4] Ambassador, Washington.   [5] Ambassador, St Petersburg.

Rome. Monson[1] goes next year and Plunkett[2] soon—so there will be a grand shuffle soon. I wish I was keener—more ambitious—cleverer and *stronger in health*.

Friday 2 October

Messenger Curzon arrived. Nothing particular in the bag—except a scheme for doing away with first Secretaries (of Legation) as a class—cont'd in a Memo. drawn up by that irrepressible and conceited Ch. Hardinge. I am asked my opinion of it—so I must study it—but I already see certain holes to pick.

Saturday 3 October

Iswolsky—Schoen (with an awful cold) Curzon and Peto dined. Iswolsky held forth a good deal on the Near Eastern question. He said that in his opinion the scheme of Reforms is no good: European control the only thing. But what he was most interesting about was when he said that in this question England and Russia—and not Russia and Austria—ought to have undertaken the job and taken the lead. He considered that a splendid opportunity of a real rapprochement between the two countries had thus been lost—and he could not understand how the people in Power in both countries had not seen this.

He said that England was not understood in Russia and that the legend of perfide Albion still held good—and that public opinion was against England always. I asked him whether public opinion had much influence in Russia—and he answered 'enormous' and that it was very difficult to control. I asked how 'public opinion' penetrated to the powers that be—certainly not thro' the Press and that there was an iron circle of Tchinovniks which acted as a wall. He admitted this rather but said 'It filters through somehow—God knows how— but it does— and not only does it have great influence but the mere fact of its having no legitimate or legal channel to flow through— like Parliament and Press in England, rendered it very difficult to control.' My conversations with Iswolsky make me think that he is very clever—but very conceited—and that he thinks that things would go better if Iswolsky was at the head of affairs.

[1] Ambassador, Paris.   [2] Ambassador, Vienna.

1904

The Goschens remained in Copenhagen until leaving for Tentschach towards the end of August. They returned in mid-September. On 21 October they set out again for Tentschach. In November they went to England, where they spent three weeks before returning to Copenhagen.

Monday 25 January

Long visit from Isvolsky—who again deplored Anglo-Japanese Alliance—and attitude of English Press. He said that a Free Press was a clumsy weapon but a controlled Press a clumsier weapon still. He also deplored this business just coming on now—when Anglo-Russian relations had been on the point of a real improvement. Now what with the Jap imbroglio—Thibetan business etc. relations were certainly not good—and that was a very bad look out for the spring— when the Macedonian question might and probably would break out again. That was where good relations between England and Russia would be useful. (Was that the reason for their approaching us so sweetly last year?) I asked him why they should be upset by our move in Thibet: and he said hesitatingly—'Well it may force us to take measures there for which the time is not quite ripe.'

Inter alia he said that he had always been in favour—and had worked to that end—of giving Japan an entirely free hand in Korea.

Scandinavian Neutrality—Martens'[1] Article in the *Revue de deux Mondes*[2] *not* inspired by Russian F.O. Lamsdorff[3] had written and told him so. Must read up this question. Isvolsky sanguine about peace— but I am not.

Friday 19 February

Ted and I went down to Gisselfeld[4] where we met with the usual kind and cordial welcome.

Monday 29 February

Ill—with Rheumatic Throat.

[1] International jurist; Goschen had known him in St Petersburg.
[2] 'La neutralisation du Danemark', *Revue des deux Mondes*, n.s., xviii (November 1903), p. 314.
[3] Russian Foreign Minister.   [4] Danneskiold's country home.

Thursday 3 March

... Heard that Hardinge was certainly going to be sent Ambassador to St Petersburg!

Sunday 6 March

Oh this E. wind.

Hardinge gazetted as Ambassador at St Petersburg. He of all men: I feel as if I couldn't stand it. It is the most ghastly unqualifiable job that has ever been perpetrated. He intrigued poor Scott out of his place and then intrigued himself into it. It is frightful and made worse by a leading Article in the *Times* applauding the appointment as a welcome change from the old system of Seniority. What can the *Times* know as to its being a good selection? Hardinge has not half the intelligence of Nicolson[1] or Howard[2]—but they have not half his pushing powers—Bumptiousness and Bounce. Of course the public *must* think that all *we* are fools and incompetent. Personally I feel disgraced while practically it reduces my chance of becoming Ambassador at any useful age.

My feelings at being passed over are intensified by my lifelong dislike of the man himself.[3]

If only I could afford to retire.

Monday 7 March

Spent whole day thinking of Hardinge—and how unnecessary it was for the people at the F.O. to tell me that I was first favourite for the place. I never thought so myself—but I *did* think Howard or Nicolson would get it....

Wednesday 30 March

King and Queen arrived....

Friday 8 April

K.C.V.O.

Old King's Birthday. We went and gratulated the dear old Boy in the morning. The King conferred K.C.V.O. on me. M.V.O. on Lister and Boyle....

---

[1] Minister, Tangier.   [2] Minister, The Hague.
[3] Goschen had already made clear in his diary his opinion of Hardinge. The extraordinary bitterness of this entry is perhaps partly to be explained by the fact that he was unwell, as the entry for 29 Feb. shows.

Monday 11 April

Big lunch for the King. . . . Most successful and food delicious. King very nice about it. He had a good talk with Isvolsky and started an 'entente' similar to that we have with France. King was pleased with Isvolsky and Isvolsky most appreciative of King's graciousness, friendliness and tact.

Going into Supper the King said as He passed 'I want to have a word with you afterwards,' and he told me that the old King had asked to confer the Grand Cordon of the Danebrog[1] upon me. The King said 'I don't often grant this permission—but in the special circs of the case—and your position here—I am going to give private permission to accept it: wh. means that you may wear it here and before us—but not elsewhere.'

Tuesday 12 April

King of Denmark gave me the Grand Cordon of the Danebrog— and I must say that it is the *one* Foreign Order I like having—because I love the dear old King and like Denmark.

Thursday 14 April

Went down with their Majesties—Crown Prince—P'ce Valdemar, P'ce and P'cess Xtian, P'ce and Princess Charles—and the Suite— in Special train to Trifolinen Dairy—and then by carriages to Gisselfeld. I drove in same carriage as the Charles and Miss Knollys—awful rag with P'cess Maud of course. Old D. drove with King and Queen. The dear six were at the door at Gisselfeld curtseying low. Dagmar[2] looked so pretty and dear little Mary rushed at me and pulled off my gloves—and seized my coat as of yore. Karen[3] looked pale but calm—and Clara excited and pretty. Magda[4] was upstairs—but Ragnhild[5] was up and looking well again. Huge lunch at wh. I had the luck to take in Dagmar—and she had *no one on the other side*. I had an awfully good time of course—and the King seated between the Queen and P'cess Alexandrine[6]—looked envious. Afterwards we went out and the King and Queen planted trees etc.

Sunday 17 April

Church. King came and sent for me afterwards and we had a long talk. I showed him a private letter to Lansdowne giving resumé of

[1] Dannebrog; Danish order.   [2] Danneskiold's 3rd daughter.
[3] His 5th daughter.   [4] His 4th daughter.   [5] His 8th daughter.
[6] Prince Christian's wife.

my conversation with Isvolsky.[1] H.M. was pleased with it and said it would work in very well with his....

Monday 18 April

King and Queen left.

Sunday 29 May

The King of Denmark left for Gmunden.[2]

Wednesday 22 June

Isvolsky came to see me this morning: he says that Alexeieff[3] never wanted war—but foresaw it and asked for masses of Troops. Kouropatkin[4] who was then Min'r of War said that Russia wanted to avoid war and that the premature sending of a large force in time of peace would precipitate it. As a compromise he sent two Brigades of European troops. These, I. says, are the only seasoned troops Kouropatkin has at the present moment—and that the great mass of his present Army are rough Siberian Levies. Two Corps d'armée are on their way—in whom perhaps the Japs will find their masters perhaps.[5] But in the meantime the Japs are making the most of their opportunities.

Wednesday 27 July

Got a *letter* from Twee saying that he had been offered Secretaryship to Sir W. Garstin[6] and had *accepted* it.... Garstin is director of Public Works and Irrigation in Egypt—the best public Dep't there I think....

Thursday 17 November

London. Arrived[7]—dense fog
The journey was very comfy but we arrived pretty late....

Tuesday 6 December

Bunt came up early for short leave. We 3 lunched at Scott's[8]—and

[1] Goschen to Lansdowne, 16 Apr. 1904, Lan. P., F.O. 800/122.
[2] Near which the Duke of Cumberland had a *Schloss*.
[3] Russian Viceroy, Far East.   [4] Russian Commander-in-Chief, Far East.
[5] Goschen's repetition of 'perhaps' was probably unintentional.
[6] Under-secretary, Egyptian Ministry of Public Works.
[7] From Tentschach.   [8] Restaurant.

then I had my picture painted by Anderson[1] from 3 to 6. B. awfully interested. It turned out a good likeness—with something queer about the eye![2]

Thursday 8 December

Left London for Copn. 8.35 p.m.

[1] Perhaps Charles Goldborough Anderson; possibly J. B. Anderson.
[2] Portrait not in family's possession; nor at National Portrait Gallery.

1905

The Goschens spent the early months of 1905 in Copenhagen. At the end of March, following his appointment as Ambassador, Goschen went to Vienna for a few days. In May he and Hosta returned to England. From 17 to 19 June they were guests at Windsor Castle. On 22 June they left for Vienna. They spent most of July and the first half of August at Tentschach, but Goschen went up to Vienna in mid-week. On 13 August they went to Marienbad for the 'season'. Goschen spent two nights in Vienna before returning to Tentschach on 10 September. He left Tentschach for Vienna on 25 October. Apart from two hunting expeditions he was in Vienna for the remainder of the year.

Tuesday 24 January

According to the papers there is the devil to pay at Petersburg—I wonder how it will all end. If it goes on like this they won't be able to get soldiers for the Far East: in any case there will be a regular reign of terror: only it will be the people—not the Aristocrats to suffer as in the French Revolution. Bad Times!

Wednesday 25 January

Crown Princess better.[1] Not much fresh news from St Petersburg—but according to the newspapers—the action of the authorities of St Petersburg in shooting down an unarmed mob who came peacefully to place their petition in the hands of the Czar—has met with the censure of the whole civilized world.

Myself I think the Czar lost a splendid opportunity—he might by a timely display of pluck have recovered all he has lost in the past by supineness and deference to the opinions and beliefs of his evil genii the Grand-dukes. He might have earned the applause and sympathy of the world—instead of its contempt. I can't help being sorry for him—He is so badly equipped for his fearfully difficult position—and *so* badly advised.

I am *sure* he has meant well—and is well meaning—but that isn't enough for an Autocrat of Holy Russia. That wretched giant has tumbled upon evil days—and who can foresee the end?

Boss is better but the doctor wouldn't let her start today.

Lady Rodd[2] turned up—a nice intelligent woman all *there* in every respect. She, Boss and I went to hear little Elman—a Russian violinist

---

[1] She had had influenza. [2] Wife of British Minister, Stockholm.

of about 14 years of age.[1] A wonderful child—but a child. No difficulty exists for him in the way of technique—*but* to compare him as some do with Kubelik[2] and even Ysaye[3] and others is simply ridiculous. I got no pleasure from his playing—but I was full of wonder at his attainments.

Friday 17 February

Gd. Duke Serge[4] assassinated

We were just dressing to go to dine with our Russian colleagues the Isvolskys—when I opened a Ritzau[5] tel. and saw that the Grand Duke Serge had been killed by a bomb at Moscow. Isvolsky came in for a few minutes afterwards to tell me that he had been obliged to put off his dinner—on account of the terrible news. He was rather overcome and I expressed to him my great sorrow that this detestable useless crime had come on the top of all their other misfortunes. He stopped and talked for a few moments— and said that he had antici- pated something of the sort—and that moreover he had great fears that this was only the beginning of a series! He attributed Serge being the first to be attacked to his being and always having been the Leader of the reactionary party in Russia. Isvolsky had never approved of his policy—which did not mitigate his detestation of a crime, useless in itself—and worse than useless as it would, like the assassination of Alexander II, put off all reform and progress for years and years. We both pitied, and sympathised with, that dear Grand Duchess,[6] whose life has not been a happy one—and who is so lovely and good. Poor Russia—I am not a Russophile exactly—but I like many Rus- sians, and I think their troubles are reaching an almost unbearable stage.

Monday 20 February

Nothing partic. Had two good walks one with Boss the other with Isvolsky. He was communicative. He said that in his own mind he was convinced that there were no Torpedo Boats (foreign) in the North Sea at the time of the Hull Trawlers incident—and that he would prefer to rest the Russian case on the evidence given by English Naval Officers as to the difficulty of distinguishing Torpedo Boats from Cruisers etc. at sea on a foggy night—rather than on the evidence given by Russian Officers. That they *thought* they saw Torpedo boats is possible—but that there *were* Torpedo Boat [*sic*]—impossible. He

---

[1] Born 1891. [2] Czech violinist. [3] Ysaÿe; Belgian violinist.
[4] Governor-General of Moscow; Nicholas II's uncle and brother-in-law.
[5] The Danish news-agency. [6] Grand Duchess Elizabeth; Serge's wife.

told me a thing I never knew before viz. that both the Grand Duchess Serge and the young Empress[1] are both [*sic*] bigoted Orthodox Churchwomen—and share the intolerance of that persuasion in a very high degree. He said that, brought up as they were, this has always surprised him. It surprised me too and I said that I thought that it was the Dowager Empress who was the most bigoted and the most under the influence of the Holy Synod—and Serge etc. He said no! She had been so more or less in her husband's life time—but that was only from her devotion as a wife—and her subserviency to *his* opinion—and not from conviction—and this she had shown since his death.

Friday 24 February

Leech[2] came back—no news except that he says that the general idea is that Gosselin will go to Vienna. But he says that O'Conor[3] is anxious to go there. Personally I doubt whether Fergus[4] will get it—because of Minna.[5]

Dined with P'e Valdemar and had quite a nice evening.... P'e Valdemar said to Boss—'What do they want to kill my poor sister (the Dowager Empress) for? Do you know? Boss said she had no idea except that she had heard that the Empress was considered to be rather hostile to the Finns. *I* think it is because she has been considered for years to be identified with the reactionary policy of Serge and Pobiedonostov,[6] and I think that is more likely. Valdemar rather scoffed at the findings of the North Sea Commission—and said 'Why every body knows that they fired on their own ships—and that there were no For: topedo boats about.' I haven't seen the findings yet—but from what I hear of them—they make the reference of questions to arbitration a farce.

Sunday 26 February

+2°. S.E. strong and cold

Got lumbago—or rather Rheumatism in the back—at breakfast. So no church. Got worse and worse all day—but still had to go and dine with Guichens[7] opposite—which was unlucky as we couldn't drive and have the carriage to go 20 yards! We had a dull evening—but Madame Guichen sang very nicely. Back awfully bad at night.

[1] Her sister, the Tsarina Alexandra.   [2] Secretary.
[3] Ambassador, Constantinople; Goschen had served under him in St Petersburg, 1896–8.
[4] O'Conor.   [5] Lady O'Conor.
[6] Procurator, Holy Synod; name also spelt 'Pobedinostsev'.
[7] He was 2nd Secretary, French Legation.

Friday 3 March

Got some news for insertion on this day later. Melchior came and gave me 'Aspirine'—whether it is that wh. has cured me I don't know—but I *am* better tonight. Perhaps it was something else.

Got the news that The King had approved my appointment to *Vienna*. Splendid—but sorry to leave little Denmark.

Friday 10 March

Crawled up but still very bad. Got a letter from Plunkett asking me whether I couldn't arrange for him to stop on till June. Rather a large order—but, seeing that they are so nice about us—I wrote to Eric[1] making the best job I could.

Sunday 26 March

Left for Vienna.

Monday 27 March

Passed through Dresden and Emmie[2] and Evy[3] travelled with us to Schandau[4]—awfully nice. Got to Vienna and received hearty welcome from Plunketts.

Tuesday 28 March

Vienna. Dull and warm

Did business all the morning with May Plunkett[2] and our future butler[6]—a nice capable man.

Dined with Alan Johnstones[7]—who asked the Duke and Duchess of Teck[8] (our future mil. Attaché[9]) Twinkle Clarke[10]—P'e and Princess Turn and Taxis[11] to meet us. Latter quite nice I thought. Js. have a fine apartment and every thing well done. Mrs Alan fatter and more pronounced than of yore. Tecks very nice—the Duchess being most amusing.

[1] Barrington.
[2] Emily von Metzsch; Goschen's sister; widow of Gustav von Metzsch; resident near Dresden; sometimes referred to as 'Emie'.
[3] Her daughter.   [4] Saxon spa.   [5] Ambassadress.
[6] Richter.   [7] He was now secretary, Vienna Embassy.
[8] He was the eldest brother of the Princess of Wales; she a daughter of the 1st Duke of Westminster.
[9] The *Foreign Office List* gives him as military attaché.
[10] Consul-General, Hungary; 'Twinkle' was a nickname.
[11] The Thurn und Taxis were a well-known mediatized family; the Prince and Princess were friends of Clarke.

Went with P. to see Ct. Goluchowski[1]—I think I liked him pretty well—he struck me as very clever—rather cynical and very obstinate: a combination of Lobanow[2] and Muraview[3]—former predominating.

Wednesday 29 March

Warmish and spring like

Lists a.m. Prater p.m. I going with May in Fiaker and Boss with Nellie[4] in Victoria. In this I saw the horses I have bought from the Plunketts and thay are *awful*. I must get some smarter ones.

Whole staff dined in the Evening—including the beautiful Mrs Bennett[5] and the Parson.[6] I liked the Tecks—Rennie[7]—Chilton[8] and Mrs Bennett: I didn't care much for Kilmarnocks[9] and the Parson gave me the creeps.

Thursday 30 March

Vienna

Finished off business and played about with Plunketts having a jolly little dinner with that dear little Nellie as Ps. were dining out.

Friday 31 March

Left Vienna 9 a.m.

Dagmar met us at Berlin—the dear thing—and drove us across the town; it was nice seeing her to say goodbye.

Saturday 1 April

Got back from Vienna—and went to a ball at Rabens[10] in the evening. . . .

Wednesday 3 May

I suppose I may soon consider myself an Ambassador as Plunkett's time is up today.

[1] Foreign Minister; Goschen had met him in St Petersburg; see Introduction.
[2] Russian Foreign Minister, 1895–6; see Diary, 1895–6.
[3] Russian Foreign Minister, 1897–1900; see Diary, 1897–8.
[4] The Plunketts' daughter.   [5] Wife of commercial attaché.
[6] Hechler, Embassy chaplain.   [7] 2nd secretary.
[8] 3rd secretary.   [9] He was 3rd secretary.
[10] The new Danish Foreign Minister and his wife.

Saturday 13 May

Presented my letters of Recall to the dear old King. I felt very choky when he talked of his regret at our going and gave me his good wishes. What a splendid old man he is.

Sunday 14 May

Went down in the afternoon to Gisselfeld to say goodbye to my dear friends there. I had the usual warm welcome from the 'six'—Dagmar being there. Very pleasant, but to bed fairly early.

Monday 15 May

Gisselfeld looking lovely—and the 6 all full of affection and kindness. After lunch I had a talk with the Count....[1]

Tuesday 16 May

In the evening we dined with the King.... He made me a pretty little speech when he drank my health and said 'We are very very sorry to lose you—and our very best wishes will go with you.' Afterwards he played on his Pianola and was like a child with a new Toy. He was delightful all the evening and when he said goodbye he added twice 'and God bless you and keep you.' There are few people whose blessing I would sooner have. I have never known a truer and simpler 'gentleman'. We are distressed to say goodbye to him and leave these nice people for the unknown!

Saturday 17 June

Windsor
Went down to Windsor—Duke and Duchess of Wellington[2]—General Kelly-Kenney[3]—Plunkett and Prince of Wales and Household including Miss Doris Vivian[4]—with whom I made great friends.

Princess Victoria[5] didn't dine. We had lovely rooms looking out on the Terrace. I took in Miss Vivian to dinner.

Sunday 18 June

Windsor
Church a.m.—in Chapel—such a pretty service—Royal Party up

[1] Concerning 'Ted' and Mary.   [2] He was the 4th Duke.
[3] Former adjutant-general.
[4] Dorothy Vivian; maid of honour; married Major-General Douglas Haig.
[5] Edward VII's youngest daughter.

in a box. Afterwards a little ceremony in which Duke of Wellington presented his Annual Banner—by which he hold S[   ][1]? Princess Victoria awfully nice. She called me aside and begged me to write to P'cess M. and do my best to persuade her to throw no objections in the way of Charles' accepting Crown of Norway![2]

Then the Queen showed us her own rooms and, hearing Bunt was coming up to lunch—P'cess V. sent for him so he saw them too. He lunched with Household and Doris Vivian took charge of him. After lunch we drove to Frogmore and Probyn[3] shewed us the gardens and afterwards his own at the Castle. Then Doris Vivian and I played golf. Prince and P'cess Alexander of Teck[4] dined—and so did Lord and Lady Knollys[5]—I took in the latter to dinner. The King and Queen were very nice to us.

Monday 19 June

Left Windsor

After a round of golf with Miss Vivian. We really enjoyed ourselves very much—it was just like staying at a big country house. One went everywhere, wh. one couldn't do in the dear old Queen's time. I forgot to mention that every morning at 8 the Royal Piper promenaded the terrace piping for all he was worth. It was rather cunning.

Thursday 22 June

Left London for Vienna—very crowded train and the Sleeping Car Co. had not fulfilled their promise of securing me a compartment. Quite a comfortable Journey in the Train de Luxe.

We had of course to leave London on practically the first beautiful warm day.

Friday 23 June

Vienna

Arrived 5.25 p.m. Rennie—Kilmarnocks—Seymour[6]—Bennetts[7] and Captain Keyes[8] at the Station—also the Consul.[9] Large Landau

---

[1] Blank in MS.: Stratfield Saye.   [2] Then breaking away from Sweden.
[3] Keeper of the Privy Purse.
[4] The Prince (later Earl of Athlone) was the youngest brother of the Princess of Wales and of the Duke of Teck; the Princess (now Princess Alice, Countess of Athlone) is the daughter of the Duke of Albany.
[5] He was Edward VII's private secretary.   [6] 2nd secretary.
[7] He was commercial attaché.   [8] Naval attaché.
[9] Goschen probably means Schoeller, the honorary Consul-General.

with the small horses conveyed us to the Embassy[1]—which we found in a most depressing state. Rennie very nice and helpful. Burchell is, thank goodness acting as my Valet.

Rather depressed altogether.

Saturday 24 June

Sultry and close

Rennie lunched. At 4 I went to see Golu—who was quite nice. He talked some time on the Moroccan question—but I expect all his arguments came from over the way and were made in Germany: he doesn't think there is any good in the discussions now going on—between France and Germany—as other Powers are also interested—amongst others Austria (having only lately discovered this). He considers that a Conference will place things on a satisfactory basis—as every Power *interested* will have its say. Personally—for me it is a matter of whether France's declarations are to be believed or not. If she is not going to interfere with the Sovereignty of the Sultan—and intends to do nothing to invalidate the most f. n. clause of the Treaty of Madrid[2]—what is there to confer about!

Tecks called—she quite charming—also Kilmarnocks and Seymour. Hechler also called—but not Bennetts.

Sunday 25 June

Fine—hot wind

Church—not bad service—but Hechler preached 25 min! He lunched with us afterwards—rather a clever well informed man—but entirely taken up with his own ideas—and terribly unctuous. Called on Tecks and Kilmarnocks—and then drove to Golf Ground and Prater in Fiaker which went like the wind. Demidoff[3] was playing golf and I was quite glad to see a friendly face.

Tuesday 27 June

Awfully hot— +20°

Received by the Emperor at 2—with the usual ceremonies: every step being regulated in a printed form. At 1.35 a young chamberlain—von der Straten—a nice chap—appeared at the Embassy with 3 Gala Coaches. Into the first two got the Staff—consisting of the Duke of Teck—Captain Keyes R.N.—Bennett—Rennie—

---

[1] In the Metternichgasse.   [2] The Madrid Convention of 1880.

[3] Secretary, Russian Embassy; previously secretary, Russian Legation, Copenhagen; Goschen had also known him before that.

Seymour and Kilmarnock—then I leapt into a huge Gilt Coach—with the Chamberlain on the front seat. The Coaches were drawn by white horses in Gala harness—and each had gala Lacqueys clinging on behind. We drove slowly to the Palace—where the Staff was deposited at one door—while I drove on to another. A couple of Court Officials conducted me up a soldier lined staircase—then I was taken charge of by another Official and conducted along a corridor lined by the gigantic Austrian Guards—fine men in fine Uniforms—then came Count Kholoniefsky[1]—Oberceremonienmeister—who conducted me through rooms lined by the too splendid picturesque Hungarian Guard—and handed me over to Count Gudēnus[2]—who showed me into the Emperor—3 bows, 3 responsive heelclicks—and then shake hands—and pretty speeches and presentation of Credentials. H.I.M. very kind and cordial. A short conversation—presentation of Staff—and reconduct to Embassy with same ceremonial. Arrived there half boiled. In the afternoon visit to Goluchowski—and colleagues—of whom more anon.

Saturday 1 July

Twinkle came up from Buda Pesth.

Sunday 2 July

Dined at Sacher's[3]—Twinkle and Seymour—afterwards went to Venedig in Wien[4]—a sort of glorified Tivoli—there met Leghait[5] and Demidoff.

Monday 3 July

Had long Hungarian talk with Twinkle and in evening had Steed[6] to dinner. A very brilliant young fellow. We discussed Apponyi's[7] letter in the *Times*[8]—in which he was rather down on Steed for seeing Hungarian action thro' Austrian spectacles.

Tuesday 4 July

Oh how hot.
Nothing partic. Twinkle left early. We enjoyed his little visit immensely.

---

[1] Choloniewski.   [2] Grand Chamberlain.   [3] Fashionable hotel.
[4] In the Prater; a pseudo-Venetian place of entertainment.
[5] Councillor, Belgian Legation.   [6] Vienna correspondent of *The Times*.
[7] Leading member, Hungarian Party of Independence.
[8] *Times*, 1 July 1905.

Wednesday 5 July

Meréy—under Sec. for F.A. called[1]—a nice ugly man—was optimistic about settlement with Hungary in the Autumn—saying he thought Emperor would make concessions on military questions! Other people don't seems to share this view.

Had a round of golf with Steed before rain came on. Count Ahlefeldt[2] and Demidoff dined.

Burchell left for Tentschach.

Thursday 6 July

Rainy day. Teck came up and brought Boss some flowers. Dined at Bristol—chiefly with Ahlefeldts—but also Meréy—Count Hardegg[3]—Müller[4] (used to know him at Const'ple)—Beck Friis—new Swedish Minister—Teck—Seymour and Demidoff. Rather fun. P'ce and P'cess A. Thurn and Taxis were there—and were very nice and cordial. Count Hardegg a very nice man—his family used to own the ruin on the way to Zweikirchen.[5]

French and German Morocco negot'ns going on well.

Friday 7 July

19°. Cool and beautiful

Called on Meréy. He told me he had good accounts from Uscub[6] of the Turkish General in command there. He seemed imbued with Western ideas and anxious to work with European officers. It is not a misfortune, Meréy added, that the Turks are active against the Bulgarian Bands. He spoke of the 3 p.c. increase in the Custom duties—which he thought w'd be necessary—tho' he knew we were against them. He seemed to think that a quid pro quo could be got.[7] He doesn't anticipate real trouble in Balkans this year—and thinks weakness of Russia keeps Bulgars—Serbs etc. on their good behaviour. Otherwise he didn't say much.

Japanese Minister[8] called on me: a quiet strong little man—with less than usual of the Jap's smiling affability. He impressed me very favourably.

He said Isvolsky didn't do much in Japan![9]

[1] Mérey; Chief of Section, Foreign Ministry.
[2] Danish Minister.   [3] Lower-Austrian landowner.
[4] Councillor, Foreign Ministry.   [5] In Carinthia, near Tentschach.
[6] Üsküb (Skoplje).
[7] That is, a 3% increase in customs duties, for which the consent of the Powers was necessary. The British Government desired further control of Ottoman finances, in order to ensure that the extra revenue should be used on Macedonia itself. See F. R. Bridge, *From Sadowa to Sarajevo* (1972), p. 275.
[8] Makino Naboaki.
[9] Isvolsky had been Russian Minister in Tokyo, 1900–3.

Saturday 8 July

V. to Tentschach, +19°. Very fine

After a fair to medium but cool journey arrived at Klagenfurt: warmly welcomed by Jim who was there for luggage and drove up in Gazarolli's Landau. . . . Tentschach lovely and *so* cool after the heat of the Vienna Embassy. Tea in the summer house delicious air—and so glad to be at home again. Mrs Jim does not look well. Bed early and *actually sleep*.

Sunday 9 July

+20°, very fine

Very cool in House but hot outside. Church at 12. Boss and I— so nice.[1] Found gardener to be a clever young man and the Kitchen garden in a promising condition. At 4 o'clock Boss and I walked over to the Jägers. Mrs Jäger *very* sprightly—clean and nice as usual. Dogs all right—and chickens and *Turkeys* splendid. No apples—but Plums and cherries very fine: the new nectarines in the Kitchen garden are full of fruit and most promising.

Jolly day.

Thursday 10 August

Left Tentschach for Vienna—very hot journey.[2]

Sunday 13 August

Marienbad

Arrived Marienbad and didn't care for rooms.

Monday 14 August

Went to see Dr Ott[3] a very nice man and said to be a 1st class Doctor. He went over me very carefully—and prescribed Kreutz Brunnen[4]—and mud baths. Met Mabel Lowther[5]—and we were mutually pleased to meet.

---

[1] Goschen presumably means that he held a service, attended by his wife, in the Schloss chapel.
[2] He had been commuting since mid-July.
[3] Fashionable physician.   [4] Kreuzbrunnen; famous mineral-spring.
[5] Probably a relative of Gerard Lowther, Minister, Tangier.

Wednesday 16 August

King arrived: he was ½ [*sic*] late owing to a lunch at Gmunden—
and this made him arrive in a shower of rain. He looked full of beans
and good spirits. As he is travelling as Duke of Lancaster—no official
reception—only the Abbot of Tepl[1] (a nice old Boy) the Burgomeister
and the Bezirkshauptmann, etc.

Friday 18 August

Service and Te deum in the Cathedral being Emperor of A.'s birthday. In the morning King conferred G.C.V.O. on me—and I wore
it for the first time at a Dinner which H.M. gave to the chief dignitaries
of the Town in the evening.

The King said some very nice words to me in conferring the
Order—and reminded me that it was on the King of Denmark's birthday that he had given me the K.C.V.O.

Tuesday 22 August

The King dined with us at Rübezahl restaurant. . . .[2] Drescher's
lovely Viennese band played and Miss Olga Leek sang—but was *not*
a success. I think evening went off all right.

Monday 28 August

Boss went

Boss's Birthday—gave her a jewel of sorts—both as a Birthday
present and to console her for not going to Tachau—Prince Windi-
schgratz's[3] place. But she had a baddish cold and it was a case of driving about 5 hours there and back in a bitter wind. She was awfully
disappointed. The King took me in His motor—and we did go—
about 30 miles in 50 minutes. I might have been nervous at the pace—
but I said to myself 'if it's safe for H.M. it's safe enough for me'! and
I thoroughly enjoyed this my first motor drive. I also knew that the
chauffeur was ne plus ultra. Windischgratzes awfully nice—3
daughters—not goodlooking but very jolly—and easy to get on with.
House enormous but lying low. Huge lunch wh the King wouldn't
let me eat because of the cure. The rest of the party by the bye was
the Stonors,[4] Fritz Ponsonby,[5] and Pom McDonnel.[6] After lunch

[1] The abbey owned much of Marienbad, including the Kreuzbrunnen.
[2] Fashionable restaurant on hill overlooking Marienbad.
[3] Alfred Fürst zu Windisch-Graetz; President, Herrenhaus.
[4] Henry Stonor and his wife; he was a gentleman usher and groom-in-waiting.
[5] Equerry, assistant-keeper of the privy purse and assistant private secretary to the
King.
[6] McDonnell; secretary, Office of Works.

drove to old Princess Matilde W.[1] quaint old place (where there was a tremendous tea) and next to it was W.'s magnificent Riding School. Afterwards to Planen—Ct. Nostitz's[2] beautiful old Schloss—which stands beautifully with a magnificent view into Bavaria. Lovely Aviary—another tea and then a brisk drive home. The King was most kind and chatty both going and coming. Wish Boss had been there and that she hadn't caught cold. Took her to Station and saw her off.

Tuesday 29 August

Cold and rainy and beastly

Had a nice little dinner with Swaine[3]—Lockwood[4]....

Miss Boss awfully—and had a dull little lunch by myself. Saw Marie Corelli[5] (and a gigantic companion in a Tam O'Shanter) for the first time. A rum little woman to look at.

Wednesday 30 August

Lunched with P'ce and P'cess Mirko[6] at Egerländer[7] to meet H.M. I sat next to Princess and found her nice but with a Servian touch that I knew well.

Marquise de Ganay[8]—who is a very nice pleasant woman gave a dinner to H.M. in the evening. When H.M. sat down to Bridge—he whispered 'Go and have a talk to Mirko and see what you can get out of him.' I did and got a good deal of boasting and bombast—of some interest for H.M. and Lord L. The chief part was his opinion of the King of Servia[9] and his heir[10]—and the possibility of succeeding them when Servia turns them out.

Consigned it all to a letter to Lord L.[11]—which I shewed to H.M. who was much interested. Pretty and amusing dinner—made acquaintance of Princesse Murat.[12]

Wednesday 6 September

Marienbad. Very fine and warm

Lunched with Campbell Bannerman to meet the King. Sir John Fisher[13] turned up and was great fun. Amongst other things the king

---

[1] Windisch-Graetz's aunt. [2] Lord high steward.
[3] Former military attaché, Berlin. [4] Colonel; Conservative M.P.
[5] Novelist.
[6] He was the second son of Prince Nicholas of Montenegro; she was *née* Constantinovic and was related to the Obrenović dynasty.
[7] Restaurant. [8] Marienbad habituée. [9] Peter I.
[10] Prince George.
[11] Goschen to Lansdowne, 1 Sept. 1905, Lan. P., F.O. 800/117.
[12] Another Marienbad habituée. [13] 1st Sea Lord.

was chaffing him and 'Oh you sailors are said to have a wife at every Port.' He answered 'Don't you wish you were a sailor Sir?'

Thursday 7 September

Marienbad. Fine and warm

King left after lunching with me at Rübezahl. Princess Murat—Mrs Stonor ... Campbell Bannerman and suites. Not bad. King distributed Forget me nots among his *best* ladies, etc. He gave me a very pretty cigarette case—Russian—and said many kind words.

Only Mirkos to see Him off besides ourselves.

Friday 8 September

Left Marienbad. Vienna

Scott[1] and I left in the afternoon. Previously I lunched with Mrs E. Stonor[2] at Egerländer Café.

Found Pom at Embassy but as our train was 1¾ hours late—only just had time for a small talk in which he promised that the Embassy should be made pretty in time.

Saturday 9 September

Vienna

Fussed about the house with Sir H. Tanner[3] and Mr Hillier[4] of the Bd of Works—and saw what was to be done—a good deal I think.

Found Boothby[5] quite charming. Dined with Freddie Clarke[6] at the Jockey Club—where I saw Mensdorff[7] and his brother—Dietrichstein.[8]

Sunday 10 September

Vienna to Tentschach. Fine

Boss met me at Station and Bunt (and dogs) up at the house. Boss has nearly got over her cold—which has been a bad 'un.

Tuesday 26 September

Old Twee came back from England.

---

[1] 2nd secretary.
[2] Wife of Edward Stonor, Henry's brother; clerk to House of Lords.
[3] Architect and Surveyor, Board of Works.
[4] Controller of Stores.   [5] Councillor.   [6] 'Twinkle' Clarke.
[7] Austro-Hungarian Ambassador, London.
[8] His elder brother. Their paternal grandmother had been Sophia, eldest sister of the Duchess of Kent.

Saturday 21 October

Boss and Twee went away—both to Cairo where B. will stay for a bit—she ought really to have come back to Vienna with me—but she will enjoy herself with her boy and it will I think do her good.

Sunday 22 October

Church—Stable—Jäger's all as usual except that I am alone without my dear Family. Tore up and wrote a lot of letters.

Wednesday 25 October

Left Tentschach. Heavy snow

Woke up to find a violent snowstorm raging—with 2 or 3 inches on the ground. Had a beastly drive down—and got to Vienna very late. But the country *looked* beautiful. . . .

Thursday 26 October

Vienna

Richter arrived in the evening and told me snow had done lots of damage. Letter from Boss written in the train. They had not as yet had a good journey.

Called on Golu who would not say a word about Hungarian affairs. Boothby and Scott both seedy. Teck and Fairholm[1] appeared and lunched. Latter most interesting about Macedonia.

Friday 27 October

+2°. Still beastly and cold

Went to the Tennis court[2] and poussai'd une balle in my boots. Arranged to play tomorrow morning. Court is small and has no tambour—but that is perhaps all the better at my age.

Saturday 28 October

Lunched with Ourosoff[3] the Russian Amb'r. D'Avarna[4] was there

---

[1] Colonel Fairholme; staff officer with the Macedonian Gendarmerie; former military attaché, Vienna.

[2] A 'real' tennis court.

[3] There are several versions of the Ambassador's name. When writing in French he signed his name 'Ouroussoff'. See his letter to Cartwright, 23 July, no year given (Cartwright Papers). He was a recluse owing to poor health. See Goschen to Grey, 13 May 1907, F.O. 371/195.

[4] Italian Ambassador.

and old Fonton—who used to be Russian Minister at Lisbon—and Bucharest and is now honorary attaché.[1] Dutch Min.? Weede[2] called on me and I liked him. Steed and Twinkle dined *and* Scott: and we had a long smoking Parliament.

Had my first game of Tennis and enjoyed it awfully.

Sultan refused the Amb'rs' demand for a collective Audience—on the ground that 1. there was no precedent 2. that it was on a subject which was a matter of internal interest only!

Sunday 29 October

Church—where I was much bothered by Hechler's antics. Then Twinkle to lunch (he is staying with me) and afterwards we went together to the Races—in order that I should make a few acquaintances.

Monday 30 October

Played tennis—then saw Sir H. Campbell-B. I think he is a nice old thing—and now that I know him no longer feel my old repugnance to his becoming Prime Minister.

The news of the day is that the Czar has granted Parliamentary Gov't and a Constitution. Witte will be first Prime Minister under new order of things. The Questions I ask myself—How about the Church—of wh. the Czar is also head—How about the Grand Dukes and will the Anarchists who have engineered the strikes and disorders allow things to calm down? Qui vivra, verra. But I doubt whether everything can be changed by a stroke of the pen.

Called on the Dutch Minister and his wife—whom I found charming. Then on Hordliczkas[3]—just the same as ever.

Henschel,[4] passing thro', lunched. He confirmed what Mirko told me about the hatred in Servia of the present dynasty: but said that Mirko was also hated as being a Montenegrin—and that the ideal of the Servians now was a German Prince with an English wife!

Twinkle had to go back to Pesth—to write about Fejervary[5] programme.

---

[1] He had the rank of Councillor.   [2] Weede van Berencamp.
[3] He had been Austro-Hungarian military attaché in Belgrade when Goschen was there as Minister.
[4] Another Belgrade acquaintance; Goschen had briefly taken lessons from him in German composition (Diary, 29 and 31 March 1900).
[5] Fejérváry; Hungarian Minister-President.

Tuesday 31 October

Nothing partic: trying to find out something about what is going on in Hungary. No one knows anything. Played a round of golf with Scott—but didn't make much of a job of it. Afterwards called on Sir H. C.-B. I found him at home with a cold and with his wife. She is slightly weird and her invalid voice is rather trying—but she seems a good sort *when* one talks of dogs. Also called on Bellamy Storers[1] but they weren't in Vienna.

Wednesday 1 November

Called on Spanish Amb'r[2]—who hadn't much to tell me that I didn't know. Also called on Ahlefeldt who asked me to dine next Monday at 7.30. Found C't. Wedel, the German Ambassador[3] who gave me his *word of honour* that Germany had nothing to do with the Articles on Lansdowne in the *Neue Freie Presse*[4]—and had no dealings with that paper. He was very angry with Steed who had said in a strong Art. in the *Times* that *Neue Freie Presse* was directly influenced from Berlin.[5] It will be rather fun talking to Steed about this—because he is equally certain!

Dined at the Jockey Club with Boothby (by the way I forgot to pay for my dinner) and met Prince Schönburg[6]—Prince Liechtenstein[7]—and a young C't. Kinsky.[8] I like Boothby very much—he *is* so pleasant and sympathetic.

Demonstration by workmen in favour of Universal Suffrage: a re-echo of Russian Revolution.

Thursday 2 November

Tecks came back and lunched. She cheery as ever. Went to see Merey—who didn't tell me much of interest—except what he *thought* were Golu's ideas of the course the Powers in S.E. Europe ought to take in consequence of Sultan's refusal to receive Amb'rs in collective audience. This was, briefly, to give the Sultan a little more time with the possibility of his taking good advice from the Germans—and then

---

[1] United States Ambassador and his wife.
[2] Duke of Bailén.
[3] Goschen wrote later that Wedel was of 'the regular type of the German soldier-diplomat', and referred to his 'rather rough and overbearing manner' (Goschen to Grey, 17 May 1907, F.O. 371/195).
[4] *Neue Freie Presse*, 18, 20 and 21 Oct. 1905.
[5] *Times*, 21 Oct. 1905; see also 23 Oct. 1905.
[6] Councillor, Austro-Hungarian Embassy, London.
[7] There were several princely members of this family.
[8] Younger brother of Prince Karl Kinsky.

if still recalcitrant (the Sultan) to proceed with Naval Demonstration englôbing all questions likely to be opposed by Porte afterwards.

2nd Demonstration of workmen—during wh. the Mounted Police lost patience—drew sabres—and charged crowd. No one killed—but considerable no. of wounded.

Friday 3 November

Messenger Ewen. Wrote a weak Hungarian desp.[1] Then went to see Goluchowski to see whether I could get anything out of him with regard to near Eastern affairs. Got nothing—except what I knew already i.e. that A.H. Government and Russian were going to propose Naval Demonst'n. I only learnt in fact that Merey's surmise as to his intentions had been wrong: I also found out and wrote to Lord L. that he didn't seem to care much about englôber-ing question in Ultimatum—and said 'Oh! If we begin to discuss such things now—the Naval Demonstrat'n won't take place for a year!'[2]

Saturday 4 November

Tennis. Then new boy Bruce[3] appeared. A good looking chap and seems nice—but he has the slight pomposity of the modern boy....

Wednesday 8 November

Tennis—had 3 rattling sets with the 2nd Marker—a strong player but out of practice. We played 3 sets and he won the odd one after a hard tussle. He made me sweat and I made him warmish too. Did accounts and am appalled at expense.

Friday 10 November

Messenger Taylor passed thro' and lunched. He told me un-employed question in England was grave: and that Balfour's answer to the women irritated rather than soothed.[4]

Monday 13 November

Tennis. Ghika[5] called and Guillemin.[6] The former a funny little

---

[1] Goschen to Lansdowne, 3 Nov. 1905, F.O. 7/1363.
[2] Goschen to Lansdowne, 3 Nov. 1905, Lan. P., F.O. 800/117.
[3] Attaché; 3rd secretary from 1906.
[4] At the Local Government Board, 6 Nov. 1905, in reply to a deputation composed largely of wives of unemployed men.
[5] Romanian Minister.   [6] Councillor, French Embassy.

clever man. Amongst interesting things he told me was that one of the reasons why the Sultan was so dead against Financial Reform was that he drew £20000 annually from Macedonia—which he feared he would lose if finances were properly administered.

Received by the King of Spain[1]—a nice boyish humane boy. Frail and ugly—but full of go—and a bright animated manner. Said he would like to shoot every day of his life! I was rather attracted by him. This is the only time I shall see him as we are not bidden to anything else. Other Amb'rs are rather shirty at this want of hospitality but I think it natural as it is a very family visit. If *not* I should think the whole reception of the King rather 'mesquin'.[2]

Tecks lunched.

Thursday 16 November

Snow

Boss arrived well and bright and early—6.30. Awfully glad to see the darling—and hear all about her trip to Cairo and about old Twee. The House will now get on.

Friday 17 November

Finish but very cold and snowy

Hofjagd at Göding.[3] Early start from Nordbahn 6.45 a.m. At the station was introduced to Archduke Franz Ferdinand—two Salvators[4]—and P'ce Philip of Coburg[5]—Golu—Wedel—Ahlefeldt—Hardegg—C't Thun of Hohenstein.[6] 14 guns. Bag:—

3 Reh—1382 Hares—552 Pheasants—62 partridges—100 rabbits—8 various—total 2107.

The Pheasants were most shot by the Archdukes who are carefully nursed—and Wedel tells me that all along their [*sic*] are boxes with Pheas. and Part. in them wh. are opened as the Archduke F. Ferdinand comes along. He likes to kill all the game and is distressed when any one else kills any. (He recently had a shoot to *himself* with 300 beaters and nets—when he killed 600 hares!)

The Pheasant drive at the end was very disappointing as they placed the guns close up to the wood and only about 5 yards between

---

[1] Alfonso XIII.

[2] Alfonso was a second counsin twice removed of Franz Joseph, to whom he was related through his mother, Queen Maria Cristina, daughter of the Archduke Karl Ferdinand.

[3] In Moravia; Czech, Hodonín.

[4] That is, two Habsburg archdukes, each of whom bore the name Salvator.

[5] Head of Hungarian branch of Coburg family.

[6] Grand Huntsman.

each gun. All the birds seemed to be blown to bits—and there was scarcely any which were allowed to get on the wing. If they went towards the Archdukes one was not expected to shoot! Not my job! Deepish snow—wet boots—no change—very cold driving back.

Lunch—a very good dinner! was served in a movable house. They did us well altogether—3 meals in the train—but the snow spoiled the sport.

Saturday 18 November

Twinkle came up from Pesth—we went out antiquity hunting.

Sunday 19 November

Got stiff in the afternoon—which turned into Lumbago and I could scarcely get upstairs to bed.

Monday 20 November

Sent for Ott—who mustard plastered my back—and ordered Masseur for tomorrow. I can't move—and I write this long afterwards.

Tuesday 21 November

Lumbago.

Wednesday 22 November

Lumbago—and so on for a long time—missing 4 days shoot—Pheasants—with Schöller[1]—and the Court Shoots.

Sunday 17 December

Hurrah! my back so much better. So I was able to start for Strassnitz[2] withScholler and party—consisting of General v. Engel (former commandant of Vienna) Col. Engel his brother—Herr von Dumba,[3] Bn. Isbary[4]—M. Czernoslavek[5]—Herr von Hartmuth[6]—Ritmeister Quirini, 9 guns with Forstmeister making 10. 3 Hours train—special carriage—fine old Schloss—good warm rooms and every thing very nice. Schöller takes his cook and servants. The numerous carriages

[1] Consul-General (honorary), Vienna.
[2] In Moravia.   [3] Councillor, Foreign Ministry.
[4] Freiherr von Isbary; textile manufacturer.
[5] Probably a business acquaintance of Schoeller.
[6] Probably another.

belong to the Schloss—which is owned by a Count Magnis—a German.[1]

Monday 18 December

Started for beat at 8.15 and had about 15 minutes drive—nice and warm in my big Schuba[2]—with my new little fur round the knees. Long line of beaters with a wing who go at right angles hauling a long string with coloured paper and feathers. Beat chiefly through vineyards. We got 506 hares—27 partridges—3 Reh—and 4 rabbits— of which I got 56 hares 8 part.

The lunch (very good) was in the open and it was pretty chilly. I *was* glad I had my little fur coat.

Pleasant dinner in the evening—but I was glad to turn in and sleep like a top.

Tuesday 19 December

Same programme

Bag 432 hares—36 part.—2 Reh—1 Rab.—1 pheasant, of which I shot 29 hares and 13 partridges. I find shooting these hares on the ploughed field at about 60 or 70 yards very difficult—it wants practice—but I shot patridges pretty well. We were much hampered by the sun in the afternoon—dead in our eyes.

Schwerin[3] and Major Bülow (brother of the German Chancellor) arrived at 2 a.m.!

Wednesday 20 December

Fine but not so much sun

Our best day

1307 Hares—63 partridges—4 Reh—6 rabbits and 96 Pheasants (cocks) of which I got 144 hares—4 partridges—1 Reh—13 pheasants—and one rabbit.

I killed a lot of my hares across a ride in a wood which is more in my line than the open.

Thursday 21 December

−1°. Threatening snow

Bag:—

556 hares—54 partridges—62 pheasants—of which I got 56 hares— 10 partridges—7 pheasants.

---

[1] Anton Count Magnis.   [2] Shuba; fur coat.   [3] Councillor, German Embassy.

We had a little wood driven for Pheasants and it was the best part of the whole shoot—as we were put far back—100 yds off the wood and the birds came really high. I only shot cocks and was proud to kill 7 off the reel and only missed one.

We came back in the evening after a jolly time which I enjoyed most immensely.

Sunday 31 December

Fine

We all stopped to communion.

It has been a splendid year for us. The top of the tree—G.C.V.O. *and* Vienna—which was our dream. We have all been well (comparatively all thro') and have an awful lot to be thankful for. We had our old Ted with us—jolly as ever—at Tentschach. But he feels his separation from Mary—and both she and he are unhappy at the uncertainty of things. Bunt is developing in every way—and is one of the very best. Keen about every thing and a universal favourite. He got 2nd for the King's Prize for German at Eton—only 20 marks behind the winner in an exceptionally good year—so the examiners said.

My dear Boss has been splendid all through the year—and is always the same dear unselfish best of mothers and dearest and best of wives.

Thank God for every thing.

In the evening we had a weird ceremony and had to go and prostrate ourselves before Liechtenstein[1] and Countess Harrach[2]—representing Emperor and Empress†.[3] Full uniform. Liked Liechtenstein immensely.

[1] Grand Master of the Court.   [2] Grand Mistress of the Court.
[3] Assassinated, 1898.

1906

The Goschens spent the early months of 1906 in Vienna. In mid-May Goschen paid a brief visit to Budapest. Soon afterwards he and Hosta had a week-end at Tentschach, where they also spent the second half of July and the first half of August. They were at Marienbad for the 'season'. They spent most of September and October at Tentschach, Goschen going up to Vienna when necessary. They then went home on leave, returning to Vienna early in December.

Monday 1 January

Staff dined and we had a jolly evening. We have the nicest staff possible—and they make it very nice and easy for us.

Wednesday 3 January

Rec'd by Archduke Franz Ferdinand—He was very nice and amiable.

Friday 5 January

Rec'd by Archduchesses Maria Therèse[1] and Annunziata.[2]

Friday 12 January

Had our official Reception (Recevimento). We had a great many people—and it was rather successful as the women stopped while their husbands went on to the Russians. I amused myself very much—Boss didn't—tho' I don't think she minded it as much as she thought she would....

It was also messenger day, wh. was a bore—as I was busy writing all day. Hungarian crisis chiefly—it was supposed to have entered a more hopeful phase—but I don't believe it much. Andrassy[3] and Kossuth[4] I believe would come to terms—but Apponyi won't—and they won't leave him.

A Heavy day.

[1] Widow of Archduke Karl Ludwig; Franz Ferdinand's stepmother.
[2] Her daughter; Franz Ferdinand's half-sister.
[3] Gyula Andrássy (the younger); founder of the Constitutional Party.
[4] Ferenc Kossuth, son of Lajos Kossuth; leader of Party of Independence.

Monday 15 January

Things keep changing here with surprising rapidity. Yesterday's papers were all Couleur de Rose as regards Hungary—today nothing could be blacker. One day Servia and Bulgaria—are treated like dogs—the next day the Bullying tone is dropped—and no one can in fact tell from one day to another on *any* subject what the attitude of Austria-Hungary is. I reported, on *excellent* authority—on Friday—that Golu's trenchant policy as regards Servia had been rejected by the mixed Council of Ministers and that milder measures were to prevail. Today I hear that Golu's original policy—i.e. 'No tearing up of the Treaty no negotiations for new Treaty of Commerce' has been adopted. Which is right? I am rather uncomfortable as to what I reported.

Tuesday 16 January

I *was* right at the time—but Golu's original policy was adopted at a 2nd Council of Ministers. I hear from Reverseaux[1] that at Council of Ministers held today Golu's policy of bullying will be again dropped. What *is* one to believe or report? Reverseaux tells me that this probable change to a peaceful policy is due to the fact that the A.H. Govt. has heard that Germany started the Serbo-Bulgar Customs Union—hoping to stir up trouble between Servia-Bulgaria and Austria—hoping thereby to profit by closure of Austrian Frontier to Servian exports. Germany has long been looking longingly at the Balkan States as an opening for Trade—and she was always anxious to increase her share of it: so it is possible that this report is true.

Called with Duchess Meg[2] on Princess Lilie Kinsky.[3] A beautiful house and a nice woman—She was very friendly. Countess Festetics[4] was also there.

Mignon in the evening. How pretty it is—but how spoilt by the 'talking' part of it—and a beast of a tenor. 'Mignon' was very good herself (Fr. Kunz) but the rest abominable. Orchestra excellent and discreet.

Scott has to go and take charge at Sofia: an awful bore just as we are getting into working order. But I can't object as it is a good chance for that excellent fellow and worker.

Wednesday 17 January

Scott ordered to take charge at Sofia—most awful nuisance—just

---

[1] Marquis de Reverseaux; French Ambassador.
[2] Duchess of Teck.   [3] Wife of Prince Kinsky.
[4] Wife of Count Festetics; *née* Hamilton.

as we are beginning to organize the work. It will be a two months job—and I expect that next month we shall have our hands full.

Went to French and Spanish days: I thought the French one rather awful and the Spanish one rather nice. But then I like the Duchess of Bailen[1] and don't care about the Marquise[2]—in the same way that I like the Marquis[3] and don't care about the Duke.[4]

Dinner at Storers.

Gulu was in good form—he is very amusing.

Thursday 18 January

Our first dinner—Golu—Storers.... A very good dinner and a particularly jolly evening.

Saturday 20 January

Our first Court Ball—Twinkle came up for it to be presented to Emperor. It was a weird entertainment. First Boss had to be dragged off to be presented by Countess Harrach. Then there was a huge cercle—Emperor and Archduchess Maria Josepha[5]—then the ball—where we men had to stand in one corner of the room for 3 hours without any supper—except the famous Marie Thérèse Bouillon which was handed round. The Ambassadresses and Ministers' wives went and had a sort of tea with the Archduchesses—Beer—water and cold chicken—*very* simple. But Boss's worst ordeal was that she had to take her turn and go and sit for about 10 minutes on an Estrade with A.D. Maria Josepha. We got home weary and worn and sad about 12.15. The Emperor was very nice and kind—and sympathetic about the Elections.

Duchess developed mumps poor dear.

Thursday 25 January

Dinner at Golu's. Diplomatic. I know these dinners *well*. I sat next to a little Jap—and worked like a trooper. She was a nice little thing and having been at Tokio I was able to get along with her. On the other side I had the dear little Duchess of Bailen—so I was all right....

Friday 26 January

Messenger Ewen. Busy all day—and wrote a poor and hurried let-

---

[1] Spanish Ambassadress.   [2] De Reverseaux; French Ambassadress.
[3] De Reverseaux.   [4] Of Bailén.
[5] Wife of Archduke Otto, younger brother of Franz Ferdinand.

ter to Sir E. Grey.[1] I told him how at the Court ball the Emperor had said to Vouitch[2]—'The conduct of your Government has been most incorrect. One does not go and make a secret convention just when one is going to make a Commercial Treaty with a Great Power.' Don't like it—think the Emperor (although Vouitch said he spoke otherwise kindly) ought [sic][3] to make such remarks in his own House to his own guest. But balls are rather fatal to H.I.M. for it was at a ball he turned his back on Apponyi and made the latter an enemy. Hence to a great extent the rocky nature of the Hungarian crisis. Latter looked as usual hopeful in the morning—before Andrassy's audience with the Emperor—but worse after it—when former told an interviewer that the situation had not improved.

Monday 29 January

Got the sad news of the Death of our dear old friend the King of Denmark....

Tuesday 30 January

Letters and telegrams and putting off dinners all day. Called on Ahlefeldt who seemed to like a letter I wrote to him last night. I wrote as I felt.

Hungarian Crisis seems to have taken a good turn. The result of Andrassy's interview with the Emperor was that he carried a message from the latter to the leaders of the Coalition to the effect that if they didn't form a Gov't and carry on the business of the country they would be responsible for *all* consequences.

This threat, but more especially the fact that the Emperor has dealt directly with them—has had its effect and they seem ready to form a Gov't under Szell.[4] There are many rocks ahead yet—but still something has been gained.

Thursday 1 February

Got a letter from George—miserable about elections. He says that he doesn't care so much for the loss of Unionist seats as for the astounding polls of the labourers. They have learnt their Power and will not unlearn it. Up till now they have never used their votes—this time they have used them with a vengeance. He says protection is killed—but with it many time-honoured institutions (probably). He considers

---

[1] Goschen to Grey, 25 Jan. 1906, Gr. P., F.O. 800/40.
[2] Serbian Minister.   [3] Negative evidently omitted.
[4] Széll, Hungarian Minister-President, 1899–1903.

the House of Lords to be in great danger. Altogether he is most depressing.

Had a long talk with Reverseaux—but didn't get much out of it. He had just seen Géza Andrassy[1]—a cousin of the Hungarian Leader J. Andrassy.[2] He was pessimistic as to peace. He said that the Coalition were ready to drop the Sprach-Commando question etc.—but would demand in return that all the Municipal Officials lately dismissed for passive resistance etc. should be reinstated! If this is true I see no present hope because the Emperor *can't* put back the people he has just turned out for disobedience to his orders!

We shall soon hear as Andrassy comes to Vienna tomorrow. The only hopeful sign is that the Coalition are both afraid (of Absolutism) and divided. A great many people think that a few months of Absolutism will bring them to their senses.

Friday 2 February

Wrote name on Infante of Spain Don Carlos de Bourbon[3] who left a card on me. That is all I did in the way of going out. Hungarian Affair sounds bad according to what I hear—no one seems to think that there is the slightest chance of a settlement for the moment. Still I think there is a step in advance and the Coalition Leaders for all their high sounding talk are in a bit of a funk with regard to where they have led the country—and are afraid of absolutism.

Sunday 4 February

Steed telephoned that the Emperor had refused the Coalition's counter proposals—and that Andrassy had left for Pesth. He considers the negotiations a failure. But we shall see—the Coalition are frightened—there is no doubt about that—and they *may* reduce their demands.

Monday 5 February

Read in the paper that Lady Grey who had a carriage accident the other day—had died.[4] Poor Sir E. Grey! We all sent a tel. of condolence.

---

[1] Nephew of Gyula Andrássy, the elder.
[2] Gyula Andrássy. 'J' stands for Julius, the English equivalent of Gyula.
[3] Brother-in-law of Alfonso XIII.   [4] On 4 Feb. 1906.

Tuesday 6 February

All coming out about Coalition job with Emperor. They had originally meant them to be milder—but Ugron[1]—a discredited Embezzler and Politician left the Coalition in consequence so the reply was altered—it was finally drafted by Apponyi and Polonyi[2]—a sharp Lawyer—and hence the sharp unacceptable language. I am sorry the Emperor didn't temporize a little and give them another chance: but one can scarcely blame him as he is greatly exasperated.

But still all this is sad for Austria: at the present moment she ought to be strong—and she is as weak as possible. Hungary the source of her chief strength in normal times is in a state of chaos—while all the different nationalities of Austria proper are tearing each others' eyes out about Universal Suffrage.

Thursday 8 February

Dined with Emperor at the Burg—not much fun. The Emperor only said the few usual words to me. But we had good oysters and the most undeniable Hock—Steinberger Cabinet Auslese 1893. Tokay didn't come up to my expectation! Sat between Wedel and Manos.[3] Dinner was at 6 and I got home at 7.45—reminded me of Copenhagen days! A lot of dips. there had dinners afterwards and got home in good time.

Saturday 10 February

Boss went off to Semmering for a day or two!

I went to see Merey who was interesting and talkative. He was furious with the Coalition—and particularly furious that they accused the Emperor's surroundings here of interfering *ag'st* peace. However, he said, they are all fighting ag'st each other now—and something may yet happen to relieve things. He doesn't believe in Banffy[4]—who he says is a most unscrupulous tho' clever dog. He thinks Szell is the only man who can take office with any chance of success. I talked to him about the *Zeit's* allegations resp'g a compact between Italy, Montenegro, Servia etc. He said the rumour was of German origin—but not necessarily Germ'n Govt. origin. He did not attach much importance to it but admitted that probably there was *something* in it.

Afterwards I went and had tea with Meg[5] and found the whole embassy there.

---

[1] Landowner from Transylvania; leader of an Independentist 'faction' in the Hungarian Parliament.

[2] Coalition politician; Minister of Justice later in 1906.

[3] Greek Minister.   [4] Hungarian Minister-President, 1895–9.

[5] Duchess of Teck.

Monday 12 February

Boss came back having enjoyed herself awfully at Semmering. She looks awfully bright and well.

Nothing partic.—except that I forgot Reverseaux's concert.

Oh Yes! Mensdorff came in and we had a good talk. He says that the King is quite well—only that he has had a good deal of cough—owing to Fogs. Doctors want him to go to Mediterranean in March. M. told me that he was furious at the day of the funeral taking such a long time to fix. H.M. said 'There is the whole family sitting there and they can't come to a decision.' M. very sad about Austro-Hungarian politics.

The Morocco Conference doesn't seems to be going quite so well!

Tuesday 27 February

Ball bei Hof. I didn't see that it was much less stiff than the Hof Ball. In fact the only difference was that we were given supper—Boss at Emperor's table—I at Archd'ss Maria Josepha. As regards the rest of the evening we were stuck up in the same places and had to remain there all the evening.

Wednesday 28 February

Called on Golu: still depressed about Algeciras—says he has done his best to urge Germany to make concessions on Police Question—as France has done her share. About Bank—on the other hand he considers France exorbitant in her demands—and made a 'faute enorme' in leaving Austria and U.S. out of her first Bank proposals.

Wednesday 7 March

Golu did not receive—so I went and saw Mérey who was interesting about Hungary—and said he thought he saw light—if only the Gov't would be sensible—not crow too much over their success in dissolving Parliament and prepare for new elections by putting situation and the results of the long continued crisis fairly and honestly before the people. He was amusing about the coalition Leaders especially Kossuth—who he said, tho' overweighted by his name was not overburdened with brains. If it were not for his name he would probably now be quite happy as a subordinate Gov't Official or even a minor Court Official.

Friday 9 March

Messenger day. Wrote desp's on Austrian Morocco proposals—Hun garian crisis—and other things.[1] Had an interesting talk with Rever-seaux. He doesn't think much of A. Hn. proposals as he considers the suggestions that the Inspector general of police should be selected by the Sultan from 3 Officers proposed by Switzerland or Holland really means a German Inspector Gen'l 'habillé en Suisse'. While I was with him he got a tel. repeating one from Bihourd[2] reporting that the Austrian Amb'r[3] after a long conversation with Bülow had said that he no longer had any doubts as to a prompt settlement by the Con-ference of the questions in dispute.

Saturday 10 March

Rest after messenger; did Tentschach accounts and find deficit of the year amounts to over 11000 Kr.! I am afraid I shall have to make a change: much as I love old Janaczek.[4]

Tuesday 13 March

Frightful toothache all day. Dentist came and said abscess was forming.

Got a telephone from Steed to the effect (i) that Ballplatz com-plained that *Times* had said latest[5] Algeciras Conference Police pro-posals had been made in Germany.[6] They said it wasn't true and that the proposals had been made by Welsersheim![7] They wanted him to correct it but not direct from here—but thro' Paris! (2) That they had heard the King was going to Montenegro which they thought w'd have a bad effect here (a) because [   ][8] (b) because of purchase of guns etc.—and supposed alliance with Italy.

Saturday 17 March

The Hungarian Gov't have dissolved the Coalition Committee. I can hardly think that is wise: it is perhaps one of those foolish steps which Merey rather anticipated would be taken.

---

[1] Goschen to Grey, 9 March 1906, Gr. P., F.O. 800/40 (strictly a letter).
[2] French Ambassador, Berlin.   [3] In Berlin; Szögyény-Marich.
[4] Bailiff.   [5] Word partly deleted; uncertain reading.
[6] *Times*, 12 March 1906.
[7] Welsersheimb; Austro-Hungarian Ambassador, Madrid, and representative, Algeciras.
[8] Blank in MS. Presumably Goschen either did not hear or could not remember what Steed had said.

Sunday 18 March

Heavy lunch at Nuncio's[1]—strictly diplomatic—and Oh so long.
But I sat next to Goluchowski and he was fairly jolly—much more
so than yesterday. He amused me by describing the Electoral Reform
Bill of his chief and colleague the Prime Minister[2] as 'de la Folie
furieuse'! What funny people they are.

Monday 19 March

Reverseaux came in the morning—and read me Bourgeois'[3] inst'ns
to Revoil[4]—which were absolutely not to give in to Austrians' proposals—or any proposal for a foreign officer in any port. They w'd
accept a Foreign inspector (without command) on condition 1st that
he is a Dane or Swiss (Reverseaux added because they knew that
neither of these would accept) 2. that he reports not to the Dip. Corps
at Tangier—but direct to the Sultan. If it is true, as Nicolson[5] reports,
that Germany won't yield an inch beyond the Austrian proposals—
it seems to me that the Conference must fail. Reverseaux says that
the French don't care a damn for that—*they* didn't call the Conference
and *they* won't lose prestige or anything else if it fails. The Germans
will—but that is *their* look out. The Moors won't think much of the
Germans after all their boasting—and their influence will be gone.
That is the French view—but as I said to R. the Emperor doesn't
swallow failures easily and He will be bound to take it out of some
one. Reverseaux also told me that Khevenhüller[6] at [*sic*][7] been to
Bourgeois and begged him to make concessions—but B. answered like
Rouvier—that is for the Conference to discuss. . . .

Went to hear *La Bohême* (Puccini) with Seymour. The music is
pretty—but not satisfying—and the piece in the last act highly
depressing.

There was a pretty little Ballet afterwards.

Tuesday 20 March

Emie arrived to look after Totty,[8] who is getting on all right.

[1] Monsignor J. Granito di Belmonte Pignatelli.
[2] Gautsch von Frankenthurn.   [3] French Foreign Minister.
[4] French representative, Algeciras.
[5] Now Ambassador, Madrid, and representative, Algeciras.
[6] Austro-Hungarian Ambassador, Paris.
[7] Word or words evidently omitted in MS.
[8] Mrs Seymour.

Wednesday 21 March

Went to see Golu—but there were so many people there that I only remained a few minutes with him. He was full of the Austrian proposals at Algeciras and quite certain all would go well.

Friday 23 March

Took Emie to *Lustige Witwe*[1] which she enjoyed immensely. I enjoyed it more than ever—as we were close to the stage and I heard it better than usual.

Saturday 24 March

Dined at Reverseaux—rather a smart dinner. Amongst others I made the acquaintance of old Princess Pauline Metternich[2]—a European celebrity in the time of the Empire! She is still all there. I didn't have much talk with her—as they all fall down and worship her here.

Wednesday 28 March

The weather is awful—and one feels an awful worm.

The conference seems to have settled the Morocco Police and Bank questions—the former having been settled on the basis of an Amendment brought in by the American Delegate[3] to the Austro-Hungarian Proposal—nothing but French and Spanish Officers—and an Inspector General (a Swiss) to inspect and report to Sultan *and* Diplomatic Corps at Tangier. So the French have got most of what they want and the Germans have to be content with the slight 'ingérence Internationale' entailed by the Inspector Gen'l reporting to Diplomatic Corps.

I wonder how William feels about it. I sh'd think sore—and I fear he won't forgive the check easily.

Monday 2 April

Got a letter from Fairholme saying that he had been appointed to a command in England—and that Teck was going to be appointed regular Mil. Att. after 13th. I am glad the Duchess is going to stay and I like Teck all right—but he is not much use at getting news—and he is a little *too* critical about things and people. Still I am on

[1] Operetta by Lehár; at Theater an der Wien.
[2] Widow of Prince Richard Metternich, Ambassador in Paris, 1859–70.
[3] Henry White.

the whole glad—though a clever Mil. Att. helps a lot as regards inform'n.

I took Lucy Kilmarnock[1] out for a drive and we had a horrible accident. The real Fiaker coachman was not there and he sent the little Piebald mare—with a substitute—who couldn't hold her. In the Kärntner Ring a cart got in the way going at right angles across the street—and in avoiding the cart—a man and a little girl who had been behind the cart got right in the way and were knocked down and run over by the Fiaker. The girl escaped with slight injuries but I fear that the man is very bad. I don't think it was the coachman's fault and even if he had been able to pull up the horses I don't think he would have been able to avoid the accident. The crowd said he was driving too fast—but we couldn't have been because we had to pull up for the cart.

Afterwards when we drove away the Coachman couldn't hold the little mare and Lucy and I finally got out and walked home.

Wednesday 4 April

Went to Golu's day and congratted him on his successful efforts at the Algeciras Conf'ce. He was very cock-a-whoop: and I must say that whether the proposals were made in Germany or not—their success has been very useful both for Golu and the Empire.

They needed a little success badly—and I think that the idea that Aust.-H. has played a considerable role in a momentous European event will have a very good effect on the Internal Affairs of the country.

I am very glad.

Thursday 5 April

I had to dine with Reverseaux—farewell dinner to Ghikas. R. made really a beautiful little speech. Afterwards there was a musical Soirée at which Brahms vocal Quartetts[2] were sung—I wish I had known they were by Brahms. There was also other music. The whole thing was entirely diplomatic—which did not add to its hilarity—but I managed to enjoy myself with the little Spanish Duchess, Me. Demidow and others. I took in Me. Ghika to dinner whom I like—*but* I had Borchgrave[3] on the other side who does not eat very nicely.

---

[1] Kilmarnock's wife.
[3] Belgian Minister.

[2] Presumably the *Liebeslieder-Walzer*.

Friday 6 April

First fine day so of course it was messenger day.

Had a busy time as it appears that the Hungarian Crisis is on the verge of settlement. The Emperor rec'd Kossuth and Andrassay today—Fejervary having had interview previously with Kossuth. It seems really all right this time.

Had a little Embassy dinner to say goodbye to Fairholme. I am sorry he is going as he would be ten times more useful than Teck. F. was very kindly rec'd by Emperor in the morning.

Saturday 7 April

Hungarian Crisis settled pro-tem. Wekerle[1] was first mentioned—then there were doubts as Clerical party was against him—and Andrassy was asked to form a gov't—finally Wekerle seems to be the favourite.

Pleasant dinner at Bailens. I took in the little Duchess and had a very pleasant time. Maritza Hohenlohe[2] was there—She was furious at settlement of Crisis and said that the Coalition Leaders instead of being given Power ought to have been hanged!

Played golf with Scott p.m. *very* badly.

Sunday 8 April

Hungarian Ministry formed by Wekerle.[3] Kossuth[4]—Apponyi[5]—Andrassy[6]—Polonyi[7] and Zichy[8] all the heads of the different parties of Coalition, have accepted Posts.

Wednesday 11 April

Went to see Golu—and as usual got but little out of him—except that Servia was behaving badly in not giving Austria a sufficient portion of its new contract for Guns. 'Our guns are as good as Krupp's and I am going to shew these gentlemen that they can't play fast and loose with Austria. No contract for guns—no Commercial Treaty.' He is very truculent and bullying about Servia. I congratted him about solution of Hungarian Crisis and he said 'Yes, those gentlemen of the Coalition have had to give way all along the line—en effet c'est une pure capitulation.' He added that he had told them a year ago

---

[1] Hungarian Minister-President, 1892–5.
[2] This may refer to any one of several members of the Hohenlohe family.
[3] Minister-President. [4] Commerce and Communications.
[5] Public Worship and Education. [6] Interior.
[7] Justice. [8] Minister *a latere*.

that the Emperor was firm and would not give way—and 'they might just as well have yielded then—as they have today—and spared the country much trouble'.

It is not so clear to me that the Coalition have not gained something—as they seem to me to have got more or less one of the things they asked for at the last attempt at reconciliation which failed—viz. that the Commandosprache should be held over for two years and then submitted to the Country!

Thursday 12 April

Very fine

Went to the Fusswaschung—where the Emperor feeds and washes the feet of 12 poor men. The latter were none of them less than 90 and the eldest was 95. The proceeding is this: the old men dressed in black—with huge ruffs—kneebreeches etc. and looking very nice indeed are led in by their relations and sat down at a long table. Then the Emperor, accompanied by Clergy and all chief dignitaries of State and the Archdukes, comes in. Then trays of food are brought in— 4 courses—each old man gets the four courses—which are served by the Emperor—and then taken off by the Archdukes—the trays being again taken out—and each dinner packed in a big box and sent to the old men's homes—nothing is eaten at the place. Then the tables are cleared away—a long white sheet is placed over the lower limbs of the old men and the Emperor kneeling goes down the whole row— dabbing water on their feet as he goes. He finally throws a gold chain over each old man's neck. It is an impressive and old world ceremony—and everything is done with military precision.

In the afternoon I teaed with Steed and met Count Dzeruscki[1] (?) the leader of the Polish party—a most interesting Don Quixote looking man. He held forth for an hour in slow but beautifully correct English and was very interesting. Too long for this book. A very cynical but amusing old man.[2]

He said amongst other things that the project of the Coalition was to bring in a Universal Suffrage Bill of so radical a nature that the Emperor would refuse to pass it. Then in return for giving it up they will ask for Commandosprache.

Monday 16 April

Emmie went back to Dresden. I enjoyed having her very much and she has been very nice.

[1] Dzieduszycki. Goschen evidently did not catch the name. His version is a mere scrawl. This rendering of what Goschen actually wrote is very approximate.
[2] Cf. Steed, op. cit., i, p. 264.

Thursday 26 April

Our first dance. About 100 people. An awful lot of refusals owing to colds—absences and mourning. But still after all we got a few Comtessen together—and as there was lots of room—and the music (Drescher) good, I think they enjoyed themselves. The young married women at all events had a good dance which is rare for them.[1]

Tuesday 1 May

Gautsch resigned[2]—and Hohenlohe[3] called to be President of the Council in his stead. The Poles made their vote for Universal Suffrage Bills dependent on conditions which Gautsch could not accept without estranging the Czechs and Germans whom he had almost squared. As he could not without the Polish vote carry his Bills—he had no alternative but to resign. Hohenlohe has a great reputation for dealing with nationalities—but he will have to do all he knows to bring them all into line now. He is a good choice—because while Gautsch was a Universal 'Suffragist' by the force of circs. and against his own convictions—he (Hohenlohe) is one by conviction. Therefore he is very acceptable to the Social Democrats—and at the same time thro' his birth and name equally so to the Conservatives—who are glad to have one of their own class in Power—even tho' he is 'Le Prince Rouge'.

Friday 4 May

Messenger Curzon left. I wrote despatch—and private letter about the coming rapprochement between Austria and Italy.[4] It is curious that just as the Emperor William's action with regard to Morocco drew France and England closer together—so his telegram to Goluchowski after the Conference has drawn Italy to Austria. His actions lately have always apparently had the reverse effect to what he intended. Boss and Goonie[5] drove to see the Rothschild's[6] gardens—which they say are perfectly lovely.

Friday 11 May

Very hot
Left for Budapesth—with Kilmarnocks. Very pleasant dinner at the Casino Club, which is very nice and much cozier than our Jockey

[1] Cf. Daisy Princess of Pless, *From my Private Diary* (1931), p. 187.
[2] As Minister-President in 'Austria'.
[3] Prince Konrad zu Hohenlohe-Schillingsfürst; hitherto Governor of Trieste.
[4] Goschen to Grey, 4 May 1906, Gr. P., F.O. 800/40.
[5] Guendolen Bertie; daughter of Ambassador in Paris.
[6] Albert Rothschild.

Club here. Festetics[1] was there—and a very nice old C't Szechenyi[2] (Father of Countess Wimpffen[3] with Archd. Isabel[4]) and other nice Hungarians.

Very comfy at Twinkle's sumptuous apartment.

Tuesday 15 May

Vienna

Came back from Pesth after a giddy whirl. I liked the Hungarians—open-handed—affectionate—easily moved—bright extravagant people.

Saturday 19 May

Went down to Tentschach—Boss and I—Richter and Fritz.[5] Everything beautifully green—lovely altogether—lilacs and Horse chestnuts in full bloom. Apple blossoms just going off. I hope to have a good apple year. Rather cold—there being lots of snow in the Mountains. All well—People dogs and horses. Lots of young chickens—and ducklings—also 10 young Turkeys. Incubator working.

Tuesday 22 May

Vienna

Back to Vienna.

Friday 25 May

Plunketts—Lady and Nellie—arrived. It is an awful bore having them at the monent—but it can't be helped and we must make the best of it.

Got a tel. from F.O.[6] stating that if 5 conspiring officers[7] are dismissed from their Posts, H.M.G. will consent to reopening diplomatic relations with Servia.

Saturday 26 May

Saw Milovanovitch[8] at 9.15 on his way to station to go to Madrid.

[1] Grand Master of the Hungarian Court.
[2] Aehrenthal's father-in-law.
[3] Lady-in-waiting to Archduchess Isabel.
[4] Wife of Archduke Friedrich; née Croy.
[5] Probably a servant.
[6] Grey to Goschen, 25 May 1906, B.D., v, n. 124.
[7] Involved in the assassination of King Alexander and Queen Draga.
[8] Serbian Minister, Rome.

I told him that he must understand that, if any of Officers mentioned were ever reemployed H.M.G. w'd. of course withdraw their Representative. He tel. to Servia accordingly.

Thursday 31 May

Big dinner for Plunketts.... After dinner Golu recd. and read a telegram saying that a Bomb had been thrown at King and Queen of Spain[1] on returning from Church where they had been married. The King and Queen were unhurt but their carriage was smashed up—and many were killed and wounded. Our poor little Princess' dress was all spattered with blood—such a horrible beginning to her married life.

Friday 15 June

Messenger day—and a very hard one—the Chancery particularly have had lots to do. Vouitch ans'd my note that app't of Whitehead[2] was agreeable to Serv'n Gov't so now our question with Servia is over.

Monday 18 June

Golu had his innings with the Hungarian Delegation—and lo! instead of being cursed he was blessed and had a comparatively great success considering what was expected. Wekerle and Kossuth seem to have calmed down Hungarian Delegates.

Wednesday 20 June

Played a monthly medal round of golf with Steed and succeeded in playing even worse than usual.

Friday 13 July

Left for Tentschach....

Monday 13 August

Tentschach
Left for Vienna en route for Marienbad.

[1] The former Princess Victoria Eugenie, daughter of Prince Henry of Battenberg and Princess Beatrice.
[2] Councillor, Berlin Embassy.

Wednesday 15 August

Left for Marienbad. Weather *not* brilliant. Hotel 'Stern' seems quite comfortable and nice.

Thursday 16 August

King arrived looking fairly well. I drove with him up to Weimar[1] in His Motor. Telegraphed to the Queen—who sent me a very nice telegram back—asking how we are.

Saturday 18 August

Emperor Francis Joseph's Birthday. We all attended Te deum in Uniform. We tried to make C.B. but he was too afraid of the Nonconformists and alleged want of Top hat as excuse! Dined with King in the Evening. H.M. proposed Emperor's Health in a charming little speech. Met P'ce Ferdinand of Bulgaria—who is a very fascinating talker—we went over a lot of old Balkan ground together—but he didn't tell me much new.

Wednesday 22 August

Lunched with Princess Clementine[2]—and her son the Prince of Bulgaria. Soveral[3] and C.B. were also there. The Princess is a very charming and interesting old Lady. She speaks English very prettily and well. Unfortunately she is as deaf as a post—and one has to write down all one has to say on tablets! One's little platitudes seem rather flat on paper. Soveral did most of the writing. Prince Ferdinand as usual most interesting—but one *cannot* feel much confidence in him. He told me that he had told Goluchowski that it was a mistake to bully the 'only respectable man in the Balkans'.

Sunday 26 August

The King lunched with us at the Kurhaus as the weather was too cold for Rübezahl—present Szaparys[4]—Soveral—Campbell B....

H.M. was in very good spirits—and asked us to his table at the Wagner Concert afterwards....

[1] Hotel.
[2] Daughter of Louis Philippe; widow of Prince August of Coburg.
[3] Portuguese Minister, London.
[4] Szápáry, Austro-Hungarian Minister, Bucharest, and his wife.

Tuesday 28 August

Mr Haldane arrived. Didn't care for him much.

Saturday 1 September

Lady Campbell-Bannerman's funeral.[1] Poor old C.B. very much distressed. King and Prince Ferdinand etc. attended.

Had a long interview with General Petrow Bulgarian Prime Minister—which I embodied in a letter to Grey.[2] Gave it to the King to read who was very pleased with it.

Prince Ferdinand and the General seem both full of pacific assurances. But Petrow thinks nothing of the Macedonian Reforms—and thinks Macedonian Bulgars unfairly treated. I advised patience but he said they had been patient long enough. I told him that Europe looked to Bulgarians as the most solid and intelligent element in the Balkans; that they looked to the present, while the other races looked to the past. I hoped that they w'd do nothing to upset our good opinion.

Sunday 2 September

Bischof Teinitz. Very hot
Motored over to Bischof Teinitz (47 miles in 1 hour 20 min.) to shoot with Trauttmansdorff.[3]

Splendid day—1000 partridges—guns King, Trauttmansdorff, Festetics, Jean Schwartzenburg[4]—Ponsonby[5] and I. King shot 200—I 120—it was my first real Partridge drive so I was fairly satisfied—but still I suppose I didn't shoot well. I had too many spectators at my first butt—about 25.

Wednesday 5 September

Shoot at Tepl. Splendid lunch—execrable shoot. Lots of Birds but driving shocking. The birds were driven *away* from the King (and me) instead of over Him. H.M. was quite furious and said afterwards—'Never again.'[6]

H.M. dined with me at 'Hotel Ott' in the evening—and we had a very cheerful little dinner....

[1] She died 30 Aug.; strictly, a memorial service, not a funeral; in the Lutheran Chapel.
[2] Goschen to Grey, 2 Sept. 1906, Gr. P., F.O. 800/40.
[3] Wealthy Bohemian landowner.
[4] Johann Schwarzenberg; Trauttmansdorff's son-in-law.
[5] See also F. Ponsonby, *Recollections of Three Reigns* (1951), p. 235.
[6] See also Ponsonby, op. cit., p. 236.

Friday 7 September

Lunch with King and saw Him off p.m. He was very nice and kind. And He went away in better health—spirits and humour—than when He came.

Saturday 8 September

Left for Vienna—travelled with Harry Chaplin.[1]

Thursday 20 September

Lunched with Seymours at Bristol and met the Leslie Melvilles[2]—secured a box at *Lustige Witwe* and took them to it.

Saw Goluchowski who was in a great rage about our new proposals resp'g conditions of our consent to 3% duties. Telegraphed and wrote.

Tuesday 23 October

Brilliant

Nothing partic.—went for a ride.

Golu has resigned and Ärenthal[3]—now A.H. Ambassador in Petersburg has been named in his place. I am half sorry only. Golu and I got on first rate socially—but he was not very communicative as Minr. for For. Aff. and it was not easy to do serious business with him. He was a pleasant man of the world outwardly—but I never thoroughly gauged his inside!

Saturday 28 October

Our last day this year at Tentschach. We both hate leaving. . . .

Tuesday 6 November

London to Bishop's Hall[4] in Lockwood's stunt motor. One hour from town. . . .

Wednesday 7 November

Col. Lockwood's

Splendid shoot, about 1200 Pheasants. Didn't shoot so badly—but I was rather nervous as there were so many 1st class. Lord Warwick[5]

---

[1] Conservative M.P.; former minister.   [2] Marienbad acquaintances.
[3] Aloys Freiherr von Aehrenthal.
[4] In Essex; the home of Colonel Lockwood.
[5] 5th Earl; Essex landowner.

(charming) was easily best—he is such a beautiful quiet clean shot. It was Lockwood's record day. Rather rainy in the morning but p.m. it held up. Lady Warwick[1] came over to tea—rather a fascinating woman I thought—but I found it hard to reconcile her smart dress and her motor and her pearls with her socialistic principles.

Saturday 8 December

Left for Vienna.

Sunday 9 December

Arrived in Vienna punctually—after a fairly comfortable journey. Found a regular Viennese wind in full force!...

Friday 14 December

Avarna called in the morning—but he didn't know much about Macedonia yet.

Beaman—*St'd* corresp'nt—also called and said he would bet heavily that there would be a dynastic Coup d'Etat in Servia before six months are out.

He told me that more than one Servian has said that they would like Teck as King! King Dolly[2] and Queen Meg—what a rag it would be!

Messenger went!

Saturday 15 December

Had Steed to lunch—he talked a lot but was not so lucid as usual. He was full of the dissolution of the German Reichstag and says that the real text of the Emperor's message was 'Ich jage sie alle zum Teufel' not 'zu Hause'.[3]

Tuesday 18 December

Boss and Bunt and latter's friend Finch Hatton[4] left for Vienna. Scarcely went out—in fact only called on Avarna. Curiously enough he doesn't know very much about the attitude of his Gov't on the Judicial Reform question. I don't quite understand it as Grey told me that the Italian Amb'r in London[5] had told him that they would

---

[1] Well-known beauty and socialist.   [2] Teck's first name was Adolphus.
[3] The Kaiser signed the decree for the dissolution of the Reichstag on 13 Dec. 1906.
[4] Oxford acquaintance.   [5] Pansa.

even prefer the Judicial Reforms to be badly administered by the Financial Commission—to well administered by Austria and Russia alone.

Got news that Bunt has passed smalls.

Wednesday 19 December

Boss Bunt and Finch Hatton arrived—all in good order....

Saw Reverseaux who told me that he had talked to Ährenthal about Judicial reforms and that the latter had said in the most decided manner that he intended to proceed on Golu's line in this matter and was determined that the elaboration and application of the Judicial Reforms should be carried out by the two Powers alone. Ouroussoff had said the same thing and was just as decided in his views. He (O.) had said that he had talked the matter over with Golu—and that if the Powers refused to adhere to their views they would tear up the Mursteg[1] programme.[2]

They both had said that refusal to confide the task to the two Powers would be an act of suspicion—as these two Powers had both signed disinterested clauses. Besides experience shewed that two Powers could move more quickly than the whole lot.

I foresee great opposition to our views.

[1] Mürzsteg.   [2] Or 'Punctation'; signed, 2 Oct. 1903.

1907

The Goschens spent most of the early part of the year in Vienna. In January Goschen went to Gmunden, staying one night. In April he and Hosta spent a long week-end at Tentschach. In May they paid their usual annual visit to Budapest. They were at Tentschach for most of July and the first half of August; once again Goschen commuted. They spent the 'season' at Marienbad, and a few days in October at Tentschach. At the end of October they left for England.

Friday 11 January

Rec'd tel. telling me I am to attend Queen of Hanover's[1] funeral at Gmunden—but that Teck will represent the King. What a curious arrangement. I shall have to give precedence to my own Mil. Attaché. Personally I don't mind—nor does Teck—but it will look bad—and puts us both in a false position.

Saturday 12 January

Bunt, Boss and I went to *Siegfried*—and had 5 solid hours of it. The first two Acts interested us orchestrally—but there are many tedious moments. Last act quite beautiful and pleased us immensely. Singing quite good. We asked Crack'thorpe[2] to come with us—he came late and went away early—saying he was hungry! Pretty cool, I thought— if he couldn't stand or understand Wagner he ought to have said so and we w'd have taken someone who could enjoy it

Sunday 13 January

Made d'Ährenthal's acquaintance at last. About Judicial Reforms—he told me that he was having pourparlers with Isvolsky[3]— w'h were not yet finished. His idea is that Judicial machinery in Macedonia is in itself not bad—only its Admin'tn is bad. To reform machinery would be interference in internal affairs of Macedonia (German idea?)—therefore it was more a question of *control*—than of Reforms. Control wd. be vested in all the Powers! This all seems to me to be quite new.

Monday 14 January

Saw Reverseaux who was as astonished as I over what Ährenthal told me. We tried to find Ourousoff but couldn't.

---

[1] Maria; widow of Georg V, last King of Hanover; mother of Duke of Cumberland.
[2] Crackanthorpe; 2nd secretary.   [3] Now Russian Foreign Minister.

Wednesday 16 January

Me Reverseaux' day. Ährenthal's first official reception. Had a supplementary talk with him and learnt that the view of the two Gov'ts was as I thought that it was not in their idea a question of reforming the Judicial System but of controlling its administration by app't of Christian Inspectors of Tribunals and dragomans attached to each court—the whole to be controlled by an International Commission. It is, that is to say, not only the fundamental Law that is to be left unchanged but the whole Judicial Machinery. He begged me that they might not be 'pushed' ('poussés trop') by H.M.G. who were, as a matter of fact, responsible to a certain extent for the delay which had already taken place!

Friday 18 January

Started 10 a.m. for Gmunden—found a very dirty compartment reserved for me—and Tecks in another carriage—most amazing. However I read *Les Réformes en Macédoine* and talked alternately to Teck—Ahlefeldt and Manos.

On arriving at Gmunden the little Cumberland girls and our old friend P'ce Harald of Denmark were at the Station to meet the Archdukes and Tecks, and they all whirled up to the Schloss.[1] We to the Hotel—some in court carriages—others in hired ones—I in one of the latter with a man I did not know! I was not much pleased.

But there was a good deal of confusion. I had a very nice room at the Hotel—with a quite beautiful view over the lake[2]—with a jolly bold snowy crag just opposite.[3] The day was divine—bright sun— no wind. As soon as luggage arrived Bailen and I drove up to the Schloss—wrote our names down on the Royalties and left tons of cards—by this time it was very dark—and we drove back to Hotel. Dinner at 7 (all gratis!) and then played Bridge with Ahlefeldt— Bailen and Manos—and won 14 Crowns. Latter the worst player I have ever seen except Prince John of Glücksberg. Bed but not to sleep as just as I was dropping off—a neighbour came next door in [*sic*] and talked so loud to a friend that sleep was impossible.

Saturday 19 January

Gmunden. Awful! Snow and rain
Jäger came in at 8 and told me we were to start for the Church at 10.50. When we got there I was put into an excellent place and had to wait there till 12.15 before Service began. In the meanwhile

---

[1] Duke of Cumberland's residence.   [2] The Traunsee.   [3] The Traunstein.

all the Royalties trooped in amongst whom I noticed—Archdukes F.
Ferdinand—and his brother?—Franz Salvator[1]—Leopold Salvator[2]—Friedrich[3]—Eugène[4]—a Bavarian Prince—a very handsome
young Duke of Würtenburg—Prince Max of Baden[5]—Prince Harald
of Denmark—and G'd Duke of Mecklenburg-Schwerin[6]—and Strelitz[7] etc. The Emperor came in at 12.15 followed by Duke and Duchess
of Cumberland—Princess Frederica of Hannover[8] and the little Cum-
berlands etc. Then the service began—wh. consisted of two hymns
and a quite interminable sermon.

Monday 21 January[9]

Had a long visit from W. T. Stead[10]—who is making a tour of the
European Capitals and touting for Disarmament and Arbitration at
2nd Hague Conference. He stayed two hours and a half—was very
fantastic and very interesting. He settled himself down on the sofa—
took a big cigar and smoked it to the bitter end.

Tuesday 22 January[11]

Awfully cold. Dined with the Emperor who was in good spirits and
chaffed me about delay in Macedonia. I let him understand that *we*
thought Austria slow. But he said—'Surely you have enough commerce all over the world that you needn't make such a fuss over the
3% duties.' He went off chuckling. I thought He would have been
in bad spirits over Hungarian latest Polonyi crisis—especially as the
latter—Min'r of Justice there—is accused of having promised to pay
(tho' he didn't) a large sum of money to* Graf Paar's (1st Aide Camp)
mistress Baronne de Schömberger[12]—if she would get out of her man
what the Emperor thought of certain events in Hungary.

* Since denied.[13]

Friday 1 February

Off day. Looked at Report and made a few visits. Weather very

[1] Archduke; Franz Ferdinand's 3rd cousin.
[2] Archduke; Franz Salvator's elder brother.
[3] Archduke; Franz Joseph's 2nd cousin once removed; inspector-general of army.
[4] Archduke Eugen; Friedrich's brother.   [5] Cumberland's son-in-law.
[6] Friedrich Franz IV; Cumberland's grandson.
[7] Adolf Friedrich V; Cumberland's 2nd cousin.
[8] Cumberland's sister.
[9] Originally entered on page for 28 Jan., and corrected by Goschen.
[10] Proprietor and editor, *Review of Reviews*.
[11] Originally entered on page for 29 Jan., and corrected by Goschen.
[12] Not identified; Goschen may have mis-spelt the name.
[13] Added by Goschen at the bottom of the page.

gloomy and cold. Got in my Tentschach acc'ts.—July–Dec. 1906. Awful. Deficit of 15000 Kr. Worse than ever. It is due to stocking farm—and erection of Saw Mill—but still it ought not to be so much. One more year's farming and if it is worse—I must stop it—and let every thing.

Saturday 2 February

Boss's first day—about 80 people—pretty good considering the awful weather. Some people stayed a long time amongst others Lillie Kinsky who is by the way quite nice this year. She can be when she likes.

Then dinner at the French—all diplomats—and no Austrians except the Ährenthals. Boss sat next to him at dinner and they talked over Wydenbruck. He said that he thought W. a very intelligent man—but rather queer. He was sorry that while so many of his colleagues had been made Ambassadors he remained on as Minister. Boss said 'But why don't you make him one? Send him to Washington.' But he said there was no vacancy and he didn't foresee any for the present. I hope the conversation has done him a good turn.

Afterwards we looked in at the Picnic Charity Ball at the Statthalterei—where we saw a good many friends. Meg gave me a bit of news about herself—beginning 'Dolly and I have got into trouble.'! Which meant that she is going to have a baby. What an unconventional person she is.

Sunday 3 February

Boss and I had a little walk in the afternoon—but it wasn't nice, and we soon came in.

Got a letter from Bunt—giving a glowing picture of his life at Oxford.... I want him not to do what his father did—viz. idle away the best years of one's educational life. Still I want the dear boy to enjoy life at Oxford too—and make good friends there....

Monday 4 February

Nothing partic. My throat Dr[1] has gone off to Sophia to attend on poor Princess Clementine—who is 90 and has influenza! P'cess Clementine is a dear old Lady. I lunched with her at Marienbad last year and found her such a charming old world Lady—*but* stone deaf.

[1] Chiari.

Tuesday 5 February

Court Ball.[1] This frightful function did not improve on acquaintance. The Cercle took an hour and a half. The Emperor was in good spirits and looked well. The Archduchess Maria Annunciata did her difficult job for the first time very well and sympathetically—*but* was too long over it. The Heir Apparent—Franz Ferdinand—never came near us. Franz Salvator—the young Orleans P'ce[2]—son of the Comte d'Eu[3]—and the Coburg Sailor Prince[4] all did the civil.

† *Thursday 7 February*†

Received awful and sudden news of dear old George's death from heart-failure.[5] I got a tel. from Charlie announcing the sad news just 5 minutes before I saw it in the Vienna Papers. It is an awful shock to *us*. . . .

We are dreadfully grieved. The head of a family always creates a very large void when he goes—and we shall all miss him terribly. I think I more than the others—as we were more in touch with each other than the others were with him: I mean only as regards foreign and other politics. The country, which he has served so well will also miss him—and he could have still, with his wonderful vitality, have [*sic*] played a very necessary and distinguished part in the House of Lords. A splendid career—tho' to himself—especially of late years it was somewhat a disappointing one. I never agreed with him in this—and consider that few modern statesman [*sic*], even tho' he was never Prime Minister, enjoyed a finer reputation both at home and *abroad*. I can't bear to think that he has gone from us—and that the fine old conservative Seacox regime is a thing of the past.

The two eldest within a year![6]

Friday 8 February

The Emperor sent me a very kind message of condolence through Count Paar. Reverseaux came to see me and was very kind and nice—and we have rec'd letters, cards or calls from nearly all Vienna. People are very kind—and the Press has had very sympathetic and appreciative obituary notices on our dear old George. He had always been admired abroad—more perhaps than in his own country—where

[1] The Hofball; to be distinguished from the Ball beim Hof.
[2] Probably Prince Peter.
[3] Prince Peter's father was the Duc de Nemours, who was born at the Château d'Eu.
[4] Prince August; captain, Austro-Hungarian Navy.
[5] On 7 Feb. at Seacox Heath.
[6] Goschen's eldest sister, Henrietta Vaughan, had died at Dresden in 1906.

some of the family looked upon him as forgotten. I never agreed with this—as he had always heaps of admiring friends. As Alic says—he had a great career—and was a great man—with a few small weaknesses, but far above most living English Statesmen in power of Intellect, incisive criticism—and absolute honesty of purpose.

He may be said to have been *too* critical and prone to go too much into details: *but* there were and are few like him. He belonged, in thought, opinions and turn of mind thoroughly to the Victorian era—and I don't think his sympathies were ever much with the new one.

Thursday 14 February

Letter from Hardinge[1] telling me that he was sure that I would be pleased to hear that Carnegie[2] had been appointed to succeed Boothby.[3] I told him in reply that I was quite sure I wasn't pleased—as both he and Theo Russell[4] had agreed with my suggestion that Clarke should come here and Carnegie go to Buda Pesth. It is too trying: we both of us like Carnegie—but Boss doesn't want Marion[5] here and nor do I. She is not at all the person for us and is ill suited to be at the most ceremonious court in Europe. I told Hardinge that the least they could have done after treating me so badly about Scott was to have shewn some slight regard to my wishes as regards Clarke.

Friday 15 February

Mr Spencer Wilkinson[6] of the *Morning Post* called—saying that he was instructed by his paper to write up the Eastern Question. I have seldom met a more disagreeable and unsympathetic man—both in appearance and manner. Twinkle Clarke wrote to me that he was dreadfully disappointed about Vienna.

Sunday 17 February

Poor old Princesse Clementine de Saxe Coburg, the mother of Prince Ferdinand of Bulgaria—died here on her way to Mentone. She has been suffering from Bronchitis—and has been very bad with her heart. But she insisted on starting for the South. She had made the journey from Sofia to here quite well—dined with her family last night in the best of spirits—dressed this morning and was on her way to her breakfast room—when she swayed—fell and died. She was a

[1] Now permanent under-secretary, Foreign Office.
[2] Councillor, Peking. He had served with Goschen in St Petersburg.
[3] Appointed Minister, Santiago; did not proceed.
[4] Grey's assistant private secretary.   [5] Carnegie's wife.
[6] Leader writer; authority on military matters.

most charming woman—full of intellect and statecraft of a sort. She has been Pce Ferdinand's chief adviser for years—and people say that it is a great deal owing to her sound advice that he has been able to weather so many political storms. I made her acquaintance last year at Marienbad—and was immensely struck with her—but she was stone deaf. But she talked most beautifully—and was quite an old world picture.

The King telegraphed in answer to my wire: 'Deeply regret that this charming and gifted Princess has passed away.'

Wednesday 20 February

Attended funeral of Princess Clementine of Saxe Coburg Gotha—as representing the King. It was at the Palais Coburg—and was quite impressive. The Emperor was there. After the ceremony we, the foreign R.R.[1] were received by Princes Ferdinand and Philip, sons and Archduchess Clotilde[2] (in a very cold room). Prince Ferdinand thanked me very much for a letter which I had written him—and said that he could quite understand the impression his dear Mother had made upon me at Marienbad. She was the best and dearest of women. He reminded me how she had sent flowers to my wife—and was altogether very much moved and affecting.

Saturday 23 February

Went out for a bit—but the cold wind touched up my neck[3] so much that I had soon to come in again. I wish I could get normal. But I always seem to have something and it interferes with my life and work.

Tuesday 5 March

Dined at a small dinner at Ouroussofs to meet Martens—the Russian Hague Conference representative. I was glad to see him again as we had been rather friends at St P. Others present were Avarna—Plehner[4]—Weede and Mérey. Had an interesting talk with Plehner: he says that the [sic] looks forward to the next Chamber in Austria with misgiving. The Peasants have given the word 'We will be represented only by peasants'—and the result will be a chamber of Peasants and shopkeepers and 'kleiner Männern'. He says they are too stupid

---

[1] Representatives.
[2] Princess Clémentine's daughter; wife of Archduke Joseph.
[3] Goschen was suffering from an abscess; it had been cut the previous day.
[4] Probably Ernst von Plener; Liberal politician; former Finance Minister.

to see that their interests can best be looked after by people of superior culture to themselves.

As regards the Ausgleich with Hungary—he thinks Beck[1] has made a mistake: he ought to have been content with a little compromise till 1917—and not gone in for one of indefinite length—and embracing every possible question. There w'd have been some hope of getting the first—while there is none of getting the second. Austrian business men would have preferred the first as they want something definite and secure. That could have been arranged for a short period but not for an indefinite one. How often big and well sounding things turn out to be impracticable when put under a commercial and financial microscope.

Friday 8 March

Got off my messenger—and with him my blessed annual report[2]— it has given me a great deal of trouble and I am afraid I did not fulfil all the rules laid down in the F.O. circ. and Memo. Otherwise, there were interesting things in it I think. But no one except Crowe[3] will read it—and it is a perfectly useless and redundant piece of work.

Reverseaux went off at 8.30 p.m. and we had to go and see them off. We took *her* some lovely flowers wh. she was too dazed to look at. *She* said goodbye looking the other way—and He said to Boss, 'Au revoir ma chère Lady Plunkett'!!

But he took a very aff'te farewell of me and said many nice things. But these beaux départs—are a mistake: neither side likes them.

Had a talk with Ouroussow who told me that Maartens was much dissatisfied with the result of his Hague Conference mission here— he could get nothing out of d'Ährenthal—and could not make him see that Germany and Austria w'd be in a far better position if they allowed Limitation of Armaments to appear on the Programme— as it would be sure to be rejected by a lot of Powers besides those two. Thus they would incur no odium. Whereas if they stand out ag'st it now and wreck the Conference—they will be held responsible. Maartens found d'Ährenthal slavish as regards Germany.

Monday 11 March

Steed telegraphed to me that Petkoff the Bulgarian Premier had been assassinated.

P'ce Ferdinand is away in Paris—I remember he told me last year in Marienbad 'Whenever I go away something either bad or stupid

---

[1] Minister-President in 'Austria'.   [2] For 1906.
[3] Senior clerk, Foreign Office.

always happens'! Under those circumstances—it seems almost a pity that he is away so much.

S. also told me that he had heard from an Italian source that the Italians had joined the Germans and Austrians in going against the 'Limitation of Armaments' being included in the Hague Conference discussions—and had sent a message here to that effect. They intended, so S. informed me to propose that a separate Conference of the protesting Powers should be held to discuss the question. This I can scarcely believe—as Italy was supposed to be with us—and a separate Conference would take too long and postpone the real one ad infinitum—at least I should say so.

The new Spanish Ambassador[1] called on me. He did *not* flow freely—and I disliked his appearance. But he may improve on acquaintance.

Tuesday 12 March

What is the weather about—we had 12° of warmth here at this time last year.

Called on Sarafow[2] to express sympathy on assassination of Bulg. Prime Minister. His theory is that it was not a political crime—but that the man who had been turned out of the Agrar. Bank by the Minister of the Interior—Ghenadieff[3]—had meant to kill the latter who was walking with Petkoff. Here I fancy they rather incline to the belief that it *was* political—and that Petkoff was assassinated because he was so down on Macedonian agitators. Petkoff was from all accounts a hard man—going straight to his points without much regard for any one who got in his way. Such a man would be sure to have many enemies.

Wednesday 13 March

Went to D'Ährenthal's official reception. Didn't get much out of him: threw a fly over him—to find out whether there is any truth in Steed's story about Tittoni[4] having suggested a separate Conference for Limitation of Armaments question. But he failed to rise—said he had never heard of any question of a separate conference (this is not true because he discussed it with Martens) and that all he knew was that the question of L. of Arm'ts was not included in the Russian Programme and that he had heard that H.M.G. wished to enlarge it! As regards Judicial Reforms—he showed no zeal whatever! Said that Turks were flesh and blood and had nerves like other people—

[1] Casa Calvo.   [2] Bulgarian agent.
[3] Appointed the previous day.   [4] Italian Foreign Minister.

that they had already had two controls forced upon them—that the Judicial Control would be a still bitterer pill as it constituted more or less an interference in their internal affairs and that the matter had to dealt [*sic*] very carefully and tactfully. If this means anything it means delay. A very unsatisfactory interview altogether. I find H.E. very slow and hesitating and difficult to bring to the point.

Teck and the boys dined with us—and Steed lunched and was very discursive—but he told me some interesting things—inter alia that Djiedyski[1] had told him that he didn't think this Gov't would last beyond September.

In the waiting room at F.O. heard some interesting Balkan conversation—how Servia had won all along the line—and that Golu was the hero of the hour in that country—as his absurd policy had made her find out she could do without Austria. They said that all was splendid—if only Servia didn't triumph too much.

Thursday 14 March

Called on Avarna and had a long talk but could not make him say anything to prove or disprove Steed's Tittoni story. Then to Ouroussow whom I found rather seedy again and very hoarse. He also said that d'Ährenthal told me quite an untruth about the Conference—as he had himself talked to Martens about a separate one—and Martens had combatted it.

Saturday 16 March

Had a pleasant visit in the afternoon from Admiral Jedina? and his wife.[2] A very nice sailor man with a deep admiration for England. He railed against Vienna want of hospitality and said that he felt outraged when he saw how Vienna society lived on the Embassies and did nothing in return. I tried hard not to agree with him—but it is *so* true.

Others came in—but he stopped on ——!

Sunday 17 March

Heard from Crackanthorpe that Crowe had said that he was pleased with the Annual Report—I didn't think much of it myself—as I finished it off rather hurriedly.

---

[1] Dzieduszycki.
[2] The Admiral and his wife are difficult to identify in view of Goschen's uncertainty as to their name.

Austria and Hungary are not getting on well for the moment: Kossuth's speech[1] refusing a long compromise and only consenting to a short one after 1917 on his own conditions—viz. completely independent Customs territory—separate Bank and settlement of Military questions—seems to have upset the coach: and if he represents the views of the Gov't to which he belongs—it would really appear to be useless for Beck and Wekerle to continue to negotiate.

Thursday 21 March

Wrote despatch—a long 'un on the Compromise negotiations between Austria and Hungary—and found when I finished it that the people for whom I wrote it would be no wiser than before. That is all right because no one knows how the cat will jump—but in my strong interior I think that Austria will finally yield—as she always does—and that there will be a compromise after all—all in favour of Hungary.

Had a short walk in the Prater and was blown to bits—and snowed upon—with the Thermometer at 8°!

Saturday 23 March

Meg and boys dined. Had a long talk to Ährenthal to whom I communicated our intention of raising question of disarmament at Conference. He was not pleased—and foresaw all sorts of bad blood and from [sic][2] our 'very inopportune wish to enlarge the scope of discussion at the Conference'. Of course he is only angry because he is told to be so from Berlin—because really the question of disarmament affects Austria very little—and she has but little to reduce—so said the Minister of War[3] last Autumn. I find d'Äh. very nice—but slow.

Tuesday 26 March

Francis[4] came round—he has heard that the Emperor intends to abdicate—or appoint F.F. regent—or Carl[5]—Maria Josepha's[6] son. We made a mutual agreement to try and find out and tell each other.

[1] To his constituents.
[2] Word or words evidently omitted in MS.
[3] Schönaich.
[4] United States Ambassador (Storer's successor).
[5] Archduke Karl; next in line of succession after Franz Ferdinand.
[6] Widow of Archduke Otto, Franz Ferdinand's brother, who had died in 1906.

Wednesday 27 March

Have come to the conclusion that Francis's story is all humbug. I have often heard such rumours before—and I have always been told that F.J. hates his heir so much that he would never abdicate. I think it more likely that Fr. F. visit to Emperor was the cause of the rumour rather than the effect of orders *from* the Emperor F.J.

Wednesday 3 April

Cold wind

Went to d'Ährenthal's day—and had a warm discussion on Hague Conference and discussion on Armaments—a still warmer one on Macedonian Reforms—when he dropped on me again for delay about Customs Duties.

'There' he said 'is O'Conor again making difficulties when we thought everything was settled—Pallavicini[1] has remonstrated with him but all to no purpose. It is really too bad—and I am in despair.' I said I was also in despair because I thought I was so tired with being scolded for delays[2]—and with having to explain the reasons for them. I said it would have been sounder—if Pallavicini, instead of blowing up O'Conor, had blown up the Sultan for not carrying out his promises about the Reforms on which our consent to the increased Deputies was dependent. We parted excellent friends.

But he is rather impossible about the Hague Conference—and persists in saying that he fears our raising the question of Armaments will create bad blood and perhaps complications.

Went to Valkyrien—which Bunt and I enjoyed immensely. The boy is frightfully keen about Wagner now—and he is doing the whole of the Ring.

Tuesday 9 April

Had D'Ährenthals to dinner.... D'Ährenthals very nice—both of them so cheery and jolly: the table was a dream and the dinner hot and good. D'Ähr. told me that Tittoni's proposals about the Hague Conference were not acceptable to A.H.G.

Thursday 11 April

Boss, Bunt and Bruce[3] went to Tentschach by evening train.

[1] Austro-Hungarian Ambassador in Constantinople; Goschen had known him in St Petersburg.
[2] Goschen originally wrote: 'I thought I had finished.' He then deleted 'had finished'. Hence the odd syntax.
[3] Now 3rd secretary.

Friday 12 April

I went to Tentschach by morning train. Had a nice journey and a nice drive up. Boss met me at foot of hill—and at the hall door were *all* the retainers.

Inspected animals after tea. House coolish—but not too cold. I slept in Fraüleinzimmer with a good fire.

Monday 15 April

Back to Vienna

Beastly journey back—the last carriage of the Trieste Express is not a pleasant conveyance. We were shaken to bits.

Sunday 21 April

Went to Church—and shivered. Hechler preached a long sermon—and I remonstrated with him afterwards....

Tuesday 30 April

Golf p.m. Ella Festetics and I against Carnegie and Leghait. I played most awfully—I can't think what can have come over me. I suppose it's age and failing eye sight—or reading *Neue Freie Presse* too much.

Many interesting Articles these days—one especially on England's Imperial Policy—which takes the new view (in Austria) that a war betwen England and Germany would spell ruin for the latter: on the other hand victory for England would mean the loss of her best market—and the jealousy of France—who would end by joining a coalition of Continental Powers to curtail the growing power of England.[1]

Thursday 2 May

Played handicap mixed foursome with Countess F. Larisch[2] and won it. I got a modicum of glory and Countess L. an enamelled buckle presented by P'ce Schönburg.[3] Before doing this I wrote despatches on Ährenthal's visit—and conference—and reviewed European situation.[4] In none of these despatches was there anything particularly new—but one has to write them.

[1] *Neue Freie Presse*, 29 Apr. 1907.
[2] Marie (May), wife of Friedrich Count Larisch, secretary, Austro-Hungarian Legation, Munich.
[3] Austro-Hungarian Minister, Bucharest.
[4] Goschen to Grey, 1 May 1907, F.O. 371/195.

It is amusing to watch how the Press dictates to d'Ährenthal what he must say, how he must look—and what he must do at Berlin. As a matter of fact the advice given is fairly sound: e.g. Don't forget that A.H. is stronger than she was when the Triple Alliance was formed. She is now a precious ally to Germany and stands between the latter power and Isolation! No need to boast—but the time for excessive modesty and self-effacement is past. 'You needn't stamp about Berlin in Cuirassier's boots—but neither need you creep about on tiptoe.' This is certainly a very proper attitude to take—but I fear d'Ährenthal *is* rather subservient to Germany—and that he will be more so after the visit to the Emperor.

Little dinner in the Evening for Forgach.[1] The latter very clever— but very cocksure. He gives me the impression when talking with him that he is being very intelligent—but when he has gone—there is but little that remains behind.

Saturday 4 May

Nothing partic.—except a little practice at golf p.m. Oh yes! Steed came to see me in the morning—having just returned from a visit to Italy. He says that there is a distinct movement in favour of better relations with Austria-H'y and that things in that direction were looking well. They would look better to [*sic*][2] if d'Ährenthal had seen his way to accept Tittoni's invitation to pay a visit to Rome. But he funks clerical displeasure—altho' T. assured him that he could square it with the Vatican. So he will go to visit the Italian King at the latter's country house at?[3]

Pallavicini—the A.H. Ambassador at Constantinople and my old St P.'friend came to see me this afternoon. He is as full of common sense as ever—and very staid for a Hungarian. Dumba told me tonight that someone had described him as a 'genial Mosaiker'— which hits him off neatly.

A pleasant dinner at Weede's—but there were no Austrians except P'cess Alexandrine Windischgrätz[4] and the Dumbas.

Friday 10 May

S. tells me Dziedyski[5] says (1) that there is a very hard 3 cornered

[1] Forgách; newly appointed Austro-Hungarian Minister, Belgrade; Goschen had known him in St Petersburg.
[2] Letter, word or words, omitted.
[3] Steed had probably referred to Tenuta di San Rossori at Cascine Vecchie, near Pisa.
[4] Sister of Prince Hugo zu Windisch-Graetz.
[5] Dzieduszycki.

fight going on between D'Ährenthal—Beck and Wekerle—about A.H. Treaties with Roumania and Servia. Wekerle insists that Treaties should be made between these countries and Austria *and* Hungary—and Beck is inclined—under certain conditions—viz. that they should be absolutely identical to agree. D'Ährenthal swears that they shall be as heretofore Austro-Hungarian Treaties. It will be curious to see who wins the day. (2) It appears that it is not yet settled whether D'Ährenthal will go to Rome or not—and that he will be guided in the matter by the Leaders of the Christo-Socialist party. (Vide May 4.) (3) Italy growing more clerical every day—or rather the Church is becoming more laical! (4) Doff says that A.H. and Germany are moving Heaven and Earth to get Russia away from France and us—and are offering goodness knows what in the Balkans—vide *N.F.P.* of May 9.[1]

My Golf Prizes were played for today—but I don't know who won them. (Carnegie and C'tess Larisch did.[2])

(5) D. said that there was a regular panic here in Gov't circles for a few days after King's[3] visit to Cartagena and Gaeta—and that they thought war was a question of days. D. calmed them.[4]

Saturday 11 May

Very hot

Left for Buda Pesth—train too hot for words. Twinkle met me and we hurried off at once to dress for dinner with the Festetics. As a matter of fact we were the first arrivals.

Other guests were—Count and Countess Albert Apponyi (he the great orator and she Mensdorff's sister[5])—Countess Karolyi[6] (very nice) with a nice daughter—Count and Countess Hadik[7]—Vilmos Festetics—a young Pallavicini etc.—a very nice party.

I had a long talk with the great Apponyi—a most charming conversationalist—but to my mind not very convincing. He sweeps away arguments with a flood of eloquent words—but one feels afterwards that he has not confuted those arguments. For instance I asked him, when he said that in order to cease being regarded as a sort of Austrian Province they must have Customs Barriers of their own and entire economic independence—what w'd become of their Agriculture—as,

---

[1] For the history of this episode see E. Walters, 'Aehrenthal's attempt in 1907 to re-group the European Powers', *Slavonic and East European Review*, xxx (1951–2), p. 213; for another view, F. R. Bridge, *Great Britain and Austria-Hungary 1906–1914*, p. 56.

[2] This sentence evidently added subsequently.

[3] Edward VII.

[4] This paragraph evidently added subsequently.

[5] Clothilde.

[6] Probably wife of Count Gyula Károlyi.

[7] Hungarian landowner and wife.

I said—Austria might on her side put high duties on Hungarian Agricultural products. 'Oh!' he said—'they surely will not do that!' 'But,' I said, 'they may!' 'Of course,' he said—'there must be a *period of transition*—before our Industries have taken the place of Agriculture.' 'But won't that period be dangerous?' It may be—but Hungary *must* be independent etc.' That is no sort of argument!

Afterwards to Rothschild's ball at Park Club. *Archduke Joseph*[1] *and wife* were there. Got presented and got home at 2 a.m. Open Fiacre—draughts etc. Pretty people.

Sunday 12 May

Big lunch at Park Club given by Polli Szapary[2]—165. Got introduced to Kossuth—pompous—I thought—and Andrassy—whom I liked and thought cleverer than K. or Apponyi. Much aged since I saw him. Also Me Wekerle[3]—and others. Sat next to Archduchess—whom I found difficult to talk to—and Countess Festetics.

Afterwards races....

Ball given at Park Club.... Got home at 3 a.m. and am already feeling seedy from this unusual 'strenuous life' the draughts and the open Fiacres in the dead of night.

Thursday 16 May

Left B.P. with regret—Boss partic. having enjoyed herself immensely.

Friday 17 May

Hard day. Crozier[4] came in the morning and fully corroborated all Steed's Demidoff information. But he doesn't see that Germany latterly has been so agreeable to France as to warrant latter making up to her—and leaving Her Entente-friends. Wrote a lot of despatches some of considerable interest—for Messenger (Watkins?).

Saturday 18 May

Interesting visit from Steed in the morning. He had lots to tell me about German and Austrian intrigues to detach France and Russia from us. He tells me that he hears from Demidoff—that d'Ährenthal is very anti-English—and talks with regard to our Limitation of

[1] Descendant of the last Palatine of Hungary.
[2] Now Councillor, Foreign Ministry.   [3] Wife of Hungarian Minister-President.
[4] French Ambassador.

Armament proposals of our 'Deeply planned naïvetés'. I must try and let d'A. see that I know what is going on—but it will be difficult. As yet I fail to see what inducements he is offering to Russia—to join them and bring France in. But he *is* offering some and the idea (of course prompted by Germany) is that there should be a revival of the old Imperial Dreibund—France thrown in. He is said to be working over Isvolsky's head! direct with the Court Party. Shares in construction and proceeds of Bagdad Railway—and partnership in Balkan and Macedonian policy way be inducements for France and Russia—but I don't see it clearly yet.

Monday 3 June

See next page.[1]

Tuesday 4 June[2]

Ball at Spaniards. Very Successful. Ouroussoff talked to me—and seemed much perturbed at it having got out about d'Ah.'s alleged intrigues. He says d'Ah. is much upset—and he wondered whether somebody has not been indiscreet! He says that H.M.G. have made a great Tapage about it and that the King had even spoken to Mensdorff about it!![3] I am glad I am going down to Baltazzis[4] tomorrow[5]— as I shall avoid awkward questions from d.Ä.

I am slightly nervous myself—but after all I had to report what I heard[6]—and Hardinge has received corroboration.[7]

(This was yesterday.[8])

Wednesday 5 June

Cold and dismal
   Went down to Napagedl[9]—Baltazzi's place to attend his sale of

---

[1] That is, the page for 4 June.

[2] Although Goschen wrote this entry on the page for 4 June, the events described occurred on 3 June.

[3] Mensdorff noted in his diary for Sunday 2 June 1907 that he had had an exhausting week. He had had unpleasant conversations with Grey and Hardinge, who had received information to the effect that Aehrenthal wanted to introduce a new grouping of the powers into Macedonian affairs; this grouping would consist of the three 'Kaisermächte', together with France, to the exclusion of England and Italy. He commented: 'Natürlich nehmen sie es übel und sind sehr schlect auf uns zu sprechen.' (Mensdorff, Tagebuch, 2 June 1907, Nachlass Albert Mensdorff-Pouilly-Dietrichstein, Karton IV, Haus-, Hof- und Staatsarchiv, Vienna.) I am much indebted to Dr. F. R. Bridge, who has kindly lent me his transcript of this material.

[4] Aristides Count Baltazzi; wealthy Moravian landowner.

[5] Wednesday 5 June.

[6] Goschen to Hardinge, 23 May 1907, H.P., 10.

[7] Hardinge to Goschen, 28 May 1907 (copy), H.P., 10.

[8] 3 June 1907.   [9] In Moravia.

Yearlings. Two hours by train—beautiful House and lovely park and first rate stables. Enormous lunch—and strong cup and Champagne to encourage bidders. The sale went well—tho' some I thought went too cheap. Mutzerli[1] had had too much cup—and woke up from a sound sleep and said 'fünfzig' nearly getting a yearling knocked down to her.

What I enjoyed most was seeing the Stallions exercised—particularly 'Con Amore'—a charming horse—and 'Gouvernant' the celebrated son of 'Flying Fox'. I think a stallion in the prime of life—fatted up for his 'business' is about the finest specimen of animal life one can possibly see.

One of the sights of the day—were the waitresses in old Moravian dress. They danced afterwards when young Reeves the trainer—and Martin the jockey distinguished themselves. A good day—but I had a tremendous headache coming back and a touch of a chill. The Beltazzis were charming Hosts. I had no idea they lived in such a splendid place.

Archduchess Elizabeth Windischgrätz[2] was there and all Windischgrätz girls under chaperonage of C'tess Szechenyi.[3]

Thursday 6 June

Important letters and desp's from Hardinge and Sir E. Grey.[4] The news made a tremendous row and H.M. Grey and Hardinge all jumped on Mensdorff—who found himself dans des mauvais draps. D'Ä denied everything—but Hardinge told him that he would have accepted his denial unreservedly if it had not heard [sic][5] from an independent source that the Russians had refused the combination proposed. They seem to have been pretty careful at the F.O. but I still think they dropped on Mensdorff rather hastily.

Went racing and won on two races—but did not do well on the whole.

Went to hear the *Contes d'Hoffmann* which sounded quite delightfully fresh to me as I haven't heard it for years. But it was better given at Copenhagen.

Friday 7 June

Avarna came to see me and pumped hard—but he didn't get much out of me. He is inclined to think that d'Ä can't possibly have meditated

---

[1] Not identified.
[2] Wife of Prince Otto Windisch-Graetz; daughter of Archduke Rudolf.
[3] Wife of Count Gyula Széchenyi.
[4] Grey to Goschen, 4 June 1907, *B.D.*, v. no. 161.
[5] Goschen originally wrote 'appeared'; hence the odd syntax.

any separate action by the 4 Powers as it would be 1. too risky a policy—2. too vile an intrigue ag'st Italy. His view is that the Mursteg[1] agreement was to a certain extent an infraction of the Austro-Italian agreement that neither Power should do anything in the Balkans without the other—but that this would be a real infraction—and would, if known to be true—create a very violent feeling ag'st Austria among the Italian Public. The only thing which leads him to think that there must be something in it is that Ouroussow in conversation with him let fall the expression that there must have been an 'indiscretion' somewhere. I quite agree if there has been an indiscretion it must mean that there has been something to be indiscreet about!

Saturday 8 June

Had a long talk with Crozier. He says that D'Ä. came here from Petersburg with the idea of the says C. Dreibund—and has been working at it ever since—of course egged on by Germany—whose vassal he is. He found that he could not get Russia without France—so he has been trying—by baits in the Balkans etc. to get France in. This *is* probably the explanation of the whole thing—and his mistake has been that he has thought it possible to draw France away from England—because of course in his combination England and Italy must have remained out in the cold. Whatever his plan was it has failed if D.[2] is to be believed: and D.'s oriental faculty of exaggeration is the rock on which my information and perhaps my place—may yet split. But I don't think so—as the information except on one point (D.'s last) comes from so many sources. The only thing troubling my mind—is whether my deductions are right—but that is after all a minor point: and it was just as well that people should see it from all sides.

Friday 14 June

Special Messenger from London bringing me instructions for tomorrow—see next page.

Saturday 15 June

Made a very important communication to d'Ährenthal—viz., that we had exchanged notes with Spain—stating that our respective policy was directed to the Maintenance of the Statu Quo and the

---

[1] Mürzsteg.
[2] For Demidoff's part in the episode see Goschen to Hardinge, 10 June 1907 (decypher), H.P., 10.

guarantee of our respective maritime possessions in the Mediterranean—and part of Atlantic washing Africa and Europe.[1] Crozier
communicated similar exchange of notes between France and
Spain—and Casa Calvo—Sp. Amb.—opened the Ball by communi-
cating both exchanges.

Casa Calvo bore the brunt—D'Ährenthal was tired and worried
by the time I saw him—but quite friendly and nice. His line was—
why all these ententes and guarantees when everything looked peaceful? Who threatened Gib. and Malta etc.? My line was that these
arrangements were directed against no one—and were no more than
the consolidation and protection of our interests—which was [sic] best
and most easily done in time of peace.

These communications were made on the same day at Berlin.

Monday 17 June

Busy all day about Crete. Started at 11.15—the Ambassadors of
the 4 protecting Powers in conclave assembled—lunched with
Ouroussov at 12.30 and then fussed about our identic note until about
5. Crozier drafted it and I didn't think much of it. I suggested one
or two very necessary alterations w'h were accepted.

Tuesday 18 June

Sent in the identic note about Crete. It seems simple enough
enough—but I shall be very much surprised if the Austrians give their
assent to the proposals of the protecting Powers without a murmur.
They are sure to make difficulties of sorts.

Wednesday 19 June

Saw D'Ährenthal at his reception—he promised to give an answer
about Crete as soon as possible.

We had a little talk about the new arrangements between Spain
and England and France. He said 'I know these arrangements are
not against us—nor against Italy—therefore they must be ag'st Germany'! I said to him that I was aghast at his bad logic. Why should
it be against any one? We were simply consolidating and protecting
our interests and possessions. D'Ä said 'But if one shuts one's door
it is against a Robber.' I said 'Not always—for I personally shut mine
against possible draughts!' 'If,' I added, 'one makes a fence round
one's property—it is to shew that it is one's property—not necessarily
against evildoers!' He was very pleasant but he insists that our

[1] Notes exchanged in London and Paris, 16 May 1907, B.D., vii, nos. 39–41.

arrangements arise from distrust. It may be so—but isn't ever policy tinged with mistrust? A big programme of Ships—increase in Armies—and armaments are all connected with mistrust of a sort—but not necessarily of any one in particular—it may be distrust of events more than of nations.

Monday 24 June

Worked hard in the morning—on 'New Triple Alliance' and Hungarian irritation at Speech from the Throne desp's.

Afterwards played for June medal—and made a bad round. Had a long talk to Charles Kinsky[1] about his conversation with Hardinge[2]—on Anglo-Austrian distrust etc. Rather interesting. Austria or rather d'Ährenthal is suspicious of us—and thinks we egg on Italy to annex Albania—and other foolish ideas. I am quite tired of explaining to Foreigners that we *never* have an intriguing policy. We seldom have a policy at all—but when we do it is always straightforward. I must try and rub this into d'Ährenthal. Of course Austria's intime intimacy [*sic*]—or subservience to Germany—must in some questions take us a little apart—but in others—such as in the Near East there is nothing that should separate such old friends.[3]

Thursday 27 June

Twee arrived. . . .

Saturday 29 June

Boss left for Tentschach in the evening.

Sunday 30 June

Ted and I went to church—then golf—then in the evening went to meet Clara and Mary. . . .

Wednesday 3 July

Tentschach

Danneskiold girls most enthusiastic about Tentschach and very satisfactory. 'No wonder that you love Tentschach' said Mary. 'I

[1] Prince Karl Kinsky; former Austro-Hungarian diplomat; also famous amateur rider, who won the Grand National, riding his own mare, in 1883; spent much time in England.

[2] In London.

[3] See Goschen to Hardinge, 28 June 1907, H.P., 10.

never saw anything so lovely.' Tour de propriétaire—Farm—
Jägers—Cow Stable and Piggery etc.

Wednesday 10 July

Came back to Vienna—much against my will. Beastly journey in
shaky train—headache. Found work waiting for me—that horrible
Crete has turned up again—*and* the Sugar question. I shall have to
go and see D'Ährenthal tomorrow.

Thursday 11 July

Went to ask d'Ährenthal by instructions whether the A.H. Govt.
agreed in principle to action proposed by H.M.G. with regard to
Sugar Convention. He was very decided about not giving an opinion
at all. He said it was not a matter to be discussed between Cabinets—
but before the Sugar Commission. He wouldn't move from that.
Wedel was with him when I arrived and the orders from Berlin were
evidently to refuse to give an opinion. Wedel told me on coming out
that he had been discussing the Sugar question—and I told him I
was going to also: and he went away. On coming out from d'Äh.
I found he had returned—and he told me that he had forgotten to
mention something to D'Ä. He asked me to keep him company for
a moment while he was waiting—and then said 'What did d'Ä. tell
you?' I told him more or less—and he took up his hat and said 'I
will walk home with you.' He forgot that he had just told me that
he wanted to see d'Ä. He had evidently come back to control d'Ä.
and see whether he had carried out instructions.

Friday 12 July

Messenger. Lunched with Ouroussof—but did not hear anything
new. He seems to think something is up between the Italian and
Austrian Gov'ts with regard to the Balkans—a sort of idea of taking
Italy into the Mursteg[1] agreement and leaving England out. There
was recently a note in the *Débats*[2] to that effect—but it hardly seems
likely that so soon after their last game had been spotted that they
would begin another.
D'Ährenthal left today for Italy.

Saturday 13 July

Left for Tentschach by 11.30 train—bringing Benjie with me. Cold
drive up.

[1] 'Mürzsteg'.   [2] *Journal des Débats*, 10 July 1907.

Wednesday 24 July

Vienna

Went up to town for Messenger—found Crete still on—but there was not much to do as Lancelot[1] had been very kind and active and had kept a good record of everything.

Supper and bed.

Thursday 25 July

Lunched with Ouroussoff and Avarna—but Crozier had gone to Paris. Avarna had still no instructions about Crete—so I telegraphed. Ouroussoff and Crozier had been going to send in independent notes—but on my representing to them that as we had been 'identic and simultaneous' before—it w'd be better to remain so—they agreed to wait.

Saturday 27 July

Tentschach

Went back to T. by the early train....

Monday 29 July

Girls and T.Wee left....

Thursday 8 August

Back to Vienna....

Friday 9 August

Did Crete with Crozier and Demidoff. We are now waiting only for the Russ. Gov't who are telegraphing to their Consul at Canea to know exactly what they *do* mean. The whole thing has been dreadfully mismanaged by the Cabinets—just as it was last year.

Wednesday 14 August

Hot

Started for Marienbad—with Benjie[2] Bruce in tow as Secretary etc. It has made Crack very discontented my not taking him—but he would have been no use.

Took up our quarters in our old rooms. Many familiar faces....

---

[1] Carnegie.   [2] 'Benjie' was a nickname.

Thursday 15 August

Visits and talks with old friends.

Friday 16 August

Cold

King arrived looking first rate—in fact better than I have seen him look for years. He was very gracious and cordial and asked me to dine in the Evening to talk over things. As a matter of fact H.M. did not talk much—but He told me the German and Austrian Visits had gone off well,[1] especially the latter. The German Emperor had not touched on politics at all! And owing to the fog in the Channel the King had arrived 3 hours late. 'So the visit was not very long—but quite long enough!'

A tel. came from German Emperor after dinner—saying that Morenga[2] had crossed into German S. Af. territory—with 400 men armed with Martini rifles—and asking that H.M.G. should *compel* the Cape Gov't to help in putting down that dangerous rebel. H.M. gave me a tel. to send to Grey—wh. I did. The whole matter was settled afterwards. But neither H.M. nor His humble servant liked the word 'compel'. 'He should choose his words more carefully' was the criticism.

Sunday 18 August

Catholic Church in the morning—full Dress. King arrived too early. Te deum. Then back to Hotel—recd. deputations—presented Liechtenstein and his merry men. Our own Church at 3 o'clock. Big dinner in the evening at the Kursaal—Head Officials—ecclesiastics—and prominent English. Broke up early.

Wednesday 21 August

Clemenceau[3] came over.[4]

Sunday 25 August

H.M. lunched with us—it was a success as the King was in excellent spirits and enjoyed Drescher's music. I had chosen the music carefully and the K. was very pleased as he said at having an Amb'r who was

---

[1] To Wilhelm II at Wilhelmshöhe, 14 Aug.; to Franz Joseph at Ischl, 15 Aug.
[2] Herrero leader.   [3] President, French Council of Ministers.
[4] From Carlsbad.

a musician. Ouroussoff came over from Carlsbad to the lunch and H.M. was very nice to him. O. and I had a good talk afterwards and he told me what was going on—wh. is not much of general interest.

H.M. asked us to his table at the Wagner concert in the afternoon— and an excellent concert it was.

Saturday 31 August

Off day. Ladies putted for my prize... K. drove to Carlsbad.

Sunday 1 September

Church at 12—when Nordica[1] sang things from *Messiah*. She sang alright but the accompaniment left much to be desired.

Marienbad is getting empty and begins to look a little bit 'triste'. Dined with Princess Murat[2] in the evening to meet H.M. Present the Duchess d'Uzès[3]—whom I didn't care about (nor did H.M. who considered her rather off hand).... A nice change having fresh people—and the evening, tho' long, was quite nice. When one doesn't play Bridge it is a bore sitting round till 11 o'clock—and *so* bad for the cure.

Monday 2 September

King's Messenger left. I had only to write about P'ce Ferdinand's proposed visit to London in Oct. King wishes it to be a private visit— as Greeks and others are already complaining that we are making too much of Bulgaria—and He does not wish this feeling to grow stronger. Therefore he wishes a private visit under travelling name if possible. 'As little fuss as possible' I wrote to Buchanan[4] and Charles Hardinge.[5]

King dined with us at Rübezahl.... Good dinner but not very cheery evening.

In the evening I had a long talk with the King—who spoke nicely of George and the services he had rendered to the country.

K. very nice to Boss in the evening.

Friday 6 September

King left at 5.30 and I at 10.
Lunched with H.M. before starting and H.M. gave me a really

[1] American soprano.   [2] Princess Joachim de Murat.
[3] Marienbad habituée. Upholder formerly of General Boulanger, later of women's rights.
[4] Agent and Consul-General, Bulgaria.
[5] Goschen to Hardinge, 2 Sept. 1907, H.P., 10.

awfully nice pin. *He* admired it awfully when I wore it at the Station: but it really is a beauty. He said *very* nice things to me and said I had been of the greatest use to him. He also praised my letter to Grey[1] about Isvolsky[2] and said that it was the best thing he had read for some time.

Saturday 7 September

Vienna in the morning after quite a nice journey.

Thursday 26 September

Duke of Connaught[2] arrived. He was met at the Station by Emperor, Guard of Honour of Regiment of Hussars[3]—with Archduke Franz Salvator. . . . The Duke looked very well in his Hussar Uniform. The Emperor had English Field-Marshal's Uniform—quite correct except that he had *Butcher* boots on and no baton. . . .

Saturday 28 September

Duke inspected his Regiment and lunched with them. I was not invited! I suppose I ought to have been—but I was so delighted to get off that I couldn't even scold Teck about it. In the evening we had a big man's dinner—military. . . . The dinner went off very well. Afterwards we all went to a supper at the Kinskeys for Grand Duke Vladimir[5] and G'd Duchess Marie Paulovna.[6] He was *much* changed and so was she—but she still has a fascinating manner and much charm. She was very nice to me and when I said that I had been afraid she would have forgotten me said that 'I *don't* forget people I like.' It was a pretty party. I sat at the same table as Marie Paulovna—Franz Ferdinand and Princess Hohenberg—his wife. She looked very pretty and nice and acted so. F.F. was also quite friendly. I had Me. Isvolsky one side and Sofka Demidoff on the other side. Boss Charles Kinsky and Farquhar.[7]

During the day we heard of death of Gd. Duke of Baden.[8] H.R.H. is going to represent H.M. at funeral—so he is going to remain on!

---

[1] Goschen to Grey, 5 Sept. 1907, *B.D.*, iv, no. 523.
[2] On 5 Sept. Isvolsky came to Marienbad and lunched with the King; he had a talk with Goschen before lunch.
[3] Edward VII's younger brother.   [4] Of which the duke was colonel-in-chief.
[5] Nicholas II's uncle.
[6] Wife of the grand duke; a duchess of Mecklenburg-Schwerin.
[7] Member of Connaught's suite.   [8] Friedrich I.

Sunday 29 September

Family dinner in the evening—Gregorys,[1] Crozier Demidoffs—
Boys and that eccentric and talkative genius Miss Ethel Smythe.[2] She
is arranging for the production of her opera[3] here. She is a strange
creature and prefers Gounod to Wagner—and *Faust* to the *Ring*! Mrs
Gregory—who is a granddaughter of Jenny Lind's told me an interesting fact. Namely that when she was about 16 she went to García—
her grandmother's singing master[4] to have her voice trained. The
Maestro who was then over 90 told her that she was then too young—
but that if she would come back in 3 or 4 years he would undertake
her musical education!!

Friday 4 October

Worked all day—with an interlude in the afternoon when I paid
a visit to Isvolsky. He didn't tell me much; but as usual he threw
out dark hints as to German action: this time it was as regards Judicial
Reform in Macedonia—and he said that he feared that they were
stiffening the Sultan's back. Isvolsky is very pleased with his visit—
and himself generally. He says that they don't seem to care much
about the Russo-English Agreement—that in Berlin where they can't
like it much—the official world is 'correct' and the Press 'aigre-
douce'—and that in Russia he has met less criticism than he
expected.[5]
The Tecks have asked me to be Godfather—which pleases and flat-
ters me very much.
Boss and Benjie left for Tentschach—night train.

Friday 18 October

Lunched with Seymour and Teck at Bristol and afterwards wrote
hard for messenger. Ausgleich and Tchirsky[6] (who succeeds Wedel
at German Embassy—Wedel is made Govr. of Alsace-Lorraine) were
the topics. I meant to apply for leave but must wait until Emperor
gets better. Rather bad account of him today.

Saturday 19 October

Emperor better again.

[1] He was 2nd secretary.   [2] Ethel Smyth; composer.
[3] Probably *Der Strandrecht* (*The Wreckers*).
[4] Manuel García, 1805–1906; Catalan singing-master; taught at Royal Academy
of Music, 1848–95.
[5] See Goschen to Grey, 4 Oct. 1907, *B.D.*, v. no. 168.
[6] Tschirschky; hitherto Secretary of State.

Sunday 20 October

Went with Clarke to the races to see the big Austria-Preis run for. It was won by a German mare—Fabula—a very handsome and racing-looking animal. A good many notable Viennese present—nearly all crabbed Tchirsky who is to succeed C't Wedel at the German Embassy here—and said that they considered it 'taktlos' of the German Emperor to send a man here whose wife scarcely belongs to even the 'Zweitegesellschaft'. Poor little Me de Tchirsky—I am afraid she will have a poor time of it here.[1]

Tuesday 22 October

Christening of the Tecks' new little boy. Archduke Frederick, Charles Kinsky, and I were godfathers....

Wednesday 23 October

Saw D'Ährenthal and told him that I was sending him a very urgent note about the position of the Anglican Church in Austria—whose members are considered 'confessionslos' and whose Churches can only exist when affiliated to Minor Faiths. He was sympathetic and promised to do what he could. He complained of delays at Constantinople and begged me to point out to Grey how important it was that the communication of the Project of Judicial Reforms should be sent to the Porte without delay. The Sultan had sent messages both to him and Isvolsky that he would never accept control—and long conferences amongst the Ambassadors would make him think that the Powers were disagreed amongst themselves and strengthened his resistance.

I telegraphed this to Grey who repeated it to O'Conor—adding that he was of the same opinion as D'Ährenthal.

Saturday 26 October

Worked hard all day—1. At a long despatch on the present state of politics, the first reading of the Ausgleich Bills—and the rotten state of Parliamentary manners in the present loudly puffed Universal Suffrage House of Deputies. 2. The Arad[2] Water Works case. I saw Baron Call[3] on the subject and he promised to warn the Hung'n Gov't of the intention of the Municipality of Arad to seize the Works. But I am personally ag'st interfering in the case at all—as the Waterworks

---

[1] Frau von Tschirschky was Viennese, but not of an aristocratic family.
[2] In the Banat.   [3] Chief of Section, Foreign Ministry.

Co. is notwithstanding the fact that *all* the Capital is British—is [*sic*]
a Hungarian Co.—and moreover the case is under Litigation. But
the F.O. would have me interfere unofficially (whatever that may
mean) and I have done so.

Baron Macchio[1] called—an old colleague at Constantinople 26
years ago—and now working in Ministry for F.A.

Countess Wedel[2] came to say goodbye. She was rather funny about
their successors the Tschirsky's and what difficulties they would have
here—from her plebeian birth and their want of means!

Sunday 27 October

Noel Buxton[3] came to see me and talked a lot of Balkan Committee
rot. He rather wants to see d'Ährenthal.

Monday 28 October

Awful day. More throaty still—I wish I had gone to Chiari last
week. Wrote a long closing desp. on gen'l situation—and tore up letters and things.

Saturday 2 November

Foggy and drizzly

Nothing very partic. Shopped a.m. and mooned p.m. I do *not* like
London on Saturdays....[4]

---

[1] Chief of Section, Foreign Ministry.   [2] German Ambassadress.
[3] Former Liberal M.P.; founder of the Balkan Committee.
[4] The diary does not give the date of Goschen's arrival in London, nor that of his
return to Vienna.

1908

Goschen and his wife spent most of the early months of 1908 in Vienna. From 29 March to 1 April he stayed at Berzencze, Count Festetics' property in western Hungary. From 8 to 14 May he was in Budapest. From 22 to 25 May he and Hosta were at Tentschach. He spent the last days of June and the first days of July at Keszthely, another Festetics property in Hungary. At the end of July he and Hosta went to Denmark for the wedding of their elder son, after which they paid a visit to King Haakon VII and Queen Maud of Norway. On 12 August, at Attnang, Goschen boarded Edward VII's train, which was bound for Ischl, and was informed of his appointment as Ambassador in Berlin. The usual 'season' at Marienbad followed, after which the Goschens spent some time at Tentschach. Goschen was in Budapest at the beginning of October. He and Hosta left Vienna for Berlin on 7 November. On 12 December they left for London.

Wednesday 1 January

The Year began with a howling tempest—and frost. Last night after the fearful ceremony of bowing down, in full uniform, before Countess Harrach and P'ce Montenuevo[1]—I invited the Embassy Staff, except Tecks who were engaged, to sup at the Bristol.... Today has been spent in writing names on all the Archdukes and calling on a few friends....

Saturday 4 January

Lunched with Tecks and the children etc.... Had a talk with Ouroussoff. The Sultan seems to have refused to prolong mandates of Financial Commission and Gendarmerie Officers. This will put the Powers in some difficulty—and I don't see yet what measures can be taken to coerce the Turks. Naval demonstrations are a bit played out. Joint occupation of Turkish Territory is a dangerous game for all concerned—especially a Mohammedan Power like us—and stopping the 3% additional tax would seem to hurt us more than the Turk. I don't like the look of things—as the Sultan is sure to kick even more at the Judicial Reforms—and the result must be renewed chaos in Macedonia. The Bulgarians may then lose patience and go for Turkey! *Then* the fat will be in the fire.

[1] Second Grand Master of the Court.

Friday 10 January

Got Messenger off. Only one desp. and private letter. Saw D'Äh-renthal—who furnished me with Text of Amendment to note, telling me that A.H. Amb'r at Const'ple[1] was now authorised to sign note as amended. Speaking of the future in case Sublime Porte remains obdurate about prolongation of Mandates and Control—he depre-cated Naval Demonstration—but said in any case the most important thing was that no means of coercion should be proposed which did not meet with approval of *all* the Powers. This of course because at the last Naval Dem'n Germany did not join.[2] Unity was the great thing and as long as Powers could present a united front all w'd be well. Personally I don't think we can talk of a united front—with Ger-many always present at our councils and then reporting everything to the Sultan!

Saturday 11 January

Dear Boss arrived after a very bad journey via Flushing—but *quite* well. I was glad to see her and have her with me again. My cough is very bad today and I can't sleep at night for it.

Sunday 2 February

Heard the dreadful news that King Carlos of Portugal[3] and that charming son of His the Crown Prince[4] were assassinated yeaterday.[5] The other boy (present King[6]) was wounded but not seriously—and the dear Queen[7] escaped unscathed—tho' she threw herself in front of her sons.

Thursday 27 February

Our ball at last came off. There were about 300 people—and every-thing went off well.... But there were too many people. The music was led by Hügel, and everybody says he is the best of all.

Saturday 29 February

Saw d'Ährenthal to have some conversation about Grey's speech[8]—he began all right by saying that with most of it he could agree. But then he got absolutely furious and said that he considered

[1] Pallavicini.   [2] Dec. 1905.
[3] Goschen had known him in Lisbon.   [4] Duke of Bragança.
[5] In Lisbon.   [6] Manoel II.   [7] Queen Amélie.
[8] House of Commons, 25 Feb. 1908.

it most unfair to him that Grey had said that his Sandjak Railway policy had caused a new situation[1]—and that he protested against it most strongly. I told him that if there was any unfairness it was the way in which Grey's speech had been distorted by the Press here— and public opinion had been misled by the Press. He said 'I have nothing to do with the Press.' I replied that not a day passed but what communiqués were sent by him to the Press when public opinion was going contrary to his wishes—and now with the text of the speech before him—he had not stirred a hand to have the gross misrepresentation made by the Chief papers set right. '*I* protest strongly against this.' This cleared the air somewhat and he said he w'd have the text published—wh. he did. He then raved on about Grey's speech and I told him frankly that it was no use saying that things were now the same as they were before the Sandjak railway incident—because they were not and he knew it. In making a review of Macedonian Affairs Grey had had to mention the Sandjak incident: moreover he never said that the situation *was* changed—but that there was *an impression* that it had changed. And I shewed him the passage which runs 'now I come to what has been called the new situation'.

Anyhow I said it was a subject that c'dn't be passed over in silence. He said 'How could I know that the Sultan would issue his Irade so quick—when the negotiations had been so long?' This was a little *too* thin—so I said—'But who put the weapon into the hands of the most skilful fencer in Europe?' Then he turned to Germany and said that in England we had Germany on the brain and thought that Germany had egged him on in this business. He assured me that the idea had been entirely his own—and that Germany had not been informed a minute before the other powers! That is as may be—but he has a loopholey mind—and is a quibbler of the deepest dye: he may not have informed Germany—but I'll bet that Germany knew—advised the S. Porte to issue the Irade—and perhaps even put d'Ä in a hole! That is quite possible. D'Ä evidently feels shaky and is beginning to be criticized here for his unskilful and untimely handling of a project quite harmless in itself and within Austria's rights.

Monday 9 March

Communicated H.M.G. proposals to D'Ährenthal. Of course he only said that he would study them objectively and give them the same attention as he would to the Russian proposals which he was expecting. He was calm today—so we had not to send elaborate messages to our wives after the interview—as we do when the conversation has been warm.

[1] Cf. Hansard, 4, clxxxiv, col. 1700.

I don't think that he will view our proposals very favourably—tho' there is not much to be said against the appointment of a Governor. But I expect we shall find—the withdrawal of the troops—and the guarantee of freedom from Foreign Attack—*when* they are withdrawn—easy either of acceptance or of execution [*sic*].[1] It is all very well to say 'We'll guarantee you from attack' but supposing Bulgaria moves when the troops are withdrawn. Who is to turn them out? Who is to pull the chestnuts out? We can't throw Ironclads into the heart of Macedonia. The Russians wouldn't move a hand against the Bulgars—France and Italy are far off—therefore it could only be Austria–Hungary!! Would that suit Russia? Would it suit anybody? That is the question.

Thursday 12 March

Dined with Casa Calvo, Sp. Ambr....
Casa Calvo committed the heinous crime of taking in Madame Montecucoli[2]—and placing the Admiral[3] opposite to him.... What Calvo meant by sending in Montecucoli before me I don't know. He must know that an Ambassador can't go in *after* other people and take 2nd place. For myself I don't care and never did—but I should catch it if it was known for not having refused to be placed where I was. I *ought* to have said something but I hate rows. But that an Ambassador of all people in the world should make such a gaffe is incomprehensible....

Friday 13 March

Got a very nice letter from Sir E. Grey thanking me for line I took with regard to D'Ä's criticisms of his Speech—and saying that he cordially endorsed every word I had said.[4] I was glad of this as I didn't get anything about it by bag—and I was beginning to think that I may have gone a little too far.

Hardinge wrote me a letter by the bag[5]—his letters are always interesting but this one did not tell me much about what I wanted to know most—namely how Russia stands exactly 1. with Austria 2. with us. But I gather that she is leaning more our way.

---

[1] Word omitted in MS.; probably 'not'.
[2] Wife of Commander-in-Chief, Austro-Hungarian Navy.
[3] Her husband.
[4] Grey to Goschen, 11 March 1908, *B.D.*, v, no. 191.
[5] Hardinge to Goschen, 9 March 1908 (copy), *H.P.*, 13.

Thursday 19 March

Poor O'Conor died at Constantinople. I am very distressed—he was a good chief to me in former years and a good friend later.

I have never been quite certain about his diplomatic ability. Able he was certainly as far as intellect went—but he was, to my mind—too original and too fantastic in his ideas to be a *safe* diplomatist. But he was full of pluck and was always ready to fight for his views. He did well at St. Petersburg—but I doubt whether he always satisfied his 'employers' at Const'ple. For an Irishman he lacked suppleness. But he was a faithful friend and a good fellow—and I am very grieved he has gone.

I wonder who they will send in his place! Bunsen[1] I should think. But perhaps Arthur Hardinge.[2] Finlay[3] would be a good man—but I suppose he is too junior.

Friday 20 March

Gregory spoke to me about staying on—which forced my hand rather. I really don't wan't them much—tho' I like them both quite well—and I seem to smell an intrigue on the part of Tyrell[4] to get him the Commercial Sec'y. app't. Personally I don't think it right to give this appt. to a F.O. man—seeing that one of the objects of the new commercial arrangement is to give secretaries in the Dip. Service experience in managing commercial affairs! The Embassy has ceased to be a pleasure to me—Crack is impossible—his wife more so—and he has been giving me much trouble about his leave—Palairet[5] the new boy is not altogether satisfactory—Carnegie is a dear good chap—but his wife make [*sic*] things impossible with her touchiness and that makes him pompous at times—and at others low. Seymour has gone—and Benjie is the only really satisfactory one from all points of view.

Saturday 21 March

Went for a walk in the Prater with Boss notwithstanding the awful wind. Ought to have written report all day but didn't have energy enough. Am I giving out? Ot is it spring coming on? I think it is Embassy worries!

I asked the Archduke F. Ferdinand to dine 3 weeks ago—as I have never rec'd an answer—I wrote to his Aide de Camp and told him 'J'attends toujours une réponse etc.' He came flying round and said

---

[1] Ambassador in Madrid. [2] Minister in Brussels. [3] Minister in Dresden.
[4] Tyrrell; Grey's private secretary. [5] 3rd secretary.

this day week. This will probably do me out of my woodcock shoot
with Festetics. But I am glad to get this invitation off my mind—
as it has prevented us asking anybody else.

Monday 23 March

Dined at the Japs[1]—She the Jap Ambassadress is a charming little
woman full of fun—and intelligent. He like all Japanese men is difficult to talk to or make talk. The d'Ährenthals were there—and I asked
H.E. whether he had done a lot of reflection at the Semmering. He
said 'Yes and I will give you the result of it on Wednesday.' Had
a long talk to Assim Bey[2]—who gave me a good doing about our
treatment of Turkey. I said 'You mustn't scold England alone—she
is only one of the Powers.' He said—'No—if she didn't push on—
no other Power would.' I asked him what in his opinion was the
remedy for the state of affairs in Macedonia. 'Give Turkey a free hand'
he said at once—though there was a better one and that was to de-
throne the Sultan—which we ought to have done long ago.[3] 'A good
sultan and a constitution is what we want.' He then told me that he
had recently had a long conversation with the Turkish Min'r of
War[4]—who said that if he had full Powers he could restore order in
Macedonia in three months. 'But if I did' had said the Minister 'every
Power in Europe would be down upon me for methods of barbarism.'
He Assim was furious at the idea of a Governor—wh. he said w'd
mean the disintegration of Turkey in Europe. 'Why don't you pacify
Ireland? Look at Egypt—since you have been there you have made
millionaires but you haven't raised the Fellaheen one bit. You have
the heaviest hand of any Power in the world—good friends but terrible
enemies.'

Wednesday 25 March

Called on d'Ährenthal. He refuses Grey's proposals regarding
Gov'r of Macedonia—and reduction of Turkish troops—but goes
about a quarter of the way towards accepting Gendarmerie proposal.
He suggests increasing that force—and giving inspector of Gendarmerie seat at meetings of Financial Commission. He and Isvolsky propose to retain Helmi Pasha[5] in his present position—but as a sop for
refusal of Gov'r proposal—has suggested to Isvolsky that in acknowledging Turkish communication of prolongation of mandates—they

---

[1] Yasuya Uchida and his wife.   [2] Councillor, Ottoman Embassy.
[3] Goschen's syntax apparently astray; 'we' presumably refers to the Turks.
[4] Riza Pasha.
[5] Hilmi Pasha, Turkish Inspector-General, Macedonia.

should state that it must be understood that Inspector General can only be removed with the assent of *All the Powers*—(instead of the two Entente Powers). As I had foreseen he asked me to tell Sir E. Grey that he thought a period of repose would be good now—as the Balkan States now that they are occupied in obtaining concessions for railways are certain to be on their best behaviour and may be relied upon for keeping their brethren in Macedonia within bounds. I don't quite know what he means—about giving the Balkan people repose—but I presume he means a period during which the Powers will mark time.

Thursday 26 March

Nothing partic.—except went to Dentist where I ought to have gone a year ago. Wrote with great difficulty a desp. upon Aust.-Hungarian views of meeting between German William and the King of Italy at Venice.[1] This opinion is that Italy will be 'folded' in the Triple Alliance and be induced to give up her strayings towards England and France.

Letter from Hardinge by Mess: he tells me that Mensdorff 'whines' greatly about England's diminished friendship for A. Hy.[2] But how can it be helped? Austria is a blind follower of Germany—refuses every thing we ask—on every question—and then expects us to love her now as then. No, my dear Mensdorff, D'Ä must change his tactics before we can be the friend of other days.

Friday 27 March

Gregory wanted to know what I had decided about the post of Commercial Secretary.... Today I told Gregory every word I had written to Tyrell—and said that I intended to make it a Head of the Chancery post for the future—and that he could have the post in the meantime until Crack goes—when it must be given up at once to the new Head of the Chancery.

Heard the *Creation* at the Science Academy—in the same room where Haydn conducted it exactly a 100 years ago.

Saturday 28 March

The Archduke Franz Ferdinand and Princess Hohenberg came to dinner. Pres't P'ce and Princess K. Auersperg (a mistake as *he* is not

---

[1] Goschen to Grey, 26 March 1908, F.O. 371/582.
[2] Hardinge to Goschen, 24 March 1908 (copy), H.P., 13; summary very approximate.

on particularly good terms with the Archduke[1]), P'ce A. Windischgrätz ... and other 30 in all. The Archduke was very pleasant and
nice—and the Princess is always charming.... Of diplomats—we had
Count and Countess Rex[2]—Tucher[3] and Beck Friis. No politics were
talked.

Sunday 29 March

Went off to 'Berzenzce',[4] C't Festetics' place on the Hungarian
frontier to shoot woodcock. Started at 10.15 arrived at 7 by Bummel-
zug. Only the family i.e. the Count and Countess, P'ce Windischgrätz
and his wife née Alex. Festetics—Countess Ella—Georgy Festetics
and 'Uncle' Vilmos Festetics. A charming House—and a most comfortable bed—into which I was glad to sneak as early as I could.

Wednesday 1 April

Berzencze to Vienna
Left for Vienna and found a snowstorm raging at Wiener Neus-
tadt!! Found Twinkle staying with me.

Thursday 2 April

Nothing doing: needn't have come back. But found that D'Ä had
already sent answer to Macedonian proposals of H.M.G. Asked him
to receive me but he can't until tomorrow.
Dined at huge dinner at Tchirskys. The Becks were there—the
Japs—I took in Me Tchirschky and had C'tess Kilmansegge[5] on the
other side: no great catch.
Dinner fair to medium. Table rather pretty: but Lacqueys fearfully
smart. Could hear nothing of any interest.

Friday 3 April

Saw d'Ährenthal, but he had nothing much to tell me that I didn't
know. He said that Bülow had approved his answer to H.M.G. but
had shaken his head over the idea of all the Financial Delegates being
placed on the same footing as the civil agents. Bülow had told him
that the Anglo-German Relations had shown improvement during
the last year—but that the two Sovereigns made it difficult. The

---

[1] There was a difference between the Archduke and Prince Karl Auerspeg over hunting rights.
[2] Saxon Minister and wife.   [3] Bavarian Minister.   [4] Berzencze.
[5] Wife of Kielmannsegg, Governor of Lower Austria.

Emperor always wanted to be friendly but that the King for some reason or other would not have it—perhaps—Bülow said—because the Emperor does not go the right way to work. He said also that Bülow had told him that Tweedmouth had furnished the Kaiser with copies of the Estimates *before* submitting them to Parliament. I *knew* this—but I wish B. had not told D'Ä. as it will now probably come out. I know the *Times* is very anxious to confirm its suspicions on the point. I had a hard afternoon's work and then went to *Cloches de Corneville*[1]—or rather two Acts of it. Twinkle and Boss went on before.

Friday 10 April

To my great astonishment there was an excellent article in the *Fremdenblatt* on our Macedonian answer to Russia—quite different from what D'Ä. had been saying—and really quite sensible and even eulogistic. About the Financial proposals—wh. is of course our chief point—they say they *hope* all will go well—and that at any rate we have shewn that our great desire is, while getting on—to preserve and promote Unity amongst the Powers. Whether the views of the *F. Blatt* are those of D'Ä. remains to be seen. I hope they are and that he is going to make 'bonne face à mauvais jeu'. But he can't be very happy—all the less so—because we know for a certainty that he did all in his power—by personal appeal even—to persuade Isvolsky to publish his proposals as joint Austro-Russian ones—and that the latter refused point blank. D'Ä. has gone to Budapesth—so I sent the *Fremdenblatt* article home to keep them quiet. It is very interesting to watch D'Ä.'s struggles—but I am afraid he is in 'des mauvais draps' and I shouldn't wonder if he fell soon. Hungarian matters will of course be the excuse. I should be sorry for this for some reasons—chiefly because his wife is so nice—but he is rather a crooked statesman.

Saturday 11 April

Lunch at Sarafoff's[2] I met Lahovary, the Roumanian Minister here. He is rather a clever but remuant creature. He told me that he liked Grey's financial proposals rather—but said that H.M.G. had overlooked the fact that the Gardes Champêtres—if organized on the former basis, would be paid by the Communes—and that their pay could not form item in Macedonian Budget. This is rather important, if true, because it is a point that forms the chief food for criticism. He welcomed the idea of the Financial Commission—and Gend. officers etc. entering nominally into the Ott. Service—because he said

---

[1] Opera by Planquette.   [2] Bulgarian agent.

European institutions always worked well in Turkey *as long* as they 'were labelled Turkish' (portaient l'étiquette Turque).

Went to a Squash at Schoellers in honour of Sir W. Ramsay[1] who had just delivered a letter on Radium.

Monday 13 April

Nothing partic. Oh Yes! A big lunch at the Bulgarian Agent's Sarafow. . . . Rather pleasant. I like Sarafow he is a good class of Bulgar.[2]

Wednesday 15 April

Went to see D'Ährenthal and got absolutely nothing out of him with regard to our Macedonian proposals.

I asked him how he had enjoyed Budapesth—and he replied that it had been a little Easter trip—on wh. his wife[3] had accompanied him. They had seen lots of old friends and dined out every night! The truth is that he went to negotiate about the Delegations and the Officers' pay question and came back absolutely empty-handed.

Thursday 23 April

Nothing exciting by bag—not even my usual letter from Hardinge—who has gone to Copenhagen with the King.

Friday 24 April

Went to see Call at Min'y of F.A. about a trifling matter—but hoping to get something out of him about Macedonian reforms and Isvolsky's speech. Of course he hadn't read it! It has been the same with D'Ä.—every time I asked him about our or Isvolsky's proposals he was always just going to read them. . . .

Monday 27 April

Had a very pleasant dinner at D'Ährenthals. Mensdorff was there—also Kinsky and Pallavicini. D'Ä told me that he wasn't going to receive on Wednesday—but that he would telephone to me on Friday if he had anything to say. But his line now with regard to the British and Russian Maced'n Reform proposals is that he has got nothing to say about them until the two Gov'ts have decided what they are going to do.

[1] Professor of Chemistry, University College, London.
[2] Evidently some duplication here; perhaps written subsequently.
[3] Széchényi's daughter.

Every one regrets the German Emperor's coming visit and people are afraid that it will tire the Emperor. He is coming with a Suite of 80 people! Our King goes with about 5, i.e., two gentlemen and 2 footmen.

Tuesday 28 April

Had a 'Crete' meeting at Ouroussow's who is looking very ill still. Owing to my foresight in drawing up the necessary note we spared him a great deal of trouble—and what is more knocked off in a quarter of an hour what generally takes us two hours.

Got a letter from Teddie stating that he has got his post at the Egyptian F.O. that he had been kindly received by his new chief Boutros Pasha[1] (who wants him to act as his priv. Sec.) but that the salary is not £600 as he had been promised—but £500. . . . Wrote to Count Danneskiold and asked whether T. and Mary might be joined in the bonds of Holy Matrimony in the Summer.

Saturday 2 May

Clarke arrived—full of beans. Saw D'Ä. late p.m. He was in good spirits. He told me he had rec'd copy of Isvolsky's answer to Grey's Memo. on Russian proposals—and that he had informed Isvolsky that he was completely in accord with his éclaircissements and that as soon as England agreed he was ready to accept Russian proposals and instruct A. Hn. Amb'r at Const'ple to begin operations. I asked him 'what operations' and he told me that the situation was that Sultan's note prolonging mandates was still unanswered. The first step now would be a rather disagreeable one viz., to inform Sultan that the prolongation of Mandates was now unnecessary (as Financial delegates etc. were to enter Turkish service) and that the Powers had other things to propose. He said that the £300000 deficit ought to be wiped out at once (as it was formed by a debt contracted before present financial arrangements came into force) and that then he was certain that the Macedonian Revenues would be sufficient to pay both Civil Adm'n expenses and the troops considered necessary by the Sultan for Macedonia.

Crete. He had not seen our urgent note despatched on Wednesday last. I told him that we had fallen in with wishes of A.H.G. as regards Municipal Taxes and provisional nature of surtax: and I reminded him that he had promised me to make no difficulties about control—if we yielded on other points. He replied 'Mais certainement.'

[1] Egyptian Foreign Minister.

Friday 8 May

I left for Budapesth—had a quiet dinner with Twinkle at the club restaurant—and got to bed fairly early.

Saturday 9 May

Buda P.

Lunch at Twinkle's—Vambery[1] and Brüll.[2] Former fairly interesting but getting a touch old. He didn't attach much importance to Mohmaud[3] rising—but thinks Persia vulnerable spot in our Eastern policy. He *hates* the Anglo-Russian Entente. On the whole he was amusing but twaddled a good deal.

Races p.m. Saw lots of friends.

Sunday 10 May

Fine and hot

Heavy day. Lunch with Szaparys at Park Club—over a *hundred*. Unfortunately Archduke and Duchess were there and I had to sit next to latter: and I never find her a very free goer in the way of conversation.... The Hungarians are much easier to get on with than the Austrians and one gets to know them much more quickly....

Thursday 14 May

Budapesth to Vienna

Lunched with Polli Szaparys—very nice—and then Polli rattled me off to the station in his motor—and so ended a most charming visit—and I went back liking Hungarians better than ever. I did not go into the official world—but Wekerle wanted me to come to lunch or dine. Luckily I was engaged too deeply—as I want to keep out of party politics and make my visits purely social. Thus I had a rattling good time: the last *really* good time I shall have as I don't suppose Twinkle will be there next year. He is very low about his prospects—and he was not as jolly as usual. Arrived in Vienna to find much cooler weather and prospect of rain. Also found that King of Denmark[4] is coming to lunch on Saturday.

[1] Vambéry; Hungarian authority on eastern affairs; paid by the Foreign Office; see Hardinge to Goschen, 12 May 1908 (copy), H.P., 13.
[2] Consul, Budapest.
[3] Mahmud Shevket Pasha; Young Turk leader.
[4] Frederick VIII.

Saturday 16 May

King of Denmark to lunch. Found him rather careworn and not so jovial as of yore. . . .

Thursday 21 May

Messenger Mulloy—but Gregory took bags on to Cons'ple. Russo-Brit. Macedonian exchange of views dragging on slowly but hopefully. But to my, and Hardinge's great regret, I find that we have rather given way as regards our Financial Proposals, wh. I thought the strongest and most practical part of our Programme.[1]

Boss and I started for a few days at Tentschach.

Friday 22 May

Tentschach. Very hot and nice

Got up to Schloss at about 8. Everything looking too beautiful for words. Meadows carpeted with wild flowers—Lilacs and Horsechestnuts in full beauty. New Verwalter, Archau, a very fine looking man. . . . Did a lot of farming with him after breakfast—inspected all the beasts etc. . . .

Saturday 23 May

Tentschach

All over the place. Two farm colts gave me great pleasure—they have grown very well.

The new pigs—Yorkshire and Kärntner mixed—promise well. . . .

Monday 25 May

Came back from Tentschach with much regret—arriving 9.30 p.m. Found nothing going on.

Sunday 31 May

Church in the morning. Hechler had very long service and sermon to match. Mrs Carnegie[2] says she is going to desert to the Scotch Church.

[1] Hardinge to Goschen, 19 May 1908, H.P., 13.
[2] Wife of Councillor.

Wednesday 10 June

Throat and cough being bad sent for Chiari.[1] He says I have Bronchitis and musn't dream of going to the Festzug![2] What a bore—but I have felt this coming on for some time.

Friday 12 June

Dullish day—being quite alone in the house—everybody else having gone to the Festzug. Hear it was an enormous success—and a very touching sight for all who were near the Emperor.

Sunday 14 June

Cold better—boils worse. Then at 5 a.m. I had been reading in bed—and as I switched off light something happened—the wires touched—there was a short circuit—flames came out with a rush and burnt my left hand rather badly. Agony for about 2 hours—applied carbolicized Vasseline [sic] on Cotton Wool—and sent for Dr Franz. He appd. treatment and said I should not be able to use hand for about a week! I am a touch unlucky and down in the mouth for the moment.

Monday 15 June

Steed came to see me and told me some curious things after a rhapsody on the Festzug which was one of the finest things he had ever seen and which shewed, he said, that the 'Austrian idea' was still alive and that the country is far more patriotic than the newspapers would seem to indicate. He told me that he learns from a 'very good clerical source' that there is an idea, when Franz Ferdinand comes to the throne, of making his eldest son[3] Duke of Alsace-Lorraine and creating it a Duchy for that purpose. This is said to have been arranged between William and F.F. It is not impossible. From this side it would remove from Vienna a young man who, under the circumstances would be there in an extremely difficult position, and who might easily become a source of intrigue etc. Archd. Carl Joseph has been too long recognized as heir to the throne of A.H. to be passed over—and altogether the idea would suit here—I sh'd think. The advantage gained by W. is harder to see. It would strengthen the ties between Germany and Austria—if the eldest son of the Emperor was made a tributary German P'ce—a Catholic State w'd be ruled over by a Catholic Prince and but [sic] is this enough?

[1] Throat specialist.
[2] To celebrate the sixtieth anniversary of Franz Joseph's accession.
[3] Maximilian.

Emperor W. tried to borrow 15000000 kr. from Emp'r F.J. but only got 5 millions. Eulenburg[1] affair has disheartened Germans very much—one said the other day 'Germany ripened too quickly and is now running to seed'—he *wept*. Entry of D. of Cumberland's son[2] in Bavarian Army was arranged directly between D. of C. and Regent.[3] Emp'r W. had nothing to do with it.

Boutros Pasha came to lunch—also Slatin Pasha.[4] Former a fat Oriental with a twinkling eye: but we had to be civil to him because he is Teddie's chief in the Egyptian F.O.

Saturday 27 June

Boss left for Festetics....

Monday 29 June

I started for Kesthely[5]—boils and all and had a warm but pleasant journey—Festetics sending his little private saloon to Balaton. He met me at the Station and was very cordial and nice as they all were. Boss had *enjoyed* herself—to my great relief—at this beautiful place.

Thursday 2 July

Left beautiful Kesthely—having had a delicious and quiet time with these kind people.

Sunday 5 July

Boss and I came down to Tentschach.

Saturday 18 July

Came to Tentschach.... Twee arrived from Egypt on Thursday evening.

Tuesday 28 July

Left Vienna 9.20 a.m. Racketty train to Berlin—and just time to drive across the town and catch Copn. train. Twee in great spirits.

[1] Philipp zu Eulenburg; friend of Wilhelm II.
[2] Ernst August.   [3] Luitpold. Bavarian Prince-Regent.
[4] Inspector-General, Sudan.
[5] Keszthely; Festetics property by Lake Balaton.

Wednesday 29 July

Copenhagen. Fine and hot
  Nice journey from Berlin—beastly up till then. Found Cop'n but little changed—and we did all the old things—shopped a bit in Oestergade[1]—and walked in Langeline[2]—but this made me so homesick for yachting when I heard the ropes running through the blocks and all the nice old yachting noises—that I could scarcely stand it and begged Boss to remove me. Dear old Copenhagen—I still like it the best of all my posts.

Thursday 30 July

Arrived at Samsö[3] in fine warm but rather threatening weather.

Friday 31 July

Teddie's wedding day
  Samsö decorated with English and Danish flags as far as one could see....

Monday 3 August

Left dear old Samsö....

Tuesday 4 August

Arrived at Xtiana at 2.30. Were met by King Haakon's Equerry....[4]

Wednesday 12 August

Teck and I fully accoutred—joined the Royal Train[5] at Attnang.[6] Very soon the King sent for me and after a few words about Queen Maud and our visit to her—made an announcement which took my breath away and changed our lives. 'I am going to give you a bit of news about yourself—which I am afraid will not be very agreeable to you—but it is one of those things with wh. Diplomats have to put up! We are going to take you from Vienna—and send you to Berlin!

---

[1] Fashionable Street. [2] Promenade.
[3] The Goschens and 'Ted' had come to the island of Samsøe, for 'Ted' and Mary's wedding.
[4] The Goschen's were on their way to pay a visit to King Haakon and Queen Maud of Norway.
[5] Edward VII's. [6] Junction for Ischl.

I know you won't like this—but you must forget all that is disagreeable in it in the thought—that being sent to the most important post in Europe is a great honour and compliment!' I said that I was quite ready to serve H.M. at any place to which I might be sent—and tho' it *was* a great blow to me to leave a Post wh. I liked so much and where we had so many friends—I would do my utmost to give satisfaction to H.M. and H.M.G. 'I am sure you will,' and he beamed *most* kindly and benevolently on me. He added that he had already asked the German Emperor whether he w'd like to have me there—and that H.I.M. had expressed himself as *most* pleased with the choice and said very nice things about me. The King told Him that I was a good sportsman and fond of shooting—and the Emp'r said he w'd be sure to give me lots of it. (I hope at all events this will be true.) H.M. was kindness itself all through the interview and did what he could to gild the blackest and most nauseous of pills. I am fearfully depressed and unhappy about it and shudder when I think what Boss will [   ].[1]

Tuesday 15 September

Left[2] early for Tentschach: old Ted met me at the station and we had a jolly drive up. Found all well and Mary looking blooming and happy.

Sunday 1 November[3]

Church. Awfully long service tho' no sermon.

Tuesday 3 November

Farewell dinner at Avarna's. Not much fun as only dips. were there and all our Viennese friends are out of town.

Wednesday 4 November

Presented my letters of recall to the Emperor. He was most charming and while regretting that I left Vienna at a time when there was a slight cloud between our two countries, he said that England and Austria were such old friends that he was sure the clouds would soon roll by. He thanked me for all I had done to make things pleasant. He was quite delightful—and it is such a pity that, as is usually the

[1] Sentence unfinished.   [2] Caslolovitz.
[3] First entry since 15 Sept. However, Goschen was not at Tentschach all that time. See Introduction.

case with dips at Vienna—that one only gets to know Him when one goes away.

There was a State Banquet in the evening for the King of Greece to which I was invited. The Emperor and the King read speeches to each other—but the effect was much marred by the King of Greece being unable to read *his*. Had a turn up with D'Ä. who lost his temper dreadfully. He told me that we in England were incurring great responsibility by encouraging Serbs—I said that he was always talking of the responsibility of others whereas he was himself entirely responsible for the whole situation and the general unrest. He was furious and began to talk about the Boers and our treatment of them—for which I gave him snuff. He said 'If Russia wants war she shall have it!' and was white with rage. I was glad to have had it out with him for once.[1]

Went home where Boss was entertaining all the Embassy.

Thursday 5 November

Went to say goodbye to D'Ä. and found him all smiles. We had quite a pleasant interview—and no allusion was made on either side to last night.

Farewell dinner at Tschirschky's. Not much fun.

Friday 6 November

Hard work getting ready for our departure. Despatches—tearing ups—and visits all day. Pleasant farewell dinner at the Tecks—p.m. went and said goodbye to Me d'Ä., who was charming as usual. Also saw Crozier and Avarna.

Saturday 7 November

Left Vienna

Black Saturday. Worked up to last minute. Beau départ—but chiefly Dips. as all Austrians are out of town. Lots of beautiful flowers. Everybody was awfully nice, especially Avarna who seemed really sorry to lose us. Like all départs of that sort our time was taken up by the wrong people and we scarcely saw the dear Tecks—and could only say very perfunctory goodbyes to them. We had tears in our heart at leaving dear Vienna where we have had the 3 best years of our Dip. life.

Chirol[2] came to see me just before I started. He gave me to

[1] Cf. Steed, op. cit., i, p. 293.
[2] Head of Foreign Department, *The Times*.

understand that Isvolsky meant to tell Duma that he would protest against annexation at the Conference. If this is true there will be no Conference to protest before: as D'A. will certainly not go to Conference in that case. If there is no Conference it is probable that Servia and Montenegro may move. And if they move—no one can tell—where movement will stop.

Sunday 8 November

Arrived in Berlin—met by the Staff consisting of De Salis[1]—very nice tho' rather deaf—Mounsey,[2] Clark[3] and to my surprise an Honorary Att. of the name of Monck.[4] By whom —or at whose request app'td I know not. Very cold at Embassy.[5] Hosta went to the Adlon Hotel[6] where she is very comfortable. I stay here where I am *not* comfortable. Both Boss and I much depressed—we don't like the House—and we miss our Vienna. Lunched and dined at Adlon—pretty good—and fussed about the House; but I slept chiefly having had no sleep at all in the train.

The Casablanca affair is the topic of the day.

Monday 9 November

Called on Kiderlen-Wächter[7] who is pro tem Min. of F.A. vice Schön[8] ill! It is a great drawback for me that Schön is away—but this man received me very nicely; though he didn't know either when Bülow or Emperor would be able to receive me. I needn't have come here so soon—as I can't do anything till rec'd. House getting warmer.

Tuesday 10 November

Cambon[9] came in for a minute and told me that he was on his way to sign the arbitration agreement with reference to the Casablanca Deserters. This puts an end to a very simple question wh. bid fair at one time to give rise to very serious complications.

It is extraordinary that the two questions which have of late caused so much excitement and even created fears of general war—have been such trifles. A general war because of a few deserters from the French Foreign Legion in Morocco—or because Servia is refused compensation for having lost nothing except a dream—would look pretty silly

---

[1] Councillor.   [2] 3rd secretary.   [3] 3rd secretary.
[4] Later Goschen's private secretary.   [5] Wilhelmstrasse 70.
[6] Adjoining the Embassy.   [7] German Minister, Bucharest.
[8] Now Secretary of State.   [9] Jules Cambon, French Ambassador.

when history came to be written! Cambon seems a nice man—but rather an old Frowst—like most French dips. of the present day.

Private financial look out—poor to *very* medium. Our books on leaving Vienna were simply frightful.

Wednesday 11 November

Boss left[1]—and it is very lonely and beastly without her. We dined together first and then puffed comfortably off to the train in a taxi. She left at 9.25.

Great debate[2] on *D.T.* interview,[3] which has irritated Germans awfully. The poor Emperor seems to have meant well—but he has offended everybody. England because he said that the great majority of his people hated us and that he amongst all Germans was almost our only friend. The French and Russians because he divulged their wishes to intervene in the Boer War—His own subjects because he said he had furnished the plan of campaign by which we eventually defeated the Boers—and the Japs because he indicated that his fleet might some day be used against them.

People are rabid here as they say he has made them ridiculous before the whole world. Bülow had to stand up and say something. Everybody is down on him too. The Conservatives say that he has said too much—the others that he said too little—and it appears that the Emperor is very angry with him too. He will probably have to go sooner or later.

The line the debate took was that everyone has had enough of the 'Personal' régime of the Emperor.

Thursday 12 November

Felt wormy owing to rain coming on. Dined at Hegermanns.[4] There were there Duke of Drachenberg[5]—and his wife—sister of Benckendorff[6]—both nice—Count Seckendorf[7]—Knesebeck—Introducteur des Amb'rs—who gave me useful information: a clever Mlle de Bunsen[8]—whom I took into dinner and who talked me to death: and our 3rd Secretary, Clark. It was rather interesting to talk

[1] For England.   [2] In Reichstag, 10 and 11 Nov. 1908.
[3] *Daily Telegraph*, 28 Oct. 1908.   [4] Danish Minister and wife.
[5] Duke of Trachenberg; Silesian landowner; head of Hatzfeldt family; chief cup-bearer to King of Prussia.
[6] Now Russian Ambassador in London.
[7] Seckendorff; formerly Grand Master of the Court and confidential adviser to Empress Frederick.
[8] Presumably a relative of Maurice de Bunsen. The German branch of the family naturally used the form 'von Bunsen'.

to Drachenberg about the *Daily Telegraph* Interview—the debate on it and the fury of the entire Press with the Emperor. I had a good Danish talk with Miss Hegermann....

Friday 13 November

Kiderlen-Wächter came to see me p.m. Pansa[1] a.m. Latter wants me to ask Bülow when I see him whether the two Emperors at their late meeting discussed probabilities of War. Kiderlen was quite interesting and agreeable—but did not refer to his fiasco in the Interview debate—when he was put up to defend Ministry of F.A. for having 'passed' Interview for publication—and was hooted and laughed at the whole time. Schön was well out of it. Kiderlen had on the same waistcoat (yellow) which excited the hilarity of the House. At 7 p.m. I went to see Bülow. He gave me a most charming reception—and talked for an hour without stopping. But in all his talk—there was devilish little to carry away with one—tho' I faked a long despatch out of it.[2] His most interesting remark that it was Isvolsky who started Ährenthal on the annexation by suggesting that if Ä. w'd support Russia in question of Dardanelles—he would support Ä. if he put into execution the much talked of project of annexation!! He was very civil about England and praised attitude of H.M.G. and Press as regards 'Interview' affair. He was glad my arrival coincided with better relations between the two countries. I enjoyed the interview but it was rather 'thin' when I came to analyse it.

Saturday 14 November

Cambon came to see me for a moment and we talked a bit. He tells me that now I shan't see P'ce Bülow again for ages. In fact he says this is an impossible place for Diplomatists. One goes to the Min'y of For. Affairs—sees Schön—and if one asks him anything really important—he says he must speak to Bülow—the latter says to Schön probably that he must refer the matter to the Emperor—and between the three the diplom't gets no answer at all. It is a higgelty-piggelty arrangement and reminds one of the time in Const'ple when Diplomats were the shuttlecocks and the Grand Vizier and the Sultan held the battledores.

But Cambon told me one very funny story, told to him by Bülow about the old Russian Amb'r Ostensacken,[3] who is a Russian Courtier of the old—very old—school.

---

[1] Italian Ambassador.
[2] Goschen to Grey, 12 Nov. 1908, *B.D.*, vi, no. 134.
[3] Osten-Sacken.

Bülow and Ostensacken were speaking of the Czar Nicolas the 1st. B. said that he admired him—but that he had been of a cold unsymp. nature. 'Never were you so mistaken,' cries O. 'He was the kindest hearted man in the world.' To exemplify this O. said that the Emp'r Nicolas had insisted on O's younger brother—a very delicate lad being sent to the Pages' school—tho' the boy's mother said it would be the death of him. B. didn't see much kind heartedness in this— and asked how the boy got on. O. replied 'Oh he died after being two months at the school—but the Emperor sent one of his Aide-de-camps to attend the funeral.'!!!

Sunday 15 November

Poor Sir Henry Bergne[1] died last night of Pneumonia. He had been here to attend the Copyright Conference.

Mounsey lunched with me. In the afternoon I went and had tea with Mrs Heath—the Naval Attaché's wife—who has two buxom daughters not out yet. She seemed quite nice. De Salis dined with me—and then we went and paid a visit to the redoubtable Princess Razowill[2]—Countess Betka Potocka's[3] Mother—who sits up every night. I liked her—she talks well—has a bitter tongue—and rather a nice face. She looked very young.

They are all very angry with the Emperor. Betka had evidently given me a good character and I was well received.[4]

Monday 16 November

Dined with Cambon. Prince Arenberg[5]—a young Neipperg[6] (Montenuovo[7])—two Secretaries. Quite a nice little evening—tho' not exciting.

Thursday 19 November

Lunched with Ostensacken, Russ. Amb'r—De Salis and secretaries. I liked the Ambassador—but not the Conseiller[8]—much. I thought him loud and familiar. But de Salis says he isn't a bad chap.

[1] Former superintendent, Commercial Department, Foreign Office.
[2] Princess Marie Radziwill; French-born wife of Polish landowner.
[3] Goschen had known her in Vienna.
[4] The Princess formed a favourable impression of Goschen. See her letter to Robilant of 17 Nov. 1908, Radziwill, op. cit., iv, p. 48.
[5] Of the von Marck family.   [6] Well-known Austrian family.
[7] Montenuovo was descended from Adam Adalbert Count Neipperg and Marie Louise.
[8] Boulatzell.

Friday 20 November

Was received in Audience by the Emperor. Not much of a show. Had to find my own way to the station here—at least I was to have—but Knesebeck the Introducer of Ambassadors gave me a lift. At Potsdam there was an open calèche with four horses for me—and rather dowdy coupés for the staff. How different from Vienna. Palace at Potsdam built by Frederick the Gt and exactly as it was. The Hall into wh we were shewn—was a study in shells! Very curious—oyster shells—mussel shells—every shell one can imagine. But there were some fine stag heads on stands down the centre of the room. Well I was shown into a long room with the Emperor standing at the far end—nearly. I bowed and bowed and bowed. But he had his Overlord face on—and never moved a muscle—not a smile, not a movement of any sort. He might have been cut out of stone. I handed him my letters with the usual words. Still not a sign—so I had to make a speech. When I had finished, at last he broke into a genial smile—shook me warmly by the hand and gave me a nice cheery welcome to Vienna [*sic*] saying all sorts of nice things. But I shall never forget those first 5 minutes. It was appalling and I nearly choked over my little speech. Afterwards I presented the Staff—I thought him genial—as he chaffed them about being young and told the burly Heath that he looked more like a football player than a golfer. But the Staff told me that for him he was depressed. Afterwards I was received by the Empress[1]—who looked very nice and has a charming manner. She was very gracious and kind. Then back. No lunch[2] altho' the time fixed was between 12.30 and 1!!![3]

Saturday 21 November

Emperor made a speech in the Town Hall—and instead of making an extempore speech as usual—he read it from a manuscript which Bülow handed him—and which he returned to the Chancellor after read.[4] This is regarded as the first step in breaking away from the Personal Regime.

Sunday 22 November

Bad
Lunched with Cambon to meet Monsieur Fauré the French composer—a very nice man, and Mrs Maddison an English woman who also composes—a sort of rival of Ethel Smythe's—but softer and better

---

[1] Augusta; daughter of the Augustenburg claimant.
[2] 'No lunch' in large letters in MS.   [3] See also Introduction.
[4] Words from 'which' onwards in large letters in MS.

looking. She *may* turn out rather a bore. She has already let me in
for a concert and a matinée. I believe her past has been a trifle stormy:
at present she adores Fauré who is indeed a nice old man. Me Car-
bonell sang some of Fauré's songs prettily enough in a little thin
French voice and way. No news. But Turk[1] called on me in the evening.
He told me that neither Bulg'n nor Austro-H'n negotiations with Turkey were going on well. He said that d'Ä.'s coup had been a violent
blow at the new Constitut'l movement. He added in answer to a
question from me—That there was no revolutionary party properly
so called—but of course there were reactionary individuals, who had
lost places and pickings by the new movement. All would go well if
they c'd only get money—as if soldiers and employés were paid—
wh. they had never been under the old system—they would plump
for the new system. But money was hard to get. (I find it so too!)
He is all for Centralisation at first and then Decentralisation afterwards.

I don't like him—but he seems clever. He has a nasty cunning face
and is not my idea of an Ott. Turk.

Monday 23 November

Rain all day

First—Deputation of British Working Men—then Chinese funeral
service for late Emperor[2] and Empress.[3] (The Chinamen looked funny
all in black—white is their real mourning colour.) It was also funny
that one signed one's name in two books, one for the dead Empress—
the other for the dead Emperor.

Then lunch with Cambon—almost alone—after lunch Bülow's
doctor came in. He said Bülow required a rest—but said he was
bothered with many things amongst them the 'America' Interview
of which a sample has been given by the American *World*.

It is stated to be false—and I should think it was as it says amongst
other things that the Emperor said to Hale[4] that when England was
thoroughly beaten as she would be in the next war—He meant to
satisfy himself with Egypt! I think this stamps the thing as I am sure
he never said that. But again other parts of the interview sound fairly
correct. But I expect we shall know soon as I look upon all these false
interviews as a prelude to the publishing of the real one. But I believe
the Germans have paid pretty heavily to have it not published. But
the Doctor's remark rather sounds as if they were nervous about it.

Jap Ambassador[5] called—not so nice as Uchida[6] but cleverer—I
sh'd think. He has a disagreeable voice.

[1] Nizami Pasha; Turkish Ambassador.   [2] Kuang Hsu.
[3] Tzu Hsi.   [4] American journalist.   [5] Sutemi Chiuda.
[6] Japanese Ambassador, Vienna.

Friday 27 November

Went to Kiderlen's reception at M'y of F.A. I talked to him about the Near East. In fact I went to get his answer as to giving Turkey an assurance that no compensation would be given to Servia and Montenegro at her expense. Of course they wouldn't. K. said that it would be no use as the Conference was such a long way off and probably it wouldn't be held at all. I said that the assurance was meant to smooth the road to the Conference and then he said 'Well we don't care tuppence whether a Conference is held or not.' I asked him whether it was indifferent to the German Gov't whether such burning questions as Ährenthal's action had raised were left indefinitely open or not: whether they didn't care tuppence about the dangers that might ensue? But all I could get out of him was that a Conf'ce might be advantageous, but was not necessary. I couldn't agree with him as to my mind a Conference which w'd regularize the situation and ratify any understandings come to between Turkey, A.-Hy. and Bulgaria is essential to the future peace of Europe.

(I wonder whether *we* are as keen about the Conference as we used to be—I can't quite make out.)

Sunday 29 November

Arranged books—a dirty job. Dined in the evening with the Schwabachs[1] (Bleichröders[2]) our extremely rich Consul General.[3] A good dinner and a pretty table. But people rather stiff—not meaning to be so—but so few people in so many gorgeous rooms. Dinner was—Schwabach's sister and brother in law—C't Seckendorff—Bassermann the National Liberal Leader[4] (and an old enemy of England in his younger days) a man whose name I didn't catch—Count Bernstorff[5] (in great spirits at having been made Amb'r in Washington) and a very nice American woman Mrs Belknap[6]—wife of the American Mil. Att.[7] to whom I froze—when I got bored with the others. She was very nice and talkative.

I shall be curious to see how I shall like the Schwabachs. At all events it was nice of them to ask me to dinner.

Monday 30 November

Seckendorff came to see me and we had a long talk. He is miserable about present state of affairs—and evidently hates Bülow—he says

[1] See Introduction.
[2] Bank; Schwabach was a partner.
[3] Honorary.
[4] Since 1904.
[5] Hitherto, Consul-General, Cairo.
[6] Belnap.
[7] Naval attaché.

that he ought to have defended the Emperor more—he *ought* to have pointed out all the great services H.M. has rendered Germany during the last 20 years: and not been so half hearted: but S. hinted that he didn't *wish* to show the Emperor in a good light and wanted to stand well with Parliament: and found great fault with his 'assurance' it consisted of mere phrases which everyone could twist and turn as they liked. He thinks the Emperor is surrounded by a bad set who flatter and don't restrain. He doesn't approve (I don't quite know why) of the visit of the King and Queen:[1] but I fancy that he thinks the Emperor will overdo it—and put himself wrong with his sub-jects—who will think he is cringing to England. He thinks the visit is forced—but that if it had been arranged in a friendly way when the Emperor was in England last it would have been a different thing. *Now Reval intervenes.* He hopes in any case that the visit will be as short as possible. He is funny about it—and said he would like, if the King wished it, to go over and talk it over with him. On one point he is quite clear—viz. that there is absolutely no doubt that the Emperor was right when he said that he stood almost alone in His Empire as a lover of England! *That* was true. His advice to me was to be stiff and reserved and not be intimate with any one. Certainly not with H.I.M.

Saturday 12 December

Left for England....

Monday 14 December

London
Comfortable journey....

Tuesday 15 December

Saw Charley Harding[2] at F.O. He advised me to go and see Asquith—who had expressed wish to see me.

Thursday 17 December

Shopped about. Afternoon hunted Grey without success but saw Hardinge (and Lady Hardinge) and Asquith. Latter seemed to me solid and sound—but with vaguish ideas on the subject of Foreign Politics.

[1] Planned for 1909.
[2] Hardinge; Goschen appears to have got over his previous rancour.

1909

*The Goschens returned to Berlin early in 1909. They took holidays at Tents-
chach in May and October. In November Goschen spent a few days in London.
Apart from an excursion to Brunswick he was in Berlin for the rest of the year.*

Tuesday 9 February[1]

King and Queen's arrival

−8°. G.C. of Red Eagle

Got up at 6.30. Weather cold—*very*—and foggy—but promising
to be bright. Went off to meet the King at Rathenow[2]—with Foreign
Suite. General Loewenfeldt,[3] Admiral Usedom[4] (nice) Gen'l v. Marschall[5]—and Trench[6] went with me. Beastly cold at Rathenow. King's
train came in too early and for once in His life the King was not ready.[7]
However the Band struck up God save the King and then we civilians
had to stand while the King got ready—the Bands playing the Nat.
Anthem about 50 times over. The King then came out tightly but-
toned up in German Dragoon Uniform with an enormous wadded
cloak. He walked up and down the Guards of Honour and then got
into the train. He sent for me at once and I had some talk with H.M.
But He did not look well—the perspiration simply streamed off his
head and he coughed a lot. After a bit He sent for Hardinge to let
me know their views about Holleben[8] and his peace society address—
and then while we were talking went off to sleep *twice*. Rather alarming I thought. Hardinge was much against His rec'g Holleben—who
he said had worked ag'st us when he was Ger'n Amb. at Washington—and had worried Pauncefote[9] into his grave. We shall have
trouble with him I expect. Some confusion at the Berlin Station—
as the Royal Train came in both too soon and pulled up wrong—
so that the Emperor and the Imp'l Family had to run! Cordial greetings—and then we separated from the others and drove to the Schloss
in the rear of the Procession. The sun shone and the U. den Linden
looked pretty—but the Guns frightened the horses of the Queen's carriage—one fell—and H.M. and the Empress had to get out. We
lunched at home and then Schön appeared bringing me the Grand

---

[1] First entry since 17 Dec. 1908. [2] Brandenburg frontier station.
[3] Lieutenant-General von Loewenfeld. [4] Vice-Admiral.
[5] Major-General. [6] Military attaché.
[7] According to Ponsonby (op. cit., p. 255), there had been a misunderstanding about
the time.
[8] Former German Ambassador in Washington.
[9] Former Ambassador in Washington. Goschen had served under him as secretary,
1893–4.

Cross of the Red Eagle—wh. I was to put on at the Banquet in the evening. I had a nice place at the Banquet—between Lady Antrim[1] (very nice) and P'cess Solms.[2] Speeches cordial—but banales—King read His speech[3] much better than the Emperor: ringing out the word 'Frieden'.

Wednesday 10 February

Heavy day. Rathaus in the morning: where everything was well arranged—the long staircase was a bore but it had to be surmounted and the King got up all right tho' somewhat blown by the time he got to the top. However there were men singing glees[4] in a gallery so H.M. had time to get his breath before he was called upon to utter. The Burgomaster,[5] in consequence of my request beforehand—made a very short speech—and then after begging the King to drink a glass of German wine (Steinberger Cabinet '68) from the hands of a German maiden—called his daughter who handed him the wine in a golden goblet. The King said a few suitable words—then more glees— Robin Adair etc.—and then while the K. visited the rooms I dashed home in order that I might be there in time to receive their Majesties. Queen arrived early—(same time as new carpet wh. we hadn't time to put down!) looking charming—passed Her on to Boss. Then King came—presented Staff—and then He came into my room a bit where I had prepared Him a *Bower* in my inner Chamber! Then He and Queen rec'd the English deputation—who were much touched by Their Majesties' kindness. They read their address (drawn up by me) and K. read His (drawn up by Hardinge).

Then lunch and I had a $\frac{1}{4}$ hr. hard work presenting people. All Amb'rs and wives—two Staffs—and Suites—Dukes and duchesses of Ratibor,[6] Trachenberg,[7] Princes of Fürstenberg[8]—Salm-Salm[9]— Pless[10]—Princess Radziwill, *Bülows* and Schöns etc. 72 head! Lunch good and my placing was much approved. The little Archduchess Salm-Salm[11] sat on one side King—Princess Bülow on other and they kept Him alive. P'ce Bülow and Szögeny[12] sat each side of Queen. Boss had Trachenberg and Fürstenberg and I Duchess of Trachenberg and P'cess Fürstenberg. After lunch while talking to Daisy Pless[13]

[1] Lady of the Bedchamber.   [2] Lady-in-waiting.
[3] In German.   [4] 'Gott grüsse dich.'   [5] Kirchner.
[6] Silesian landowners; she was a lady-in-waiting.
[7] Previously referred to as 'Drachenberg'.
[8] Grand Master of the Court; friend of Wilhelm II.
[9] Westphalian landowner.   [10] Silesian landowner.
[11] Strictly, 'Princess Salm-Salm'.
[12] Szögyény-Marich; Austro-Hungarian Ambassador. Goschen had much difficulty with the spelling of this name.
[13] Princess of Pless; English by birth; *née* Cornwallis-West; for an interesting account of the King's visit see her *Daisy Princess of Pless* (1928), p. 173.

King lost consciousness for a few seconds! Awful! However he recovered almost directly and called for a fresh cigar! I was frightened. He was alright directly we unbuttoned his tight mil. collar. He came into my room before He went away—said everything had gone off admirably—and that the only fault had been that the room was hot—but it wasn't as a matter of fact. It was bronchitis and smoke that had made him ill. In the evening there was a Court Ball—very lugubrious to my mind—but of course a pretty sight. The King looked ill and tired—the Queen brilliant. Hardinge told me he had had his eye on the King when he felt bad—that H.M. had certainly lost consciousness for about 30 seconds—and that He, Hardinge, had thought that it was all over and that H.M. was dead! How *awful* to think of. We both agreed that we were very anxious about him and shouldn't be happy until we get them back to England.

Thursday 11 February

The King lunched with His Regiment[1]—happily it all went off well and the King made a nice little speech. I saw Him in the p.m. and He said he was better—but confessed to being tired. He therefore asked me to try to arrange that the Cercle after the Gala Opera should be cut short. This I did—and it *was* cut short. The Gala performance was *Sardanapolus*.[2] Not very interesting—music poor and orchestra very mediocre. But House very pretty and brilliant. I never saw the Queen look so splendid as she did at the Cercle—everybody was in ecstasy about her. The Emperor told me afterwards that He had no idea that She took such an interest in things—that she had asked the most intelligent questions, wh. seemed to *surprise* Him.

Friday 12 February

Cold and bright

Took Mrs Ponsonby p.m. to see Fritz—waited for hours as was with the King. Only saw him for a few minutes but she had time to get his permission to go to Paris. We had just time to get home and go to the Station to see Their Majesties off. King looked very stuffy and seedy—and moreover the Prussian Uniform and especially the Prussian Pickelhauber[3] is too small for his expansive head. He thanked everyone who had done things for Him at the Embassy—but He rather forgot to thank *me* who had all the work and responsibility. Well—He was ill poor man. But I do hope he will get well soon—

[1] 1st Dragoon Guards.
[2] The Kaiser himself was responsible for this work.
[3] Pickelhaube.

as he rather alarms me—and He would be such an irreparable loss if He was to pass away.

Saturday 20 February

Went to Schoen and asked Germany to join us in making representation at Vienna.[1] He said, as I had of course foreseen, that he had every sympathy with the step—that they were considering it and would learn the Emperor's decision tomorrow—when he would give me definite reply. He said the same to Cambon and Ostensacken. Cambon saw Bülow afterwards upon another affair—and Bülow said that in principle he agreed with our move—but that it was difficult to join without offending Ährenthal. He was going to talk it over with the Emperor—and perhaps a form might be found!

Tuesday 23 February

Went to see *Henry IV* with the Emperor and Empress—there was also P'ce Friedrich Wilhelm[2] in the box. A most interesting and thorough performance—costumes most correct and handsome. Emperor asked my opinion of the German rendering. I said that in the way the Germans did it the *Play* gained rather—and there was perhaps more lucidity—in fact it was like a very high class modern Play.

Monday 1 March

H.R.H. that nice little Princess Alice of Teck—and her husband came to lunch. She *is* a jolly little thing.

Monday 15 March

Baddish news from the Near East—Servia's note[3] having been very badly rec'd both here and at Vienna.[4] War seems very likely—and *yet* I can't believe it will come—it would be too foolish. There seems to be some idea that it may be localised: but I am afraid of the Russian Slavs. If they chip in—then Germany will have to move and then France: but we I expect will be very doubtful starters. Bülow said to Cambon, 'We must localize hostilities if they occur: it would never do if we were to begin cutting each other's throats.' Cambon said,

---

[1] As instructed by Grey; see Grey to Goschen, 18 Feb. 1909, *B.D.*, v, no. 583.
[2] The Crown Prince.
[3] Of 10 March 1909.
[4] It did not recognize the annexation of Bosnia-Hercegovina.

'Tout de même il ne faut pas que vous coupiez la gorge aux autres (Russes).'!!

Very pleasant dinner at the Palace—but we arrived a bit late! Nice music after dinner—and tremendous conferences going on all over the room. The Emperor didn't say a word of politics to me—but he told Cambon that it was France with whom rested the question war or not war: as if France didn't lend Russia money—latter could not go to war.

Cambon did not make the obvious retort.

Saturday 27 March

Agreement arrived at between Cartwright[1] and Ahrenthal upon Form of Note to be addressed [   ][2]

Sunday 28 March

by Servia to Austria. The papers here says [sic] that 'England has accepted Austria's formula unreservedly': this is not so—as the formula now arranged is a compound of the two—but Grey has been more lenient than he would have been, because he has learnt that Austria *desires* war—therefore he has tried to avoid all excuse [   ].[3]

Wednesday 14 April

Had a dinner party at home—3 Szögenyis—3 Pansas. . . .

Much discussion with regard to the military revolt in Turkey: but it is early days to foresee the results. It seems directed against the Young Turks Committee—who have swollen heads. If the result is the doing away of the present 'incognito' Gov't—it will, in my opinion, do no harm. But if it is an Islamite movement it may prove serious. Macedonia may break out again: Bulgaria seeing Turkey in a state of chaos may want to use her efficient army for getting a slice of Macedonia—or a bit of Servia—in fact the whole dangerous E. Question may be revived—and we may yet have a lively summer.

Tuesday 20 April

Did Schoen's official reception day. Nizamy Pasha appeared again (as the Young Turks are getting the best of it). He held forth a great deal and said that there would be no effusion de sang et que rien

---

[1] Goschen's successor in Vienna.
[2] Entry continued on following page; 28 March 1909 was in fact the correct date.
[3] No full stop in MS.; sentence unfinished.

ne sera changé. On which of course old Szögenyi asked 'Et le Sultan?'
Nizamy turned the question by saying that no one knew yet *who* was
responsible for the revolt. He bragged a lot about the manner in which
the Committee had moved up 40000? troops from Salonica in a few
days without disturbing the ordinary train service. It must be
admitted that they have been pretty smart.

Thursday 22 April

Lady Nicolson[1]—Guen[2] and her governess arrived.

Young Turks seem to be having it all their own way and have surrounded Const'ple.

Nothing going on here. Cambon has come back—he tells me that
he has refused to be present at a lecture to be given by d'Estournelles[3]
(the French peace man and F'h representative at last Hague Conference) on 'a rapprochement between France and Germany a
guarantee of the peace of the World'. He is furious—he says a lecture
of that sort is fearfully ill timed at a moment when Germany is doing
all she knows to split up the Triple Entente.

Lady N. says that Nico thinks Isvolsky will stay on: but my information is that he won't and that he will go to Madrid. Nico thinks his
going bad for our Entente—and he would like us to go further in the
direction of an alliance. 'Not my place—Sir.'

Friday 23 April

Announced to Schoen that we were recognizing Independence of
Bulgaria. He said that he wished they could too—but as they hadn't
seen the Turco-Bulgar Protocol and therefore didn't know whether
the Railway part of it was satisfactory they had to wait a little. But
they would make no difficulties.

Pansas dined as they are old colleagues of Lady Nico's.

Sultan's fate still undecided—Schön thinks Young Turks will make
a great mistake if they hurt him and even if they depose him. In their
place *I* sh'd keep him on—*I think*—but he is a wily old devil and I
suppose, if kept on, he will be always trying to get back his Power.
But it is marvellous to me how such a clever man can have miscalcu-
lated the strength of the Young Turks so much.

[1] Wife of Arthur Nicolson, now Ambassador in St Petersburg.
[2] The Nicolsons' daughter.
[3] Former French diplomat; winner of Nobel Peace Prize, 1909.

Saturday 24 April

Very fine and warm

Got off a rather empty messenger. Sir Hubert Jerningham[1] turned up and lunched. He talked to me a lot about combination which he seems to think Germany and Austria are trying to bring about—*after* death of Francis Joseph by 3 Empire Alliance—by which Russia is to have a free hand Const'ple way—Austria Salonika way and Germany Trieste. I had not time to point out all the difficulties namely that Austria would never give up Trieste without a war—that Russia would never allow (if she c'd help it) Austria to go to Salonica—so that the only gainer would be Germany. But of course I have no doubt but that Germany is trying to detach Russia from us and France. This may happen if Isvolsky goes and Goremekin[2] comes in—but the Czar seems very firm for the Triple Entente.

Lady Nicolson, Guen and Miss Parminter[3] departed at 10.30 p.m. but I went to a Beethoven Concert directed by Mottl.[4] The VII Symphony was splendidly played.

Heavy fighting going on at Constantinople: situation is still very obscure—and nothing seems decided about the Sultan.

Tuesday 27 April

The Sultan Abdul Hamid dethroned today and Reshad Effendi[5] proclaimed in his place under the title of Mohammed IV.[6] No news yet as to what becomes of the old one. I foresee troubles both in Macedonia where Bulgarian and Greek Bands are making a reappearance—and more especially in Asia where they cannot have much sympathy for the Young Turks. Should there be, which is not impossible, a Jehad—it is a bad look out for us in India and Egypt—and for the French in Morocco. But I hope I am wrong.

Dined with the Hills.[7] I do not often dislike people—but I cannot stand Mrs Hill. She is the very worst kind of boastful American.

Presented the 'Mt. Mfumbiro'[8] delegates—Colonel Close[9] and Captain Behrens[10]—to Schön. Latter took gloomy view of Eastern Affairs. I think the Germans are sorry Genl. von der Goltz[11] has given such good military instruction to Young Turks.

---

[1] Former member of Diplomatic Service; former colonial governor.
[2] Russian Prime Minister, 1906.   [3] Governess.
[4] Director, Munich Opera.   [5] Abdul Hamid II's brother.
[6] Muhammad V.   [7] He was United States Ambassador.
[8] The Mfumbiro (or Virunga) Mountains in East-Central Africa.
[9] Head of geographical section, War Office.
[10] Royal Engineers.   [11] Instructor, Turkish Army.

Saturday 8 May

Started for Tentschach....

Sunday 9 May

Tentschach
Not such a bad journey on the whole—anyhow we were so glad
to get to dear old Tentschach that we didn't mind anything....

Thursday 14 May

Farm—Kegel—but no walk owing to rain.

Wednesday 6 October[1]

Our dear children, Twee and Mary, left having enjoyed their stay
as they always do....

Sunday 10 October

Bunt and I left Tentschach.

Tuesday 12 October

Went to Schön's day and had a talk with him. He didn't say
much—as he wished me to see the Chancellor[2] first. He doesn't seem
to me quite so keen as B. Hollweg: perhaps owing to his diplomatic
experiences he sees more difficulties.

Thursday 14 October

Had a long talk with Chancellor which was supposed to be an in-
formal preliminary conversation. But I did not see much informality
about it—as Schön was present as short hand writer and tried to take
down every word—and the Chancellor made a long set speech. S.
reported *him* correctly—as well he might—but he made fearful gar-
bage of what I said: and I had to correct his report freely. This is
a new departure in diplomacy and I didn't much like it.

---

[1] First entry since 14 May; however, Goschen was not at Tentschach all that time,
as his correspondence shows.
[2] Bethmann Hollweg; Bülow's successor.

Friday 15 October

S. came round and I revised Procès verbal—wrote a long explanatory desp.[1] for the Messenger—and altogether both I and the Chancery had a heavy day. I had a talk with Schoen and by dint of badgering got some important things out of him with regard to what B. Hollweg called 'a relaxation in the tempo' of shipbuilding. His ideas seem to be fairly sound but I ha' me doots. If they stick to their present programme an arrang't. is difficult.

Tuesday 2 November

Got a tel. from Twee[2] announcing the fact that I am a grandfather and that Mary has a little girl.

Saturday 6 November

Left for England via Hook of Holland. . . .

Sunday 7 November

Arrived at 40 Portman Square.[3]. . .

Monday 8 November

Went to F.O. and had preliminary talk with Hardinge—Grey being away. H. had not seen my desp.[4] yet—so we couldn't go into things much. . . .

Friday 19 November

Back to Berlin.

Sunday 12 December

Teddie Seymour went away—quite satisfied with regard to Richard's health. He is a nice chap and it was a great blessing having him here.

Monday 13 December

Sir E. Cassel[5] arrived on Bagdad business. Before I saw him I saw

[1] Goschen to Grey with enclosure, and to Hardinge, 15 Oct. 1909, B.D., vi, nos. 200–1.
[2] In Cairo.   [3] Clarke's residence.
[4] Goschen to Grey, 4 Nov. 1909, B.D., vi, no. 204.
[5] Wealthy London banker; native of Cologne.

Cambon—who was rather excited and said that he was under impression that England, France and Germany were working together in this business—and now it appeared that Cassel had come out here to negotiate—he did not think it 'quite gentlemanlike'. I soothed him down but I was rather in an awkward position as I didn't know whether the French Govt. had been spoken to on the subject tho' I thought it rather likely they had—as Grey had certainly exchanged views with Isvolski—and the latter had not been best pleased.

Tuesday 14 December

Saw Schön—who said that it didn't follow that if Cassel and Gwinner[1]—came to an agreement that the Imp'l Gov't would consent to it—at all events at once! And he gave me to understand that they would want a Quid pro Quo from us—before they consented. He says without this the Gov't couldn't face the Reichstag. The alleged inability to face that assembly or public opinion unless they can show that they have done some one in the eye and got the best of a bargain —has become chronic.

Wednesday 15 December

Went to Brunswick for marriage of Prince Regent[2] to P'cess Elizabeth Stolberg Rossla.[3] Had to get up at 5.30. Train at 7. Pansa and Szögenyi and I. Changed into uniform in the train and arrived just in time to be in our seats in the Cathedral at 11.30 a.m. Such a gem the said 'Dom' dating from the time of Henry the Lion. Everything beautifully warmed. We had places in the choir—and had a splendid view of the wedding procession. The Emperor headed it with the Grand Duchess Marie Paulovna[4] (whom I was glad to see but could have no speech with). Then came King Ferdinand with the Empress—Gd. D. of Mecklenburg[5] with Queen of Bulgaria[6]—and heaps of Mecklenburgers and Reuss-es.[7] Also Grand Dukes Boris and André.[8] Afterwards a short court when we congratulated the happy pair. She about 20[9] and he 50[10] à peu près. Then an excellent lunch at wh. I was very lucky as I sat next to the nicest and prettiest woman there—Mme de Bülow—wife of the Prussian Minister there. On the other side I had the youngest sister of the Bride—about 14. After

---

[1] Director, Deutsche Bank.
[2] Duke Johann Albrecht of Mecklenburg-Schwerin; Regent of Brunswick in the enforced absence of the Duke of Cumberland.
[3] Princess Elisabeth of Stolberg-Rossla.   [4] Sister of the Regent.
[5] Mecklenburg-Schwerin.   [6] Queen Eleonora; née Reuss.
[7] The Mecklenburg-Schwerin and Reuss families were related.
[8] Cousins of Nicholas II.   [9] Born 1885.   [10] Born 1857.

lunch—which lasted till 4—scurry for the train and back to Berlin again. Acquaintances made—von Klenke the Brunswick Minister of State[1] (very nice) his wife (poor to medium), the reigning Princess Reuss[2] and a Princess Charlotte of Reuss? Heavy but not bad day.

[1] Von Klencke; Marshal of the Court.   [2] Princess Elise.

1910

The Goschens were in Berlin for most of the early months of 1910. In April Goschen paid a brief visit to Neustrelitz. In May he went to London for the funeral of Edward VII. Early in August and again in November he spent a few days at Trachenberg, in Silesia. On 20 December he left for a short stay in England.

Saturday 1 January

New Year's Day—not a good day to start the year with. Too much uniform and too many visits. Went in 'Gala' to the Schloss in the morning—Georg and Paul[1] looking rather noble behind the coach. Ours is the quietest looking turn-out—tho' I think the neatest. Emperor in good form—he bullied me about the Speeches in England—and said 'Not much of the Peace and Good Will over there such as we expect at this Season. You have all gone mad and you seem to think that I am always standing with my battle-axe behind me waiting for an opportunity to strike.' He said what amazed him most was that the worst speeches were made by the Upper Classes. I told him that I had already been scolded by the Chancellor—on which he clapped me on the shoulder and said 'I am glad he did scold you—he is very angry.' H.M. never gave me a chance to get anything in. He was in excellent spirits and said all the above cheerfully even boisterously. But he *is* annoyed I know and wants to make me feel it. The Empress was very nice.

Visits all the afternoon and then Pansas (5) and a few others to dinner. Danced and played games—but I had a horrible t--my-ach- —which is running thro' the whole stable.

Sunday 23 January[2]

Boss and I went to Weimar—where I presented my letters and attended State Banquet (next to May Fürstenberg) and Gala Opera. . . .

Monday 24 January

Back from Weimar in a very cold train

Fête at Cambons—very successful—Emperor and Empress—C. Prince and Princess—and a lot of swells. Sat between Countess Brockdorf and Madame Hegermann.

[1] Presumably Embassy footmen.   [2] First entry since 1 January.

Thursday 27 January

Emperor's Birthday. Church in Schloss in morning and congrats to Emperor.

Dinner at Bethmann Hollwegs—between Cambon and my bête noire Varmbüller.[1] Then Gala Opera—where Boss had to sit behind all the other Ambassadresses and where I couldn't see the stage or even the Orchestra—was as cross as two sticks and slanged poor old Knesebeck. When the Emperor asked me whether I liked the scenery I said I hadn't seen it—so he said 'Ah! You were asleep.' I said No! and that I had enjoyed the music. Then he scolded me again for the speeches in England and w'd not listen when I wanted to tell him that it was more admiration for Germany's activity and strength than abuse. Then he uttered the cryptic phrase '*I* am not the strong man—that is some one else!!' *I* don't know to this minute what he meant. I don't feel that I am doing good work here—but it may be that I feel that because I have a bad cold!!

Friday 4 February

Pom arrived last night about the New House.[2] He has been over it and likes it.

Saturday 5 Feburary

Went over No. 19 Thiergarten St. with Pom. Excellent House with garden and any amount of room.[3]...

Sunday 6 February

The Duchess of Wellington and Lady Eileen Wellesley[4] arrived. Pom stays on till tomorrow morning. He has been a delightful companion and we had fine talks together.

Monday 7 February

Our big ball. 400 invitations—350 came and 326 stayed to supper! A strain on the organisation, but it all passed off well. Four sons of the Kaiser were present—and the wives of the married ones.... People stayed late as I had a special train for the Potsdam division—this had a 'succès fou'. The whole thing was, I believe, a success and

---

[1] Varnbüler; Württemberg Minister.   [2] For the Embassy.
[3] The contemplated move did not take place.
[4] Duchess's daughter.

it went with a snap. One of the successes of the evening was the Flowers on sledges being dragged in by the Embassy dogs—'Daisy', 'Jones', 'Raffles' and Mrs Trench's[1] toy Bulldog.

Tuesday 8 February

Court Ball—and rest from yesterday. I rather enjoyed it. I sat next to the Empress—who talked 'Danneskiold' to me—and was very nice indeed. All the young Princes and their wives sat at a table together and they collected flowers from it and sent them to Boss (who was at the next table with the Crown P'ce) drinking her health at the same time. It was rather pretty of them.

Thursday 10 February

Dinner to Crown P'ce and Princess[2]—Guests: Duke and Duchess of Arenberg, P'ce and P'cess Lowenstein,[3] P'ce and P'cess Münster,[4] P'ce and Princess Pless—P'ce Salm-Salm—Duchess of Wellington, Lady Eileen Wellesley, Lady Annesley[5] and C't Seckendorf—C'tess Wedel (Lady in waiting) and Captain v. Plainitz (equerry). A very pretty lot of women and nice men. Little May Harrison[6] played the violin *quite* beautifully—and Daisy Pless sang like a bird and *did* enjoy it. *But* Boss disappeared for a few minutes without anyone knowing it and had a nose bleed.[7]

Friday 11 February

Duchess and Lady Eileen left for St P.

Tuesday 1 March

Poor C't Seckendorff died—after a few days illness. Only heard of it this morning and rushed down to inquire. Met Knesebeck who told me that it was a hopeless case. Double pneumonia and a weak heart. He passed away peacefully in the evening. We are very sorry—he was always kind and nice to us—and he was a real good friend to England.

[1] Wife of military attaché.
[2] Princess Cecilie; *née* a duchess of Mecklenburg-Schwerin.
[3] He was a Bavarian landowner; she a daughter of Lord Pirbright.
[4] He was the son of a former German Ambassador in London.
[5] Wife of 6th earl.
[6] Young English violinist; resident in Berlin.
[7] This marks a stage in Hosta Goschen's long and ultimately fatal illness.

Did not feel much inclined to go to P'cess Henckel Donnersmark's[1] musical evening—but had to—very good music. Got a nice corner with a lot of Austrian friends: then Crown P'cess sent for me and I had to 'sit up' for the rest of the time. But she was very jolly and friendly as she always is.

Wednesday 2 March

Court Concert. Full dress. Who can enjoy music in Breeches and white stockings? Sat between the two Japs! Which was not very inspiring either. A woman sang Handel's Largo out of *Rinaldo* most beautifully—and that and the March of the Men of Harlech—was what I enjoyed most. The latter had 'Bruch' opposite to it in the Programme as if *he* had written it. Must take an opportunity of speaking to the Empress about it. Took Me. Polo[2] into supper! but sat next to the Crown Princess who said as I sat down by her, 'How jolly! but I feel as if I was going to have a fit of the giggles.'! *She was* jolly—but on the other hand Me. Polo told me all about the last illnesses of her recently deceased relations.

Thursday 3 March

Musical evening at P'cess Radzivill: a banging French Pianist—a *fair* violin—and a good singer—Padilla.[3] Emperor and Empress were there. The former sat on a sofa at the back and talked to one man the whole evening through the music and everything. The Empress talked to me about Hosta very nicely.

Friday 4 March

Duchess of Wellington and Lady Eileen returned and are going to stop till Monday. Bad day for Messenger. They arrived—the Boys all dined at Potsdam with August Wilhelm[4] and had a tremendous orgie—and I dined at usual Ambassadorial dinner at the Palace.... Then up till 2.30 a.m. with Messenger work.

Both Emperor and Empress sent kind messages to Boss. H.M. did not talk politics to me—only music. But to Heath[5] he did—expressed pleasure that German scare seemed to be over in England, then went over old ground and said that he had during 22 years striven to be England's best friend—and that no one in England ever seemed to believe it. He couldn't understand the English he felt inclined to ask

---

[1] Donnersmarck; wife of Guido Fürst Donnersmarck, Silesian landowner.
[2] Spanish Ambassadress.   [3] Spanish baritone.
[4] Kaiser's 4th son.   [5] Naval attaché.

them in the words of the old song 'Oh Juli*ar*—Oh Juli*ar*—why are you so peculi*ar*?'!!¹

Szogenyi said the Russo-Austrian negotiations were going on well—and that Isvolski seemed to be coming round to Ährenthal's views as to publication of result. Cambon told me that the Russians had told him *just the contrary*!

Saturday 5 March

Went to poor old C't Seckendorff's funeral—at wh. I represented the King. Not very impressive service. P'ce F. Leopold² represented the Emperor. Church bitterly cold.

Thursday 17 March

Went to Noë's³ Concert where May and 'Baba'⁴ Harrison were playing Brahms double concerto for Violin and Cello. They played a beautiful composition beautifully—but I didn't care about M. Noë's style of conducting. Benjie went with me and we left early as we didn't care about the next things.

Letter from Hardinge saying that things were going from bad to worse in England—that the present idea was that there would be elections in June—and that the Conservatives w'd come in with a large majority owing to disgust of nation at Liberal and radical tactics.⁵

Saturday 19 March

Boss went off to Wiesbaden. Weather fair to medium. Don't like her going much—but then again I don't think that here she would ever get strong: . . .

Had a violin lesson with May Harrison—got on a little better—but my wrist won't waggle the way she wants it to.

Monday 21 March

Pretty cold but fine intervals. P.m. went and called on Harrisons—charming flat—Mrs Harrison⁶ told me that the man who conducted the orchestra at the concert the other day had committed suicide because the critics had been so down on him. On the other hand they had praised the girls.

---

¹ Cf. Heath to Goschen, 7 March 1910, *B.D.*, vi, no. 335, enclosure.
² Kaiser's 2nd cousin.   ³ German conductor.
⁴ Barbara Harrison; 'cellist; younger sister of May Harrison.
⁵ Hardinge to Goschen, 15 March 1910 (copy), H.P., 21.
⁶ Mother of May and Barbara.

Tuesday 22 March

Cold bright then rain

Went to see Schön—1st time for a month. He had nothing to say—neither had I. He defended Tirpitz[1] (who is angry with McKenna's[2] speech[3] and w'd scarcely speak to Heath) because he said McKenna *would* say that the Germans accelerated. I said that all McKenna had said was that the *Nassau* was built in 2 years and 2 months—and that *if* the Nassau could be built in that time other ships could.[4] I told him we *must* take possibilities into account—a first Lord w'd have a very poor time if he didn't. The fact is the Germans count a ship laid down—when the money is found for her—we count it from the time her keel is laid. Another fact is that Schön knows nothing about it.

I also told him that the police had had the audactiy to fine my chauffeur. He tried to laugh it off, but I said that though I did not intend to make a fuss about it—the principle must be upheld of the ex'territoriality of Ambassadors' servants etc. When he saw I was in earnest he took a note of it and said he would speak about it.

Sunday 10 April

Went down to Mecklenburg Strelitz to see the Princess of Wales.[5] Stayed at the Schloss. The P'cess was very cordial and nice; and the old Grand Duchess[6] very graciously pleased to see me and talk over B'sh Politics. She said she would like to give Lloyd George a bit of her mind. I wish she could—for She has the aptitude of her old brother the late Duke of Cambridge for calling a spade a spade! A very pleasant dinner after which I talked some distance into the night with the Dugdales.[7]

Sunday 17 April

Met Princess of Wales,[8] and took her to Hohenzollern Exh'n—then to Durhams![9] and then she came and dined with me and left for London 9.13. She was awfully cheery and nice—and sent affec'te messages to Boss. We had a very nice dinner—all the Embassy appearing.

[1] Secretary of State, Navy.   [2] First Lord of the Admiralty.
[3] House of Commons, 14 March 1910.   [4] Hansard, 5, xv, col. 50.
[5] She was a cousin of the Grand Duke Adolf Friedrich V.
[6] Augusta Caroline; daughter of 1st Duke of Cambridge; widow of Grand Duke Friedrich Wilhelm; mother of Adolf Friedrich V.
[7] He was an equerry; she a lady-in-waiting.
[8] In Berlin.
[9] He was an honorary attaché; his wife, Lady Agnes Durham, was a friend of the Princess.

Friday 6 May

The King died at 11.45[1] after a reign of only 10 years. A great national calamity. A great King and a great personality has disappeared from the scene—a Man respected and loved and admired throughout Europe—and an immense 'force' and influence.

To me he was always kindness itself and I owed much to Him—so I feel his loss privately as well as nationally.

I only heard He was ill this morning early when Schön came round to tell me of his conversation with Isvolsky.

He worked almost until he became unconscious—as the following lines indicate.[2]

Saturday 7 May

Chancellor and Schön came early to express sympathy—followed by all the Amb'rs except the Turk—and Ostensacken. Then a stream of visits throughout the day. Heaps of telegrams and a great deal to do.

Only got news of H.M.'s death at 2.30 p.m.

Sunday 8 May

Church. Nearly all Embassy attended. Church hung in Black—but choir all in coloured dresses and hats—and scarcely anybody in mourning in the whole church! Organist awful.

The Emperor came to see me at 3 o'clock and stayed an hour and a half.[3] He was very sympathetic and kind: and afterwards talked on every subject under the sun. Navy—relations—Old Age Pensions—Zeppelins—Poverty and Press!

For once he talked a little bit of politics and pointed out a few mistakes England had made. 1. We had built Dreadnoughts and thus opened competition fr. other nations. 2. When we had built our first Dreadnought—the entire Press had said 'Now we can lick Germany into a cocked hat.' This had put Germany's back up and made her say—'We will see about that we can build Dreadnoughts as well as they' and they did so. Fisher—H.M. said, had quite forgotten that the Nation which could build huge liners could equally well build huge Battleships etc.

---

[1] P.m.; Goschen evidently made this entry subsequently.

[2] There follows a cutting of some verses printed in *The Times*, 7 May 1910.

[3] According to Bruce (op. cit., p. 111), this was the Kaiser's only visit to the Embassy during Goschen's ambassadorship.

Monday 9 May

Went to the Reichstag where the President made a sympathetic little speech about the King which was listened to by the Members standing. The Vice-Presidents came to the Diplomatic box and expressed their condolences.

Tuesday 10 May

Called on President and Vice-Presidents of the Reichstag and thanked them for their sympathetic action.

Sunday 15 May[1]

The Emperor called and stayed an hour and a half. He was very sympathetic and nice about the poor King. Then he talked on every conceivable subject. About Anglo-German Relations—Poor Laws—Pensions—pauperism—everything. Finally he told me he attributed no military value to Airships, as in a wind over 8 knots they were helpless. Useful for reconnaissances perhaps—but certainly for maps and surveys. He was very nice. But I suppose the length of his visit was calculated and for effect in London.[2]

Tuesday 17 May

Left for London to attend the Funeral, via Hook of Holland.

Wednesday 18 May

Arrived 8 o'clock at 40 Portman Square where Twinkle received me with open arms. . . . A.m. went to the F.O. and saw Grey and Hardinge—both satisfactory—Persian question seems to be settling down.

Wrote my name down at Buckingham Palace. King Haakon saw me from the window—and Queen Maud sent for me and was very nice indeed. Rather sorrowful of course, poor dear.

Thursday 19 May

More F.O. Went to meet the Emperor at 3. Teck drove me there. I knelt down and kissed the King's hand when he arrived at the

---

[1] Goschen must have made this entry in error; he is evidently relating what had occurred during the Kaiser's visit on 8 May.

[2] Cf. Bruce, op. cit., p. 111.

station: he was very nice indeed—and seemed to me to have his wits about him very much.... The Emperor looked wellish but a bad colour. Saw old Leopold Swaine for a moment—who was in attendance on H.I.M.

Friday 20 May

King Edward's funeral.... On arrival at Windsor we found lots of carriages and were driven straight up to the Chapel and both took our places in the Nave—where we had to wait an hour and a half before the Procession came: but during the wait the organ played beautiful funeral marches—Beethoven—Schubert's and others. Then we heard the muffled drums coming nearer and nearer and we had a chokey moment. Then came the procession and the remains of our dear old King. One can scarcely imagine him *gone*. The Queen (Alexandra) was a pathetic figure—swathed in crape and with a white set face. With her came the King, then the Emperor and Duke of Connaught—and then about 8 other Kings. Amongst these was King of Bulgaria who rather spoilt solemnity by mopping himself all the way up the Chapel....

Saturday 21 May

Rather tired from standing so long.... Saw Hardinge in the morning and had a good talk with him. Germans don't want to go on with Persian question for the moment. Why? It is [*sic*] because A. Hy. has shown no sign of backing up?

Tuesday 24 May

Had an audience with the King[1] after seeing the Emperor off. Latter told me how nice everybody had been—how sympathetic he had found the King and how he had admired the decorum and reverence of the enormous crowds who had assembled to see the Procession. 'England sh'd be proud of her people *and* her police.'! The King was charming and talked to me for an hour—he seemed quite up in For. Aff. and spoke most sensibly about them. He said that nothing could exceed the kindness and thoughtfulness of the Emperor during the visit—adding that he should do his best to keep up the best private and public relations with Germany. But he didn't seem keen about a definite understanding on German lines! He gave me interesting details of row between His Father and Emperor—re Crown Prince

[1] According to the King this interview took place a day earlier; cf. R.A., King George V, Diary, 23 May 1910.

not having been allowed to accept an invitation to come to England. Queen Mary came in and was most cordial and gracious and said many kind words about her visit to Berlin the other day.

Wednesday 25 May

Left for Berlin....

Thursday 26 May

Arrived Berlin. Found Boss better but not looking as well as she ought to yet.

Friday 1 July

Caught Schön just as he was starting for Travemünde[1] to see Emperor. I told him Special Mission to announce King's accession wanted to come here middle of this month. Schön said he w'd ask Emperor—but that he didn't think the Emperor could possibly manage it as he would be away cruizing in the North until *end* of month. It is very awkward for all parties—and I don't like it much either—particularly if it is put off till September!!

Saturday 2 July

The Chancellor sent for me to say goodbye as he is going away for a month or two. He had nothing much to say—except that Russia had made no signs about the Persian Railway matter and that we didn't seem much inclined for conversation! I think he is rather upset about all the papers saying that now Kiderlen is to replace Schön[2]— the Imperial Foreign Policy will be stronger. He said to me as he said to Cambon—more or less: Don't you trouble about Kiderlen's senti-ments—it is I that direct the Imp'l For. policy—'et c'est moi qui in-spire les sentiments'. This was in response to a remark of mine that I hoped he would be as nice and friendly as Schön.

Tuesday 5 July

Saw Schön—he maintains that Wilhelmshöhe[3] in the middle of August will be the best for the Special Mission—I only hope they won't come in September. There was nothing much to talk about

---

[1] Near Lübeck.   [2] Appointed German Ambassador, Paris.
[3] Kaiser's summer residence, Kassel.

either with him and the colleagues whom I met there. Everybody talked about Crete but there was nothing new to say about it.

Thursday 7 July

Letter from Hardinge—only interesting about Home politics: he says that everything points to the formation of a centre party.[1] This is awful. Every Foreign nation envies us our two big parties system. The Labour party is bad eno' and now we are to have another one. I honestly believe that our dear old country is deteriorating in every way. I don't believe that the proper sort of patriotism exists among the masses; professionalism—and vicarious exercise—is dominating our sports—and in fact I don't like the look of things at all. *But* I have hopes that King George will have a good influence—give a good example in many things and arouse a proper spirit thro'out the country.

Friday 8 July

Smallish Bag. Could only write one despatch and that upon internal affairs. The changes in the Ministry—my last conversation with the Chancellor and my opinions and those of the Press.[2] Things are in a queer state and I can't make out what Bethmann is up to—is he coquetting with the National Liberals—or is he working at getting them back into the old block? I don't think so—and think rather that he is trying to get rid of all the old Bülowites surround himself with men of his own choosing and try to put into practice his theory of governing over the heads of the parties. But will he be able to do so? I say emphatically *no*.

Saturday 9 July

Nicolson arrived on his way to Petersburg to wash up—preparatory to his taking on Permanent Under Sec'yship at F.O.[3] Of course he was full of it. He tells me he didn't want to accept it—but Grey put it in such a way that he had to: besides his wife wanted him to accept it. He said that Lowther[4] had been offered Petersburg but had refused—and that this had put the F.O. into a hole as they want to get him away from Const'ple. They have not been satisfied with his work there for a long time. Nico seemed to know what they were going to do with him—but he wouldn't say. But he did tell me, under the

---

[1] Hardinge to Goschen, 6 July 1910 (copy), H.P., 21.
[2] Goschen to Grey, 3 July 1910, *B.D.*, vi, no. 379.
[3] In succession to Hardinge.   [4] Now Ambassador, Constantinople.

seal of secrecy that Buchanan[1] was going to Petersburg! he passes over 18 of his colleagues—but in point of length of service he is senior to all of them except Elliot.[2] Nico tells me that both King, Grey and Hardinge had all said that I musn't leave Berlin and had spoken highly of my work here! We talked a good deal about situation and he told me many interesting things about Isvolsky—saying that he had never lied to him but seldom told him the *whole* truth. When he yielded to the Germans last year—he told Nico that Pourtalès[3] had presented him with a sort of Ultimatum and exercised the greatest pressure (Buchlau protocol?) to Louis[4] the new French Amb'r he said that they had used no pressure at all—only given friendly advice! He is a slippery creature is Isvolski.

Sunday 10 July

Nico all day. He talked incessantly—and it is very difficult to get one's own oar in. He said that King Edward had expressed the wish that Kitchener[5] should go to India as Viceroy—and that after H.M.'s death they had almost decided to send him in deference to the King's wishes. Morley[6] had however not wished it (I can fancy why—as Morley likes to have his own way in India) and had held out—so they finally appointed Hardinge who was Morley's candidate. Hardinge is certain to ride roughshod over his Council—but he will find Morley a tough customer.

We had Schöns, Pansa, Berckheim[7] and most of the Embassy to lunch—and Niko had a long talk to Schön—the only part of which I heard was that 'Germany, as I have often told Goschen, only wants to save her face in Persia'. P.M. Nico, Boss and I motored to the Grünewald and had a charming walk there—and a good bask in the unaccustomed *sun*. The Lake was a very pretty sight. Benjie B. joined us at dinner and Nico and I had a long bout of reminiscences up to his departure at 11 p.m. He was very bright and nice—but as I said before he is so full of his own subjects that one can't ventilate one's own. But he is very clever and as Grey said in a letter to him—he will bring to the F.O. the 'gift of wisdom'.[8]

Tuesday 12 July

Nothing partic. Schön didn't receive. Crete seems to be going all right—tho' personally I think that the adjournment of the Assembly

---

[1] Now Minister, The Hague.
[2] Minister, Athens.
[3] German Ambassador, St Petersburg.
[4] French Ambassador, St Petersburg.
[5] Former Commander-in-Chief, India.
[6] Secretary of State, India.
[7] Councillor, French Embassy.
[8] Not traced in N.P.

(after voting for the readmission of the Mussulman deputies without oath to the King of Greece) without having a sitting at wh. Mussulmans c'd attend—was rather a piece of cheek and may not satisfy Turkey. Press much excited about telegrams in English papers resp'g a letter addressed by the Kaiser to the President of Nicaragua. This telegram makes out that America is furious because the Emperor called President his good friend—thereby shewing that he wants to mix himself up in Nicaraguan Affairs—and so in S. American republics. This appears to be rather rot—as letter was evidently an official one in usual form—in answer to President's announcement of his accession to office.

It appears that we consulted U.S. first before answering—but Germans say that it doesn't matter to them in the least what other Powers did. If they choose to recognize President without consulting U.S. why shouldn't they? Certainly why shouldn't they? I consider *Daily Chronicle's* telegram[1] deplorable.

Had a round of golf—but got lumbago at first hole and couldn't play a bit.

Wednesday 13 July

Weather warmer. Great storm in a teacup going on about a letter addressed by Emperor to President of Nicaragua—acknowledging latter's accession to office and beginning in usual form on such occasion 'Grosser und Guter Freund'. *Daily Mail*[2] and *Chronicle* have published tel's from their U.S. correspondents stating that letter is regarded in U.S. as an interference in Nicaraguan affairs a violation of Monroe Doctrine and Goodness knows what. Fearful outcry in the German Press. England accused of trying to make mischief between Germany and U.S. etc. Facts are that France and we have not answered President's letter and consulted U.S. first. This Germany did not do—and cut in on her own hook—probably intentionally—but probably not with the intention, as asserted in the *D. Mail* etc. of currying favour with Nicaragua in order to get a coaling station out of them. Of course they are angry here at this absolutely formal letter being given such a black construction.

Thursday 14 July

Wrote a long desp. on Russo-Japanese Treaty[3]—giving Press opinions etc. Saw Schoen p.m. to ask him whether Emperor can receive Special Mission about August 27th. We talked about the

[1] *Daily Chronicle*, 12 July 1910.   [2] *Daily Mail*, 13 July 1910.
[3] Agreement on Manchuria, 4 July 1910.

Emperor's Nicaragua letter. He told me that the fuss was all over. Affair had been begun by the Nic'n Gov't having published Emperor's purely formal letter and represented its opening words 'Great and good friend' as a token of the Emperor's partic. esteem and affection! U.S. had officially stated that they regarded the letter as a formality and saw no reason for demanding explanations either from Germany or Nicaragua. Germany had not approached U.S. Government before ack'ing letter—because they saw no reason why they should—but they had consulted German Amb'r at Washington—who had told them there could be no objection as State Department had as a matter of fact a high opinion of new President.

Schön speaking of *Tägliche Rundschau*, who had published violent anti-English article respecting Russo-Jap Treaty, said that they had long been trying to get it into their hands—but had not been able as Editor was too independent. I must have caught Schoen napping—as every one, from Bülow and Bethmann downwards, have always told me that they never try to, or can, influence the Press in any way!

Friday 15 July

Wrote long despatches[1] on Nicaragua incident and Russo-Jap treaty—and on German comments on Asquith's speech on Naval Estimates.[2] It has made a splendid impression here—as he spoke of the great friendly German Nation, admitted that Germany required a strong navy—with her commerce and World Power increasing every day, and buttered them up generally. He however maintained his point about the possibility of Germany having 17 Dreadnought[3] ships in 1912—and that may make a little row as Tirpitz and Bethmann etc. have always said that they will only have 13. Moreover, they *can* have 17—and we have to reckon not with what they say they will have—but with what they *can* have and what they *would* have sh'd circ'es require it.

Saturday 16 July

Nasty boil on my face—saw Doc

German papers still full of Asquith's speech and *most* appreciative....

Cambon came to see me having just come from Paris. He said that Grey had talked to his brother Paul Cambon[4] about the necessity of

---

[1] Goschen to Hardinge, 15 July 1910, H.P., 20 (strictly a letter).
[2] House of Commons, 14 July 1910.
[3] 'Dreadnought' added by Goschen above line.
[4] French Ambassador, London.

telling the Turks to behave themselves now that the Cretans have given in at the rquest of the Powers—and not to go on trying to goad Greece into doing something which might give Turks an excuse for War. Paul Cambon had reported to Pichon[1] also Grey's suggestion that Germany and Austria sh'd be invited to join Powers in talking to Turkey to the above effect.[2] My Cambon (Jules) told me that he had advised Pichon to let B'h Ambassadors at Berlin and Vienna do it—on the plea that we should have a better chance. I told him that I didn't like it as it was running after a refusal—and I didn't see why we alone sh'd incur the odium. He is a nice, sly old dog.

Monday 18 July

My old birthday. Boss awfully sweet and nice and had a table for me with 'just the things I wanted'. We had a nice walk in the Grünewald with the Dogs and a tête-a-tête dinner—when B. made a speech and drank my health. When one is 63 Birthdays are not such a joy as they once were! But there is a good side which is the thankfulness w'ch I feel that I have been allowed to have 63 Birthdays—and that during that time I have had so much happiness and achieved a fair little career.

Went to Schön and asked him whether Imp'l Government would join in pressing the Porte to stop boycott and other provocative measures against Greece. I pointed out that the Cretan question had been settled pro tem: and every satisfaction had been given to the Turks. They now said that Boycott waś justified by action of Greek committees and meetings in Macedonia and other Turkish territories. As this was a matter which concerned all the signatories of the Berlin Treaty H.M.G. hoped they w'd join in pressing Turks to put a stop to a situation, which might at any given moment bring about a war. Schön agreed that the Turks were unreasonable and wanted pulling up. But he said he could not answer until he had consulted Chancellor and their Ambassador at Const'ple.[3] (Cambon has therefore had history.)

He found rather fault with Asquith for having stated in his speech that Imp'l Government had informed H.M.G. that public opinion in Germany w'd not support modification of Naval Programme.[4] He anticipated trouble in the Reichstag and awkward questions as to whether and what negotiations have taken place. *Tageblatt* says that there have been evidently negotiations and they ought to be published.

---

[1] French Foreign Minister.
[2] Paul Cambon to Pichon, 11 July 1910, *D.D.F.*, 2, xii, no. 358.
[3] Marschall von Bieberstein.   [4] Cf. Hansard, 5, xix, col. 638.

Tuesday 19 July

Schön did not receive—and when asked why by Berckheim said that he had some visits to pay. I expect he thought I might press him for answer about Crete.

Friday 22 July

Austria has refused to join in Grey's collective remonstrance at Constantinople. Äh. says that Turks are not so very satisfied at Cretan settlement—that Ott. Min'r for For. Aff.[1] is bluffing when he says that Boycott is justified by action of G'k Committee in Macedonia—that he is afraid of being drawn into the Cretan question—and therefore must refuse. Grey has sent an angry tel. to Vienna—reproducing reasons why remonstrance was necessary—and saying that under circ'es he withdraws from initiative.

I fear this will create rather a coldness again—and I think (and thought) that it was a pity Grey ever asked Germany and Austria to join. Their refusal was a dead cert. Schön has not answered yet—but it will be the same as Austria's answer.

(Went and had my boil lanced.)

Wrote to F.O. on subject of Asquith's speech—and the German Press. Liberal Press in favour—and Pan German Press agin. Asquith rather gave the show away and has put German Public on track of negotiations.

Sunday 24 July

Bossie left for Tentschach.

Had a good game of Golf with Twee after a morning at Tentschach accounts. Boss and T. left by the 8.45 train to Villach über München. A new train. Doesn't seem to me to have many points. They have to turn out of their sleeping car at Munich and they have to change at Villach. Distressed not to be able to go with them—but *without leave* it meant all travel and no stay: with leave far too expensive in our present stony condition.

Monday 25 July

House very dull without Boss and Teddy and Berlin is in itself unspeakably dull. I wrote a note to Schoen today asking him for an answer to my representation about Grey's collective step at Const'ple. Stumm[2] came round and told me that the answer had been sent to

---

[1] Rifaat Pasha.   [2] Councillor, Imperial Foreign Office.

Metternich.[1] I told him gently that as I had spoken to Schoen about it I might have been informed! It amused me rather that he spoke of Grey's proposed collective step on the subject of the Cretan question. I told him that I had particularly pointed out to Schön that it had nothing to do with the Cretan question which was for the moment settled—but with the Macedonian question in wh. all six Powers were interested. I said that Grey's point had been that as the Cretan question had been (temporarily) settled in a manner satisfactory to the Turks—and as the Ott. Min. of Foreign Affairs had justified continuation of the Boycott by the action of the Greek Committees in Macedonia—and as moreover, notwithstanding settlement of the Cretan question Ott. Gov't (or rather Young Turk Committee) seemed determined to provoke Greeks—he had thought that all the Powers sh'd give a word of advice. Stumm said that if Germans interfered and things went wrong—everyone in Paris and London would say that it was Germany's fault as usual—so it was better for them not to take a hand in it. I said that in London and Paris, if Turkey made war, they would be much more likely to say that Germany was responsible as in order to curry favour with the Turks—they had held aloof at a critical moment....

Tuesday 26 July

Boil.

Cambon turned up—and I dined with him. He didn't have much to tell me—except that the Bulgarians are protesting ag'st Turkish treatment of Bulgarian Macedonians and want the Powers to remonstrate at Const'ple. I don't think Grey will take the initiative this time!
    The only interesting thing now going on is the meeting of Ährenthal—Kiderlen—Grand Vizier[2] and perhaps Isvolski at Marienbad.

Wednesday 27 July

Combon lunched—also Count[3] and Benjie. Latter a mistake as he didn't utter except in an undertone in English to the Count. Cambon was interesting about Schön's appointment to Paris. He thinks he will be a failure as he will promise everything and do nothing—while Me S. qui est (il faut dire les choses comme elles sont) un peu snobinelle— will go in for the Faubourg St. Germain—and neglect the Ministers' wives and think them—as they most of them are old and fat and dull.

---

[1] German Ambassador, London.   [2] Hakki Pasha
[3] De Salis.

Now Radolin,[1] who was a real grand seigneur 'a fait une cour acharnée à toutes les femmes officielles' and nevertheless had a position in both worlds. As regards Kiderlen he said that his own opinion was that we should have a great change and that the Chancellor would have nothing to say in Foreign Politics. To this I answered that my opinion of the Chancellor was that he was just weak enough to want to appear strong and that for that reason Kiderlen might find it difficult to get his own way. . . .

Got a letter from Hardinge telling me that my last annual report[2] was excellent and just the sort of thing they wanted.[3]

Friday 29 July

Fairly early Messenger. I wrote a long desp. about Naval Affairs[4]— but it is no good. I preached on the text that as it is known by everybody that the Germans intend to carry out their Fleet Law—and that we are going to build a sufficient number of ships to ensure our supremacy at sea—there is no more to be said—and violent articles quite unnecessary.

They might have been necessary once—on *the German side* to rouse the enthusiasm necessary to make the German public put its hand in its pocket for a big fleet; on our *side*—to rouse our public opinion to a sense of the danger which threatened our Naval supremacy. Now Press violence only embittered relations and rendered any moderating influence quite powerless. Them's my sentiments.

Had a bad round of golf with Benjie.

Schoen came in to say goodbye and was very pleasant and Schönish. It has been very pleasant having him at the Imp'l F.O. and I am sorry he is going.

Kiderlen-Wächter will be another pair of shoes—and I doubt if they will fit me so well. Mais nous verrons! and it is possible that it may be advantageous having a man who will take a line of his own—and talk out even tho'—brutally.

Monday 1 August

Had a nice letter from Boss saying how much she was enjoying Tentschach and what good it was doing her. In the afternoon called upon old Szögyenyi; he didn't tell me anything much—said that Kiderlen and d'Ährenthal had decided that the summer and autumn

---

[1] German Ambassador, Paris, 1900–10; Goschen had been on friendly terms with him in St Petersburg.
[2] *B.D.*, vi, p. 319.
[3] Hardinge to Goschen, 26 July 1910 (copy), H.P., 21.
[4] Goschen to Grey, 29 July, *B.D.*, vi, no. 386.

would be peaceful—and also that I sh'd find K. very well disposed towards good relations with England. I am not certain about either of these things. I don't think things look particularly well in Macedonia—and I am not certain about K. Of course if we yielded everything Germany wants we could have an understanding tomorrow.

Tuesday 2 August

Left for Trachenberg (Silesia) to stay a day or two with the Duke and Duchess of that Ilk. Long journey and hottish. An hour and a half's wait at Posen gave me an opportunity of looking at the New Royal Schloss in that town—of which the Germans think much. I thought it heavy and hideous—so do the Trachenbergs. (Arrived at 5 o'clock and rec'd a warm welcome from these nice people. Had tea and then a beautiful drive through lovely oak woods. The estate is 20000 Hectares! The Schloss is quaint and huge—but hardly pretty. It is yellow and white! It dates from the time of Frederick the Great— but the Tower which stands by itself—is much older and very fine.

Count Maltzahn[1] and Frau v. Bülow[2] and her daughter came to dinner—having motored over from C't Maltzahn's place about 50 Kil. I had a beautiful Bedroom sitting room bath room and dressing room—and a splendid bed. Very sumptuous, all the modern improvements—and *most* comfy. Glad to find Trachenbergs like to go to bed early 10.30! Yi.

Wednesday 3 August

Trachenberg

Still finish. Visited Fisch Verein—where a learned Professor shewed us all sorts of things in Fish life and subaqueous plants. We also visited Carp ponds and saw how they are bred and kept and sold. Motored and drove all day—devoting afternoon to a visit to Augusta Maltzahn the C't's unmarried sister—who has a charming little house, whose garden etc. has been created by the hands of the Lady herself. She seemed very nice. Frau v. Bülow and her daughter were there—and also a Pole, with his wife and daughter (whose name escaped me). Duchess told me that this was the *first* time they had been asked to meet a *Polish* family—and said that it was evident that it was devised by Augusta Maltzahn to bring about a marriage between the Polish daughter—and Hermann Hatzfeldt—the Trachenberg son.

Bad night owing to change of weather.

[1] Andreas Graf von Maltzan; Silesian landowner.
[2] The Bülow family had numerous ramifications.

Thursday 4 August

Trachenberg. Rainy

Farmed all day. Home farm in the morning—main farm in the afternoon. At the former the cows were so-so. Black and white Dutch-Oldenburg breed. At latter Holstein breed dark red (like Danish only bigger)—beautiful cows and one or two splendid Bulls. Pigs very well housed—and as usual. Country bred ones prolific—and imported ones less so. A few pure bred Berkshires looked well—but farmers inveighed against them as being small and growing slowly. They (farmers in Germany and Austria) prefer the *long* narrow—long-legged pigs to the *broad* English breeds. In fact they seem to go in for length altogether. I enjoyed my farming day very much—but the weather turned rather cold.

Friday 5 August

Back to Berlin after a very pleasant visit found lots of disagreeable work—quite unsuitable to the time of the year! Cambon came to see me and nobbled me for dinner tomorrow! pish![1]

I am not very pleased with contents of the bag—and Sir E. Grey's private letter did not fill me with joy, as it rather went ag'st what I have been telling the Chancellor—by his and Hardinge's inst'ns—for the last year. Moreover it did not strike me as having been penned by Sir E. with great pleasure—and I expect that he has had pressure put upon him by the radical wing of the Cabinet.

Saturday 6 August

I asked for a farewell audience for Heath about 3 weeks ago. Today I rec'd an answer saying that the Emperor regretted not to be able to receive him owing to his other numerous engagements! Now the Emperor was in Berlin for several days and rec'd the Chinese and others—so it is evidently a 'parti pris'—probably worked by Tirpitz. They all (apparently and I know Metternich does) hold Heath responsible for what they consider McKenna's mis-statements in the House of Commons respecting the German Navy.

Called on Harrisons. 'Baba' played 'Cello Elégie of Fauré and 2 movements out of a 'cello concerto—*most* beautifully. She is really first class and 'May' accompanied her charmingly. I arranged for a Violin lesson on Monday.

---

[1] According to Bruce (op. cit., p. 121), 'pish' was Goschen's favourite expression; in the Chancery and in a canine context he was known as 'Uncle Pish'.

Tuesday 9 August

Went to Kiderlen's reception. I found him rather boutonné—and tho' I gave him a chance he did not say a word of Anglo-German relations. As regards Macedonia he said things looked better—I said I presumed since King of Bulgaria returned to Sofia from *Vienna*. He said probably so—but he didn't much care *what* had improved the situation as long as it *had* improved. I asked him whether supposing there was war he agreed with Ährenthal in thinking it would be localised. He said 'Yes—if you keep your friends back!' I said 'What friends?' and he said 'The Russians.'

Stumm asked me to come to his room and told me that he had just received a message from Wilhelmshöhe saying that the Emperor would receive *Heath* and Watson[1] on Sept. 1 !! He said that there must evidently have been some stupid mistake about the first message. He admitted that he had thought that the Emperor had for some reason or another not wished to receive Heath—and he was glad to see that it was not so. I asked him to explain why the Emperor had deliberately (after weighing his reply for a fortnight) said only 3 days ago that he was unable to receive Capt'n Heath before latter left Germany and now (when he must know that Heath had left), said he w'd receive him three weeks hence. He c'd not explain—but said that Kiderlen had said in his note 'before the Emperor left Berlin'—this was not true and I proved it to him.

Stumm then gassed a good deal about Anglo-German Relations. He started a new theory which was that it was not the Naval question w'h upset relations—but our policy. I asked 'What policy?' He said 'Well your policy of being friends with Russia and France.' I said 'My dear man—we might as well complain of your policy of being friends with Austria and Italy.' He admitted that he had no belief in the Balance of Power theory.

Wednesday 10 August

Nothing partic. and nothing of any interest by Messenger—except printed copy of my Report for 1909. It has been much praised by F.O. and I must admit that on reading it through I was surprised to find that it was not so bad as I thought. *But* they have asked me to try and send it in earlier!!

Thursday 11 August

Noting partic. Tels. from Sofia seem to point to trouble in the near future. But King Ferdinand has evidently had a talking to at

[1] New naval attaché.

Vienna—and he may soothe his people down. Here they are most optimistic but I don't know on what ground—particularly if they get the same information as us.

Friday 12 August

Rather seedy—think a very cold drink when I was very hot yesterday upset my tummy. I was going to the Villa[1] tomorrow to see Emmie—but telegraphed I would rather come Sunday: it is no good going if one is seedy and can't eat. Then Stumm came round and said that the Chancellor would me [sic][2] to come to Hoch Finnow[3] on Sunday—and as I have got to see him I couldn't refuse. So had to tel. to poor Em to put off my visit.

Saturday 13 August

Got off my Messenger in good time—having written a very dull uninteresting letter to Grey overnight.[4] Glad I hadn't much to do this morning as I have had a vile headache all day. There was thunder and rain all the afternoon. I went up to Golf but the rain came down in torrents and I came back—and called on the Chinaman.[5]

Polo[6] came to see me—being here for a day! He told me that Kiderlen had said that he had been very much annoyed by an article in the *Temps*. He did not know whether it was officially inspired—but if it was—it was quite contrary to all the assurances of goodwill wh had been given by the French Govt.! I have not seen this article.

Sunday 14 August

Went out to see Chancellor at Hohen Finnow[7]—a quaint old house with fine ceilings and a nice old fashioned garden—with old fashioned flowers and beautiful avenues of old lime trees. Farm—about 200 cows not up to much—and badly kept. Some good pigs—Deutsche Edelschweine chiefly—but not many.

Had a long talk with Chancellor on Anglo-German relations. He did not understand Grey's 3rd suggestion—no increase to German programme and reciprocal information as to ship building. between two Admiralities. He asked exactly the question I knew he w'd ask— 'But what will G't Britain do meanwhile?' I said that I was not clear

---

[1] His sister Emily's home near Dresden.
[2] Word apparently omitted; probably 'like'.
[3] Hohenfinow; Bethmann Hollweg's country-house.
[4] Goschen to Grey, 12 Aug. 1910, Gr. P., F.O. 800/62.
[5] Chinese Minister, Liang-Tcheng.   [6] Spanish Ambassador.
[7] Hohenfinow.

either but that I thought—as our great object was to reduce the great expenditure on armaments—we should reduce our expenses to the minimum of what we considered necessary for safety. He asked me to thank Grey for the communication[1] but to say that he w'd have to study Memo. before giving an opinion—in any case he was grateful for goodwill and friendly tone.

I had quite a nice afternoon—tho' it was beastly cold sitting out in the garden before dinner—Me B.H.'s sister was there—young B.H. a nice lad educated at Oxford and a very pretty Governess—Miss Clark: also that dull fellow Flotow[2] and Stumm.

Tuesday 16 August

Kiderlen did not receive—so nothing partic.—except that the British, French and Belgian buildings at the Brussels exhibition have been burnt to the ground.

Wrote a very tiresome despatch on the German Minister's[3] game at Teheran—where he tried to interfere in the fight between the Gov't troops and the Fedais.[4] The Russian papers have abused him like a pickpocket—and say that he has made himself and the country he represents the laughing stock of Europe. Therefore the papers here are up in arms in his defence and say that he at least displayed humanity—while the B'h and Russian R.R. were callous and indifferent to the shedding of blood.

He evidently tried it on—and if he had succeeded would have scored heavily.

I wonder what they think of it at the Imp'l F.O. I know that they have not a very high idea of his discretion.

Wednesday 17 August

Lesson with May Harrison—at which I was very stupid—and then played golf by myself. I wish I could find out something about Djavid's[5] mission here—but there is no one here to tell me anything. Boil suddenly appeared and got bad and painful in the twinkling of an eye.

Thursday 18 August

Sent a tel: to the old Emperor Francis Joseph for his 80th birthday—and got a nice answer from Him.

[1] Enclosed with Grey to Goschen, 29 July 1910, *B.D.*, vi, no. 387.
[2] German Minister, Brussels.   [3] Quadt-Wykradt-Isny.
[4] Followers of Satta Khan.   [5] Turkish Minister of Finance.

Orsini[1] and Berckheim came to lunch but they didn't know anything—except they had both heard that Isvolsky contemplates going to Paris and *not* Rome.

Messenger in. Two letters from Grey—one telling me to call him 'Grey' and not 'Sir E. Grey', and the other talking a little about affairs.[2]

Didn't go out all day as my boil is painful....

Friday 19 August

Wrote private letter to Sir E. Grey[3]—a rather interesting one *I* think—and I hope he will think so too.

Good lesson from May Harrison—just as an interlude in the Messenger work.

Benjie is doing very well—and wrote some excellent drafts.

Boil bad and painful.

Tuesday 23 August

Much better—owing to having taken Aspirin last night....

Saw Kiderlen—who told me that the Chancellor required a little time for reflection—verb sap.

Milovanovich (Servian Min'r for F.A.) came to see me this morning and was very interesting. He told me inter alia in answer to an observation from me that the military situation between Turkey and Bulgaria was very different, in Turkey's favour, from what it was two or three years ago, that that was true to a certain extent; but that the Turks were neither so strong as they thought themselves nor as a great many other people thought them. Their men were good— but their officers—notwithstanding v. der Goltz deplorable: as venal and inefficient as they were in Abdul Hamid's time. Still they c'd cope with Bulgaria alone now—but not he thought with Bulgaria *and* Servia—besides they had no money—and it passed his comprehension how they could go and buy two old ships from Germany when there was so much financial pressure at home. He scoffed at the idea that it was to make them safe ag'st the Greeks 'Who ever thinks of the Greeks now?' There had been and perhaps still was a chance that Turkey might move ag'st them: but it w'd be a promenade which w'd bring them no military prestige and w'd perhaps put powers ag'st them. They fully realized this—that is to say the sober heads. No! he thought that Turkey had bought the ships to put Germany in a

[1] Councillor, Italian Embassy.
[2] Grey to Goschen, 11 and 16 Aug. 1910 (copies), Gr. P., F.O. 800/62.
[3] Goschen to Grey, 19 Aug. 1910, *B.D.*, vi, no. 395.

good humour and to get their support: and in this they had probably
succeeded as 'L'Allemagne a fait une bonne affaire'. He then made
a little disquisition on Turkey's relations with the Powers. When first
the new regime had started—the Turks were all for the liberal and
constitutional Western Powers. Then gradually they had realized that
Austria was a near neighbour with whom it was well to be on good
terms—'Ils n'ont pas la maladie des souvenirs, Messieurs les Turcs'—
and that Germany was not only the strongest Power on the continent
as shown by the rôle she played in the Annexation business—but also
a power looking for fresh markets and ready to make sacrifices to get
them. Therefore she had turned to them. He added that he wasn't
so sure about Germany—but that he was absolutely certain that there
was a sort of unwritten Entente or alliance between Turkey and
Austria. This brought him to Ährenthal and Isvolsky. Speaking of
the former he said that before the A.H.—Servian trouble had got
acute he had gone to Ährenthal and said 'Look here what do you
want us to do—we will do *anything* to place things on a friendly footing—only let us know what *you* want—because what we want is good
relations with you and time and opportunity to develope our country.'
But that Ährenthal had merely given him a strong stare (I know that
stare) and refused to discuss. By the way I asked him about the Commercial Treaty with Austria—which I had heard was not considered
very satisfactory on either side. He replied 'Well no it isn't *very* satisfactory: but I didn't want it to be so—as if it had been it would have
tied us too much to Austria. I didn't want this as I am anxious to
keep open the new lines of Trade wh. we opened at the time when
Austrian frontiers were closed to us.' Talking of the Adriatic Railway
he said that he had discussed it with the G'd Vizier once. Who had
said that they wanted it as much as the Serbs did but that they wanted
to construct it themselves—as if it was put in the hands of Foreigners
it meant an influx of the latter with consequent interference with
Turkish Affairs like under the old Régime. This meant clearly, Milovanovich said, that the line would never be constructed—and that
it was just as well as a line constructed and managed by Turks and
Turkish methods would be worse than no line at all. But he was most
interesting about Isvolsky and his dealings with Ährenthal.

Wednesday 24 August

Nothing partic. except that I played trios of Haydn with May Harrison and 'Baba' (cello). They went off quite well and I enjoyed
it. Afterwards Baba played one or two things very prettily—she
is to be a very fine player—and then May H. played beautifully

notwithstanding that Baba was not such a *very* good accompanyist. Otherwise packed up chiefly.

Tyrell turned up for dinner—Count, Benjie and Molloy[1] also dined.

Thursday 25 August

Left for Tentschach—Linz way....

Monday 29 August

Emperor of Germany seems to have overdone the divine right job in a speech he made at Königsberg[2]—I am afraid it will only help Socialists.

Wednesday 31 August

German Emperor has been talking about 'Divine Right' and the papers (German and English) are full of it. His speech was of course directed ag'st the Socialists—but I expect it will do more harm than good!

Friday 2 September

Twinkle Clarke arrived from Gastein....

Friday 30 September

Tel. from Grey telling me he would like me to go back as soon as possible. But my cold is still too bad. Must try and get off Tuesday or Wednesday. Awful bore as the weather is beautiful.

Wednesday 5 October

Left Tentschach for Berlin via Gastein etc....

Read in the train that King Manuel[3] had been driven out of Portugal and the Republic declared! Poor little chap—but ought he to have left the country? I trow not. He fled with his Mother our dear Queen Amélie to Gibraltar—where they were joined by Queen Maria Pia[4] and Duke of Oporto.[5] The latter appears to have fought.

The selfseeking and selfishness and political ineptitude of a long series of Portuguese Conservative statesmen is sufficient to account

---

[1] King's Messenger.   [2] On 25 Aug. 1910.   [3] Manoel II.
[4] Widow of Luis II.   [5] Uncle of Manoel II.

for the Revolution. Even when I was there 20 years ago they were doing their best to bring one on.

Thursday 6 October

Arrived Berlin—rain!...

Wednesday 12 October

Tremendous talk of 2 hours with the Chancellor—an excellent exercise for the memory which I was able to check afterwards by notes supplied.[1]

Sunday 16 October

Lunched with Emperor and presented my letter of credence.[2] He has not often talked politics with me but on this occasion he did it with a vengeance and gave me a good doing. He would have gone on for ever only the Empress put her head in and said that they were all dying with Hunger—and couldn't wait for luncheon much longer. It was very interesting but too secret for this book.[3] Empress very nice and so was the little Princess.[4]

Monday 17 October

In the morning P'ce A. of Teck and his delightful little wife Princess Alice (of Albany) turned up to lunch on their way through to Gotha.[5] Between luncheon and their train Dolly Teck telegraphed to me to try and catch Alex'r and advise him to return as their brother Francis[6] was seriously ill. So P'cess went off to Gotha and Alex'r of T. stayed on, dined and went straight home by Flushing. Other guests at dinner—Kiderlen—Lerchenberg[7]—2 Thurn und Taxis—Russells[8]—Watson and boy. That was all I could scrape up. It was very gay and pleasant—and the old P'ce enjoyed Kiderlen's Roumanian stories.

Tuesday 18 October

Went to Kiderlen's day—had a short argument with him about

[1] Memorandum, enclosed with Goschen to Grey, 12 Oct. 1912, *B.D.*, vi, no. 400.
[2] As Ambassador of George V.
[3] Cf. Goschen to Grey, 16 Oct. 1910, *B.D.*, vi, no. 403.
[4] Viktoria Luise.
[5] Where the Princess's brother, Charles Edward, was the reigning duke.
[6] 2nd Teck brother.   [7] Probably Lerchenfeld.
[8] Military attaché and his wife.

the Journalists who were maltreated by the Police in the Moabit riots.[1] I wanted him to allow the Journalists to publish the expression of regret (contained in Stemrich's[2] note). K. said but I am not sorry—they brought it on themselves. I said that the Imp'l Government speaking thro' Stemrich had expressed their regret: and what was the use of their doing so if no one was to know it? Finally he agreed that as soon as their communiqué giving the substance of the Police enquiry was published—the Journalists might do as I asked.*

* Oct. 23. The beggar has not published the communiqué!! Cambon's estimate of K. is: 'Dans les petites affaires il sera très coulant—mais dans les affaires importantes il est capable de nous faire des grandes cochonneries.'!![3]

Wednesday 19 October

Work on Emperor's conversation.

Tiresome bag in from London. Lots of small things to do—but little information. But a good long letter from Nicolson—chiefly about forthcoming meeting between Emperor and Czar—wh. means Sazonow and Kiderlen![4]

German Bank project in Egypt?

If Turkey continues to threaten Greece—do I think Germany w'd join in remonstrance? No I don't—but I also don't think that Turkey means to make war. They might have done so earlier—but now, as they have accepted Venizelos as Pres't of Greek Council[5]—they have not a shadow of an excuse. That's what I think and it has been confirmed to me by G'k Ch. d'Aff. Theotoki.[6]

Thursday 20 October

H.M.G. express their views as regards recognition of Portugal. Current affairs to be treated with de facto Gov't—recognition to wait definite expression of National will.

Told Kiderlen who agreed—particularly with Grey's wish that all Powers should act unanimously in this business.

Also had it out with Kiderlen as regards certain expressions of Emperor re a Naval Agreement. He had seen Chancellor who explained what Emperor had *meant* to say—but wh. as a matter of fact he had *not* said!!

[1] In September 1910; in Moabit, a district of Berlin; the outcome of an industrial dispute; there were clashes between the police and strikers, and between the police and British and American journalists.

[2] Under-secretary, German Foreign Office.

[3] Added subsequently by Goschen at foot of page.

[4] Nicolson to Goschen, 18 Oct. 1910 (copy), N.P., F.O. 800/344.

[5] Appointed October 1910.   [6] Secretary, Greek Legation.

Friday 21 October

Hard work for Messenger all day. Long letter to Nico explaining things. This *is* a responsible and Heavy Post.

Empress's birthday. Teld. and got a nice answer—also I and whole staff wrote names down.

Saturday 22 October

Polished off Messenger, but didn't go out in beastly E. wind. Berckheim came to see me and reminded me of Emperor's remark to Lord Reay[1]—speaking of Crown Prince's visit to India he said 'This will be the unique opportunity for my son to study the effect which Greek art had upon that of India.'!! I can't help being amused at the idea that the Crown Prince is going to *study*: they attribute all sorts of ideas to him—how he is going to win over China—separate Japan from England etc. and take Professors and Experts with him who will turn his studies into the right direction. If I know the Crown Prince His only idea is to have a jolly good time in India and kill lots of tigers etc.

Poor Francis of Teck died this morning. I didn't know him well—but I am sorry for Teck. Tel'd. sympathy to him and the Queen.

Sunday 23 October

Went to general rehearsal of Mischa Elman's concert with Jimmy[2] and Lady Agnes.[3] Elman played Brahms' violin concerto—very beautifully very easily and with a sweet tone. But—pace J. and Lady A., who thought it quite perfect, I felt there was something wanting. The critics said it was lovely—but not Brahms and I expect that is about right.

May Harrison opinion is that he is a magnificent Fidler—with lots of temperament, but lacking in education—musical and otherwise.

Tuesday 25 October

Nothing partic., but on the next day[4] (whose page is full) I had a lesson from May Harrison—and played Spohr and Tartini with her. She swears I have improved enormously. Afterwards she played the Spohr with Jimmy and then we three discussed Governess Home Concert.

[1] Former Governor of Bombay and parliamentary under-secretary, India.
[2] Durham.   [3] Durham's wife.   [4] 26 Oct. 1910.

Wednesday 26 October

Dined at the Chancellor's to meet the Crown P'ce and Princess. I sat next to the latter and as usual we had a merry talk. She is furious at not going all the way with the Prince—but says she means to have a 'jolly good time' going out to Ceylon. She had never been, she told me at the Reichskanzlei before: the Bülows had never asked them! There was one of the Cabinet opposite to us and she asked me who it was. I told her and said that she ought to have known. 'Don't give me away' she said. She said she liked sitting next to me as like most Englishmen she had met I had such a strong sense of humour. The Crown Prince was like a boy just going home for the holidays. He could talk of nothing but Polo, tiger-shooting and all the joys he was going to have in India. 'I know I can get on with Englishmen,' he said. Kiderlen says 'This journey of the Crown P'ce is giving me a lot of bother. The Emperor looks upon it as an opportunity given to the Prince for scientific study and research. The Press and the Public look upon it as an opportunity for him to draw closer commercial and political ties between Germany and the countries he is going to visit. The Crown Prince himself looks upon it as a pleasant outing and an opportunity for sport. How am I to find an entourage representing all these points of view?'

Chancellor very friendly and I took an opportunity of giving him a message from Grey.

Thursday 27 October

Boss arrived from Tentschach looking very much better than she has looked for a long time....

Letters from Grey[1] and Nicolson[2]—latter said that there was but one opinion in F.O. viz. that I had managed my difficult conversations with Emp'r and Chancellor very skilfully. Yi!

Saturday 29 October

Norah Drewett Concert. She played well—Cellist Beyer-Hané—so-so. Good programme—and an early Cello Sonata by Strauss surprised me by its beauty and grace.

---

[1] Grey to Goschen, 26 Oct. 1910 (copy), Gr. P., F.O. 800/62.
[2] Nicolson to Goschen, 26 Oct. 1910 (copy), N.P., F.O. 800/344.

Monday 31 October

Had a long and interesting talk with Cambon this evening. He agrees with me that the idea of lending money to the Turks is very disagreeable to them here and if they can get out of it they will. He is not easy in his mind about Kiderlen—and says 'Ah! Mon ami—nous avons mangé notre pain blanc dans la Personne de Schoen—avec Kiderlen nous n'aurons que du pain noir!' He does not think we shall get anything out of Ostensacken or Schebeko[1] with regard to Sazonow's[2] visit. He had asked Ostensacken whether Sazonow would call upon us—and O. said 'No'. He told me that Schön's speech to Fallières[3] had been drawn up in much warmer terms by the Imp'l F.O. but that Schoen had modified the warmth a good deal saying that he was already regarded by the German Public as too Francophil! Cambon added that the Emperor and His Gov't were trying to suck up to them—but that a few friendly words and the fact that the Emperor had lent pictures to the French Exhibition at Berlin did not make the French people forget 1871–3!

Tuesday 1 November

Durham and May Harrison lunched—and we settled a good deal about the Governess's Home concert, wh. May H. is getting up and wh. is to be held on Dec. 3.

Afterwards I had a very good lesson from May H.

Boss does not seem *very* well these days, but perhaps it is only the weather which is muggy and rainy with the lowest Barometer possible.

Sazonow arrived and met Chancellor and Kiderlen at lunch at Ostensacken's. It will be very difficult to find out what he is up to here.

Tuesday 8 November

Went to Kiderlen's day—he gave me a very jejune account of his conversations with Sazonow—Statu Quo in Balkans—support of present Turkish Gov't 'Faute de Mieux' (wh. he explained by saying that a Gov't directed by an anonymous Committee was not an ideal one!)—localization of quarrels amongst minor Balkan States—and necessity of making latter understand that sh'd Internal troubles arise in Turkey it is not *their* affair but that of G't Powers. About Persia he said but little merely that he had told Sazonow that as long as integrity of Persia and open door was guaranteed Germany had nothing to do with 'Persian Question'.

[1] Councillor, Russian Embassy.
[2] Russian Foreign Minister; Isvolsky's successor.
[3] President, French Republic.

I called his attention to Article in *D. Chronicle*[1]—which gives practically everything that has been said to me on the subject of Anglo-German relations by Chancellor—it was sent by Special Correspondent of that paper from here—where he had seen Kiderlen (and I think *Pansa*).

Thursday 10 November

Boss left for London.

Sunday 13 November

Left for Trachenberg[2]—feeling rather a worm. Throat very sore—feverish.

Monday 14 November

Trachenberg

Shoot—guns—P'ce and P'cess Hatzfeldt[3]—Prince Solms,[4] Prince Lignowsky,[5] C't Strachwitz[6]—Count Hatzfeld[7]—Heintze (Oberjägermeister) and C't Lerchenfeld and I. Fine day—1500 Pheasants etc. Keen E. wind. Felt fairly all right in the Evening. I shot about 220.

Tuesday 15 November

Returned to Berlin. Throat sore again and fit for nothing. Much fussed and worried about concert.

Thursday 1 December

Bunt came to hear the beautiful Brahms double concerto played by May and Baba H. under Stransky's[8] Bâton. The girls played it quite beautifully but I didn't think much of either the Orchestra or its leader. I love the 'Double' more and more—and I want to hear it some day with Kahn[9] at the Piano.

Saturday 3 December

Concert at Embassy.[10] Great financial success £140! Also musically an enormous success—*but* it was too long. . . .

---

[1] *Daily Chronicle*, 7 Nov. 1910.   [2] For this outing see also Introduction.
[3] Son and daughter-in-law of Trachenberg.
[4] Grand Chamberlain.
[5] Lichnowsky; Silesian landowner; formerly on staff of German Foreign Office.
[6] Silesian landowner.   [7] Younger son of Trachenberg.
[8] Conductor, Hamburg Opera.   [9] German pianist.
[10] In aid of the Governess's Home.

Sunday 4 December

May and Baba Harrison came to tea at Mrs K.'s[1] request. They made me play and I played very badly being nervous. Later on Bunt and I gave a recital to Emmie and Mrs K. and I played all right and pleased them.

Saturday 10 December[2]

Went to Baba Harrison's concert with Philharmonic Orchestra under Becker.[3] Bunt and Lascelles[4] came up for it[5]—and we sat with May and Bébé Harrison.[6] It was a great success and I never saw so much enthusiasm in a Berlin audience. Afterwards we all went to supper with the Harrisons and I was much interested to make Becker's acquaintance. A fine musician and a most intelligent man. He told me that Baba was already a splendid cellist and would be greater still.

Sunday 11 December

Bunt—Lascelles and I dined at the Harrisons—and we had lots of music. Bunt and I began—then Bunt played his new sonata—and then May and Baba H. played a lot. But poor old Baba was rather tired I think, tho' she insisted on playing the Dvorak Concerto—a very jolly evening.

Tuesday 20 December

Left for England and picked up Bunt at Hanover.[7]...

Wednesday 21 December

Arrived at 40 Portman Square....

Thursday 22 December

Saw Nico. Nothing new—but found him rather upset about Sazonow. *I* think latter is not behaving well. He seems to think that I have done all right....

[1] Kahn's wife.   [2] Entered in error on page for 5 Dec.
[3] Probably Hugo Becker.   [4] Alan Lascelles; friend of 'Bunt'.
[5] From Hanover.   [6] Margaret; the 3rd Harrison sister.
[7] Where he was preparing for the Diplomatic Service examination.

1911

Goschen was in Berlin until 12 May, when he left for London to be present at the unveiling of the memorial to Queen Victoria. After returning to Berlin he again left for London on 14 June to attend the coronation of George V. He was back in Berlin on 9 July. In August he went to Homburg for the unveiling of a memorial to Edward VII. On 8 October he left for Tentschach, arriving back in Berlin on 1 November. On 17 December he set out for Arco in Tyrol, where he joined his wife. He got back to Berlin on 31 December.

Sunday 1 January

The year opened with a dull dark day—not very inspiriting for one with his little family in 3 different parts of the earth.[1]

Went to Emperor at 'etwa' 11.30 a.m. driving to the Palace in my state coach. All 8 Amb'rs present—all making tender inquiries after Boss, and expressing regret that she had not come back with me. Emperor *very* friendly. Said he had exchanged very cordial letters with the King etc. Bewailed the state of politics in England—and said he had received many very 'violent' letters from his friends in England on the subject. Added that he had great confidence in the conservative instincts of the British people being sufficiently strong to prevent any too radical change. H.M. expressed great gratification at the reception His son the Crown P'ce had met with in India—and told me how 'awfully' the latter was amusing himself. The Empress was, as usual, most kind and inquired lots after Boss. Cambon chaffed me afterwards at the 'Cour' made to me by their Majesties—and attributed it to our new 'Alliance'. !!

Tuesday 3 January

Saw Zimmermann[2] in Kiderlen's absence: had nothing to say to him except wish him a happy New Year. I alluded to Press Arts. respecting answer of Russian Gov't to German proposals of 1907: but he said they had rec'd *nothing* in writing. This is not *quite* the case as they have rec'd Sassonow's draft memo. resp'g Bagdad R'way and other matters discussed at Potsdam. He told Pansa the same thing—adding that such a note as that alluded to in the *Novoe Wremja* and French and English Press—would be far too comprehensive for what has taken place up till now between the two Gov'ts. This is strange:

---

[1] Hosta was in England; 'Ted' in Egypt.
[2] Councillor, Imperial Foreign Office.

for while Zimmermann is saying this—the German Press (inspired and otherwise) is fulminating ag'st what it considers to be an attempt on the part of the French, Russian and English Press to attenuate the Chancellor's statement in the Reichstag—viz. 'That it has again (at Potsdam) been made clear that neither Country will join any combination having any aggressive point ag'st the other.' (The *Novoe Wremja* limited this to 'Persia or Turkey'—while the German Press regards B.H.'s statement as a general 'entente' not to join etc.) It is a matter of opinion which of the two statements is strongest—the general one—or the one wh. specially mentions two countries.

Sunday 8 January

Mackenzie[1] came to see me after lunch: and discussed production in *Evening Times*[2] of alleged note from Russian Gov't to German Gov't. As a matter of fact this is a tolerably correct reproduction of the *draft* Memo. embodying the Potsdam and Petersburg negotiations: which was sent some time ago (a fortnight?) by Sassonow to German Government without submitting it *beforehand* to either B'h or F'h Ambassadors—or (apparently) to Czar. It contained the Art. I about the Bagdad R'way which has caused so much annoyance and disapp't to French and us, as by it Russia practically detaches herself from us as regards B'd Railway. He told Buchanan[3] that he only meant 'Railway *as far* as Bagdad', but there is no doubt that Kiderlen will hold him to the letter and won't allow him to wriggle out—i.e. without a row—because there is nothing signed yet.

Called on Harrisons—and met Herr Buchmeyer[4] of Dresden, the Bach expert and digger out of 17th century dances etc. He played an almost unknown Violin Sonata of Bach with May—a gorgeous thing: and then for an hour played old dances—French, German and English with consummate skill and expression. He is going to arrange them for violin—and May is delighted as they will be for her alone and Kreisler has not got them.

Monday 9 January

A Revolting day—but a very good violin lesson—and heavy practice. Press still hot about Potsdam Interview. The situation is very confused. Officially French tranquil and certain that nothing has passed either at Potsdam or St Petersburg which need disturb their minds as to solidarity of Russo-French alliance. But really they are

[1] Berlin correspondent, *The Times*.
[2] Goschen presumably means some Berlin newspaper.
[3] Now Ambassador, St Petersburg. [4] Richard Buchmayer; musicologist.

furious and consider that a great blow has been struck against the Alliance and that Sassonow has been made to go much further than he meant, by Kiderlen. I share this view and so does Cambon.

Tuesday 10 January

Fine

Shoot with Schwabach at Lenke.

After a deluge of rain in the night the day proved fine. Motored down with Schwabach and Russell[1] on a very slippery road at 8.15. 14 guns—only hares. . . .

Friday 12 May[2]

Left Berlin for London.[3]

Saturday 13 May

London

Arrived at Lennox Gardens,[4] and had a *second* breakfast with Alic and Laura.[5] Found a telephone from Nicolson asking me to come and see him at once. So went down to F.O. at 12. Had a good talk with Nico: but found him rather depressed and of course unable to give me news of any decided policy. Drift seemed to me to be the order of the day—as there is a decided revirement for Germany in British Public Opinion—and the idea of the Gov't seems to be to take count of this by spreading negotiations over a long time—even tho' they know that no definite agreement is likely. This is an unpleasant position—1. for H.M. Amb'r at Berlin. 2. for Nico whose child the Triple Entente is. I am to see Grey on Monday. A little bit of Lords[6] in the afternoon and then tea to 117 Sloane Street[7] where I found Charlie very fairly well—and Nellie[8] likewise. Quiet dinner with Alics and bed early.

Sunday 14 May

Alic and I had a quiet morning—in fact quiet day. We went over

---

[1] Military attaché; Trench's successor.

[2] First entry since 10 Jan. Goschen made this entry on page for 19 May, but it clearly relates to 12 May. The succeeding entries down to and including that for 22 May were all made on pages for the wrong days, and subsequently corrected.

[3] Goschen was on his way to London for the unveiling of the memorial, erected in front of Buckingham Palace, to Queen Victoria.

[4] Alexander Goschen's London home.   [5] Alexander's wife.

[6] Lord's Cricket Ground.   [7] Charles Goschen's home.   [8] Charles's wife.

and saw Dates[1]—I made some visits and then in the late afternoon we went for a charming walk through Chelsea—by the river etc.—which I had never done before. Weather delightful.

Dined with Charlie—little Mabel[2] was there looking as pretty as ever.

Tomorrow the scurry begins.

Monday 15 May

London

At Station at 12.45. Immense crowd but got through fairly easily. Found Lascelles and old Swaine—and others there. Then came King and Queen and Prince of Wales—Duchess of Argyle[3]—the Schleswig-Holsteins[4] all complete—Duke and Duchess of Connaught—P'cess Patricia[5]—Alexander Tecks etc. King and Queen both said a few nice words to me. Train badly measured didn't draw up right! The Imperial party all looked in good spirits and as if they meant to enjoy themselves. P'cess Victoria Luise radiant. After a short hand shaking they drove off to the Palace. Emp. and Empress both asked after Boss.

Then lunch at Venetia's.[6]... Very pleasant party. Spent afternoon in writing name down on Royalties—and a very nice interview with Grey—at wh. we discussed lots of things—chiefly unclear part of Chancellor's Memo.

Quiet dinner at Lennox.

Good conversation with Sir E. Grey: but I don't see the way clear ahead—nor does he!

Tuesday 16 May

Unveiling ceremony. Very beautiful and very impressive. But the singing of the hymn 'Oh! God our help in Ages past' was rather lost. The 3 choirs the soldiers all sang but everything was drowned by the massed bands of the Guards. Still the last verse with a continuous roll of the drums was very fine. The march past was splendidly done—especially by the Cavalry. Münster who was next to me said that the wheeling of the 9th Lancers was the most perfect thing he had ever seen. Altogether a splendid ceremony—the Archbishop[7] read the prayers most beautifully—even I heard every word.

[1] Former companion of Goschen's mother.
[2] Charles's daughter.
[3] Duchess of Argyll; Victoria's 4th daughter.
[4] Prince Christian and Princess Helena and family.
[5] Of Connaught.
[6] Mrs Venetia James; Marienbad acquaintance; wife of John Arthur James, J.P.
[7] Davidson.

Garden party at the Londesborough's[1]—to which Venetia James took me in her motor. Very pretty—the Emperor and Empress most amiable. Saw Margaret Talbot and her general[2]—they were very pleased at the Emperor's remembering them.

Banquet at the Palace. I sat next to Grey who was very nice.... Queen talked to me and said that she had nearly wept during ceremony thinking how King Edward would have liked it. She said she had to cover her mouth to prevent people seeing how it was twitching....

Wednesday 17 May

Command performance of *Money*[3] at Drury Lane most interesting—but had great difficulty in getting there owing to the crowd. I had a very good place in the Royal Box sitting between Countess Brockdorff[4] and the Duchess of Westminster.[5] The latter was very nice indeed and rather good looking. (The Duke[6] is a heavy looking chap.) The play was well done—by Hare, Alexander Tree (who rather overdid it—but was good) Charles Wyndham—looking very old— and Cyril Maude. The women were also good—partic. Irene Vanbrugh and Alexandra Carlisle. I saw Charlie Hawtry amongst the supers.[7] The Emperor said he had never seen better acting.

Thursday 18 May

Lunched with Grey. The party being He, Asquith Nicolson and myself. Most interesting and rather alarming. We did have a good talk—and I found Asquith and Grey quite sound on For. Pol. I wish I could say the same for their internal ones. Grey drew me out a good bit for the Premier's edification—and I responded freely and did not *hide* my own views. Asquith is a charming man to meet—with a very pleasant manner: as a matter of fact one can't help liking him *when one is with him.*

Friday 19 May

Court Ball. Very crowded—beautiful sight—lovely faces—splendid jewels—lots of old friends. Diana Manners[8] mothered me and got

---

[1] 2nd earl and his wife.
[2] He was a former military attaché, Paris.
[3] By Bulwer Lytton.
[4] Grand Mistress of the Court.
[5] *Née* Cornwallis-West; sister of Princess of Pless.
[6] Duchess of Teck's brother.
[7] The persons named were all well-known actors and actresses.
[8] Daughter of Duke of Rutland; now Diana Viscountess Norwich.

me supper—as I couldn't penetrate the crowd at the Buffet....
Rather a rag altogether.

Musical afternoon at the Harrisons—crowds of people. A man sang
indifferently and the girls played splendidly. May looked very
wretched and ill.

Saturday 20 May

Went down in the evening to spend week end with the Ponsonbys
at Tangley Manor....

Sunday 21 May

Tangley

Played golf all the morning at New Zealand links—great fun. After
lunch went round the garden with Lady Fritz—both she and the aza-
leas being in great beauty! There is nothing in the world like English
faces and English Country. Had a putting tournament on the Lawn.
Fritz and I in the final—he just beating me at the last hole!

Monday 22 May

London

Had an audience with the King. He was most gracious and kind
and talked with me for an hour on German and other affairs. He
told me that only on the last day just before going had the Emperor
talked politics with him—and on the subject of Morocco. The K.
seems to have kept his end up very well. He is dead against any bind-
ing naval or pol. arrangement—and told me to try and stop it!...

Wednesday 14 June

Left for London[1] but before starting got a letter from the Prime
Minister telling me that the King had been pleased to give me

G.C.B.

I *am* glad as that is *the* best thing of *that* sort to have. All the Chancery were awfully nice about it.

Left Berlin in heavy rain and found gale blowing at Hook—rough-
ish passage.

---

[1] Goschen was again leaving Berlin for London; on this occasion to attend George
V's coronation.

Tuesday 20 June

Boss arrived from Folkestone.

Thursday 22 June

The Coronation.[1]

Saturday 1 July

Went down to Ballards with Bunt—for Xtening (tomorrow) of Syb's[2] new baby. May and Baba came down later in their motor. . . . Had a thoroughly musical evening and the playing of the two girls was much admired.

Sunday 2 July

Christening of Syb's babe. . . . May got a telephone from her mother saying that Elgar was coming on Tuesday to play his concerto with her. She was awfully pleased but had to practice all day wh. rather spoilt her fun. They and we all went to the Xtening p.m. . . .

In the evening we had lots more music—and kept it up late. They made me sing Odds Bobs—and Bunt and I played Op. 3—Küssen ist keine Sünd[3] and other pieces. I also played Op. 4. I may say that they were all astonished at the progress I had made. The Harrisons have to motor up to town early tomorrow and propose to take Bunt with them.

Monday 3 July

Oxford and Cambridge. . . .

Tuesday 4 July

Oxford and Cambridge match all day. . . .

Wednesday 5 July

Oxford and Cambridge at Lords in the morning—then a very jolly little lunch with Lady Molly Crichton[4]—poor dear—and back to Lords to find match finished Oxford winning by 3 wickets. Rather a sell for me not to see the end of it. But it was a good match—and

---

[1] Written in large letters in MS.   [2] Charles Goschen's daughter.
[3] Popular Viennese song.   [4] Duchess of Teck's sister.

no walk over for Oxford who had a great reputation but did not show themselves to be a very sound team.

Before going up to Lords I went to F.O. to see Grey and had a good talk about Morocco. I also took opportunity of thanking him for recommending me for G.C.B. He said that I had well deserved it—and that he had been delighted to find that the Prime Minister was just as pleased that I should have it as he was.

Thursday 6 July

Invested by the King with *G.C.B.* at St James Palace. He said something to me while I was kneeling in front of him—I didn't hear what it was but it frightened me so that I kissed his hand standing instead of kneeling!

Lunch with Venetia—rather a nice party—a nice French woman on one side and a nice Englishwoman on the other—but I forget who.

Made some hurried visits afterwards and left Venetia's hospitable home at 4 and went down to Ballards. Henrys[1] dined and were very nice. Had a final talk with Nico: and we were very satisfied with Asquith's declaration in the House of Commons[2] that the desp. of the German ship to Agadir created a new situation—and that if it raised international questions—and a German occupation was threatened—we should be solid with France and keep a sharp eye on every thing that might affect B'h interests. Our idea is that France paid us for letting her alone as regards Morocco—by giving us free hand in Egypt: if Germany goes to Morocco—situation changed because she has paid us nothing.

Saturday 8 July[3]

Went down to Folkestone with Boss—and found Bunt already there having gone by an earlier *and* quicker train. Cheery little dinner and evening.

Left Folkestone for Berlin—Boss and Bunt seeing me off. Weather quite fresh not to say cold. Awful crowd on the steamer—but they kinder melted away after a bit.

Sunday 9 July

Arrived Berlin. Dogs at all events glad to see me.

[1] Henry Goschen and his wife.   [2] 6 July 1911.
[3] Entered in error on page for 7 July and corrected by Goschen.

Monday 10 July

Long talk to Cambon, who told me everything that had passed—
which was in fact and in brief that after a conversation with Kiderlen
at Kissingen in which latter had made certain proposals with regard
to compensation outside Morocco—Cambon went home to lay these
proposals before his Gov't—and before he could do so (owing to
change of Gov't) and only 3 days after Kid.'s proposals—Agadir
happened.

Cambon furious naturally. Went raving to Schoen and gave a bit
of his mind as regards K.'s proceeding.

He then came back here—and had a conversation with K. which
beginning, naturally, very stiffly ended by the same proposals as K.
had made at Kissingen.

Both Cambon and I are very sceptical about settlement being
arrived at once—as everything looks so easy.[1]

Twinkle arrived from the Taxis'—looking well and portly: but he
is a little low about his health.

Thursday 13 July

C. and K. met again and had again rather hot conv'n.

The demands are shocking—wh. may—or may not be—K.'s fault.

K. sent for me and talked about meeting of B'h and German Squad-
rons at Molde[2] under H.M.'s eye!

He took a line which I sh'd not have expected: but in wh. *I* quite
agreed.

Friday 14 July

Heavy Messenger—as I had so much to write and tell. All of which
the F.O. will also hear from Paris. *But* in my priv. letters I gave some
pungent details.[3]

Saturday 15 July

Another interview between C. and K. but again not much biz
done—at all events according to C. K. wants apparently whole of
French Congo coast line. C. asked then how are we to get to the sea.
'By a railway which we shall build,' said K.

Twinkle left at 11 p.m.

---

[1] Doubtful reading; Goschen corrected the word that he had originally written; the
final version is only partly legible.
[2] In Norway.
[3] Goschen to Grey, 14 July 1911, *B.D.*, vii, nos. 383–4; to Nicolson, 14 July 1911,
N.P., F.O. 800/349.

Monday 17 July

Count departed.[1] We were both sorry to say goodbye. He has I think liked being with us—and I certainly have found him always ready and willing to give any sort of help. Besides I am fond of the nice quaint creature personally.

One very good point in our relation was that he loved the things that I hate most. He loved Statistics, Finance and Commerce—and boundaries—while I was only too glad to place all such matters in his capable hands.

Tuesday 18 July

Kiderlen did not receive—he never does.

Had a lonely birthday (64) but had nice letters from Boss and Bunt and others—and a spirit lamp toast rack from Bunt!

Thursday 20 July

Very awkward discovery. A private letter from me to Nicolson[2]— containing very important and secret matter—which I wrote for last bag—came back to me from the Imp'l F.O. [sic] *opened* and returned as insuff'ly addressed.

Benjie gave it to Heinrich[3] to seal and put in the bag. Heinrich sealed it—but left it on his table and sent it by Post in the evening. It was marked priv. and conf'l and addressed F.O. without London. Benjie went to the Imp. P.O. about it—and they told him it was quite out of the question that it had been read—as the opening and finding the address of the sender is a purely routine matter performed by only *two* clerks who have to deal with a mass of such letters every day. They had neither time nor inclination to read—and their inst'ns are agin it. I hope it is all right but one can't help feeling nervous as for once in a way it mattered!!

Morocco. Went to see Kiderlen who told me that Colonial Minister[4] was making difficulties and asking too much—and that he Col. Min.[5] could not understand that as Germany was claiming compensation for giving up not what they possessed but what they felt they had a right to possess—they must not be too grasping and must in fact be ready—for the sake of public opinion in France to give up a little bit of German territory. This sounds unlike K.—but it is what he said. He chaffed a good bit—and said that the real difficulty lay in the

---

[1] To Cetinje, as Minister.
[2] Goschen to Nicolson, 20 July 1911, N.P., F.O. 800/349.
[3] Embassy servant.   [4] Lindquist.
[5] 'Col. Min.' added above line.

fact that Germany France and England all pronounced Agadir in
a different way.

Friday 21 July

Ted arrived a day late owing to Quarantine. The dear boy looked
very well and is in splendid spirits.

Had to get Mess. off: rather a nasty job telling Nico of the con-
tretemps of yesterday[1]—and I am not quite sure I was right in doing
so.

Cambon not at all satisfied as to way things are going. K. says that
he won't go on negotiating if every thing they He and Cambon[2] say
is communicated by French Govt. to French Press. C. says that it
is *rather* true that de Selves[3] talks to [*sic*] much and doesn't clothe
his thoughts in Dip. language.

Saturday 22 July

Awfully hot

Boss arrived having had a very hot journey: and therefore rather
tired. It was hard for her to receive such a warm welcome from the
three dogs and they nearly knocked her over which did not improve
matters.

Ted and I met her at the station. She looks pretty well.

Sunday 23 July

102 in shade

Hottest day known for years. But Ted and Benjie played golf—
and Boss and I drove up—had a look at them—and then had a charming drive in the shady Tiergarten.

Sat out on Balcony all the evening.

Tuesday 1 August

This was the day when Bunt should have gone up for his exam.[4]
But we got a letter from Tommy Lascelles yesterday saying that Bunt
had gone up in a balloon on Saturday—that the landing had been
bungled—and that Bunt had concussion of the brain! Same post
brought a letter from Morison[5] saying the same thing—that he would
have to lie up for some time and that all idea of the exam would have

---

[1] Goschen to Nicolson, 21 July 1911, N.P., F.O. 800/349.
[2] 'He and Cambon' added above line.   [3] French Foreign Minister.
[4] For the Diplomatic Service.   [5] Family Doctor.

to be given up. He added that there was no cause for anxiety but that he must be kept quiet.

An awful disappointment. Wrote to Tyrell and explained matters—and asked whether the regulations as regards age could be waived in this case.

The news upset Boss who was none too well before.

Thursday 3 August

Heard from Teddie who had been to see Bunt. He said he seemed all right and was to be allowed to go to Ballards on Monday.

Boss very seedy all day. Oh dear, Oh dear!

Saturday 5 August

Boss left[1] in the evening—still very seedy—and we didn't have a good start as there were 1000s of people at the station and we couldn't find her carriage. . . .

Thursday 10 August

Murray—the Premier of Victoria came to see me today—a great big Burly Colonial—but quite a nice chap. He is in business connected with the electrical Railways in Melbourne—*but* he and I talked cricket and he was very interesting.

Cambon saw K. yesterday—he seemed to think things were going better. He told me that K. said 'look here I am to see the Emperor on the 18th—let's settle all the chief points by then—and then you write me a letter, wh. I can shew to the Emperor saying that you must go to Paris for a week to settle about the form to be given to the transaction. I'll tell you why I ask this! it is because *I* want some leave too!' A small thing but it looks as if K. meant to settle.

Friday 11 August

Had to hurry up with my messenger and left for Homburg by the 11 p.m. train—to be present at the unveiling of the King Edward Memorial[2] by the Emperor at 10 a.m. tomorrow! Awfully hot journey: if I had the window open I was nearly blown out of my bed—if I shut it I was boiled.

Saturday 12 August

Homburg
Arrived at 7.50 but my luggage didn't turn up till 10.20 and by

---

[1] For Tentschach. [2] In the English church.

the time I got into my frock coat and tall hat the ceremony was over!
What a sell! Lunched at de Meister's[1] to meet the Emperor—and my
mishap was a godsend to him—he chaffed about it all the time—and
said finally that I had turned up in bathing drawers and a jersey with
a Union Jack painted on it and that the Bishop[2] had turned me away
as the Church drew the line at that costume![3] I sat next to the Duchess
of Sparta[4] who was there with Princess Frederic Charles.[5] Lascelles
and the Bishop ran things as regards King's telegram and answer—
and didn't consult me much.

Dined at Friederichshof[6] in the evening—on the terrace—but it
was so hot it didn't matter. After dinner (not good) the Emperor took
me aside and gave me a good doing for $\frac{3}{4}$ of an hour. He was rampant
about Lloyd George's speech[7] and our interference—and said that
without that Germany and France would have arranged matters long
ago. I reminded him of Agadir and we had some warm work: he
abused us like pickpockets. And said that if France didn't give him
the compensation he wanted he would have every French soldier out
of Morocco by force if necessary.

Tuesday 15 August

Came back to Berlin. Kinsky motored me over to Frankfurt. . . .
Cool journey.

Wednesday 16 August

Quite cold—a very sudden change. Found the Moroccan negotiations no further advanced—Cambon and Kiderlen still haggling.

Thursday 17 August

Signed two Treaties with Kiderlen—one for combating sleeping
sickness in S. Africa—another extending Colonies' extradition to Pro-
tectorates.[8] Kiderlen depressed and serious—told me that French
were reducing their offers and increasing their demands—and that
early indiscretions of French Press had rendered it extremely difficult—if not impossible—for him to reduce his demands. German

---

[1] Meister; President, Wiesbaden Province.
[2] Bury; Bishop for Northern and Central Europe.
[3] For the Kaiser's side of the story see Wilhelm II to Bethmann Hollweg, 12 Aug.
1911, *G.P.*, xxix, no. 10638.
[4] Wilhelm II's 3rd sister; wife of eldest son of King of the Hellenes.
[5] Wilhelm II's youngest sister; wife of Prince Friedrich Karl of Hesse-Cassel.
[6] Friedrichshof: Schloss near Kronberg.
[7] Mansion House, 21 July 1911.   [8] *B.F.S.P*, civ (1911), pp. 153 and 155.

public opinion, he said, was up in arms—not only Pan Germans but every one.

Cambon saw him directly after me—he also found K. depressed and he put it down to a conv'n between de Selves and Schön—in which de Selves had spoken rather categorically. The two negotiators made no progress in geographical negotiations—but Cambon obtained satisfactory assurances as to what was meant by 'giving France free hand in Morocco'. K. goes to Wilhelmshöhe today—where he and Chancellor will talk things over with the Kaiser. K. wants 10 days leave—he wanted C. to write a letter wh. he could shew to Emperor—saying that he (C.) wanted to go to Paris and stay 10 days. Naturally the wily C. would not *write* this—but the end of it was that they arranged to be away until the 28th. *I* think this interruption a pity—there will be so much talk in the Press! but this is perhaps what K. wants.

Friday 18 August

C. gave me an account of his yesterday's conv'n of wh. I tel'd the heads.[1] (This tel. was sent to Bertie[2] who took it to de Selves—and it made rather a row. It is a bore Nicolson is not at the F.O. for *he* knows that it is not wise to let the F'h Gov't know that C. tells me everything!)

Saturday 19 August

Cambon came to see me before he left for Paris. Very depressed—but chiefly about Paris—where he says too many cooks are spoiling the negotiations *broth*. Szogyëny back from Wilhelmshöhe told C. that Emperor had told him that the situation was very grave but that a solution *must* be found. Sz. added that the Kaiser was far more down on England than on France and said that now Liberals and Conservatives were all in the same bag.

C. thinks that France is not at all indisposed to war: that the people are tired of 'Alertes' like Casablanca and Agadir—and are beginning to say 'better finish it off now—we may be beaten—but any thing is better than this perpetual worry and unrest.'

Went for a solitary walk in the woods—where I brooded over dear Boss's state of health.

---

[1] Goschen to Grey, 18 Aug. 1911, *B.D.*, vii, no. 478.
[2] Ambassador in Paris.

Monday 21 August

Botkine[1] called being in Berlin on his way to Tangier. He talked a lot about Morocco and seemed to me to be rather German than otherwise. I had tea with his nice wife in the afternoon. He is going to stay here a week and I wonder why? except that Me. Leghait is coming here on Saturday.

Berckheim in charge of Fr. Embassy. He is just back from Paris—and is not sanguine. I told him I regarded the present situation like I regarded Ghosts—I don't believe in them but am frightened of them. So I don't believe there will be war—but I am deadly anxious about it.

Tuesday 22 August

W. Tyrell arrived on his way to Radolin's.[2] Very interesting about L. George whom he admires immensely. King congrat'ed him on his speech (the famous Agadir one) and he said to Tyrell—'I got no congrats after my Limehouse speech.' T. says he will never make a Limehouse speech again.

He seems to be singularly outspoken about his colleagues. Talking of Morley,[3] Lulu Harcourt and another member of the Cabinet who are against the line taken by the Gov't in the Morocco Crisis—he said 'I only wish they would go, we can get on perfectly without them.'!! He seems to be singularly human—and with a great sense of humour—I almost feel as if I c'd like him—if I could only forget his earlier speeches. Tyrell says that he doesn't think the French will fight—that the French will make some rotten agreement—and that we shall have to bear the brunt of German hatred. The latter will be the case whatever happens. Saw Zimmermann today—he was rather excited about Morocco—and said 'Who is Lloyd G. that he should dare to dictate and try to terrorize a Great Power like Germany?'

Tuesday 19 September[4]

Cambon came round to give me an account of his yesterday's conversation with Kiderlen. They had he said made a great step forwards and he regarded the Morocco part of the affair as nearly settled: K. had been in a very good humour and had sent for a bottle of Port wine, which they drank while negotiating! C. said that he considered that as far as *he* was concerned the question was finished—i.e. that

---

[1] Russian Minister, Tangier.
[3] Now Lord President of the Council.
[2] He was Tyrrell's brother-in-law.
[4] First entry since 22 Aug. 1911.

he considered himself responsible for the Morocco part of the business—and the F'h Gov't for the Congo part wh. was yet to be settled. He said that the French Gov't and Press were so much in the hands of Colonial financiers that he could not answer for what w'd be done. He hoped H.M.G. would counsel generous concessions—as it would be a pity if what had been obtained as regards Morocco were to be lost by unwillingness to make a certain amount of sacrifice. This unwillingness was due partly to sentiment but chiefly to private interest of a small but rather powerful group.

Friday 29 September

War declared by Italy against Turkey—and a damned shame too. They gave 'em no chance. Goodness knows what it will lead to. It is bad for everybody including Italy herself—who may find she has gone lightheartedly into a thing which may cost her dear. As Nizamy put it to me—there are 100000 Italians trading in the Turkish Empire—earning about 10 francs a day—that meant a loss to Italy of a million Francs a day. It doesn't mean that at all—but the poor devils may have a pretty bad time. But the worst of it is that it may lead to the whole Eastern question being brought up again—and for us it is anyway embarrassing with our millions of Mussulman subjects. And the Italian methods have been simply brutal—and more those of Brigands than of a respectable people. The Germans are in an awkward position. The Pan Germans say that we started it—1. to break up the Triple Alliance—2. To break down German influence in Const'ple. What fools they are—can't they see that any difficulties between Xtians and Mohomedans hit us much harder than anyone?

Cambon came in very découragé—he says that they are playing the fool in Paris.

Nizamy and Polo came in.

Saturday 30 September

Nothing partic. Waiting for news. H.M.G. have told Italy that as they had formerly given her carte blanche as regards Tripoli—they would remain perfectly neutral. It. Amb'r tried to get more out of Grey but failed. The fact is that neither France's nor our hands are quite clean in this matter—as we practically gave Italy leave to do as she liked with a country wh. did not belong to us—and wh. moreover forms an integral part of the Ott. Empire. But at all events we did not and do not encourage her to do it—and I am glad to say that the B'h Press almost unanimously condemns her somewhat brutal and precipitate action. The French *have* told her that she has their entire sympathy—and that has made a deplorable impression both here and in Turkey. I hope it wont interfere with the French Morocco negotiations of wh. the end was in sight! The Pan German Press is saying that the negotiations ought to be adjourned sine die!

Sunday 1 October

All we have heard as yet is that the Italians have sunk a Turkish Torpedo Boat off Prevesa[1]—and that the Austrians are furious thereat. There is also a rumour that the Italians have landed troops on the Albanian Coast. I don't believe it but if they have Austria will kick up a jolly good row I expect.

It is rather pathetic to think that the Triple Alliance to two members of which Turkey has been kotowing so long—should be just the ones to bag her territory in defiance of the Treaty of Berlin. First Bosnia and now Tripoli! It ought to bring that old weather cock Turkey round in our direction again.

Saturday 7 October

Cambon told me Morocco part of arrangement finished—all except two words!

Sunday 8 October

Left for Tentschach.

Monday 9 October

Tentschach
Arrived after goodish journey. Train was so hot that it did my lumbago good....

Monday 16 October

Beautiful weather still.... No beastly politics—perfect peace.

Friday 20 October

Lovely weather still continues.... Heard from Granville[2]—things seem quiet in Berlin. Congo still on—also War. There seems to be

---

[1] Preveza; on the coast of Greece.
[2] Councillor and chargé d'affaires; de Salis's successor.

an idea that Italy acted quickly because she was afraid Germany wanted to buy Tripoli! Don't believe it.

Wednesday 25 October

Heard from Granville that Congo was on the point of being settled but that the Italo-Turkish War showed no signs of stopping.

Monday 30 October

Our this year's last day at dear old Tentschach—and we are both miserable about going away. We have had, my dear Boss and I a lovely two weeks together.... But I hope that Arco[1] will do her lots of good and set her right again....

Tuesday 31 October

Left Tentschach on a bright cool day. Boss and I travelled together as far as Villach.... I *was* so sorry to leave her and come back to old Berlin.

Wednesday 1 November

Arrived Berlin—cold and damp as usual. Had a bath and went to bed for an hour or two. Found instructions for me to lose no time in speaking to the Chancellor about the Press as Grey is going to say some thing in the H. of C. next week.[2] I hate the job—as it will do not an atom of good and will lead only to recrimination. Our Press is not much better than the German—except that our good papers are not so vulgar as the German good papers—and perhaps for that reason ours are more irritating. However—that is not *my* business—so I wrote to Chancellor at once and asked him to see me. All Staff here except Benjie.

Thursday 2 November

Chancellor received me and greeted me warmly. I hadn't seen him before for six months *nearly*. After compliments we went at it hammer and tongs for about $\frac{1}{2}$ hour. Lots of recriminations on his part and lots of raking up old grievances—just as I expected. I dosed him with

[1] In the extreme south of Tyrol; Hosta Goschen was to say there in the hope of recovering her health.

[2] Grey to Goschen, 10 Oct. 1911, *B.D.*, vii, no. 657.

the MacKenna[1] and Cartwright[2] incidents and he fed me up with *Daily Graphic*! Articles[3] and the *Times*' Military Corresp't's[4] Articles on the German Army[5] (which seem to have caused not unjustifiable irritation). However I told him that criticisms, however unmerited and irritating, were not in the same category as gross fabrications and abuse founded on them—like in the case of MacKenna (certainly) and Cartwright (perhaps!). However he said that if I would go and tell Kiderlen all about it—he would discuss with him Grey's suggestion that the Chancellor should join him in giving some public warning to the Press of the danger to good relations between the two countries caused by gross fabrications and misleading reports. Had a still more disagreeable interview with Kiderlen who, with some reason said that before deciding whether he could act on Grey's suggestion—it w'd be necessary for Chancellor to know exactly what Grey was going to say. Telegraphed.[6]

Called on Harrisons—found May and Baba blooming and had a very pleasant dinner with Granvilles.

Friday 3 November

Very heavy Messenger day—complicated by visits from Cambon—Pansa and Polo (together) Leishman—the new American Ambassador and others. Had therefore to write late into the night.[7] Didn't care much for Leishman—he is more genial than Hill but also more vulgar—at least so it appeared to me. He stopped and jawed for ever—and I was *so* busy. Cambon was most interesting—he has initialled the Morocco Arrangement and will sign it tomorrow. He is satisfied—at all events relieved—but does not feel quite at ease about the Congo part of it—he thinks that France has given too much. But as the Colonial Minister here has resigned because he thinks Germany has not received enough—and as Kiderlen is being abused by most of the Press—I think Cambon *can* be *quite* satisfied. Pansa depressed—he doesn't like the War—and the Press here is as much against the Italians as it was against us in the Boer War. Polo looked pale and ill—whether from bad health or because *his* troubles about Morocco are now going to begin—I don't know.

---

[1] McKenna's speech at Abersychan, 26 Sept. 1911.
[2] On 22 Aug. 1911 the *Neue Freie Presse* had published a sensational article by Siegmund Münz in the form of an interview with an unnamed ambassador. See F. R. Bridge, *Great Britain and Austria-Hungary*, p. 179.
[3] *Daily Graphic*, 25 Oct. 1911.   [4] Repington.
[5] *Times*, 12, 14, 17, 19, 24 and 28 Oct. 1911.
[6] Goschen to Grey, 2 Nov. 1911, *B.D.*, vii, nos. 659 and 660.
[7] Goschen to Grey, 3 Nov. 1911, *B.D.*, vii, no. 661.

Saturday 4 November

Finished off Messenger—but had a lot of other work. Still had a splendid lesson from May and a long talk with her about Music and the thousand concerts they are to going to [sic] give. She is delighted that they are going to play at Vienna and that Steinbach[1] is going to conduct the Orchestra. She was very interesting about Elgar—who seems to me to be an A 1 Poseur and awfully spoilt—but he was very kind to her and praised her rendering of his Concerto—especially the Cadenza.

Morocco arrangement signed.

Sunday 5 November

Very wet cold day

Nothing partic. but we all had to do a good deal of work to get some pressing things off by post. One thing especially which was a very sharp attack on Nicolson and Bertie—saying that while Grey had been all right—these two had done all in their power to egg on France ag'st Germany and to hamper negotiations. I thought Grey ought to see it before he speaks next Tuesday. He can't use it of course—but he might keep it in reserve for future.

Monday 6 November

Called on Nizamy Pasha—who fulminated against Italy. He is always somewhat truculent—but he said one or two things that are difficult to contradict. Why did Italian [sic] called [sic] Turkish subjects rebels when they were only defending their country? How can Italians declare the country annexed while its owner was still defending it and successfully? People complained of weakness of Turkish Gov't. Which was the weaker Gov't the one which was unable to resist public opinion and was driven ag'st its will into a costly doubtful and criminal adventure in a time of profound peace? Or the one which when its people were urging refusals and the expulsion of Italians—remained perfectly calm and refused to be intimidated into doing things of which it did not approve?

He talked a lot about the Italian 'atrocities'—and said that he was sure that at all events in England public opinion would be revolted: for he said if the English mistrust Turkish reports they will at all events believe their own correspondents. (I suppose there is *some* truth in these so called atrocities—and they are probably due to nervousness among the troops owing to continual night-attacks. But one must

---

[1] Cologne conductor.

remember that both in Egypt and in the Boer War we were continu-
ally accused of atrocities without the slightest foundation—*and* by
For. correspondents.)

Late at night got tel. giving text of what Grey is going to say in H.
of C.[1]

Nizamy said prospects of peace were remote—but wished some
friend of Italy's wd. recommend armistice and point out that if things
were arranged now she might get something out of Turks—which we
[*sic*][2] won't if she goes on.

Tuesday 7 November

Called early on the Chancellor. He was perfectly satisfied with what
Grey is going to say—and only suggested one rather meticulous altera-
tion—which I tel'd to Grey.[3] (He adopted it.) Chancellor said that
he would have to allude to Lloyd George's speech but that he didn't
intend to criticize either Ll.G. or the speech itself—and was only going
to refer to the intense irritation caused throughout Germany by the
interpretation put upon it by the British and French Press. I also saw
Kiderlen and gave him a copy of Grey's speech. He seemed to think
it all right.

He told me that he had just rec'd a telegram from German Amb'r
at Const'ple stating that Min'r of War[4] had rec'd a desp. signed by
Enver Bey[5] and Sheick of Senussi saying that the Turkish Troops had
recaptured Derna defeating the Italians and bagging a lot of guns
and munitions of war! I wondered if it was true. K. was inclined
to believe it as he did not think that Enver would dare to *sign* an
absolutely false declaration. The Italians deny it however—I heard
afterwards.

Called on Pansa—and Polo—latter much excited about Franco-
Spanish negotiations.

Wednesday 8 November

Got following tel. from Grey. 'I highly approve your language to
Chancellor and Kiderlen—you have acted with great tact and firmness in a very delicate situation.' Yi—the best I ever had.

Tuesday 14 November

Ill.

[1] Grey to Goschen, 6 Nov. 1914, *B.D.*, vii, no. 663.
[2] Goschen no doubt intended to write 'she'.
[3] Goschen to Grey, 7 Nov. 1911, *B.D.*, vii, no. 665.
[4] Mahmud Shevket Pasha.
[5] Young Turk leader; had a command in Libya.

Wednesday 19 November

P.m. Played trios with May and Baba—they went fairly well—but we laughed so sometimes that we had to stop. My Pizzicato seemed to tickle them very much. But playing is a nice change from the endless work.[1]

Came downstairs for the first time and it was today I played Trios with the H. Girls. I enjoyed it fearfully—but I did not feel at all well—and May told me afterwards that they had *not* thought me looking at all well. Still we had great fun—they are always so bright and nice and frank with me.

Friday 24 November

Awful day and night—wrote up till 3—*translating* Kiderlen's 2nd Statement and speeches in the Budget Committee.[2] So much to do I couldn't even write my private letter. K.'s statements are very one sided and it is obvious to me that he is trying to persuade public opinion that England gave way before Germany's firmness and thus draw a red herring across the track of his own shortcomings—or rather those shortcomings which are attributed to him and Bethmann by their countrymen. The papers here are dreadfully abusive. They are at their old game, these Germans. After reviling us uphill and down-dale—and rattling the sabre: they now say 'Well Grey is going to speak on Monday and we shall probably judge by that whether England will be friendly or not.' They do not or will not realize that they have done all in their power to render us unfriendly—and if we made the slightest reply they will at once talk of anti-German Hetzerei—and say that we are provoking war!

Saturday 25 November

Rested. Besides we can't do much more until Grey has spoken: then I expect we shall have lively times—Grey himself will be very careful—but I doubt if private members will: especially those who read the German Papers or have seen the Reichstag speeches.

Monday 27 November

Grey made a very fine speech.[3] It was a most awfully difficult job and he did it splendidly. If he had been too conciliatory—they would have said here that it was because he was face to face to face [*sic*]

---

[1] This paragraph entered on page for 12 Nov. 1911, and corrected by Goschen.
[2] 17 Nov. 1911.   [3] House of Commons, 27 Nov. 1911.

with a United Germany—and had been made to mind his Ps and
Qs—and change his tone by the firm and patriotic language of the
German Press. But he steered a middle course. Asquith was also good
and Bonar Law also—in fact the debate was for once on a high level,
untainted by party spirit, and worthy of the occasion and the Mother
of Parliaments.

Personally I thought the speech very friendly on the whole.

Tuesday 28 November

The German Press was not at all satisfied with Grey's speech. They
say it was all words and contained nothing to show that friendly acts
were to follow them. 'We want acts and not words' was the parrot
cry of the whole Press. The papers also say that the speech confirmed
the idea that England arrogates to herself the right of having the
deciding word in the affairs of the whole world. I asked Stumm what
he thought of it—and he said that there was nothing in it to efface
the effect of Lloyd George's speech. But it was a foregone conclusion
that the speech would not satisfy public opinion here—as the latter[1]
did not *want* to be satisfied. Some of the papers praised very highly
the elegant form and language of the speech—and the high level of
the whole debate—and the *Post* said it wished they could have the
same sort of thing in the Reichstag. A skilful Statesman enunciating
a skilful policy—amidst the discriminating applause of an attentive
House: instead of an unskilful Statesman trying in vain to defend a
foolish policy and being laughed at for his pains in an apathetic
assembly.

Tuesday 5 December

Chancellor made a speech[2] in answer to that of Grey. It was not
a very cordial one as far as England was concerned: met Grey's
friendly words by saying that he wanted words not deeds [*sic*]—and
that England must shew in her policy that she really desires to be
friends! It has not calmed public opinion here in the least rather the
contrary: but it has appeased the Conservative Party here and will
be useful for the Elections.

Wednesday 6 December

I ought to have gone to Pless[3] to shoot today—where I should have

---

[1] Goschen originally wrote 'it'; then substituted 'the latter'.
[2] In the Reichstag; see *B.D.*, vii, no. 739.
[3] In Silesia.

met many friends including Betka and Duchess of Arenberg: but I couldn't go—and it is well I didn't—as I must write on the desp. of yesterday. Besides Granville has gone to shoot with the Crown Prince.

Thursday 7 December

Watson gave me rather a shock today: he told me that P'e George of Greece[1] when lunching with them the other day had said that 'Sir E. Goschen was not the right sort of person for Br. Ambassador at Berlin!' Where did he get it from? That is the question! I suspect Abby[2]—who has been staying at Potsdam and who has just come back from Primkenau[3] where the Emperor has been shooting. Considering the milieu in which P'ce George lives the remark has left an unpleasant impression upon me! I shall tell Nico.[4]

Wednesday 13 December

Got a very nice letter from Nico.[5] He told me that I could be perfectly indifferent to what either P'ce Abby—P'ce George or any one else said about my not being the right person for Br' Amb'r at Berlin— as both Grey and H.M.G. generally were thoroughly satisfied with the way I conducted the Embassy. He added that no one could do better than I and that they would all be filled with dismay if I talked of going etc.

I was very glad to hear this as I see from Acton[6] despatches that P'ce Henry[7] told him that it was a great pity that Lascelles had not been at Berlin all this time! Acton added that perhaps this might be regarded as a compliment to the 'efficiency of his successor'. But still all this is not pleasant!

I confess I don't think all the Court people like me: the Emperor doesn't I am sure. The Crown P'ce I think does—and I generally get on well with Eulenburg[8] and Countess Brock and certainly with the Empress. The Chancellor and I are I think very good friends. But of course there is a great deal of diff'ce between me and Lascelles—and the times are different.

---

[1] 2nd son of the King of the Hellenes; nephew of the Kaiser.
[2] Prince Albert, son of Prince Christian and Princess Helena of Schleswig-Holstein.
[3] In Silesia.
[4] Goschen to Nicolson, 8 Dec. 1911, N.P., F.O. 800/352.
[5] Nicolson to Goschen, 12 Dec. 1911, Go. P.
[6] Minister, Darmstadt; previously, secretary, The Hague.
[7] Of the Netherlands; consort of Queen Wilhelmina.
[8] August zu Eulenburg, Minister of Royal Household.

Saturday 16 December

Had a violin lesson and general rest after the Messenger.

Dined with the Chancellor. Pansa was the other Ambassador. I took in Frau v. Klugmann[1] and sat on left of Frau v. Bethmann H. The *Schwerins* were of the party, and heaps of people whom I didn't know and asked tenderly after Boss. After dinner I talked for ages with the Chancellor. It began by my asking him whether he was doing much music. He said there was too many [*sic*] discords in the atmosphere—for him to play harmonious music.[2]

Sunday 17 December

Had my usual Trio afternoon—and May and Baba to tea: then started off for Arco at 10.30.

Excellent Schlafwagen.

Monday 18 December

Arrived at Arco after an excellent journey. Found Boss very white but much better. I found out afterwards that it was the first time she had been out of her bedroom for weeks. But she was very cheerful and bright and we had a nice little supper together.

Sunday 31 December

Berlin

Arrived Berlin 8 a.m. After greetings from Daisy and warm welcome from Richter.

Saw the New Year in at the Esplanade with O'Beirnes[3] Chilton[4] B. Hope[5] and Mackenzie of the *Times*. Granville was at another table. Benjie not returned yet.

1911 has been a bad year—with a few streaks of light—such as G.C.B. and a certain amount of credit. But Bossie's health has been a perpetual anxiety and worry: Bunt's balloon accident prevented him from going in for his exam: and thus ruined his chance (a small one) for the Dip: Service; and there has been too much work and

---

[1] Klügmann; wife of Minister representing the Hanse cities.

[2] Goschen wrote Grey, 17 Dec. 1911, Gr. P., F.O. 800/62: 'I dined with the Chancellor last night and we had a little friendly conversation together upon recent events. We have one great thing in common which is love of music. I asked him whether he had had time lately to play his usual Beethoven sonata before going to bed. He said "My dear Friend you and I like classical music with its plain and straightforward harmonies; how can I play my beloved old music with the air full of modern discords?"'

[3] Councillor, St Petersburg, and wife.

[4] 2nd secretary.   [5] 3rd secretary.

too little leave. Germany and France over Morocco and Congo: Anglo-German very fishy relations and wars, rumours of war, Revolutions and Strikes all over the World! But little leave: 3 weeks only at Tentschach—and 10 days at Arco! On the other hand the Coronation was splendid—and we had a nice time there—seeing and making many English Friends. Family events few.... But a poor year—overshadowed by Bossie's illness.

Goschen was in Berlin until 4 February, when he went to London, having been summoned back by Grey in connection with the forthcoming Haldane mission. His stay in London was extremely brief. He was already back in Berlin when Haldane arrived on 8 February. On 15 February Hosta died at Arco. Goschen went to Arco and from there to England for the funeral at Flimwell. He did not resume his diary for over five months. He was in England during part of the summer, and in August took a cure at Nauheim. He spent September and part of October at Tentschach, and the rest of the year, apart from a trip to Leipzig, in Berlin.

Monday 1 January

Usual job at Palace. The Emperor appeared in good spirits. To me he said not a word of politics—to Cambon he said that tho' the French Press was abusing him (Cambon) now for conduct of Morocco-Congo negotiations—in a year's time they would be erecting a statue to him in Paris. He also made a remark of a not very friendly nature—to us!

In the evening had a dinner at home to which the whole Embassy came plus May and Baba—who played to us afterwards. Then we had a musical rag—when May played Wagner.

Thursday 11 January

Went to Russian Ballet. They dance beautifully but the men too loathsome for words. Saw *Pavillon d'Armide Carneval* (music by Schumann) very pretty and beautifully danced—and *Cleopatra*[1] wh. I considered *revolting*: Mrs O'Beirne who sat next to me said 'sickening'. Nijinsky the first man dancer is a loathsome brute—but the finest dancer I have ever seen.

Friday 12 January

Got off Messenger. One important desp. giving my opinion as to timeliness of reopening Exch. of N. Inf.[2] which *I* consider sound.[3] I hope they will at F.O. too. Otherwise nothing much.

Reichstag Elections take place today.

[1] Three Diaghilev ballets; choreographed by Fokine.
[2] Exchange of naval information.
[3] Goschen to Grey, 12 Jan. 1912, *B.D.*, vi, no. 485.

Saturday 13 January

—14°

Got up at *six* and started for shoot with Schwabach at 7.30.... Bag 500 hares (about) and a few pheasants of which I shot 8. Only cocks....

Yesterday's elections favourable to Socialists—but most of their seats were won from the National liberals. The supplementary ballots still to come.

Sunday 14 January

Lunched with Princess Titi[1] and met Countess Hatzfeldt, the American wife[2] of Count Hatzfeldt[3] (George's old colleague at Const'ple[4]) her daughter and Grand daughter, Ratibor and others. Ballin[5] came in afterwards—also Duke of Trachenberg—who told me things between England and Germany were looking better. This scarcely tallies with the attitude of Conservative and Pan German Press.

Played trios with May and Baba all afternoon—played a new Haydn one—which was quite delicious. Saw some of their latest criticisms (German) all *most* complimentary—indeed one said Baba was by far the greatest woman 'cellist and would probably in the near future be one of the first of all 'cellists!

Monday 15 January

C. told me last night with ref'ce to the proceedings against the *Post* etc. that he had been furnishing the German Govt. with 'Pièces'. In one of these despatches he had mentioned that Kiderlen had asked for Mogador. The Imp.l Gov't. asked that the sentence mentioning this might be suppressed as it would place K. in a very awkward position. Cambon said that if they liked he would alter it to 'a port in Morocco'—this they said would be just as bad—the whole thing must be suppressed. Cambon was against this suppression as the fact that K. had demanded Mogador explained why France had offered compensation. But de Selves had very weakly given in.

Tuesday 16 January

Called on Prof. Robert Kahn to see whether he w'd play with May and Baba on the 25th.

[1] Von Thurn und Taxis.   [2] Widow.
[3] Former German Ambassador, Constantinople.
[4] Where George Joachim Goschen had been Ambassador, 1880–1.
[5] Director-General, Hamburg–America Line.

Spring Rice[1] turned up—and stayed the night. Springy was very interesting and told me all about Caillaux'[2] proceedings behind the F. Gov't.—and how long before Agadir he and German Financiers had arranged about Congo etc. It strikes me that we shall very soon know all about what Emperor meant when he talked about France and Germany having almost settled every thing till Ll. George's speech put a stopper on things and bucked France up! There seems to have been a lot of shady work in France.

Zimmermann rec'd.! (Kiderlen being away.) He seemed rather preoccupied about China and hoped there would be no mil. intervention by any Power—as that might lead to spheres of influence— to wh. Germany had strongest objection. She wanted China to remain as she now is i.e. territorially intact. Of course he was alluding to Japan.

Wednesday 17 January

Bunt arrived—looking jolly and well and full of enthusiasm for his new duties.[3]

Attended reception at American Ambassador's and presented the whole staff....

Grey is being much attacked by radical Press in England for not being better friends with Germany.

Friday 19 January

Schleppen Cour.[4] Bunt's uniform not arrived alas!

So he couldn't go. I enjoyed it more than usual because my shoes didn't hurt me....

Saturday 20 January

Valentine (now Sir[5]) Chirol came to see me at three—and stayed till 5.30 when the Radolins came—he then stayed on with them so I had him from 3 to 7. He was very interesting for some time!

Sunday 21 January

'Ordensfest' at Palace. Usual long sermon and beautiful music— and heavy lunch. Emperor gay and in good spirits. Empress looked tired and seedy. Sat next to Pansa and a deaf German General. Cambon—who as usual is off to Paris—is very angry with the Italians,

---

[1] Minister, Stockholm.
[2] President, French Council of Ministers.
[3] As honorary attaché.
[4] When the ladies wore long trains.
[5] Knighted, 1912.

'qui se conduisent comme des cochons' for holding up French ships. I expect there will be a row about it. P.m. went with Bunt to Harrisons and heard Baba play the St. Saens Concerto which she is to play at Dresden on the 23rd. She played it well—but I have heard her play better. I didn't care for it as a composition—though there were beautiful bits in it. She also played a lovely thing by Glazounow—which showed off her beautiful Cantabile playing. Then we went to tea with Me Pansa—and in the evening Bunt made his first bow to Princess Radziwill. To our surprise there were a lot of people there—two rooms full! I have never before seen more than five! I think the old Lady was delighted.

Monday 22 January

Thaw

The Speaker James Lowther arrived. Had a good talk with him. He is on his way with the big deputation to the Duma to St Petersburg.

Sunday 4 February

—16° Reaumur

Left for London. The train was quite comfortable but it was cold work getting on to the boat—*and* on it. Excellent passage—the rather strong breeze being with us.

Monday 5 February

Arrived punc. 8 a.m. after the usual good breakfast in the train. Had a bath and then bed for an hour and then down to the F.O. to see Nico: whom I found in despair. He told me everything—and it is worse than I feared. The idea of negotiations between the two Gov'ts being opened by Cassel and Ballin makes me sick: and Nico more so. The whole thing reminds me of the French Gov't. and Caillaux. Nico lunched with me and we had a good talk—he evidently feels that *my* position in all this is most disagreeable. I can see that I have been sent for to save my face—tho' they put it more kindly to 'consult' as to future developments!

Saw Grey at 6, and spent the interval in going to tea at Charlie's....

Grey talked to me a lot and I told him a good deal of what I thought—but he told me that Haldane was going over to talk etc. I dined with him at Haldane's[1] tête-à-tête (oysters and '92 champagne) and we had a very pleasant talk. Then Haldane came in and we talked till about 12.30. I said that I presumed Cassel and Ballin

[1] 28 Queen's Gate.

would now drop out—and Grey backed me up—but Haldane said
they were too useful! Pah! Underground work.

Thursday 15 February[1]

I lost my poor darling Bossie today.[2]

Tuesday 20 February

Tuesday—left sad little Arco.

Wednesday 21 February

Arrived Dover....

Thursday 22 February

Motored over to dear Seacox....

Friday 23 February

My darling Bossie was laid to rest here today....

Thursday 1 August[3]

Left London for Berlin.

Friday 2 August

Arrived Berlin.

Sunday 4 August

Left for Nauheim.[4]

Thursday 29 August

I left for Berlin—feeling very much better than when I arrived....

Saturday 31 August

Left for Tentschach.

[1] First entry since 5 Feb.
[2] Hosta Goschen died at Arco; Goschen was in Berlin at the time.
[3] First entry since 23 Feb.   [4] Spa.

Sunday 1 September

Tentschach

Arrived in fairly fine weather and old Ted met me at the Station—
and Mary on the landing where my darling always used to be. Felt
very sad and missed my Hosta fearfully.

Thursday 12 September

May Harrison arrived in good health and spirits but in shocking
weather.

Tuesday 17 September

May H. left to join her family at Bozen. It was very nice having
her here—and all liked her. We didn't have much music—but I had
some good lessons. I think she enjoyed her stay.

Wednesday 25 September

Heard that poor Marschall v. Bieberstein who has only been Amb'r
in London for a few months[1]—has just died at some Bavarian watering
place.[2] And he was to do so much! He is an enormous loss to Germany.
Telegraphed condolence to the Imp'l Chancellor.

The Kramer pond was emptied and the Carp taken out. . . .

Thursday 10 October[3]

War seems almost certain in Balkans—but I think Powers will keep
out of it.

Thursday 17 October

Got a letter from Nicolson cont's friendly hint that I had better
return to my Post: King had said he presumed all his Amb'rs were
at their posts—and Grey had spoken in much the same sense. Well!
I meant to go on Monday—and now I shall go on Saturday.

Saturday 19 October

Left dear of [sic] Tentschach in glorious weather. . . .

[1] He had succeeded Metternich in June 1912.
[2] Badenweiler; on 24 Sept.
[3] Originally entered on page for 3 Oct., and corrected by Goschen.

Sunday 20 October

Arrived fairly fresh after the shakiest journey I ever made. That train is a scandal—old Italian carriages—and a badly laid line. The conductor called it 'ein böser Zug'.

Monday 21 October

Slight sciatica.

Thursday 12 December

Went down to Leipzig with Benjie and Bunt to hear May and Baba play the 'double Brahms concerto' with Nikisch's Orchestra at the Gewandthaus.

They played splendidly and had a great deal of applause—much more—so the Committee told me—than is usually vouchsafed to strangers by that particular Leipzig audience. Afterwards we had a huge dinner at a Mr Fiedler's[1]—to which the Committee and their wives were invited—and of course Mrs Harrison and May and Baba. Mr. Fiedler proposed May and Baba's health in poetry!...

Monday 30 December

Poor Kiderlen-Waechter died suddenly at Stuttgart. An awful loss for Bethmann Hollweg and the Emperor—particularly at this difficult moment in Foreign Affairs. I wonder who will succeed him as Sec. of State for F.A.

He had gone to Stuttgart for his Xmas holidays and only a few days ago he said to me in joke 'Do you think you can spare me for a few days at Xmas?' I told him that I could spare him for more than a few days as there was always less work when he was away!

He lived very hard. Took no exercise, eat, drank and smoked too much. I finished by liking him very much. He was a good hearted chap—and though he could be very hard and even rude—he could also be very nice; and we got on together first rate ever since we had a bit of a row together about 2 years ago. I am *very* sorry he has gone.

Tuesday 31 December

The last day of the saddest year of my life.

Saw the Chancellor and conveyed Grey's message of sympathy about poor Kiderlen's death.

For the first time of my life the clock strikes twelve on New Year's eve with me 'Mutterseele allein' as Bunt has gone up to bed!!

[1] Max Fiedler; conductor.

1913

Apart from trips to Dessau in March and to Neustrelitz in May, Goschen was in Berlin until 5 July, when he left for England, getting back to the German capital on 17 August. He spent most of September and the first week of October at Tentschach. On 19 October he left for Copenhagen in connection with a family matter; he was back at his post on 21 October. On 30 November he went to stay with Lichnowsky in Austrian Silesia; he returned on 3 December. He spent the rest of the year in Berlin.

Wednesday 1 January

Came a little out of my shell—and had Pansas, Chiltons, Gurneys,[1] B. Hope and Benjie to dinner. Chilton sang and I in a deadly funk— played the Violin Obligato[2] of the Braga—and Ave Maria. Pansa had to go off early to attend Kiderlen's funeral at Stuttgart.

In the morning went to the palace in State Coach to wish Kaiser and Kaiserin a happy New Year. Former was very affable and talked to me so long that all my colleagues were on the Qui Vive to know what he had been talking to me about. As a matter of fact he made a proposal—or said he had instructed Lichnowsky[3] to make one— to the effect that England and Germany should exercise joint pressure on the S. Porte to make them more reasonable in their peace negotiations. He said that the Peace Conference looked rather dicky and that we *must* prevent resumption of hostilities—if Peace Conference were to break down it would be a 'Blameage'[4] for H.M.G! I didn't see why—but had no chance of discussing the point with him.

The Empress was very nice and spoke *most* kindly and sympathetically about my Hosta.

Friday 3 January

Radolin came to see me and talked for an hour on Polish question and court matters etc.

Saturday 11 January

Messenger.

Saw Zimmermann who is anxious about Roumania and Bulgaria— and had teleg'd to German Minister at Bucharest[5] to preach modera-

---

[1] He was 2nd secretary.   [2] Obbligato.
[3] New German Ambassador, London.   [4] Blamage.
[5] Waldthausen.

tion and calm—and in fact to tell them that they *must* keep quiet. Unfortunately it is such a splendid opportunity for them—tho' a most ill chosen moment for Europe. The Roumanians know the Bulgars too well to expect anything from them when peace has once been signed—but until that moment comes it would place Bulgaria between two fires if Roumania moves. The tension between the two countries is evidently at the bottom of the Turks saying that collectives Démarches or even Naval Demonstrations will have no effect on their determination not to give up Adrianople. Turkish Ch. d'Aff.[1] was told by Zimmermann today that they *must* give in and make peace: and that the Powers were quite united in this decision. The Ch. d'Aff. replied 'Then we must look for help elsewhere.' Z. said 'Where?' And the Ch. d'Aff. 'From Roumania.'

A violent Article appeared in an Alsace paper against poor Kiderlen—and it was given out that the inspirer of the Article was no less a person than Cambon. The papers have taken this up and say 'that the Min. of F.A. should have no further dealings with a dip. who can write such things etc.' C. spoke about this to Z. and said 'Never talk to me about the F'h Press again: because at all events it doesn't make personal attacks on Foreign Dips.' Z. is going to issue démenti in papers. The real author of Article was—*Oppersdorff*.[2] What annoys Cambon most is that French papers say he cd. have written it because is [*sic*] trop allemand.

Saturday 15 February

Just a year since Hosta was taken from us. Bunt and I spent a very quiet day alone—and everybody was most considerate and kind. The Empress sent me a charming telegram to say she had not forgotten the day and was thinking of me with much sympathy. Countess Broćkdorf also sent me a very very nice little letter.

Sunday 9 March

In the evening had my first little party since—! It was just a few people to hear May and Baba and Kahn play classical music—Brahms C minor trio—Beethoven A major Sonata and Bach's 4th Sonata in E major.... We had the Chancellor—Cambons—C'tess Harrach—P'cess Lowenstein and her sister—the Roeders[3] and some of the Embassy—and a very good supper afterwards.

[1] Galib Kemali Bey.
[2] Silesian landowner; keen golfer; mother *née* Talleyrand-Périgord; wife *née* Radzivill.
[3] He was a chamberlain.

Chancellor rather grumpy—and asked what Grey was doing that he couldn't finish the Albanian frontier question—and to Cambon he said the same thing—adding something about his being always fishing!! This is H.I.M.

Monday 10 March

Got a telegram from Ted saying that Lord E. Cecil[1] offered Bunt private secretaryship at £300 per annum—and wants him as soon as possible.

A splendid opening for Bunt....

Wednesday 12 March

... I had to go to that tiresome Ambassadors' dinner at Court.

My dinner went off all right.... The Emperor didn't say much to me—it was Cambon's turn—and I thought it w'd be—owing to the violent anti-French Article in the Kölnische Zeitung:[2] he also talked to Sverbéef[3] a good bit. To me he said only that he had a nice letter from the King—who had told him that the P'ce of Wales was coming to Germany—and was going to stay a few weeks at Stuttgart with the King of Wurtenberg.[4] The Emperor said that it wasn't much of a place for learning German and that the Prince w'd return to England with an accent like Kiderlen Waechter. The Empress wasn't present owing to mourning (Hohenlohe Langenburg)[5] and the Crown Princess took her place. I was told off to sit next to her afterwards wh. was very nice for me....

Thursday 13 March

The Balkan States accepted mediation of the Powers—but on terms of a bigger slice of territory than they are likely to get—and an indemnity wh. they are certain not to get.

Scutari[6] not yet fallen—but I'm afraid it will soon and if it does before peace is made the Montenegrins will go in—and then it will be a case of turning them out. Djakowa[7] looks a little brighter.

Friday 14 March

I went down to Dessau to present my letters of Credence (2 years

[1] Financial Adviser to Egyptian Government.
[2] Kölnische Zeitung, 10 March 1913.
[3] Russian Ambassador; Osten-Sacken's successor; name also spelt Sberveev.
[4] Wilhelm II; Queen Mary's 3rd cousin.
[5] The Empress's mother was born a princess of Hohenlohe-Langenburg.
[6] Shkodra; near the lake of that name.   [7] Djakovica; north of the Drin.

old) to the Duke of Anhalt.[1] Bunt in attendance as Secretary! We
had an excellent time. We were put up at the Schloss and done well.
A nice Chamberlain called Eude was attached to me and looked after
us first rate. The Audience was at 3.30. No speech but a friendly reception. We talked Music most of the time—the Duke being a good musician and, I believe, an excellent pianist. The Duchess—a princess of
Baden was also very nice. At 4 there was a gala dinner. . . . The dinner
was excellent—and the Plate and flowers lovely. After dinner we went
back to *our* Schloss in *our* Gala carriage—and then very shortly it was
time to dress for the Opera. The duke had ordered *Madame Butterfly*
which he said he thought we would like. It was quite good—an
excellent tenor and a very fair Prima Donna who was also a good
actress. The orchestra very good too. The Duke goes every night and
superintends all the rehearsals too.

In the Entreacte we went and conversed with the Royalties again
and then retired to our rooms where we had a most *excellent* supper
with our Chamberlain and the Ober Hofmarschall.[2] Everyone was
very nice and Bunt and I enjoyed it.

Saturday 15 March

Back from Dessau by 12—both Bunt and I being a little the worse
for wear. Went with Bunt to say goodbye to May and Baba who leave
tomorrow for England. Baba frightfully excited at the idea of playing
with Eugène d'Albert.[3] He was asked for a certain big concert at
Vienna to select any artists he liked to play with him and he selected
our Baba. This I fancy is besides the three concerts—i.e. London in
May—here—and Vienna. It is a big thing for her but I don't much
like it.

Boghitchevitch[4]—the Serb Ch. told me a curious story. Namely
that he had rec'd instructions from His Gov't which he had just
carried out—to say that it was strange that Jagow[5] had said (wh. he
had done a few days before) that Italy was just as angry as Germany
about the Servian Gov't having said that whatever the Powers might
decide—Servian troops w'd only leave Dhakova if turned out by
force—as the Italian Min'r of F.A.[6] had told the Servian Min'r
in Rome[7] to urge his Gov't to 'push their claims with more
vigour'. !!

---

[1] Friedrich II.   [2] Auer von Herrenkirchen.
[3] British-born composer; Director, Hochschule für Musik, Berlin.
[4] Secretary, Serbian Legation.
[5] Secretary of State, German Foreign Office; Kiderlen-Wächter's successor; previously Ambassador in Rome.
[6] San Giuliano.   [7] Vouić.

Tuesday 18 March

Just as Bunt and I were playing a Sonata of Bach—I got a telephone from a newspaper correspondent telling me that the King of Greece was assassinated this afternoon at Salonica. I hope it may not be true—but I fear it sounds bad.

Wednesday 19 March

It is true and the King of Greece was murdered yesterday by a Greek anarchist just at *the* moment of His long and difficult reign—when fortune smiled on him most. Our poor Queen Alexandra how she will suffer—He was her favourite brother—and I fear that this blow coming so soon after the loss of the other Brother—King of Denmark under such queer circumstances[1]—will affect her terribly....

One thing is that the New King[2] ascends the throne on a wave of popularity owing to his Military successes. Had this happened even a year or two ago—his throne would have been more dicky.

Heard Beethoven's Mass in C at the Gedachniss Kirche[3]—also a cantata of Bach—both splendid and well given.

Saturday 22 March

Messenger who came last night—brought desp. according to which an advance towards a settlement of the Albanian question has certainly been made—even if it doesn't go very far.[4] Anyhow it is better than I thought it was. But my own idea is that however ready Sazonow is to give Scutari to Albania—Pan-Slavism has to be reckoned with: and if Scutari were to fall—I doubt if Sazonow would be allowed to consent to the Montenegrins being turned out by force. Nous verrons!

Sunday 23 March

The Morning Service at Church was very nice.

... Went out for a solitary walk p.m. and felt very sad altogether. But before Bunt went out to supper to meet Pucini[5]—he and I had our usual music and we found a lovely largo of Bach in his 5th Viol. Sonata—quite gorgeous.

---

[1] In Hamburg; May 1912; the circumstances were certainly queer.
[2] Constantine I.   [3] Gedächtniskirche.
[4] Perhaps a copy of Grey to Buchanan, 20 March 1913, *B.D.*, ix, 2, no. 741.
[5] Puccini.

Monday 24 March

Lunched at 2.30 with my Italian colleague[1] to meet Pucini—the composer—a very nice man. They tried to get him to play and he wouldn't—quite rightly because Bunt who met him last night at the Schusters[2] says the he could not even read his own music. . . .

The papers this morning said that Austria and Russia were agreed as to Scutari and Dkakowa—but Bolati[3] seems to think that things are not going so very smoothly—and shook his head over the Austrian Naval Demonstration—wh. he said was looked at askance both here and in Italy.

Wednesday 26 March

Saw Jagow. He is still suspicious of Russia's policy—admired Grey's speech[4]—but didn't like Winston Churchill's Naval Estimate speech[5]—which he thinks will pull out all the Naval programme question again from its quiescent state where it had been placed by Adm'l Tirpitz's estimate speech. He is, in fact, afraid that the papers will begin again on both sides. Winston Churchill's proposal that there should be a 'year's inactivity in Naval construction'[6] for everybody is not liked here—ostensibly because the idea is unworkable—but really I expect, because it is an offer which they can't very well accept—and which may make them liable to be told later by us— 'We have made you an offer and you wouldn't accept it.'

Personally I think the proposal *almost* ridiculous—and I also wish that he had not mentioned the 16 to 10 proportion. *I* begged Nicolson to prevent all allusion to that if possible.

The most interesting thing in my conversation with Jagow was that he suddenly looked up and said 'Your King and Queen are coming here for the Royal Wedding in May.'!!![7]

Friday 28 March

O'Beirne turned up. He told me that the Austrian Naval Demonstration—or rather her threats to Montenegro had irritated the Russians very much and that the Czar had never been so angry about anything in his life.

---

[1] Bollati; Pansa's successor.
[2] He was a German conductor and musicologist.
[3] Bollati.   [4] House of Commons, 25 March 1913.
[5] House of Commons, 26 March 1913.   [6] Cf. Hansard, 5, 1, col. 1757.
[7] Wedding of the Kaiser's daughter, Princess Viktoria Luise, to the Duke of Cumberland's son, Ernst August. This would mark an at least partial Hohenzollern–Welf reconciliation.

Saturday 29 March

Emmie arrived for lunch from Dresden: very worried about poor little Evie—but very bright on other subjects. She is 73—but having so many people to look after seems to keep her young. May H. came to tea and Bunt and I played some Bach to her and Emmie—but as usual when May is there I played shockingly. After dinner Bunt and I played to Emmie alone and everything went much better.

Emmie *does* like to come here and have a talk sometimes—it takes her out of her somewhat narrow Saxon groove—and freshens her up a bit.[1]

A week ago I thought the Albanian question was on the point of settlement. But now things still look dicky—as Montenegro holds firm—Russia's policy is still obscure—and Naval demonstration seems on the Tapis. It appears that Russia has joined other Powers in telling Montenegro that she must give up Scutari and stop the siege—but if coercive measures have to be resorted to to make her do so—or to turn her out should Scutari fall—Russian Panslavists will surely not allow Russia to join in them. The *Matin* adds a very pertinent question viz. 'What if, as is not at all impossible, the Naval Demonstration has no effect on Montenegro? Will Europe make war on her? The Great Powers have in this Crisis more than once played a ridiculous role—but surely such a war would be too ridiculous even for them!!'

As a matter of fact nothing seems to be going well for the moment.[1]

Sunday 30 March

Attended service in the Greek Church at 12 for poor King George of Greece.

Saw Emmie off at 4.30 and then Bunt and I went to Harrisons—where May Baba and Bunt played till nearly 7. M. and B. went off to Vienna tonight where on Tuesday they play the 'Double Brahms' for the 50th time in public.

Bogitchevich told me that collective representation had been made at Cettinje but not yet he thought at Belgrade.

Got off my messenger with difficulty owing to the Greek service. Wrote a very dull letter to Nicolson.[2]

Tuesday 1 April

Situation still uncertain as to Naval Demonstration. It seems

[1] These two paragraphs originally entered on page for 28 March, and corrected by Goschen.

[2] Goschen to Nicolson, 29 March 1913, N.P., F.O. 800/364.

French are not sending ships—but I am kept badly informed. Jagow told me tonight that the Germans were sending one; that the Emperor had told him he might either send *Groeben*[1] (their best Dreadnought) or smaller one. He had sent the smaller one because he did not want German to be Senior Officer! or to put themselves forward in any way. He said that Grey seemed to think that they didn't want to send ship. I told him I had reported exactly what he had said to me viz. that Imp. Gov't thought that one other Power of the Triplice ought to stand out if Russian Gov't decided not to join—and that they didn't care whether it was they or Italy.

Saw Camdon in the morning—told me that Greeks were furious with Italians—also that they (the Greeks) and their allies had suggested that a plebiscite of towns Italy wanted to go to Albania should be taken by an Intern'l Commission. Jagow had replied that Imp'l Gov't could not approve of such a proposal—as it w'd form such a bad precedent. (Alsace Lorraine.)

Wednesday 2 April

Situation in Near East more obscure than ever—owing to funny policy of Russia and therefore France. C—n told me that Russia had been pushing France to join in Naval demonstration—but that France had said that they would do so—only on condition that Russia would do so too—or cause herself to be publicly represented by France in Demonstration. What I can't understand is that Zimmermann told both Gueshoff[2]—Theotoki[3] and Boghichewitch that Germany was certainly not going to send a ship—while Jagow the day before had told me that they would stand out from, or go in for, the demonstration just as it suited. It was all the same to them. Jagow's idea was that as Russia was standing out—one other Power should do so—from the Triplice—so that it would leave two Triplices and two Ententes—so as to give appearance of no division amongst the Powers. But now there seems a chance of its being 3 Triplices (if Italy joins) and one Entente viz. ourselves. Well! What will happen if Montenegro captures Scutari and occupies it and the demonstrating Powers have to land troops to turn them out? Will Russian Panslavist [*sic*][4] force Russia to move? And if she does—which is a not impossible chance—what happens to us if *we* have landed troops? It is an awful embroglio. Gueshoff thinks if Scutari falls—Powers will still let Montenegro keep it—and quoted Powers who said at beginning of war

---

[1] *Goeben.*

[2] Bulgarian Minister; his name is sometimes spelt 'Guechov'.

[3] Secretary, Greek Legation.

[4] Goschen may have omitted a word after 'Panslavist'; or he may have intended to write 'Panslavists'.

to allies—however victorious you may be you shall have no increase of territory!!

Thursday 3 April

My dear old Bunt left for Egypt to take up his appointment as 2nd Sec. to Financial adviser at £300 per annum! It is a good opening so I musn't repine....

Situation still confused. Grey says that if Russia and France don't join in demonstration—England can't very well either. But I think he is rather angry about the whole thing as he says it is rather nonsense that people approve of Naval Demonstration and then won't take the steps necessary to carry it out.[1] It *is* humbug—and if possible tragedy was not on tapis—it would be the most comic thing in the world. Austrian, Italian and perhaps German and English Men of War cruizing off Antivari—and King Nikita[2] bombarding Scutari gaily! A Cettinje correspondent writes that when the Austrian Fleet appeared—Nikolas was having his afternoon nap. The Officer on duty woke him up to tell H.M. of it. But he said 'don't disturb me with such trifles' and went to sleep again! This is probably not true— but it is quite in the picture. Beldiman—the Roumanian Minister came in to see me—very gloomy and not seeing the way out of this maze. He is very anti-Russian and says Russia is in a very bad state and capable for the moment of any folly. Just the same state as she was before the utterly useless and mad Japanese War!

Friday 4 April

Depression!

Saturday 5 April

Big dinner of 30, of whom the Trachenbergs were the chief German guests....

The sensation of the evening was the Roumanian Minister's waist-coat. The Naval Demonstration is now in order—as the French have joined. It is rather an outrageous proceeding—as, as a matter of fact the Allies are still at war with Turkey—and Scutari is a Turkish Fort occupied and defended by Turks. But I suppose there are arguments to support the demonstration: and of course as the Powers have made up their mind that Scutari is to belong to Albania—there is not much point—except for Military Prestige—in Montenegro taking it. But

[1] Grey to Goschen, 2 Apr. 1913, *B.D.*, ix, 2, no. 790.
[2] Nicholas of Montenegro.

still——! Well! I am a little sorry for Montenegro—as she has
made enormous sacrifices—for nothing—all because Austria wants
it for the capital of an impossible Albania!

Sunday 6 April

We hear very little of what is going on from the F.O. Montenegro
swears she won't give in about Scutari—and apparently doesn't care
tuppence for the Naval Demonstration. But the King seems inclined
to accept a *money* compensation. Cambon has suggested that the Turks
should hand over Scutari to the Powers who at the conclusion of the
war could hand it over to Albania. That w'dn't change things much—
but it w'd 1. regularise the position of the Powers and 2. perhaps offer
a bridge to King Nicolas for a dignified retreat.

Monday 7 April

Chancellor made a big speech in defence of the Wehrvorlage (to
the tune of a milliard of marks).[1]

The Press here have given it a good reception except the Socialists—
who maintain (with some justice) that he didn't produce a shadow
of a reason for the contemplated enormous mil. expenditure. I say
with some reason—for the chief part of his speech was devoted to
showing how excellent the relations between Germany and all other
powers are at the present moment. But his justification was that there
are large numbers of the German population who might be called
upon to serve—and who up till now have *not* been called upon to
do so. What he practically says is that Germany ought to be as strong
as her means and men allow her to be—they don't want a war—but
if it comes—they want to win it. He talked a lot about French Chauvinism and Russian Panslavism—and said that as Turkey has retired
from the Scene—and her place has been taken by virile Slav nations—
circs render it necessary for Germany to take every precaution. A good
lot of his speech was good—but I never think that sabre rattling and
patriotic platitudes ring true in the Chancellor's mouth—and he has
to do it. He was partic. civil to England in general and Grey in particular: but there were tons of butter left for Russia and France. Still
his remarks about French chauvinism will set the ball of newspaper
polemics rolling.

Tuesday 8 April

Lumbago baddish. Very busy getting off trans. of Chancellor's
speech.

[1] Reichstag, 7 Apr. 1913.

Wednesday 9 April

Lumbago worse.

Bulgar came to see me. He told me one interesting thing. I asked him whether he did not think that Peace would help the settlement of other questions. He said yes! So I asked why they didn't make it then. I reproached him for not accepting conditions of the Powers. He said that practically they had done so. I said that they insisted on indemnity—and refused the frontier line Enos-Midia. He replied that he didn't think there would be much difficulty about the indemnity now that they were going to be allowed to take part in the Paris Conference on Financial matters. As regards the line he told me that the line his Gov't. had submitted to the Russian Gov't. was the Enos-Midia line with certain deflections to Bulgaria's advantage. Sazonow had accepted this line—and the Bulgars had asked him to submit it to the Amb. Conference in London. This he had *promised* to do—but instead of doing it he had submitted the *straight* Enos-Midia line. That was what Bulgaria was haggling about—but it was a very small question and would not cause much difficulty. He was not sure—being a very careful man—whether Sazonow submitted the wrong line by mistake or deliberately.

Tuesday 15 April

Weather at last a little better—and I went out for a short walk in the sun—and felt all the better for it.

Cambon came to see me, and we talked about the Nancy Affair—when a lot of French Students seem to have ballyragged and hooted a couple of Germans at a Café Chantant.[1] No one seems to know the rights of the matter—but the papers here are furious, partic. the *Lokal Anzeiger*—which published a very disagreeable article about France. The papers in fact write of nothing else—and questions have been asked in the Reichstag—and Jagow made really a rather foolish little speech considering he didn't know the facts—speaking of the results of French Chauvinism. In fact they have made it a national affair. It is so like the Germans: during the Boer War—English people were hooted and hustled at every moment—at Leipzig, Hanover and all the chief towns—and England never said a word. When the same thing happens to them they cry like spoiled children.

Cambon was rather bitter about it and said 'Tout cela doit venir—nous ne pouvons pas continuer ainsi.' Indeed sometimes one cannot help thinking that people are right who say 'War *must* come.'!

[1] 13 Apr. 1913.

Thursday 17 April

Dined with the Japanese Ambassador[1]—very nice little people both of them—but never have I seen so many of my pet aversions gathered into the same room.

Sunday 20 April

A truly dull and lonely day—of which the monotony was relieved by a visit from poor Nizamy Pasha—whose successor[2] arrives on Tuesday. He doesn't know where he is going—because his instructions are not to leave before a certain business he has on hand is finished and then to wait for instructions. He thinks that this means that he may perhaps be sent to London for peace negotiations. Theotoki also came to see me—and talked about the islands.[3] His views as to their coming to Greece en bloc are not unsound: as if they go to Turkey they will all become 'Cretes'. And he rather ridicules Jagow's idea that the Greeks of the islands would intrigue with the Greeks on the Asiatic mainland and bring about the Asiatic question. He says, and not without reason—that their proximity to Asia is no argument—because after all—all continental countries are closer to each other than the Turks and the Greeks—as there would be a channel between them.

Monday 21 April

Dined at Cambons.... There doesn't seem to be anything fresh going on in the Balkans. The Greek transports are taking the Serbian troops away from Scutari—but old King Nicolas seems to hold out— and he swears he wont be bought off! But I have known people refuse tips stoutly and take them all the same.

The 'Nancy' affair—though officially settled—has taken fresh impulse from a speech of M. Barthou F'h Président du Conseil: who talked of German Chauvinism—and said that France did not want lessons from anyone. The *Post* of this Evening had the worst article I have ever seen ag'st France and the French—and says amongst other things 'If the French want war—why don't they make it—instead of talking so much! But they neither can or will attack Germany by themselves—and will only attack if they could get a coalition to join them at a moment when they might find Germany isolated.' Talk of Chauvinism! The article is also heavily written and full of sort of schoolboy abuse.

Hermite[4] said to me tonight, 'This can't go on—we can't stand it much longer.'

[1] Sugimura.   [2] Mahmud Mukhta Pasha.
[3] In the Aegean; as a result of Turkey's wars their future was in doubt.
[4] 2nd secretary, French Embassy.

Thursday 8 May

Went down to Mecklenburg Strelitz—to present my letters to the Grand Duke. He met me at the Station and was awfully nice and kind—but he had no idea that I was going to present my letters—and was quite aghast when I handed them to him: he said he ought to have been in full uniform and rec'd me in State. But I told him that the Emperor had also rec'd me informally as it was only a case of renewing letters. 'At all event' he said 'I went to meet you at the Station.'!

I had a charming talk with the dear old Dowager G'd Duchess—92 years old![1] She was as fresh as a daisy. Called the Great Powers 'the great weaknesses' and was very amusing all together. A wonderful memory—and such charm in conversation. She was awfully down on the Suffragettes and said—referring to the Hunger Strikes—'Why don't they let 'em die if they want to?' Had a very pleasant lunch with the Grand Duke—and then took Bruce up to present him to the Old Lady. He fell quite under her charm. She is the only surviving grandchild of George III.

Not much news by Messenger.

Sunday 11 May

Messenger in the morning—only interrupted by old Hechler—our old parson in Vienna—whom somehow or another I was glad to see. Then I went and talked over King's and Czar's visit[2] with Sverbeef. Then I went to Harrisons—to say goodbye. I had a good play with May—and then I heard Baba play the d'Albert concerto wh. she is going to play with the composer here in the Autumn. It is a quite lovely piece of music and beautifully written for the 'Cello. Baba played it quite wonderfully—with temperament, feeling, strength and breadth all mixed up. I enjoyed it most awfully.

Monday 12 May

Lord Morley lunched. A Quaint dried up old man—but all there. But he was excessively unsound on the Suffragette question on wh. Granville and I drew him. He said he was *for* violent measures—but had none to suggest.

Wednesday 21 May

Arrival of King and Queen. I went down to Rathenow to meet

[1] Born 1822.
[2] For the wedding, on 24 May, of Princess Viktoria Luise and Prince Ernst August.

them with the German Suite. For this I had to get up at 6.15 in order to get into my big uniform—as it was to be full dress at the Station! Travelled back with King and Queen, who were both charming to me. He talked a lot, always with good honest sailor expletives. He said that Haldane and other colleagues—but partic. he—wrote a lot of 'd—d tommy rot'—because they got so thoroughly biassed by staying too long in one place. Every body at the Station in full uniform—and I drove in the procession to the Schloss with Lichnowsky. The populace were cordial—and it was the fashion aft'ards to say—enthusiastic—but I don't think it was any thing out of the way. The King's Suite were Lord Annaly[1]—Stamfordham[2]—Fritz and Adml. Keppel[3] and Henry Verney:[4] the Queen's Lord Shaftesbury[5]—Duchess of Devonshire[6]—Lady Minto.[7] very nice selection.

Hung about the Palace for a bit—and then came home. In the evening there was a dinner at the Palace to wh. Granvilles and I were invited—while Lady Fritz and Mary and Benjie and Co. went to the Wintergarten! The Queen looked wonderfully well and handsome. I don't remember much about it except that we got a cigarette afterwards.

Friday 23 May

King and Queen lunched at the Embassy....
People said luncheon was an enormous success. Well! I think the flowers were lovely and the people nice.

Saturday 5 July[8]

Left Berlin for England.

Sunday 6 July

Arrived at Lennox Gardens. Found Alic well and cheery.

Saturday 16 August

Left for Berlin....

Sunday 17 August

Arrived Berlin....

[1] Lord-in-waiting.
[2] George V's private secretary.
[3] Equerry.
[4] Groom-in-waiting.
[5] Lord Chamberlain to Queen Mary.
[6] Mistress of the Robes.
[7] Lady-in-waiting.
[8] First entry since 23 May.

Saturday 30 August

Prince of Wales arrived at the Embassy—He and his suite i.e. Cadogan[1] and Prof. Fiedler[2] a good chap and brother of the Brahms and Beethoven conductor. They are stopping here for the night.…

Sunday 31 August

Prince of W. lunched up at the Golf ground after Church. I had Prof. Fiedler (travelling with H.R.H.)—the brother of the great Brahms conductor—to lunch alone. He is excellent company. About 2 o'clock! Granville—Watson and I got invitations to dine at the Palace. Prince left here at 5 p.m. He gave me a charming cigarette box and a photo of his nice little self. He is really a charming boy and directly his shyness wears off—he talks very intelligently. Like his August Father he prefers talking to listening. But he is very lovable.

We had rather a jolly little dinner at the Palace. I sat next to the Emperor—and tho' he looked a little tired after his *tremendous* doings— he was in perfectly *tremendous* spirits. To my great surprise he knew *Midshipman Easy*[3] by heart almost—he considers it as I do 'a classic'— and we made merry over the Triangular duel and other incidents in the book. The Empress was as usual perfectly charming to me— but she not only looked tired but *was* tired—so she didn't come to the opera to which we all went—*Aida*—most *superbly* mounted— lovely dresses and splendid masses of Eastern colour—but badly sung except by Rhadames (Knüpfer[4]) and the Soprano. Latter *most* excellent—the best singer I have heard for ages. She was singing 'als Gast' but I told the Emperor I hoped he would keep her and he said most certainly He would. The tenor—that fellow Jadoklow[5]—was awful and yet they love him here and he gets 100000 marks for 3 months!!

Monday 1 September

Prince of Wales left 8.25.

Tuesday 2 September

Left for Tentschach.…
Got a tel. from Ted announcing birth of a *Boy*[6]—mother and child as well as possible.

---

[1] 3rd secretary, Vienna Embassy.   [2] Professor of German, Oxford.
[3] By Frederick Marryatt; published, 1836.
[4] German bass.   [5] Jadlowker.   [6] In Copenhagen.

Wednesday 3 September

Arrived Tentschach. . . .

Tuesday 7 October

Left for Berlin—in lovely weather.

Wednesday 8 October

Arrived Berlin—sands.[1]

Friday 17 October

Heard from Mary. . . .[2]

Saturday 18 October

Worried . . . all day—but the situation in the Balkans with Austria threatening Servia with an Ultimatum takes up one's time. I have decided to go to Copenhagen tomorrow night. . . .[3] But it is difficult to get away now and I can only be a few hours absent.

Zimmermann very excited—he is angry with Austria for not consulting Germany—but says of course they can't ask her to stop—all the more that she has said 'In diesem Fall werden wir *nicht* nachgeben.'

Sunday 19 October

The Austrians *have* sent an Ultimatum to Servia.[4] I expect the latter will give way—if Russia advises her to especially—but this separate action on the part of Austria is very bad—and may of course lead to very serious consequences! A.-Hy has behaved badly all through.

Monday 20 October

Copenhagen
    Left last night for Copenhagen. . . . The steamer lost Warnemünde in the fog and I didn't get to Berlin till [   ][5]

---

[1] A family expression; indicating satisfaction.
[2] This entry records the receipt of bad family news from Mary, who was in Copenhagen.
[3] In order to be with Mary.
[4] On 18 Oct. 1913, demanding the evacuation of Albanian territory.
[5] No full stop in MS.; entry continued on page for 21 Oct.

Tuesday 21 October

Berlin

8.30[1] instead of 6.30 a.m....

Saw Zimmermann at 6. He told me a little of what had passed between him and Sassonow but not much.

Thursday 30 October

Isolde Menges[2]—the violinist came and played to me—rather good—but not so good as people and the Papers make out. I can't go to her concert tomorrow as Baba Harrison has hers on that night.

Saturday 1 November

Dined at a small dinner at the Chancellor's. He was dull and I thought looked very seedy.

Sunday 30 November

Left for Lichnowsky's place in Aust. Silesia—Grätz. Arrived there at 4.30 and was ushered into a large suite of rooms on the ground floor of the nice old Castle—with a nice open fire place. Lichnowsky found me and we had a good talk. Princess[3] only turned up at dinner time— 8.30. I like her so much she is so engagingly quaint—and very nice always to me....

Monday 1 December

Grätz

Pheasant shoot—very well arranged. About 1200 pheasants—30 hares etc. I got 260 pheas. for my share. The birds flew well in a high wind—but should have got more if sun had not been in my eyes all the time before lunch. The 'Strecke' was in the woods round a huge bonfire—it was a pretty sight....

Tuesday 2 December

Hare Shoot.... I got about 90—not quite my share—but I shot them much better than usual....

[1] Continued from previous page.   [2] Young English violinist.
[3] Mechtilde Lichnowsky.

Wednesday 3 December

Back to Berlin—after a very pleasant visit. Princess L. travelled with me from Ratibor to Breslau. We had a charming motor drive from Grätz to Ratibor—but as she had a dog, a cat and a child with her—we separated when we got into the train.

Found much excitement in Berlin owing to the debate on the Zabern[1] affair. An interpellation—amounting to a vote of censure ag'st Chancellor—will be voted tomorrow in the Reichstag.

Thursday 4 December

Zabern affair

Vote of censure passed by 293 to 54!! but it will make no difference to Bethmann's position.

Saturday 20 December

P'e Wied[2] lunched and I had to tell him that Grey thought he ought to make a communication as to Loan and conditions direct to the Powers who had supported him.[3] He told me he didn't quite see his way to this as this had been done thro' Roumania 6 weeks ago.

Finished my annual report for *1912*—at wh. I have been working day and night.

Saturday 27 December

Downstairs again[4]—and Jagow came to see me and we had a long talk of Wied, Islands and Military mission.

[1] In Alsace; French, Saverne.
[2] Prince Wilhelm zu Wied; the Powers' choice as King of Albania.
[3] Grey to Goschen, 20 Dec. 1913, *B.D.*, x, 1, no. 95.
[4] Goschen had been confined to his bed with influenza.

1914

Apart from visits to Dresden at the beginning of May, Brunswick a few days later, and Neustrelitz and Weimar in June, Goschen was in Berlin until 23 June, when he went to Kiel for the 'week'. On 30 June he left Kiel for England, where he remained until 26 July. He was in Berlin from 27 July until 6 August, when he left for London. The entries in his diary for December 1914 were made when he was living in Chelsea.

Thursday 1 January

Thaw

The year opens with some nasty rocks ahead—Islands— and German Mission.

Went to Palace to wish Emperor and Empress a happy New Year. Had no conversation of any account with H.M. The Empress very nice to me as usual. Owing to the thaw and the enormous amount of snow I didn't have my Gala Carriage out—I was sorry as all the others did: but I thought it would be cruel for the horses. Rattigans[1] to lunch: she *is* very pretty—and he seems quite a nice chap.

Jagow came to see me—and we discussed German Mil'y Mission (amicably) and question of Italy's intrigues with Turkey about islands. He was very friendly and nice and I think he would like to settle the Mil'y Mission question with Russia in a friendly manner— but he says it will be impossible if 1. Entente Powers try to exercise pressure. 2. If the Russian and French papers make so much fuss that the German papers will recriminate.

Tuesday 6 January

Didn't go to Jagow's day—because Mrs Gerard[2] and her nice sister came to tea with me—and at 7.30 I went to *Parsifal* with May Larisch.[3] I loved every note of it—though it lasted till 12.30. I like the music better than any of Wagner's other operas—and even enjoyed the 'longueurs' of which there are many especially the feet washing. But the music was entrancing and there are such wonderful contrasts between the religious, the mystic—and the earthly music. A great evening—but strenuous.

[1] New 2nd secretary and wife.
[2] Wife of new American Ambassador.
[3] Her husband was now Councillor, Austro-Hungarian Embassy.

Wednesday 7 January

Went to see Jagow—to ask him to convey the 'views' of H.M.G. as to the procedure to be adopted by Wied on going to Albania. Jagow told me that the intrigues of Turkey in favour of Izzet Pacha[1] as Prince—and the certainty that both Essad[2] and Kemal[3] are mixed up in them—would probably retard Wied's departure and anyway he was not much in favour of giving him too much advice! Jagow shuffled a bit about Enver Bey's appointment as Turkish minister of war—but finally admitted that it caused him considerable anxiety. He still thinks Turks are sure to go to war for Chios and Mytilene—but not yet.

Took the Rumbolds[4] to Princess Radziwill—and found her alone. She was very nice and quite interesting. She was awfully down on the Enfant terrible, as she calls the Crown Prince, for his interference in the Zabern affair. She did not think that if the Chancellor goes he would be succeeded by Lichnowsky—as Schwabach maintains. She said that if the Chancellor went and she did not believe he would—he would be succeeded by either Rheinbaben[5] or Schorlemer.[6] She maintains that Lichnowsky has neither the Head, the appearance, nor the eloquence to be a Chancellor.

Saturday 10 January

Jagow again. He told me that Triplice answer to Grey's Island proposals had not yet been sent in—but that Grey knows its tenour from Lichnowsky. I have a sort of feeling, that though he maintains that the delay is caused only by alterations in the rédaction—there is some hitch—probably on the part of Italy.

Monday 12 January

Walked over to see Bolati—who rather confirmed my idea that it was not only question of rédaction which was causing delay. *He* said that the answer had been about to be presented when Jagow telegraphed to Lichnowsky to wait a bit—as Turks were addressing a note to the Powers asking them not to send their answer in yet as they were anxious to negotiate directly with the Greeks! I hope to hear more of this tomorrow.

---

[1] Turkish Minister of War.
[3] Turkish military attaché, Sofia.
[5] Former Prussian Finance Minister.

[2] Defender of Scutari.
[4] New Councillor and wife.
[6] Prussian Minister of Agriculture.

Thursday 15 January

Prince Wied came to see me—and was much preoccupied about the Loan—but Grey is away and Asquith is away—and nothing can be settled on our side until the Cabinet has been consulted. But this delay about the Loan places Wied in an awkward position—and I have told them so at home.

Sunday 18 January[1]

'Ordensfest.' Reischach[2]—vice Eulenburg—on duty for the first time. *He* hasn't got the right Courtier's walk yet. No truck with the Emperor except a few banalities. He seemed in good spirits and was full of 'Minauderies'—but the Empress was not looking well. In the afternoon I took the whole staff to Mrs Gerard's official reception of the Dip. Corps.—in the new American Embassy—which looked very smart.

Monday 26 January

Malcolms[3] arrived. She is so pretty and nice and they both seem anxious to do everything and enjoy everything.

Tuesday 27 January

Emperor's birthday—usual games. Malcolms went to the Gala Opera and had fair places. I managed with great difficulty to present them in the Foyer—to the Emperor and Empress, Crown Princess, Princess Henry[4] and others. The Emperor talked a long time to the Malcolms—and old Prince Solms said to me directly he saw H.M. begin to talk to Mrs. M. 'Jetzt is alles aus'—because there were hundreds of people waiting—and he knew he wouldn't leave a pretty Englishwoman in a hurry.

Friday 30 January

Went to Isolde Menges concert with Mrs Malcolm and Mrs Rattigan—and finished up with supper at Bristol—awfully good evening and we all three enjoyed it. Isolde played well—except the Chaconne wh. I thought she ought not to have played.

[1] Entered on page for 20 Jan. and corrected by Goschen.
[2] Master of the Horse.
[3] Probably Ian Malcolm, Conservative M.P., and his wife, Jeanne Marie, daughter of Lily Langtry.
[4] Wife of Kaiser's brother.

Wednesday 4 February

Malcolms departed to our *great* regret.

Tuesday 10 February

Went to Jagow and after congratting him on his being engaged to be married—had a talk with him about the answer to the Triplice—*not* very satisfactory as I c'dn't persuade him that it is foolish to give out decisions, without deciding beforehand what one will do if they are not respected.

Wednesday 25 February

Venetia left.[1] Dinner at the Crown Prince's—for the Ambassadors—a dull affair—carriages ordered 9.45—smoking room till then—then good night to the C. Princess and home. Sat between Me Polo and Mrs Gerard.

Thursday 26 February

Ambassadors' dinner at Palace—exactly the same party as last night—and I sat between the same people.

Emperor took us into the room where Frederick the Great was born to smoke—and I was chilled to the bone there. I don't think it's been aired since that 'stupendous birth'! Concert afterwards—but I was so cold that I couldn't enjoy it.

Hobhouse[2] arrived.

Friday 27 February

Lunched with Me Botkine[3] for Blinis[4] and Caviar—but the cold I caught last night got so bad in the afternoon that I finally had to go to bed—with throat and everything very sore.

Tuesday 3 March

bed

Hobhouse left. I saw him in my bedroom to say goodbye. He is not a bad chap—but I rather resent having been asked to put him up.[5]

---

[1] She had arrived on 16 Feb.   [2] Postmaster-General.
[3] Wife of secretary, Russian Embassy.   [4] Pancakes.
[5] See Introduction.

Thursday 5 March

Better—but very low as Böhme[1] finds my heart very weak—and it keeps stopping. He makes me drink old Rhine wine—and won't let me do any work.

Tuesday 17 March

Had a dinner for the Chancellor—6 people sent excuses between 3 and 6!! Mrs Chancellor amongst others.[2] Rather a ghastly party.

Wednesday 18 March

Went out for a walk in Grünewald—heart didn't trouble me so much as last time.

Wednesday 15 April

Cambon came in to see me—he told me that little Boghietchevich had told him that there was going to be a meeting between Cz. and Kr. this year—at demand of latter and that motive of demand was weakness of A.-Hy!

Saturday 2 May

Went down to Dresden with Foddles[3] arriving about 6.30, met by George[4] Evy and Verena[5]—who took me to Bellevue Hotel. Unluckily this was all we saw of George because he was on duty with the King away from Dresden all the time.

Sunday 3 May

Found Emmy very white—and as her servant put it 'nicht besonders wohl'—but Evie very well indeed. We had a nice 'family' day and lunched and dined with Emma and Evie. Foddles and I played a lot to them after dinner and I really believe they enjoyed [   ][6]

Monday 4 May

I went back to Berlin and Florrie remained another day at Dresden

---

[1] Physician.   [2] Cf. diary, 11 May 1914.
[3] Charles Goschen's daughter, Florence; also known as 'Florrie'.
[4] Emily von Metzsch's son.   [5] His wife.
[6] Sentence incomplete.

and then went home to England. It was awfully nice having Florrie
with me—and she was a dear—but I wish she would get rid of her
suffragette ideas.

Friday 8 May

Rumbold and I went down to Brunswick for the Xtening of the
Brunswick heir[1]—I representing the King[2] and taking his Xtening
present with me. Found very comfortable quarters taken for us at the
Park Hotel—*all gratis*. Had an excellent dinner and good bed. But
my tummy was only in fair order.

Saturday 9 May

Brunswick, very cold wind

Called on Min'r of For. Aff.,[3] who was quite alone in his enormous
F.O. Rumbold lunched with the Household. I by myself quietly at
Hotel—after a walk through picturesque old Brunswick—nice narrow
streets—old timbered Houses with carved and painted Balconies—
lilacs and laburnums everywhere—but a bitter wind which brought
my old chill back. At 3.15 presented my letters at a very cordial and
pleasant audience with the Duke and Duchess. Then gave 'em the
King's Xtening cup which was greatly admired and rightly as it was
a lovely one. Then a short walk with Rumbold when we got cut off
from our Hotel by the Crowd—and had to walk miles to get round
and got to the Hotel just in time to dress for the Xtening—very pretty
Ceremony—P'cess Olga of Cumberland,[4] looking charming brought
the Baby in—Empress and Duchess of Cumberland held him by turns
at the Font. Too long a sermon—at wh. the baby very rightly roared
lustily. Then a gratulation's Cour—and then a gala Banquet. After
dinner had nice talks with P'ce Waldemar of Denmark—the Duchess
of Cumberland and the Empress. Didn't get speech with the
Emperor—but sat opposite to him at dinner—when he drank my
health—very cordially—and said 'Mind I expect you at Kiel.'[5]
Torchlight procession—and 'Dutch' Chorale sung by about 2000
voices. But it was too cold to enjoy it. Ill all night with chill.

Sunday 10 May

Back to Berlin—feeling rather a wreck—but nearly all right again.

[1] Son of Duke and Duchess.   [2] George V was to be a godfather.
[3] Probably Hartwig, Minister of State.
[4] Duke of Cumberland's youngest daughter.
[5] For the yachting week.

Monday 11 May

Poor Me Bethmann Hollweg—who had been ill for some time—died this morning.[1] She was such a nice good woman—and we had always been most excellent friends. I am awfully sorry for poor B.H. as his private life has been so happy—and his political life the reverse—and the latter is all he has left now.

Wednesday 13 May

Funeral service for poor Me B. Hollweg. The Empress was there and at the close of the dreadfully long and harrowing sermon—she knelt down with the Chancellor before the coffin—it was very touching. There is no one more sympathetic in grief as [*sic*] the Empress—as *I* know.

The flowers were lovely—and the service was held in the room where the Berlin Congress used to assemble.

Thursday 14 May

Jagow made the statement on For. Aff. wh. the Chancellor was to have made. It was a good, tho' naturally a rather optimistic one in some things (Balkans etc.)—as he had to follow the lead of Berchtold. The only interesting part was his dressing down of the Russian Press for their Anti-German campaign. Speech very well received in Reichstag and Country.

Monday 15 June

Teck arrived to represent the King at funeral of Grand Duke of Meck'b'g Strelitz[2]—wh. takes place tomorrow. He stayed of course with me—and I had Rattigans to lunch and Rumbolds to dine. T. and I had good talks of old times.

Tuesday 16 June

Awfully hot

Teck and I went down to Neu Strelitz—the Emperor just came for the funeral service—but had time to spot Teck's new uniform as Gov'r of Windsor[3] and ask him what it was. After the service there was a lunch—(like a wake) and I sat next to two very pleasant

---

[1] It is tempting to speculate as to whether Bethmann Hollweg's handling of the situation in July and August 1914 would have been more prudent, if his wife had still been alive. Cf. *D.A.B.*, ii, p. 214.

[2] The late duke was Teck's first cousin.   [3] Windsor Castle.

people—one a Bavarian Prince and the other the Duke of Meck'b'g-Schwerin who is Gov'r of Togo.[1] He was pleasant but not *too* modest about his attainments his strength of character and his power of governing natives. I made the acquaintance of T.'s 'naughty cousin'[2] whom I found quite an agreeable woman—and of a Grand Duchess of Meck'b'g-Schwerin whom I never knew. There were many Royalties of that sort that they all asked me what we were going to do against the Suffragettes. Then the widowed G'd Duchess[3] sent for me and was very sad—she told me the King and Queen had been very pleased that I had kept them informed about the G'd Duke's state without being told to do so.

Then my dear old G'd Duchess Augusta Caroline sent for me—notwithstanding her 92 years she was, tho' sad and upset, as fresh as a daisy. She said she had buried 3 Grand Dukes and wondered why *she* was not taken: she said 'it must be for some purpose—and if I could only help my dear *old* country in its present difficulties—I should die happy.' She told me that she regarded me with 'a true and deep affection'.

Tuesday 23 June

Kiel

Reached Kiel 6.23. Had to change into a frock coat and tall hat—and was recd. by Admiral[4] with Guns—Guard of Honour, Band and much pomp all together: *but* I rather enjoyed it as I like all shows! Admiral very kind and nice and pleasant set of Officers. Dined with P'ce and P'cess Henry of Prussia[5] in the evening.

Bunt joined me at Kiel Station.

Thursday 25 June

Had a splendid sail on the *Meteor*—the Emperor very cheery. He rather hoped that I should be seasick as there was a spanking breeze—but I told him that as the representative of a Maritime Nation I was afraid I must disappoint him. Old Tirpitz—Eisendecker[6]—Warrender—Goodenough[7] and I were the guests—besides one or two others. The Yacht did not win. She carried away her main Jackyard Topsail yard on the way down—then lost a minute and a half at the start—and was, I thought, not well sailed in the race. P'ce Henry

---

[1] Adolf Friedrich.

[2] Maria, daughter of the late duke. For details see Pope-Hennessy, *Queen Mary* (1959), p. 341.

[3] Elisabeth; a princess of Anhalt.   [4] Warrender.

[5] He was the Kaiser's younger brother.   [6] Eisendecher; commander of *Meteor*.

[7] Commodore.

was of the same opinion and said that H.I.M. had got rid of his English skipper and crew too soon. We had a jolly good lunch after the race.

Sunday 28 June

While the Emperor was racing in *Meteor* she received a wireless to the effect that the Archduke Franz Ferdinand and His Consort had been assassinated at Sarajevo by Servian agitators![1]

This is a dreadful business and Heaven knows what it may lead to—as the Austrians have for ages been looking out for an excuse to trample on Servia and to punish her for her continual agitation. Personally, too, I am very sorry as the Archduke was always very nice and kind to me—and His Wife was charming. It was a most determined assassination—as the conspirators missed more than once—and a third attempt had been planned if the 2nd had failed. Too awful!

Monday 29 June

The Emperor left Kiel. Ad'l Warrender and I went to see him off at the station. He was very depressed and angry. He told me that the assassination was a dreadful blow to him—both because it was only a fortnight ago that he had been staying with them and seen their happy family life—and because it was such an upset of everything they had planned and arranged together. He didn't know who the next successor was and didn't care—and the Emperor Francis Joseph was so old—the Crown of Austria–Hungary would soon be in the hands of an unknown and inexperienced boy! He said he was going to Vienna if the Emperor wanted him. But he didn't go—and altogether it turned out that the funeral was a disgraceful affair— owing I believe to Montenuevo[2] who hated, and was hated by, the poor Archduke.

In the evening there was a big dinner at the Yacht club at which P'ce Henry presided instead of the Emperor. There were no speeches—except that P'ce Henry said a few words of goodbye to the Guests.

A sad end to a very jolly week.[3]

Tuesday 30 June

Left Kiel in the *King G. V*, accompanied by Battleships—*Centurion*— *Ajax* and [   ][4]

---

[1] The wireless message was in fact received by *Hohenzollern*.
[2] Grand Master of the Court since 1909.
[3] At least part and perhaps the whole of this entry was evidently written subsequently.
[4] Sentence unfinished.

The Cruisers left the same day but went through the Canal—perfect weather. Passed all the big Yachts going out for their last race—and exchanged greetings with them: sent wireless messages to Prince Henry—and Admirals—expressive of good will and thanks for hospitality etc.—and got very warm and cordial answers.

Monday 6 July

Oxford and Cambridge—very dull.[1]

Thursday 23 July[2]

Austria sent in Ultimatum to Servia stating her demands and saying that unless they were satisfied entirely in 48 hours dip. relations w'd be broken off and Servia invaded.

This Ultimatum, as Bollati—the Italian Amb'r told me afterwards—was drawn up in such a manner that no independent Power could swallow it: he, Bollati, had drawn up the Italian Ult'm to Turkey on similar lines and with the same intent—namely that it should be refused.[3] Austria means business—and personally I doubt whether anything will stop her.

In fact I met Mensdorff and Ch. Kinsky in the evening—and they both told me that Servia had made them mobilize 3 times for nothing—and that this time Austria–H'y—would certainly move.[4]

Friday 24 July

Went down to F.O. and found Nicolson and Grey very anxious as to situation.

Saturday 25 July

Servia sent answer to Ultimatum—accepting nearly the whole of Austrian demands—but making certain reserves with regard to the Austrian demand that A.H'n officials sh'd participate in Servian Judicial proceedings.

The reply went further in direction of satisfying Austria than anyone (incl. Germany) thought possible: but nevertheless the Austrian Minister[5] left Belgrade in the evening and Servia therefore

---

[1] Cricket match at Lord's.   [2] First entry since 6 July.
[3] In September 1911, when he had been secretary-general, Consulta.
[4] Last two paragraphs and perhaps whole entry evidently added later.
[5] Giesl.

ordered general mobilisation. Sir E. Grey told me this and asked me
to go out to Berlin tomorrow morning—as the situation looked serious
to a degree. So off I go.

I heard also that Rumbold had reported that Jagow had given him
his word of honour—that the Ultimatum had not been submitted to
the German Gov't before its despatch.[1] I feel I am in for a heavy
time—instead of going to Nauheim for my cure as I had intended.

Sunday 26 July

Left for Berlin via Flushing—strong wind but fair. Got *last* sleeping
berth on the train—a very small one just over the wheels. Most uncomfortable. Ballin[2] who of course had the best compart't showed me
a telegram en route stating that the Austrians had already crossed
the Servian Frontier. This proved to be untrue. Rather low in my
mind—as Russia can under the circs hardly remain indifferent—and
then * * *?

Monday 7 December[3]

Bunt was warned for the Front. I am very astonished—as he has
had only 3 weeks training!! But it had to come sooner or later: any
way I expect he won't go out before Xmas. He is of course delighted.
Chris[4] is warned too—so I hope they will go out together.

Tuesday 15 December

As Bunt and I were playing Mozart Violin Sonata—No. 6, a large
envelope was handed to Bunt containing his Order to start for France
next Thursday morning at 9.25!! I was awfully flabbergasted as I
thought that he would be with me for at least another month. He
has had a bare month's training. We shall have our time cut out to
get everything—i.e. his War Kit ready. It is ordered but none of it
has come yet. We were going to dine both of us at Nicolson's—but
Bunt's Captain *begged* him to go and dine on guard as he wanted to
talk things over. So I went to Nicolson's alone—and got lots of sympathy from them for Bunt's early departure.

[1] Goschen is presumably referring to Rumbold's telegram to Grey, 24 July 1914
(*B.D.*, xi, no. 103), reporting that Jagow had denied to Jules Cambon having had
any previous knowledge of the terms of the Austro-Hungarian note.
[2] For an account by Beyens of what he claimed Goschen had told him of his conversation with Ballin on board the Flushing steamer see *D.A.B.*, ii, p. 252.
[3] First entry since 26 July.   [4] Henry Goschen's son.

Thursday 17 December

My Bunt left for the Front. Went to see the dear Boy off to the station. Henry was seeing Chris off....

Monday 28 December

Got a telegram from the War Office telling me that my darling darling boy Bunt was wounded and has been missing since the 24th. So that he must have gone into action almost directly he got to the front. I am heartbroken—and find it difficult to hope! Oh dear—that bright merry boy—who only a fortnight ago was with me so splendidly enthusiastic and in such high spirits. It was awful that he should have been sent to the front so soon.

Wednesday 30 December

Was fairly hopeful all day—because every one told me that all the chances were in favour of Bunt having been taken by the Germans who w'd be sure to look after him well. *But* tonight I got a dreadful letter from his Colonel which takes away *all* hope. He said that when last seen he was unconscious but still alive—but that he was sorry to say that he could give me no reason to hope that he was still alive—and he sympathies [*sic*] with me for my great loss. But he doesn't know *what* a loss it is to me. That darling darling boy—who has been such a loving, bright and always cheery companion to me. So full of bright hopes, of promise, of talents—and such Joie de Vivre.

APPENDIX A

The genesis of the Daily Telegraph *'interview'*

Goschen's diary and letters bear witness to the seriousness of the repercussions in Germany of the publication in the *Daily Telegraph* on 28 October 1908 of the famous 'interview', given by Wilhelm II. The papers left by Colonel—subsequently Brigadier-General and finally Major-General—Montagu-Stuart-Wortley are an indispensable source for a study of the genesis of this well-meant 'communication'.[1] A letter written by Montagu-Stuart-Wortley to the editor of the *Daily Telegraph* in 1930, and printed in that newspaper, although, understandably, not accurate in every detail, constitutes a useful supplement to the contemporary documents.[2]

Colonel (as he then was) Edward Montagu-Stuart-Wortley was the owner of Highcliffe Castle, a large country-house close to the Hampshire coast and a short distance to the east of Christchurch. A regular army officer, he had served as military attaché in Paris for three years, including the time of Edward VII's famous visit in May 1903. His wife, Violet, *née* Guthrie, also had connections with the diplomatic world. Her sister, Lilias Georgina, was the wife of Rennell Rodd, Minister in Stockholm from 1905 to 1908. The Kaiser's most recent biographer has drawn attention to the curious fact that she was also a first cousin once removed of Houston Stewart Chamberlain.[3]

In the autumn of 1907, when Wilhelm II, accompanied by the Empress, was about to pay a state visit to Edward VII and Queen Alexandra at Windsor Castle, William Tyrrell, Grey's private secretary, wrote to Violet Montagu-Stuart-Wortley, informing her that the Emperor was 'in search of a place on the South Coast where he could spend a fortnight quietly on leaving Windsor'. 'Do you think you could let Highcliffe for a fortnight inclusive of servants and everything else?' he asked, adding a request for an answer 'by tomorrow in case there is a chance'.[4] I have not been able to trace any reply, which, in view of the short time available, may quite possibly have been made either by telephone or by telegraph. However, an endorsement to Tyrrell's letter states that Montagu-Stuart-Wortley answered

---

[1] Papers concerning the *Daily Telegraph* Incident, Bodleian Library, Oxford, MS. Eng. hist. d. 256. All manuscripts and typescripts of the years 1907–8 mentioned in the footnotes to Appendix A are in this collection. Mr Alan Palmer has used the documents in the collection for his account of the incident in *The Kaiser* (1978), from which I have greatly profited.

[2] Montagu-Stuart-Wortley to Editor, 7 July 1930, *Daily Telegraph*, 8 July 1930.

[3] Palmer, op. cit., p. 129.

[4] Tyrrell to Violet Montagu-Stuart-Wortley, 8 Nov. 1907.

that 'he would not let Highcliffe but that he would *lend* the house
to H.I.M. on condition that he remained on the spot to look after
the Kaiser himself', and that 'the condition was accepted'. The
endorsement also states that the Colonel had never met the Kaiser,
but that King Edward knew Highcliffe well, and that it was at his
request that the Foreign Office made its approach.[1]

In due course, the Empress returned home, and Wilhelm proceeded
to Highcliffe. The Colonel took up his quarters at a nearby farm-
house—Nea Farm.[2] His wife went away—evidently to stay with her
sister.[3] From the point of view of the historian her absence was fortunate, as it occasioned an interesting succession of letters. On 1
December the Colonel wrote, relating that he had that morning received a letter from a friend, asking him to arrange an interview with
his imperial guest for the journalist, W. T. Stead. When, after consulting Metternich, who was also at the castle, he read this letter to Wilhelm, it evoked a firm refusal—'I have made it a hard and fast rule
never to accord any such interviews.' The Kaiser, he added, then took
him 'into the library window', and there declared:

> When history is written, it will be shown that the British public
> has misjudged me.
>
> At the commencement of the Boer War, when everything was
> going wrong for you, the Queen wrote me a letter, saying how
> anxious she was about the state of affairs. Although nearly all my
> people were in favour of the Boers, from a purely sentimental point
> of view—(a bible-reading, protestant people being oppressed by
> a great nation of a like religion) personally I knew that the majority
> of the Boers were not bible reading and I realised, with a view to
> the future of my own Colonies the extreme importance of the ulti-
> mate victory of the mother Country.
>
> I immediately set to work with my general staff—and having
> considered the situation as it was, I recommended a certain line
> of military action—Queen Victoria thanked me most deeply.
>
> I do not wish to say that it was owing to my advice—but the
> strategy followed by Lord Roberts on arrival in South Africa, was
> exactly that which I had recommended.[4]

The Colonel went on to recount further remarks. He promised to
write again the next day, and concluded with the injunction: 'Show

---

[1] I have been unable to identify with certainty the author of the endorsement. It
may, however, have well been Montagu-Stuart-Wortley's daughter, Louise, wife of
Sir Percy Loraine.

[2] Montagu-Stuart-Wortley's movements can be deduced from his letter of 1 Dec.
to his wife, quoted below.

[3] Ibid; see also below.   [4] Ibid.

this to Rennell—it is very Confidential.'[1] This injunction Violet Montagu-Stuart-Wortley evidently carried out.[2]

On the following day the Colonel implemented his promise, reporting observations concerning Bismarck's dismissal, the Russo-Japanese War and French activities in Morocco. 'Rather an interesting Conversation!' he commented.[3]

Five days later he wrote again, describing a walk, in which his guest claimed to have foreseen the 'yellow peril' twenty years previously and explained that that had been his reason for building his fleet—'just to be ready to lend a helping hand'. 'I could not gather to whom he meant to stretch this helping hand,' commented the Colonel.[4] Eventually, after an enjoyable stay of three weeks, far removed from the world of Maximilian Harden, the Kaiser left for home.

Some six months later, in June 1908, Montagu-Stuart-Wortley, now a Brigadier-General, received an invitation from the head of the German imperial household, Count August zu Eulenburg, to be present, as the Kaiser's guest, at the manœuvres that were due to take place 'in Lorraine' from 8 to 10 September.[5] He attended the manœuvres, and had a further conversation with his host, the circumstances of which he more than twenty years later described in a letter, also published in the *Daily Telegraph*. After referring to 'the German manœuvres at Saarbrücken', he continued:

> On the concluding day of the manœuvres the Emperor sent for me. He was on his horse in the middle of a ploughed field. He told his staff to clear away for some distance, and proceeded to recount to me all that eventually appeared in the interview which was published.[6]

Despite having been written so long after the event to which it relates, this graphic letter deserves quotation. Montagu-Stuart-Wortley's statement that he had a further conversation with the Kaiser in Germany in September 1908 is confirmed by contemporary documents.[7] Nevertheless, it is evident that much of what 'eventually appeared in the interview which was published' was based on the conversations that had taken place at and near Highcliffe Castle in the previous year and of which Montagu-Stuart-Wortley had a written record in the form of his letters to his wife.

[1] Ibid.
[2] J. R. Rodd, *Social and Diplomatic Memories, 1902–1919* (1925), p. 101.
[3] Montagu-Stuart-Wortley to his wife, 2 Dec. 1907.
[4] Montagu-Stuart-Wortley to his wife, 7 Dec. 1907.
[5] August zu Eulenburg to Montagu-Stuart-Wortley, 14 June 1908.
[6] *Daily Telegraph*, 8 July 1930.
[7] Montagu-Stuart-Wortley to Wilhelm II, 23 Sept. 1908 (copy); Wilhelm II to Montagu-Stuart-Wortley, 15 Oct. 1908.

On his return to England Montagu-Stuart-Wortley, according to his subsequent account—which in this connection there seems to be no reason to question—got into touch with a friend of his, Harry Lawson, son of Lord Burnham, the proprietor of the *Daily Telegraph*, and at his request a member of the staff of that newspaper, J. B. Firth, came to his rooms in Clarges Street and took down word for word all that he had to relate; this account was then typed.[1] On 23 September he wrote direct to the Kaiser, acknowledging the great honour that the latter had done him both at the recent manœuvres and also during his stay at Highcliffe 'in talking so openly concerning the most regrettable tone of a portion of the Press of this Country', and suggesting that it was high time for the sincerity of his good feelings and intentions to be placed prominently before the British public through the medium of a leading newspaper. He revealed that he had been in touch with the son of the proprietor of the *Daily Telegraph*, 'a paper which has never adopted the tone concerning Your Majesty which is so much to be regretted', and enclosed what he called the 'draft of a supposed communiqué ... made at my instigation, veiled as from a retired diplomatist'. The draft, which has been preserved, is typed on paper of excellent quality; the first page is embossed with the title and address of the *Daily Telegraph*.[2]

When the typescript reached the Kaiser he was at Rominten, his shooting-box in East Prussia. Jenisch, a member of the imperial entourage, and also Bülow's nephew, dispatched it to his uncle, who sent it to the German Foreign Office. As Schoen, the Secretary of State, was ill at the time, the typescript was read by Stemrich, the under-secretary, who passed it on to Klehmet, of the Political Section. Klehmet made a number of corrections, before returning it to Bülow, who then sent it back to Jenisch.[3] Eventually the corrected version reached Montagu-Stuart-Wortley,[4] together with a letter, dated 15 October and signed by the Kaiser, authorizing him to make a discreet use of the article in the manner that he thought best, and expressing the hope that it would have the effect of bringing about a change in the tone of some of the English newspapers.[5]

On the day on which the 'interview' finally appeared in the *Daily*

---

[1] *Daily Telegraph*, 8 July 1930. The role ascribed by Montagu-Stuart-Wortley to Firth has been attributed by several historians to Harold Spender. However, there seems to be no reason to doubt Montagu-Stuart-Wortley's statement concerning Firth, who was a member of the staff of the *Daily Telegraph* both in 1908 and 1930.

[2] Typescript, undated, MS. Eng. hist. d. 256, f. 43.

[3] For a good account of what happened to the typescript in Germany see L. Cecil, *The German Diplomatic Service 1871–1914* (Princeton, 1976), p. 304, to which I am much indebted.

[4] The typescript bears a number of corrections in ink, presumably made by Klehmet, and a few minor ones in pencil, in the handwriting of Montagu-Stuart-Wortley.

[5] Wilhelm II to Montagu-Stuart-Wortley, 15 Oct. 1908.

Telegraph Lawson wrote to Montagu-Stuart-Wortley. He thought that no newspaper had 'ever had a more important or a more interesting contribution', the appearance of which would 'entirely make for good'. 'The British public will,' he affirmed, 'taken as a whole, be fully convinced of the Emperor's sincerity and the desire will be strengthened to make our relations with all classes of the German people more natural and friendly.'[1]

[1] Lawson to Montagu-Stuart-Wortley, 28 Oct. 1908.

APPENDIX B

'A scrap of paper'

In conclusion, some discussion of a number of questions that have been raised by historians and other writers in connection with the famous phrase, 'a scrap of paper', attributed to Bethmann Hollweg by Goschen in his account of his last days in Berlin, may be of interest.[1] These questions are: In what language did Bethmann Hollweg and Goschen talk to each other at the Imperial Chancellery on the evening of 4 August 1914, and, more particularly, since they may have used more than one language in the course of their interview, in what language did the Chancellor refer to the Belgian treaty? Was it English, which Bethmann Hollweg, like many other educated people in Berlin, certainly spoke, or German, which Goschen knew, or perhaps French, which both men knew and which was then the normal language of diplomacy? What were the precise words that Bethmann Hollweg uttered with reference to the Belgian treaty? Finally, what connection, if any, is there between the words attributed to Bethmann Hollweg by Goschen and the play by the French dramatist, Victorien Sardou, *Les Pattes de Mouche*, first produced in 1860, the English translation of which is entitled *A Scrap of Paper*?

As far as the linguistic point is concerned, neither the Foreign Office's version of Goschen's final telegram of 4 August 1914 nor his subsequent report, dated 6 August 1914, is of any help. The telegram, if one may call it that, contains no reference to paper of any dimension. Neither in his memorandum of 4 October 1914 nor in his *Betrachtungen zum Weltkriege* did Bethmann Hollweg specifically state in which language he made his famous slip. The two documents give different German versions of the key words. In his letter to Hardinge of 11 August 1914 Chirol did not mention the language spoken at the interview. He merely quotes Goschen as having said that Bethmann Hollweg referred to 'a bit of paper'. On the other hand, Rumbold declared explicitly in his 'Rough Account' that the Chancellor made his remarks in English and that the words that he used were 'a piece of paper'. However, in *The War Crisis in Berlin* he took the view that Bethmann Hollweg had probably spoken in German on this occasion; he also discussed the possibility of the Chancellor having spoken in French.[2]

The testimony of Jules Cambon also deserves mention. He travelled

---

[1] Butterfield, *George III and the Historians* (1957), p. 32; A. J. P. Taylor, *Politics in Wartime* (1964), p. 90; for other writers see below.

[2] See Introduction.

from Berlin to Copenhagen and thence to London, where, as he later, after his return to Paris, reported to Doumergue, the new French Foreign Minister, he saw Grey, who described Bethmann Hollweg's reception of Goschen as 'brutal'. The Chancellor had told him that his country 'faisait la guerre pour une feuille de papier'.[1] Cambon does not in this report mention having seen Goschen himself while in England. His account of the famous interview appears to have been derived from Grey. Among the papers of Simon, the then Attorney-General, there is a typewritten copy of a diary-entry, recording that, at a dinner-party at Mrs J. Astor's on 18 August 1914, Jules Cambon assured him that, when Goschen took leave of the Chancellor, Bethmann Hollweg 'expressed some irritation that England should go to war with Germany over "un morceau de papier" '.[2] In his autobiographical *Retrospect*, published nearly forty years later, Lord Simon, as he had now become, repeated this story, but with two variations: the dinner-party took place at Lady Horner's, and the words attributed to Bethmann Hollweg are given in English—'a scrap of paper'.[3] After returning to Paris, Jules Cambon went on to Spiez in Switzerland, where he met Berta de Bunsen, who in her diary for 3 September recorded that he had informed her that Bethmann Hollweg had told Goschen that 'the Treaty was a mere bagatelle and shd. be torn up'.[4] Interesting as these statements are, not one of them is conclusive.

The first professional historian to interest himself in the linguistic point appears to have been the distinguished French medievalist, Charles Bémont, for many years joint editor of the *Revue Historique*, to whose 'Chronique' of happenings in the historiographical world he regularly contributed a section on Britain. In the 'Chronique' that appeared in the number of the *Revue* for January–April 1915 Bémont asked rhetorically in what language the by now famous conversation between Goschen and the Imperial Chancellor, related in the former's report, which now constituted No. 160 in 'The British Diplomatic Correspondence', had taken place. He supplied his own answer: 'En anglais, m'assure-t-on, c'est donc en anglais que le "le chiffon de papier", le *scrap of paper*, sera buriné dans l'histoire.'[5] He did not disclose the source of his information. However, on 27 May 1924, after Goschen's death, Hubert Hall, the archivist, formerly of the Public Record Office, revealed in *The Times* that Bémont had asked him to obtain for the *Revue Historique* authentic information as to the language in which the phrase had been uttered; he added that the question had been submitted by the Foreign Office to Goschen himself, who

[1] Jules Cambon to Doumergue, 22 Aug. 1914, *D.D.F.*, 3, xi, no. 793.
[2] Simon, Diary 5, 18 Aug. 1914, Simon Papers.
[3] Viscount Simon, *Retrospect* (1952), p. 96.
[4] Berta de Bunsen, Vienna Diary, 3 Sept. 1914, de B.P., B.B./III/a.
[5] *Revue Historique*, cxviii (1915), p. 24.

stated that the whole of the conversation with Bethmann Hollweg had been conducted in English.[1]

Valentine Williams, a former Reuter correspondent in Berlin, also contributed a letter to *The Times*, published on 29 May 1914, in which he stated that Goschen, after returning from Berlin, had told him that the conversation with Bethmann Hollweg had been in German and that the words of which 'a scrap of paper' were a translation were 'ein Stückchen Papier'. In a subsequent letter, published in the same newspaper on 3 July, Williams added that Goschen, although he disliked speaking German, knew the language well.

One other piece of evidence deserves to be mentioned, despite the fact that it did not appear in print until twenty years after the event. In 1934 Arnold Wahnschaffe, who had been under-secretary at the Imperial Chancellery at the time of the outbreak of war, related in the *Berlinermonatshefte* that when he entered Bethmann Hollweg's office after the interview, the Chancellor, still hot with rage—'noch heiss vom Zorn'—told him that he had not hitherto known that he could speak English so well—'dass er so gut englisch sprechen könnte'.[2] It is difficult to believe that Wahnschaffe invented this story.

What precisely were the words uttered by Bethmann Hollweg on the evening of 4 August 1914 with reference to the Belgian treaty is something that we shall probably never know for certain. In the first place, Goschen, as entries in his diary for 23 March 1906 and 16 May 1911 indicate, had for some time been getting somewhat hard of hearing. The report in which he attributed to Bethmann Hollweg the phrase 'a scrap of paper' must have been composed some time after the interview had taken place. Moreover, he reported the Chancellor's remarks in *oratio obliqua*. He did not claim, by the use of quotation marks, that his words constituted the latter's *ipsissima verba*. Indeed, he may no longer have recalled what exactly the *ipsissima verba* had been. On balance, the evidence suggests that on the occasion in question Bethmann Hollweg spoke English and that he made a reference to paper of some dimension or other.

In his letter to *The Times* of 29 May 1924 Valentine Williams also raised the question of a connection between the words used by Goschen in his report and Sardou's play. After explaining, as has been seen, that 'a scrap of paper' was a rendering of 'ein Stückchen Papier', he added:

The phrase was so much more felicitous than any other rendering

---

[1] See also H. Hall, *British Archives and the Sources for the History of the World War* (1925), p. 314, n. 2.

[2] A. Wahnschaffe, 'Gesamtverantwortung', *Berlinermonatshefte*, xii (1934), p. 651.

that I asked Sir Edward how he came to use it. He then confided
to me that he thought he must have had in mind Sardou's play
thus named....

Whatever the language in which the Chancellor expressed himself
and whatever the precise words that he uttered on the evening of 4
August 1914, the story related by Valentine Williams did not lack
foundation. The fact that Goschen, while in Washington, had
recorded in his diary having on 16 March 1894 seen a performance
of *A Scrap of Paper*, in which William and Madge Kendal had acted,
has already been mentioned. Moreover, a certain Lady Haversham,
the widow of a Liberal politician, in a letter published in *The Times*
on 3 June 1924, recalled that Goschen himself had once taken a leading part in an amateur performance at Seacox Heath:

> I well remember Sardou's play, *A Scrap of Paper*, being acted in
> private theatricals at Seacox Heath, the seat of the late Lord
> Goschen (then the Right Hon. George Goschen), who, I think, was
> First Lord of the Admiralty at the time. His brother, Sir E.
> Goschen, acted a principal part in the play, which was voted an
> excellent one and very well acted.

Lady Haversham's recollection of the office held by George Joachim
Goschen at the time of the performance was inexact: he served twice
as First Lord of the Admiralty. Nevertheless, there seems to be no
reason to question the general truth of her story.

Goschen does not mention the Seacox Heath performance in his
diary, but he does relate having once, when in Lisbon, taken part,
albeit reluctantly, in amateur theatricals (Diary, 23 January–25
February 1892). In writing his report he may well have been influenced in his choice of words by his recollection of a play in which
he had seen well-known actors perform and in which, on another
occasion, he himself had taken part.

No doubt one could pursue the question of derivation almost indefinitely. Granted that Bethmann Hollweg made a reference to paper
in the course of his interview with Goschen on 4 August 1914, did
he, for his part, derive the notion, to which he so unwisely gave expression, from some earlier source? In the previous year the Chancellor's
assistant, Kurt Riezler, had, in his book, *Die Erforderlichkeit des Unmöglichen*, commented on the testimony of events, arbitration treaties
and the extension of international law notwithstanding, to the ease
with which international paper is torn up—'die Geschehnisse
bezeugen immer von neuem, wie leicht das internationale Papier

zerrissen wird'.[1] It is interesting to speculate as to whether Bethmann Hollweg's words to Goschen were prompted by what Riezler had written and perhaps also said.

[1] K. Riezler, *Die Erforderlichkeit des Unmöglichen* (Munich, 1913), p. 230. I owe this reference to I. Geiss, *July 1914* (1967), p. 340.

INDEX

Principal references are italicized

(1911), 233–4; at Homburg, 242;
and Balkan War, 263; and Prince of
Wales, 265; and Mrs Malcolm, 283;
at Kiel, 288–9; mentioned, 26, 33–
4, 37, 48, 65, 129, 144, 178, 195, 201,
224, 226, 256, 277, 284, 287
Wilhelm II of Württemberg, King, *265*
Wilhelm zu Wied, Prince, *280*, 282, 283
Wilkinson, Spencer, *136*
Williams, Harold, 56
Williams, Valentine, 300–1
Wimpffen, Countess, *124*
Windisch–Graetz, Prince and Princess,
99, 100, 167
—, Alexandrine, *144*

—, Elisabeth, *148*
—, Matilda, 100
Witte, 81, 103
Wolff, 47
Wydenbruck, *76*, 79, 134

Yellow Peril, 81, 295
Young Turks, 24, 190–2
Ysaÿe, *89*

Zabern, *280*, 282
Zeit, Die, 115
Zichy, *121*
Zimmermann, 46, *230*, 244, 258, 263, 278,
279